THE BIBLE, PROTESTANTISM, AND THE RISE OF NATURAL SCIENCE

PETER HARRISON

School of Humanities and Social Sciences
Bond University, Gold Coast, Australia

CAMBRIDGE
UNIVERSITY PRESS

PUBLISHED BY THE PRESS SYNDICATE OF THE UNIVERSITY OF CAMBRIDGE
The Pitt Building, Trumpington Street, Cambridge, United Kingdom

CAMBRIDGE UNIVERSITY PRESS
The Edinburgh Building, Cambridge CB2 2RU, UK
40 West 20th Street, New York, NY 10011–4211, USA
10 Stamford Road, Oakleigh, VIC 3166, Australia
Ruiz de Alarcón 13, 28014 Madrid, Spain
Dock House, The Waterfront, Cape Town 8001, South Africa

http://www.cambridge.org

First published 1998
Reprinted 1999
First paperback edition 2001

Typeset in Baskerville 11/12½ pt [VN]

A catalogue record for this book is available from the British Library

Library of Congress Cataloguing in Publication data
Harrison, Peter, 1955–
The Bible, Protestantism, and the rise of natural science/Peter
Harrison.
p. cm.
Includes bibliographical references and index.
ISBN 0 521 59196 1 (hardback)
1. Bible and science. 2. Protestantism–History. 3. Science–
History. I. Title.
BS650.H37 1988
261.5′5′09 dc21   98-20967
CIP

ISBN 0 521 59196 1 hardback
ISBN 0 521 00096 3 paperback

Transferred to digital printing 2003

For Carol

πάντα λόγον ὥσπερ ζῷον συνεσάναι
A discourse should resemble a living creature
Plato, *Phaedrus*, 264c

Contents

Acknowledgements

During the seven years which this book has taken to reach completion, I have accumulated numerous debts. I am grateful to the staff of Bond University Library, and in particular the document delivery officers, for their generous assistance in locating and retrieving research materials. The University of Queensland Central Library, which houses the Early English Books collections on microfilm, was also an indispensable part of this project, and I am especially appreciative of the efforts of the Reference and Inter-Library Loan staff there. Staff at the Bodleian Library were particularly helpful during my time at Oxford in 1996, and their friendliness and professionalism made my researches there both fruitful and enjoyable. The British Library is an incomparable resource, and it was my good fortune to have been able to spend several months in the North Library, spread across the years 1991, 1994, and 1996, mistakenly thinking on each visit that it would be my last. I am therefore grateful not only to the staff there, but also to those responsible for the construction of the new library, whose ponderous progress has allowed me to develop attachments to the old one.

My home institution, Bond University, has been generous in providing research awards in the years 1991 and 1996, enabling me to travel to England to consult materials unavailable in Australia. To my colleagues there I am grateful for providing a convivial environment for teaching and research. The Australian Research Council also provided a Small Grant, which again made possible a trip to the British Library in 1996. I also wish to express my gratitude to the Principal and fellows of Harris Manchester College, Oxford, whose hospitality I enjoyed as a visiting fellow in the summer of 1996. Final revisions of the book were carried out there, and a better environment for such a task I cannot imagine. A special thanks is due to those long-suffering souls who either volunteered, or were imposed upon, to read various drafts of the book: James Ferguson, David Pailin, Philip Almond, Scott Mandelbrote. The anony-

mous readers for Cambridge University Press also offered perceptive
and helpful criticisms. I owe countless debts to members of the Depart-
ment of Studies in Religion at the University of Queensland, an aca-
demic home away from home, where I usually spend some months each
year. Particular thanks are due to friends and colleagues there: to Ed
Conrad, for his constant reminders that the Bible does not describe a
world, but creates a world; to Michael Lattke for numerous references
and helpful discussions of classical and patristic materials; and most of
all to Philip Almond who shares my interest in ideas of the early modern
period, and with whom I have had extended and fruitful discussions on
numerous aspects of this book.

This book is dedicated to my wife Carol, who during its creation has
been a source of unfailing support, encouragement, and love.

Abbreviations

ANF	*Ante-Nicene Fathers* (Edinburgh: T. & T. Clark, 1989)
Aquinas, *ST*	Thomas Aquinas, *Summa theologiae*, Blackfriars edn. (London, 1964–76)
BJHS	*British Journal for the History of Science*
CCSL	*Corpus Christianorum series latina*
CHLMP	*Cambridge History of Later Medieval Philosophy*, ed. Norman Kretsmann, Anthony Kenny, and Jan Pinborg (Cambridge University Press, 1982)
CSEL	*Corpus Scriptorum Ecclesiasticorum Latinorum*
FC	*Fathers of the Church* (Washington: Catholic University of America Press, 1947–)
HMES	Lynn Thorndike, *A History of Magic and Experimental Science*, 8 vols. (New York, 1923–58)
JHB	*Journal of the History of Biology*
JHI	*Journal of the History of Ideas*
JHP	*Journal of the History of Philosophy*
LCL	*Loeb Classical Library*
NPNF 1	*Nicene and Post-Nicene Fathers*, first series, ed. Philip Schaff (Grand Rapids, 1956)
PG	*Patrologia cursus completus, series Graeca*, ed. J.-P. Migne (Paris, 1857–1912)
PL	*Patrologia cursus completus, series Latina*, ed. J.-P. Migne (Paris, 1844–1905)

Page numbers for references to classical and patristic sources are given in brackets if a direct quotation from a particular translation has been made. For other works divided into sections, page numbers given in brackets refer to the particular edition which appears in the References. Biblical quotations are usually taken from the Authorised Version (1611) or the Revised Standard Version (1952), depending on context.

Introduction

For the whole sensible world is like a kind of book written by the finger of God – that is, created by divine power – and each particular creature is somewhat like a figure, not invented by human decision, but instituted by the divine will to manifest the invisible things of God's wisdom. But in the same way that some illiterate, if he saw an open book, would notice the figures, but would not comprehend the letters, so also the stupid and 'animal man' who 'does not perceive the things of God', may see the outward appearance of these visible creatures, but does not understand the reason within.

Hugh of St Victor, De tribus diebus

Philosophy is written in this grand book, the universe, which stands continually open to our gaze. But the book cannot be understood unless one first learns to comprehend the language and read the letters in which it is composed. It is written in the language of mathematics, and its characters are triangles, circles, and other geometrical figures without which it is humanly impossible to understand a single word of it.

Galileo, The Assayer

In 1678, Cambridge naturalist John Ray published *The Ornithology of F. Willughby*, a tribute to his friend and colleague Francis Willughby, who had died unexpectedly at the age of thirty-seven, some six years previously. Ray and Willughby had collaborated on a number of projects involving the study and classification of flora and fauna in England and on the Continent, and before Willughby's untimely demise, they had together made pioneering contributions to natural history. Although the book on birds does not enjoy the same exalted status in the history of biology as Ray's later work on the classification of plants, it nonetheless represents something of a watershed in the field of ornithology.[1]

---

[1] Ray's *Methodus Plantarum Nova* (1682) laid the foundation for modern botanical taxonomy.

I

The preface gives some indication of its import. Here Ray announces that he and Willughby have 'wholly omitted what we find in other Authors concerning *Homonymous* and *Synonymous* words, or the divers names of Birds, *Hieroglyphics, Emblems, Morals, Fables, Presages* or ought else appertaining to *Divinity, Ethics, Grammar,* or any sort of Humane Learning'. The reader is presented instead 'only with what properly relates to their Natural History'.[2] The list may seem a curious one – not for the fact that Ray chose to exclude this information – but because it was ever thought pertinent to the subject of natural history in the first place. Yet we do not have to look far to find the 'other authors' whose labours are the subject of Ray's reproach. Earlier seventeenth-century works of natural history unambiguously locate themselves within the sphere of 'humane learning', or the humanities. Wolfgang Franzius, in his *Historia animalium sacra* (1612, 1670), provides descriptions of animals 'cum Commentariis & Supplementis, Observationum ex recentiori Historia naturali, Similitudinem, Emblematum, Hieroglyphicorum' (with commentaries and supplements, observations from recent natural history, similitudes, emblems, hieroglyphics). Edward Topsell's *Historie of Foure-footed Beastes* (London, 1607, 1653), announces in similar vein that 'the story of euery Beast is amplified with Narrations out of Scriptures, Fathers, Phylosophers, Physicians, and Poets: wherein are declared diuers Hyeroglyphicks, Emblems, Epigrams, and other good Histories'.[3] For Franzius and Topsell, the literary context of the living creature was more important than its physical environment. Animals had a 'story', they were allocated meanings, they were emblems of important moral and theological truths, and like the hieroglyphics of ancient Egypt they were to be thought of as the characters of an intelligible language. The elucidation of the natural world in this tradition calls for an interpretive, rather than a classificatory or mathematical, science. It is the assumption that natural objects have a meaning, and the view of the world that this entails, which is challenged by Ray's list of omissions. 'Proper' natural history, he insists, must be divorced from the human sciences. It is my aim in this book to explain how the systematic study of nature came to be incorporated into the humanities

[2] John Ray and Francis Willughby, *The Ornithology of Francis Willughby* (London, 1678).
[3] See title pages. An English translation of Franzius appeared in 1670, *A History of Brutes* (London, 1670). William Ashworth uses the expression 'emblematic world view' to describe the mentality which informed the work of Topsell and Franzius. He nominates John Johnston's *Historia naturalis* (1650–3) as the work which first represents a breach with that world view. See his 'Natural History and the Emblematic World View', in David Lindberg and Robert Westman (eds.), *Reappraisals of the Scientific Revolution* (Cambridge University Press, 1990).

in the first place, and to document those events which led to its eventual independence.

The kind of transition evident in Ray's new method for the natural sciences is foreshadowed in Galileo's earlier remarks about 'the book of nature', and how it is to be understood. Physical objects, in Galileo's view, are related to each other mathematically, and if nature is to be rendered intelligible at all, it must be interpreted according to the language of mathematics. The familiarity of Galileo's famous metaphor tends to obscure the radical departure from prevailing conceptions of 'the book of nature' which it represents. Writing in the twelfth century, Hugh of St Victor provides a typical example of the traditional under-standing of the metaphor – an understanding which was virtually universal in the middle ages, and which persisted right up until the seventeenth century. All of the elements of the empirical world, says Hugh, are 'figures', which have been invested with divinely instituted significance. The creatures, then, are natural signs.[4] It is this hieroglyph-ic conception of nature which undergirded the medieval belief that there were two books – the book of nature and the book of scripture.[5] The interpretation of the two books, moreover, took place as part of an integrated hermeneutical practice, premised on the principle that the meaning of the words of scripture could not be fully known until the meanings of the objects to which the words referred were also known. Linking the words of scripture with the objects of nature was the universal medieval practice of allegorical interpretation. Allegory was not, as we sometimes tend to think, a strategy for reading multiple meanings into the words of texts, but was rather a process through which the reader was drawn away from naked words to the infinitely more eloquent things of nature to which those words referred. Determining

[4] Full references for the two quotations are Galileo, *The Assayer*, in *Discoveries and Opinions of Galileo*, tr. Stillman Drake (New York: Anchor, 1957), pp. 237f.; Hugh of St Victor, *De tribus diebus* 4, (*PL* 122, 176.814 B-C).

[5] For discussions of 'the two books', and medieval book metaphors, see E. R. Curtius, *European Literature and the Latin Middle Ages* (London: Routledge and Kegan Paul, 1953), pp. 319–26; William Madsen, *From Shadowy Types to Truth: Studies in Milton's Symbolism* (Yale University Press, 1968), pp. 124–44; Robert Markley, *Fallen Languages: Crises of Representation in Newtonian England 1660–1740* (Cornell University Press, 1993), pp. 39–45; Benjamin Nelson, 'Certitude, and the Books of Scripture, Nature, and Conscience', in *On the Roads to Modernity: Conscience, Science and Civilizations*, ed. Toby Huff (Totowa, N.J.: Rowan and Littlefield, 1981), ch. 9; Steven Shapin, 'Robert Boyle and Mathematics: Reality, Representation, and Experimental Practice', *Science in Context* 2 (1988) 23f.; Eisenstein, *The Printing Revolution in Early Modern Europe* (Cambridge University Press, 1983), pp. 185–276; Michael Buckley, *At the Origins of Modern Atheism* (Yale University Press, 1987), p. 69. Specifically on Galileo's use of the trope, see James Bono, *The Word of God and the Languages of Man: Interpreting Nature in Early Modern Science and Medicine* (Madison: University of Wisconsin Press, 1995), pp. 195f.

the reference of a word was merely the starting point of a procedure which would terminate in speculations about the manifold meanings of creatures. A denial of allegory is thus the message of Ray's preface; denial of allegory is the assumption of Galileo's mathematical language of nature.

The emergence of 'proper' natural history, however, was not simply the result of stripping away unwanted and extraneous symbolic elements, leaving a core of pure and unadulterated science. Rather a new conception of the world, itself premised on a particular view of the meaning of texts, was to drive a wedge between words and things, restricting the allocation of meanings to the former. Only then was a genuine science of nature, at least as Ray conceptualised it, gradually able to occupy the territory vacated by the humanities, ordering the objects of nature according to new systematising principles. The new conception of the order of nature was made possible, I shall argue, by the collapse of the allegorical interpretation of texts, for a denial of the legitimacy of allegory is in essence a denial of the capacity of things to act as signs. The demise of allegory, in turn, was due largely to the efforts of Protestant reformers, who in their search for an unambiguous religious authority, insisted that the book of scripture be interpreted only in its literal, historical sense. This insistence on the primacy of the literal sense had the unforeseen consequence of cutting short a potentially endless chain of reference, in which word refers to object, and object refers to other objects. The literalist mentality of the reformers thus gave a determinate meaning to the text of scripture, and at the same time precluded the possibility of assigning meanings to natural objects. Literalism means that only words refer; the things of nature do not. In this way the study of the natural world was liberated from the specifically religious concern of biblical interpretation, and the sphere of nature was opened up to new ordering principles. The mathematical and taxonomic categories imposed by Galileo and Ray on physical objects and living things represent an attempt to reconfigure a natural world which had been evacuated of order and meaning. It is commonly supposed that when in the early modern period individuals began to look at the world in different way, they could no longer believe what they read in the Bible. In this book I shall suggest that the reverse is the case: that when in the sixteenth century people began to read the Bible in a different way, they found themselves forced to jettison traditional conceptions of the world. The Bible – its contents, the controversies it generated, its varying fortunes as an authority, and most importantly, the new way in which it was read by Protestants – played a central role in the emergence of natural science in the seventeenth century.

Over the past sixty years, a number of attempts have been made to establish causal connexions between the Protestant Reformation and the scientific revolution. The first and best known of such attempts – the 'puritanism and science' thesis – made its appearance in the 1930s, when Dorothy Stimson put forward the view that puritanism was a key element in the philosophical reforms initiated by Francis Bacon. The suggestion that puritanism might have acted as a catalyst in the development of modern science was subsequently adopted by R. F. Jones in *Ancients and Moderns* (1936), and Robert K. Merton, 'Puritanism, Pietism, and Science' (1938).[6] These seminal works have exercised a profound influence over subsequent discussions of seventeenth-century science, particularly in the English context, and the relatively recent revision of the thesis, in Charles Webster's monumental *The Great Instauration* (1975), has added considerable strength to this long-standing view.[7] The hypothesis was first prompted by the discovery that Protestants, and puritans in particular, were disproportionally represented in the ranks of seventeenth-century scientists. Merton observed that of the ten scientists who formed the nucleus of the Royal Society during the period of the Commonwealth, seven were puritans. In the year 1663, moreover, sixty-two percent of the members of the Royal Society were similarly

[6] Dorothy Stimson, 'Puritanism and the New Philosophy in 17th century England', *Bulletin of the Institute of the History of Medicine* 3 (1935) 321–4; R. F. Jones, *Ancients and Moderns*, (St Louis, 1936); Robert Merton, 'Puritanism, Pietism, and Science', *The Sociological Review* 28 (1936) 1–30; 'Science, Technology, and Society in Seventeenth-Century England', *Osiris* 4 (1938) 360–632. For discussions of the thesis see G. A. Abraham, 'Misunderstanding the Merton Thesis', *Isis* 74 (1983) 368–87; Charles Webster (ed.) *The Intellectual Revolution of the Seventeenth Century* (London: Routledge and Kegan Paul, 1974); R. Hooykaas, *Religion and the Rise of Modern Science* (Grand Rapids; Eerdmans, 1972), pp. 135–60; P. M. Ratansi, 'The Social Interpretation of Seventeenth-Century Science', in *Science and Society 1600–1900*, ed. Peter Matthias (Cambridge University Press, 1972) pp. 1–32; Richard Greaves, 'Puritanism and Science, *JHI* 30 (1969) 345–68; Douglas Kelmsley, 'Religious Influences in the Rise of Modern Science', *Annals of Science* 24 (1968) 199–226; Leo Salt, 'Puritanism, Capitalism, Democracy, and the New Science, *American Historical Review* 73 (1967) 18–29.

[7] Charles Webster, *The Great Instauration: Science Medicine and Reform 1626–1660* (London: Duckworth, 1975), see esp. pp. 484–520. For a more recent restatement, see Webster, 'Puritanism, Separatism, and Science', in David Lindberg and Ronald Numbers (eds.), *God and Nature: Historical Essays on the Encounter between Christianity and Science* (University of California Press, 1986), pp. 192–217. Further discussions may be found in John Brooke, *Science and Religion: Some Historical Perspectives* (Cambridge University Press, 1991), pp. 82–116; Richard Kroll's introduction to *Philosophy, Science and Religion in England 1640–1700*, ed. Richard Kroll, Richard Ashcroft, and Perez Zagorin (Cambridge University Press, 1992), pp. 1–28; Lotte Mulligan, 'Puritanism and English Science: A Critique of Webster', *Isis* 71 (1980) 456–69; Elizabeth Eisenstein, *The Printing Press as an Agent of Change*, 2 vols. (Cambridge University Press, 1979), II, 636–708. Also see numbers of these journals devoted to the topic: *Isis* 79 (1988), and *Science in Context* 3 (1989).

identified, and this at a time when puritans were in a minority in the general population.[8] While this general correlation seems to be beyond dispute, the provision of a satisfactory explanation for it has proved more elusive. Merton invoked the Weber-Tawney thesis, which links the rise of capitalism with 'the Protestant work ethic'. Scientific pursuits, on this account, turn out to be a special case of good works, which act as a sign of election. Merton claimed that the same 'this-worldly asceticism' which inspired puritans to greater economic activity also motivated them to diligent and painstaking scientific enquiry.[9]

Not all historians, however, have concurred with this analysis. The designation 'puritan', it has frequently been pointed out, does not sit well with a number of individuals who are identified as exemplars of the thesis.[10] Leading figures of seventeenth-century English science, it is argued, are better designated 'latitudinarians' or simply 'Anglicans' than 'puritans'.[11] Acceptance of these new labels, in turn, requires the relinquishing of a central element of the thesis as it was originally formulated – the nexus of the Calvinist doctrine of election, the Protestant work ethic, and scientific activity.[12] Even more damaging to the puritanism and science thesis is the fact that on most accounts, modern science had its rise well before the puritan revolution in 1640, and was by no means restricted to England or other Protestant countries. As Theodore Rabb has pointed out: 'By 1640, with the work of Galileo, Harvey and Descartes virtually complete, one can safely say that science had risen.'[13] The puritan form of Protestant religion, on this view, may well

---

[8] Merton, *Science, Technology, and Society in Seventeenth-Century England* (New York: Harper, 1970), pp. 113f. Stimson offers similar evidence. For criticisms of this statistical analysis, see T. K. Rabb, 'Puritanism and the Rise of Experimental Science in England', *Cahiers d'Histoire Mondiale* 7 (1962) 50ff.

[9] Merton, *Science, Technology, and Society*, pp. 56f.; Max Weber, *The Protestant Ethic and the Spirit of Capitalism* tr. T. Parsons (New York: Charles Scribner's Sons, 1930); R. H. Tawney, *Religion and the Rise of Capitalism* (New York: Harcourt, Brace, and Co., 1926).

[10] Kearney, 'Puritanism and Science: Problems of Definition', in Webster (ed.), *Intellectual Revolution*, pp. 254–61; Godfrey Davies, 'Arminian versus Puritan in England *c.* 1620–1650', *Huntington Library Bulletin* 5 (1934), 157–79; Nicholas Tyacke, 'Puritanism, Arminianism, and Counter-Revolution', in *Origins of the English Civil War*, ed. Conrad Russell (London: Macmillan, 1973).

[11] Barbara Shapiro, 'Latitudinarianism and Science in Seventeenth-century England', in Webster (ed.), *Intellectual Revolution*, pp. 286–316. James R. Jacob and Margaret C. Jacob, 'The Anglican Origins of Modern Science: the Metaphysical Foundations of Whig Constitution', *Isis* 71 (1980) 251–67. Also see Kroll et al. (eds.) *Philosophy, Science and Religion*; John Gascoigne, *Cambridge in the Age of Enlightenment: Science, Religion and Politics from the Restoration to the French Revolution* (Cambridge University Press, 1989), passim.

[12] For problems with the 'latitudinarian' thesis, see Lotte Mulligan, 'Anglicanism, Latitudinarianism, and Science in Seventeenth-Century England', *Annals of Science* 30 (1973) 213–19.

[13] T. K. Rabb, 'Religion and the Rise of Modern Science', in Webster (ed.) *Intellectual Revolution*, p. 263.

have provided fertile soil for the growth of science, but its germination dates from an earlier period. The great advances in astronomy, physics, and anatomy which we designate 'the scientific revolution' had taken place well before puritanism reached its zenith, and this revolution was presided over by individuals of diverse religious commitments.

In the light of such criticisms, some have retreated to a more general thesis: not *puritanism* and science, but *Protestantism* and science. Proponents of this wider view have identified a number of elements of Protestant ideology not restricted to the puritan party, which may have provided important stimuli for the new science. According to the Protestant doctrine of the priesthood of all believers, for example, all individuals have direct access to God and the Bible without the necessity of official priestly mediators or sanctioned interpreters. Carried over into the sciences, it has been argued, this principle granted to students of nature direct access to the book of God's works, liberating them from both a slavish adherence to classical writings and the censorship of ecclesiastical authorities. Allied to this new freedom was a suspicion of scholastic philosophy which led to calls for educational reforms and for an end to Aristotle's domination of the university curriculum.[14] The theological voluntarism which lay at the heart of Calvin's doctrine of election has also been proposed as an important factor behind the new emphasis on empirical investigation of the world. Calvin's sovereign and distant Deity had laid down arbitrary laws which conferred upon the sphere of nature the same deterministic inevitability which existed in the sphere of grace. This meant that the operations of nature were regular and lawful, but these laws of nature, resting upon the divine will rather than the divine reason, could only be discovered through research and experimentation. Protestant demystification of the world also promoted the mechanical conception of nature. Scepticism about Catholic miracles, the denial of sacramental magic, the challenging of the special status of priests, saints, and supernatural intermediaries, have also been plausibly proposed as aspects of Reformed theology and ecclesiology which contributed to the emergence of the lawful and deterministic universe which is the prerequisite for scientific investigation.[15] For other critics of the 'puritanism and science' thesis, it was not Protestant doctrines which encouraged

[14] Phyllis Allen, 'Scientific Studies in the English Universities in the Seventeenth Century', *JHI* 10 (1949) 238.

[15] Richard Westfall, *Science and Religion in Seventeenth-Century England* (Yale University Press, 1958), pp. 5–7; Greaves, 'Puritanism and Science'; Hooykaas, *Religion and the Rise of Modern Science*, pp. 98–114. Specifically for the influence of nominalism, see Eugene Klaaren, *Religious Origins of Modern Science* (Grand Rapids: Eerdmans, 1977), pp. 32–52.

scientific activity, but rather the social and political conditions which resulted from the Reformation. The Protestant Reformation, in other words, might have indirectly influenced the fortunes of science. Christopher Hill has observed in this context that 'what mattered for the development of science was not so much Protestant doctrine . . . as the breaking of clerical monopoly control.'[16] On this view it was reformation challenges to entrenched authorities which indirectly paved the way for a new approach to the natural world. Richard Greaves has argued along similar lines that the Puritan revolution gave rise to conditions favourable to the development of experimental science. 'There is a relationship between Puritanism and science', writes Greaves, 'but it is not a direct one. The mediating link is revolution.'[17]

The present work, then, falls into this last category, for I shall be arguing for an indirect, even diffuse, influence of Protestantism on the development of modern science. The specific agent which I wish to identify as having been a major catalyst in the emergence of science, however, is the Protestant approach to the interpretation of texts – a central feature of the Reformation which up until now has received surprisingly little attention in literature on the relationship between Protestantism and science. While I do not wish to be seen as setting out a monocausal thesis for the rise of modern science, for there is no reason why a range of factors should not play some role, yet I shall argue that of these factors by far the most significant was the literalist mentality initiated by the Protestant reformers, and sponsored by their successors. In sum, this book addresses three overlapping concerns: first, the Protestantism and science thesis; second, the related question of the timing and place of the emergence of modern science; and third, the broader issue of the interactions between science and religion, particularly in the early modern period.

Many histories of science have tended to work backwards, beginning with the modern conception of the discipline of science, and projecting it back in time. Historians of science, as Paolo Rossi has observed, frequently concern themselves with 'an imaginary object', constructing it from a variety of texts and heterogeneous disciplines.[18] It is of course inevitable that in order to understand the past we must understand it

[16] Hill, 'William Harvey and the Idea of Monarchy', in Webster (ed.), *Intellectual Revolution*, p. 180.
[17] Greaves, 'Puritanism and Science', p. 368.
[18] Paolo Rossi, *The Dark Abyss of Time: The History of the Earth and the History of Nations from Hooke to Vico* (University of Chicago Press, 1984), p. vii.

through modern conceptions. At the same time, it needs to be recognised that 'science', as we understand it, does not have a history which can be traced back beyond the seventeenth century. Accordingly, what I have sought to do in this book is to work forwards, in as much as that is possible. For virtually the first fifteen hundred years of the common era the study of natural objects took place within the humanities, as part of an all-encompassing science of interpretation which sought to expound the meanings of words and things. This work is therefore not a history of science, if for no other reason than that science did not exist for much of the period under study. Thus we shall at first be concerned more with the history of hermeneutics – broadly conceived as the general science of interpretation – for the study of the natural world up to the seventeenth century was an integral part of just such a science.

From time to time, readers might find themselves in what seems to be rather familiar territory, particularly in the later chapters of the book. The role of humanist philology in the development of science, the predilection of late seventeenth-century English naturalists for physico-theology, the motivation provided to natural philosophers by certain passages of scripture – these are stories which to some extent have already been told by others. What I hope to have done in my presentation of this material is to shed new light on its significance by showing its intimate relation to the business of biblical interpretation. I must also confess what will soon become obvious to the reader – that there are gaps in the narrative of this book. Rather than trace continuities in detail, I have resorted to a focus on those discrete times which I believe to have been important historical moments of transition. The study thus deals with North Africa in the patristic period; France in the twelfth century; Europe generally in the sixteenth century, and England in the seventeenth. This procedure is less than ideal, but for practical purposes unavoidable. Doubtless there are numerous relevant developments in those times and places which I have omitted from this study. But for the purposes of outlining a broad thesis about the relation between biblical interpretation and the rise of natural science, I trust that I have covered sufficient ground to make a convincing hypothesis.

The structure of the book reflects this focus upon discrete times and places. The first chapter deals with the development of the symbolic view of the world and the allegorical approach to texts, concentrating on the work of the third-century Alexandrian writer Origen and the contributions of that luminous genius of the fifth century, Augustine of Hippo. The second chapter is concerned with the twelfth-century renaissance and the rediscovery of nature. In the third chapter, the relevance of fifteenth- and sixteenth-century advances in philology and textual criticism for the study of nature will be considered. Here too, I spell out in detail the central thesis that the Protestant Reformation brought about changes to the interpretation of both the book of scripture and the book of nature, and suggest how these changes in the methods of biblical interpretation might have led to new approaches to the natural world. The next three chapters are concerned in various ways with the implications of the literal approach to texts for the study of nature. Chapter four shows how in the seventeenth century scripture, now read almost exclusively for its literal sense, was thought to contain historical and scientific information, and how that information was utilised in speculations about the beginning and end of the world, and the birth, death, and resurrection of human bodies. The subject of chapter five is the physico-theological tradition, and the process by which explanations of the meaning of the things of nature came to be replaced by the search for their practical utility. The final chapter gives an account of how new literal readings of scripture, and of the first chapters of Genesis in particular, were to inform and motivate scientific investigations of the natural world.

CHAPTER I

Worlds visible and invisible

For the invisible things of him from the creation of the world are
clearly seen, being understood by the things that are made.

Romans 1.20

I think that He who made all things in wisdom so created all the
species of visible things upon the earth, that He placed in some of
them some teaching and knowledge of things invisible and heavenly, whereby the human mind might mount to spiritual understanding and seek the grounds of things in heaven.

Origen, *Commentary on the Song of Songs*

. . . after many generations and many conflicts there is strained out
at last, I should say, one system of really true philosophy. For that
philosophy is not of this world – such a philosophy our sacred
mysteries most justly detest – but of the other, intelligible world.

Augustine, *Against the Academics*

THE WISDOM OF THE WORLD

Visitors to modern Athens, if they were to approach the ancient monuments of the Acropolis from the Pláka area, might notice before the final
ascent to the ruins of the temple of Athene Nike a set of steps cut into the
side of a large granite outcrop which lies below and to the West of the
Acropolis. The site is the Areopagus – literally 'Mars Hill' – where for
the first time in their own city Athenians encountered the new faith of
the Christians. To the right of the worn steps is a large brass plaque
which bears in Greek the words of the seventeenth chapter of the book
of Acts, which recount the events which took place there, probably in
the autumn of the year AD 50. This first contact between Christianity
and Greek culture, despite its impressive physical surroundings, was not
auspicious. St Paul was passing through Athens – in the first century still
the symbolic centre of ancient learning – and having struck up conversa-
tion with philosophers in the market place, was taken to Mars Hill,

ominously dominated by temples to the Greek deities, to address a larger audience. The Epicurean and Stoic philosophers who were present on this occasion were not impressed by the Jewish teacher, describing him as a 'babbler' and 'a preacher of foreign deities', and his assertion of the resurrection of the dead was met with general ridicule. Few converts were made, no church was established, and what might have been a powerful symbolic moment in the fortunes of a developing Christian faith failed to realise its latent potential. Authorities retrospectively attempted to salvage something out of this otherwise disappointing event by attributing to Dionysius the Areopagite, one of two Athenian converts specifically named in the book of Acts, a body of profoundly influential writings, but as it turned out, the documents attributed to the Areopagite actually date from the late fifth century, and thus could not have been the works of Paul's Athenian disciple. It was perhaps his experience at Athens which later led Paul, when writing to the Church at Corinth, to observe that the Christian message was 'folly to Greeks', implying that the converse was also true. God, wrote the apostle, had 'made foolish the wisdom of the world' and had 'brought to nothing the cleverness of the clever'.[1] This assessment, bearing the weight of apostolic authority, was to exert considerable influence on subsequent Christian thinkers, and despite favourable treatments of Greek philosophy from Alexandrian theologians, tended to become the norm for writers of the Christian West.

'Serves him right' was Tertullian's unsympathetic verdict on the fate of the father of Greek philosophy, Thales of Miletus, who had fallen headlong into a well while gazing up at the stars. There was a lesson in this for students of nature, according to the second-century theologian: Thales' mishap was 'a figurative picture of the philosophers', who 'indulge a stupid curiosity on natural subjects, which they ought rather (intelligently to direct) to their Creator and Governor'. Pagan philosophy, Tertullian thought, was the parent of heresy.[2] Subsequent Christian writers, while less hostile to pagan wisdom than Tertullian, were nonetheless unenthusiastic about the study of nature. Basil the Great, typically, dismissed Greek science as 'idle chatter' which was 'not at all useful for the edification of the Church.'[3] Ambrose of Milan, explaining

---

[1] Acts 17, I Corinthians, I, 19–27.

[2] Tertullian, *Ad nationes*, IV (*ANF* III, 133); *De praescriptione haereticorum*, 7 (*ANF* III, 246).

[3] Basil, *Hexameron*, 1.8, 11; IX.1 (*FC* 46, 14, 19, 136f.). Cf. Irenaeus, *Against Heresies*, II.xiv.2; Origen, *Letter to Gregory Thaumaturgos*, 13.1. Augustine, *De Genesi ad literam* II.9, 10. A comprehensive refutation of Greek cosmologies was provided by Hippolytus (170–236), *Refutation of All Heresies*, I. A more positive attitude had been expressed by Clement of Alexandria. See *Stromata*, I.ix, xiii; *Exhortation to the Heathen*, VI.

why the scriptures had little to say on scientific matters, wrote that 'there was no place in the words of the Holy Spirit for the vanity of perishable knowledge which deceives and deludes us in our attempt to explain the unexplainable'.[4] Augustine was hardly more enthusiastic, declaring that 'the knowledge collected from the books of the pagans, although some of it is useful, is also little as compared with that derived from scripture.'[5] Tertullian, Basil and Augustine all agreed that Greek philosophers had contradicted each other, and that their disagreements stood in stark contrast to the harmony of scripture.[6] The final humiliation for the natural philosophy of the Greeks came from the universal assumption of the Church Fathers that Moses and the prophets had pre-dated the great thinkers of the other ancient cultures – Hermes Trismegistus in Egypt, and Thales, Socrates, and Plato in Greece – and that whatever there was of value to be found in their writings had been plagiarised from the Mosaic tradition.[7]

Despite this generally negative appraisal of the approach of the Greeks to the natural world, some of the specific issues which were to exercise the minds of the Church Fathers – why, for example, there was a material world at all, and why it had the particular features it did – bear traces of the philosophical concerns of the Greek philosophers. And while the Fathers of the Church sought answers to these questions by speculating about the motivations of an all-good and all-powerful divine agent, Greek dialectic and ontology, as well as helping to provide the means by which those questions might be addressed, also furnished the technical language in which their solutions might be expressed. Indeed, in the application of the principles of pagan philosophy to the raw materials of a faith, the content of which was expressed in those documents which were to become the New Testament, we can discern the beginnings of Christian theology.

One of the central concerns of the first Christian theologians was the doctrine of creation. Granted that God had created the material world, why had he created it, and why were this world and its inhabitants marred by imperfections?[8] This question was made all the more urgent by the fact that the various systems of gnosticism which sprang up in the second and third centuries had already provided a plausible account of

---

[4] Ambrose, *Hexameron*, VI.ii.8 (*FC* 42, 232).
[5] Augustine, *On Christian Doctrine*, II.xlii.63 (p. 78); Cf. *City of God*, XIV.28.
[6] Basil, *Hexameron*, I.II; Augustine, *City of God*, VIII.41; Tertullian, *Treatise on the Soul*, III (*ANF* III, 183).
[7] Tertullian, *Ad nationes*, II; Augustine, *City of God*, XVIII.37-9. Cf. Augustine, *On Christian Doctrine*, II.42, *Confessions*, VII.x.
[8] For differing formulations of this problem, see Origen, *De principiis*, II.ix.4; Augustine, *De genesi contra Manichaeos* I.XVI.25 (*PL* 34, 185).

the origins of the visible world. For them, the present world was the work of some lesser deity, and the embodiment of living things the consequence of a cosmic catastrophe. The aim of the gnostic was to escape from this evil world of matter into the spiritual world which lay beyond. While many Christian thinkers, then and since, have shared the gnostics' distrust of the flesh and of things material, gnosticism collided directly with the positive view of the creation set out in the Hebrew scriptures. The gnostic systems of Marcion, Valentinus, and Basilides, touted by their proponents as legitimate expressions of Christian faith, thus came to be identified by the orthodox as a major threat to a nascent Christian theology. Indeed the perceived threat of gnosticism provided a major impetus for the systematisation of Christian thought.

Irenaeus of Lyons (c.130–c.202), the first Catholic theologian, saw as his primary task the refutation of the claims of the gnostics. In his chief work – *Against Heresies* – he put forward an alternative account of the creation, suggesting that the material world had been created as a venue for the moral development of free beings. Of necessity, he explained, it was imperfect, for all things that are created must lack at least some of the perfections of the creator.[9] In their first estate, our original parents, too, had been imperfect. Yet their inevitable fall had not been an unmitigated disaster, for it had been the intention of the Creator all along to allow his creatures the freedom to err, and like children under the guidance of a benevolent parent, to mature gradually, and slowly to put on the accoutrements of deity.[10] Created in the image and likeness of God, our first parents had lost this likeness. They and their children had been placed in the world in an 'unfinished' state in order that they might be gently encouraged to develop towards perfection and regain the divine likeness which they had lost. In their earthly sojourn they were not bereft of resources: their teachers were to be the world and the word – nature and scripture. 'God formed all things in the world, by means of his word', wrote Irenaeus, 'His works do declare him, and his word has shown that in many modes he may be seen and known.'[11]

That the reading of scripture might lead to moral edification is relatively unproblematic. Explaining how the world might be read in a comparable way required some elaboration. As it happened, the dualistic platonic tradition which had served as a point of departure for the

---

[9] Irenaeus, *Against Heresies*, IV.xxxviii.1.

[10] *Ibid.*, IV.xxxviii–xxxix, II.xxii; *Proof of the Apostolic Preaching* 12. Also see John Hick, *Evil and the God of Love*, (London: Macmillan, 1985), pp. 211–15, 253f.

[11] Irenaeus, *Against Heresies*, IV.xx.1 (*ANF* v, 439).

various systems of gnosticism also held out for the Fathers of the Church the possibility of demonstrating the value of the material world. Plato had argued that this visible world was but an inferior, transient, and decaying image of an eternal, spiritual realm – a realm in which ultimate truth and reality were to be found. Christian writers of the second and third centuries were to replace the temporal, eschatological dualism of the first Christians with the ontological dualism of Plato, for they had found in this latter conception a means of ascribing value to the visible world by asserting that it provided the key to an understanding of the invisible. God was said to have infused the created order with symbols, the highest purpose of which was to point beyond themselves to the superior world of spiritual realities. By attending to the spiritual meaning of physical objects, the soul might become familiar with higher truths.

The conviction that physical objects were tokens of spiritual truths was only part of the story, however, for it was clear that despite the efforts of the best pagan philosophers, the most profound meanings of the natural world had remained hidden. To be sure, Aristotle and the Stoics had progressed to the point of realising that the purpose of the world was to minister to the physical needs of the human race, but they had failed to move beyond this. The world was designed not only to nourish the body, but to edify the soul. What was wanting in pagan philosophy was a science of interpretation, a hermeneutical method by which natural things could be made to yield up their secret meanings. In the first three centuries of the Christian era such a method was developed by the Platonists of the Alexandrian school, and brought to perfection by the third-century Church Father, Origen. This universal hermeneutic was to provide interpretive strategies for dealing with both texts and objects in the physical world. It lay at the foundation of the 'symbolist mentality' of the middle ages, and was the *sine qua non* of the medieval image of the 'book of nature'.

THE THREE SENSES

Origen (c.185–c.254) is the most colourful of the Church Fathers. His home was Alexandria, second city of the empire, site of the famous library, and a metropolis which numbered amongst its inhabitants the largest Jewish community of any city in the ancient world. Origen's brilliance and originality, combined with an ambivalent acceptance of some of the tenets of Platonism, rendered much of his theology suspect in later centuries. Such was his personality, that when he erred, it was not on the side of caution. His suggestion that human souls might have 'pre-existed' before embodiment, and his generous extension of salvation to Satan and his minions, were condemned as heretical by the Council of Constantinople in 543.[12] The rumour, put about by his opponents, that he had taken too literally that passage of scripture which refers to 'those who have made themselves eunuchs for the sake of the kingdom of heaven' further eroded his prestige, and the vast majority of his original works have been lost. (Jerome generously numbered Origen's works at two thousand, Epiphanius mentions the figure of six thousand.)[13] Not until the Renaissance was Origen in some measure rehabilitated.

Despite the considerable suspicion with which Origen's theological writings were viewed during the Middle Ages, he exerted an enormous influence on medieval thought through his methods of interpretation.[14] The approach of medieval thinkers to both world and text derive ultimately from Origen. The foundations of that method are set out by Origen in his commentary on The Song of Songs:

Paul the apostle teaches us that the invisible things of God are understood by means of the things that are visible, and that the things that are not seen are beheld through their relationship and likeness to things seen. He thus shows that this visible world teaches us about that which is invisible, and that this earthly scene contains certain patterns of things heavenly. Thus it is to be possible for us to mount up from things below to things above, and to perceive and understand from the things we see on earth the things that belong to heaven. On the pattern of these the Creator gave to His creatures on earth a certain likeness to these, so that thus their great diversity might be more easily deduced and understood.[15]

---

[12] Origen, *De principiis*, II.ix.3–4; *Against Celsus*, 1.32; Henrici Denzinger, *Enchiridion symbolorum* 37th edn (Friburgi Brisgoviae: Herder, 1991) paras. 403–11 (pp. 189f.).

[13] Jerome, *Against Rufinus* II.22; Epiphanius, *Haereses*, LXIV.63.

[14] On the influence of Origen's hermeneutics in the Middle Ages, see B. Smalley, *The Study of the Bible in the Middle Ages*, (Oxford: Blackwell, 1952), pp. 13f.; H. Flanders Dunbar, *Symbolism in Medieval Thought and its Consummation in the Divine Comedy* (New York: Russell and Russell, 1961), pp. 11–25; G. R. Evans, *The Language and Logic of the Bible: The Road to Reformation* (Cambridge University Press, 1985), p. 42; Henri de Lubac, *Exégèse Médiéval: Les Quatre sens de l'écriture* (Paris, Aubier, 1959–64), 2 vols., I.1, 187–97.

[15] Origen, *The Song of Songs, Commentary and Homilies*, tr. R. P. Lawson (London: Longmans, Green and Co., 1957) p. 218. The reference to Paul is Romans 1.20. Cf. Irenaeus: 'But it is congruous that these earthly things, indeed, which are spread all around us, should be types of the celestial, being [both], however, created by the same God. For in no other way could he assimilate an image of spiritual things [to suit our comprehension].' *Against Heresies*, IV.xix (*ANF* V, 436f.).

In principle, this Platonic understanding of the created order made possible an elaborate semiotics of the natural world, in which every visible feature of creation corresponded to some reality in the unseen, heavenly realm. 'Each of the manifest things', said Origen, 'is to be related to one of those that are hidden . . . all things visible have some invisible likeness and pattern.'[16] For his successors, Origen had demonstrated how the physical world could be rendered intelligible through a process of laying bare the spiritual realities which material things signified. By the fourth century there was general agreement amongst Christian theologians from both East and West that the world was indeed designed to be a school for souls, and that the things of this world, for all their transience and imperfections, could serve to edify the soul in search of salvation. Basil the Great (c.330–379) thus declared the material world to be 'a training place for rational souls and a school for attaining the knowledge of God because through the visible and perceptible objects it provides guidance to the mind for the contemplation of the invisible'.[17] Ambrose of Milan (c.339–397), the great Doctor of the Latin Church and mentor of Augustine, taught similarly that 'the beginning of the ways of God is in His work, so that the race of men might learn by Him to follow the ways of the Lord and to perform the works of God'. 'Heaven and earth', Ambrose declared, 'are the sum of the visible things which appear not only as the adornment of this world, but also as a testimony of invisible things' and as 'an evidence of things that are not seen'.[18] For the Fathers of the Church, then, the material world was designed to minister to the human needs both physical and spiritual. The things of nature, in this latter role, were regarded as signs. Henceforth, explanations of physical phenomena will be to do with signification, rather than causation. What becomes important about the features of the visible world is not how they function, nor how they interact causally, but what they signify. The world, like a text, will have a meaning, and systematic accounts of the objects encountered in it will belong to a science of interpretation.

The principles upon which interpretation of the world was based closely parallel those which were employed in the study of scripture. Origen had argued that both the world and scripture have embedded within them potent symbols. 'This relationship [between the invisible and the visible] does not obtain only with creatures', he insisted, 'the

---

[16] Origen, *Commentary on Song of Songs*, p. 220.   [17] Basil, *Hexaemeron*, 1.6 (*FC* 46, 11).
[18] Ambrose, *Hexaemeron*, 1.iv.6 (*FC* 42, 15f.)

Divine Scripture itself is written with wisdom of a rather similar sort.'[19] Scripture, no less than the world of appearances, required a method for determining the references of its symbols: it stood in need of a means of interpretation which could transport the reader beyond the threshold of literal truth to hidden spiritual truths which lay beyond. The key was provided by allegory. Allegorical methods had long been employed by Greek philosophers in order to sanitise the fables and myths of the gods related by Homer and Hesiod.[20] 'If everything he wrote is not an allegory', wrote Heraclitus of Homer, 'everything is an impiety.'[21] In the first century, the Alexandrian Jew, Philo (c. 20BC – c. AD50), applied similar methods to the text of the Old Testament, and by this means was able to discover much in the Hebrew scriptures which was consonant with his beloved Greek philosophy.[22] Alexandrian Christians, immersed as they were in the hellenistic thought world, came quickly to be persuaded of the advantages of the allegorical method. Through allegory such embarrassments as the immodesty of the inebriated Noah and the opportunist incest of Lot's daughters could be accounted for, the exuberant eroticism of the Song of Songs subdued, and most important of all, the wrathful and vengeful Yahweh of the Old Testament reconciled with the loving God of the New. With Origen, the method of allegory was raised to the level of a science.

Scripture, according to Origen, had three senses: 'For as a man consists of body, soul, and spirit', he wrote, 'so in the same way does Scripture.'[23] The first sense in which scripture was to be taken was the

---

[19] Origen, *The Song of Songs*, p. 223. Even John Chrysostom, leading exegete of the Antioch school (which generally took a dim view of allegorical interpretation) could concede Origen's point: 'let us not stop short at the literal level; instead let us reason from the perceptible visible realities to the superiority of spiritual realities'. *Homilies on Genesis* XIV.4 (*FC* 74, 182).

[20] Subsequently in the Christian era Ovid and Virgil were to sustain similar interpretations. Erasmus, e.g., remarked that 'as divine scripture has little if you persist and cling to its literal sense, so Homer's and Virgil's poetry has considerable value if you remember that all of it is allegorical', *Enchiridion militis christianit* (London, 1533), p. 63, qu. in Marie-Dominique Chenu, *Nature, Man and Society in the Twelfth Century* (University of Chicago Press, 1968), p. 110, n. 29. Also see L. P. Wilkinson, *Ovid Recalled* (Cambridge University Press, 1955) pp. 366–444; L. K. Born, 'Ovid and Allegory', *Speculum*, 9 (1934) 362–79; de Lubac, *Exégèse Médiéval*, II.2, 237f.

[21] Heraclitus, *Allégories d'Homère*, tr. F. Buffière (Paris: Société d'Edition 'Les Belles Lettres', 1962), I.1 (p. 1), qu. in David Norton, *The History of the Bible as Literature* (Cambridge University Press, 1993), p. 55.

[22] Philo, *De opificio mundi* 157 (p. 22). For Philo's influence on patristic exegesis, see J. Daniélou, *Philon d'Alexandrie* (Paris, 1958); H. A. Wolfson, *The Philosophy of the Church Fathers*, 2 vols., 2nd edn (Harvard University Press, 1964) I, ch. 2; David Runia, *Philo in Early Christian Literature* (Minneapolis: Fortress Press, 1993), pp. 163–71, 292f., 325f.

[23] Origen, *On First Principles*, IV.i.11 (*ANF* IV, 359); *Homilies on Leviticus*, v.3 (*FC* 83, 89). Cf. Clement of Alexandria, *Stromata* I.xxviii; Jerome, *Commentariorum in Ezechielem* v.16.30-1 (*PL* 25, 153D); *In Amos* II, 4.4–6 (*PL* 25, 1027D–1028A); Augustine, *City of God*, xv.xxvii, xvi.ii. The biblical warrant for

literal sense, which was the 'body' of scripture, or the obvious or historical sense. For the simple carnal man the literal sense might be the
highest level of knowledge to which he could aspire. The *moral* sense, the
'soul' of scripture, communicated to more advanced individuals how life
was to be lived. The *allegorical* sense, the spirit of scripture, was the
highest sense, and contained timeless theological truths.[24] So influential
was this hermeneutical scheme that over one thousand years after
Origen's death, Dante was still employing a system of interpretation
which in its essential details was the same. Explaining the three meanings of the exodus of the Israelites from Egypt, Dante wrote: 'If we
consider merely the letter, the meaning is the exodus of the children of
Israel from Egypt . . . if we look at the allegorical signification, it is the
Redemption by Christ; taken in the moral sense it indicates the turning
of the soul from the sorrow and misery of sin to the state of grace.'[25]

One the chief advantages of such a method was that it could bring
sense to passages which, when read literally, seemed nonsensical. A
literal reading of scripture will bring to light inconsistencies and contradictions, and narratives whose sense is obscure. It will uncover complete
books – such as the Song of Songs – which, on a naive reading, seem
totally devoid of religious or historical significance. Origen went so far as
to suggest that certain passages of scripture have no literal sense at all,
and that others, when taken literally, could reasonably be dismissed as
'absurd and impossible'.[26] Given the existence of these 'hindrances and
impossibilities' which mar the literal text, typological and symbolical
methods of interpretation provided a means by which scripture could be
shown to be authoritative in every detail: nothing was false, superfluous,
or meaningless. The Word was on no occasion void. At the same time,
the possible meanings of scripture could never be exhausted. The
mysterious world of the Bible to which Origen felt himself irresistibly
drawn was like an uncharted ocean of truth.[27]

The physical world was likewise open to various levels of interpretation. Natural objects, understood literally, pertain to the body of man,
taken spiritually, they pertain to his soul. The significance of the lower

---

allegory was provided by Paul, Galatians 4.24; I Cor. 2.6–7, 3.1–2, 9.9, 10.4; 2 Cor. 3.6; Rom.
15.4.   [24] Origen, *On First Principles*, IV.i.11.
[25] Dante Alighieri, 'Letter to Can Grande', qu. in R. Allers, 'Microcosmos', pp. 328f. In the
manner of medieval exegetes, Dante refers to a fourth, anagogical sense: 'anagogically viewed, it
is the exodus of the saintly soul from the slavery of corruptibility to the liberty of glory eternal'.
[26] Origen considered these 'stumbling blocks', 'hindrances and impossibilities', to have been
deliberately placed in scripture to ensure a spiritual reading. *On First Principles*, IV.ii.5, 9; IV.iii.4.
[27] J. Daniélou, *Origène*, (Paris, 1948), p. 174.

orders of creation, at a literal level, was plain. Animals and plants had
been given to mankind to provide for his physical needs as food or as
'helpers'.[28] The pagans with their darkened minds had managed to
establish this much. Yet on this literal reading, some aspects of nature,
no less than some passages of scripture, seemed senseless. Origen
himself had noted that 'he who believes the Scripture to have proceeded
from him who is the Author of Nature may well expect to find the same
sort of difficulties in it as are found in the constitution of nature'.[29] The
interpretation of nature according to which the purpose of lesser creatures was solely to serve man's physical needs had somehow to come to
terms with predators, parasites and pests. Armed with awkward and
indisputable facts about noxious or apparently useless creatures, critics,
both pagan and Christian, cast doubt upon the interpretation of nature
according to which the sole purpose of the creatures was to serve the
physical needs of mankind. If the gods had 'made animals for the sake of
us', wrote the Neoplatonist Porphyry, 'in what do we use flies, lice, bats,
beetles, scorpions, and vipers?' Such an assumption, he went on to point
out, leads to the conclusion that we were generated 'for the sake of the
most destructive of animals, such as crocodiles, balaenae, and
dragons'.[30] Celsus, the famous second-century critic of Christianity, had
used similar examples to ridicule what he considered to be the immoderate claims of Christians and Stoics.[31] It was not only critics of divine
purposes in the world who found the existence of certain creatures
puzzling. Neophyte Christian writer Arnobius candidly admitted to
being embarrassed by the existence of flies, beetles, bugs, dormice and
weevils – creatures 'so needless, so purposeless, nay more, at times even
hurtful, and causing unavoidable injuries' that their existence was inex-
plicable.[32] Even the most innocuous of creatures found their purpose in
the created order being questioned. No less a luminary than Augustine,
apparently innocent of the most rudimentary ecological considerations,
thought that the earth had no need of those winged creatures produced
on the fifth day of creation.[33]

Under the system of interpretation outlined by Origen, however,

---

[28] Origen, *Against Celsus*, iv.lxxiv; Methodius, *Discourse on the Resurrection* i.x; Lactantius, *Divine Institutes*, vii.iv; Augustine, *Catholic and Manichean Ways of Life*, 1.20. Cf. Genesis 1.28–30; 2.18f; 9.3.

[29] Origen, *Philocalia*, qu. in Joseph Butler, *The Analogy of Religion to the Constitution and Course of Nature* (London: Religious Tract Society, n.d.), p. 7.

[30] Porphyry, *De abstinentia* iii.20 (p. 130). The Manichees made a similar complaint, Augustine, *De Genesi contra Manichaeos*, i.xvi.25 (*FC* 84, 72–4).   [31] Origen, *Against Celsus*, iv.

[32] Arnobius, *Adversus Gentes*, ii.47, 59–60 (*ANF* vi, 452, 456f.); Cf. Origen, *Against Celsus* iv.lxxv.

[33] Augustine, *Confessions* xiii.xxi (p. 290).

these 'difficult' elements could be invested with moral or figurative significance and thereby be shown to contribute to divine purposes in the creation. St Basil was thus to conclude that 'all poisonous animals are accepted for the representation of the wicked and contrary powers'.[34] Augustine found a use for the winged creatures – they signified believers who had been given instruction in the Christian faith and were thus enabled to soar into the heavens.[35] Of course, some features of the world might successfully resist such interpretations. Those who adapted the methods of Origen to the study of the natural world were at times forced to admit, with Origen himself, that the ultimate 'purpose' or 'intention of the Creator' which had been 'concealed in each individual being', could not be fully known in this present life.[36] Yet the general import of this powerful interpretive framework was clear: the natural world was ordered in such a way as to meet man's physical requirements, and at the same time serve as a repository of eternal spiritual truths. In the words of Irenaeus: 'For with God there is nothing without purpose or due signification.'[37] Those natural objects for which no mundane purpose could be discovered became signs and were invested with meaning.

Origen devoted his exegetical skills, for the most part, to the interpretation of scripture, although in his homilies he occasionally provided allegorical interpretations of the significance of certain animals, based on the natural histories of Aristotle and others.[38] More extensive examples of higher level interpretations of nature can be found in the hexaemeral literature and in the *Physiologus*. The moral or 'tropological' interpretation of nature is represented most strongly in the hexaemeral literature, writings which take the form of commentaries and homilies on the six days of creation. Fourth-century writers Basil the Great and Ambrose of Milan produced the most influential works of this kind. While these works contain some elements of allegorical interpretation, in the main their purpose was to present relatively straightforward moral and theological truths.[39] Already, the nature and habits of various animals and plants had, on occasion, served the purposes of moral

---

[34] Basil, *Hexameron* XIII.6 (*FC* 46, 207); Cf. Augustine, *Confessions* XIII.21; Jerome, *Homilies* 30 (*FC* 48, 225–7). [35] Augustine, *Confessions* XIII.xx (p. 289).

[36] Origen, *De principiis*, II.xi.5 (*ANF* IV, 299); John Chrysostom agreed that 'there is nothing which has been created without some reason, even if human nature is incapable of knowing precisely the reason for them all.' *Homilies on Genesis* VII.14 (*FC* 74, 100).

[37] Irenaeus, *Against Heresies* IV.xxi.3 (*ANF* I, 493).

[38] See, e.g., Origen, *Homilies on Jeremiah* 17.1, frag. 3; *Song of Songs*, p. 147.

[39] Basil had actually voiced some reservations about unrestricted allegorical interpretation. *Hexameron*, IX.1 (*FC* 46, 136f.).

exhortation in classical and Hebrew writings. In the Jewish Wisdom literature, animals exemplify virtues or vices to be imitated or avoided, hence the familiar injunction in Proverbs: 'Go to the ant, thou sluggard' (6.6), and the advice of the book of Job: 'But ask now the beasts and they will teach thee; and the fowls of the air, and they shall tell thee. Or speak to the earth, and it shall teach thee, and the fishes of the sea shall declare unto thee.' (12.7f.). But nowhere in scripture do we encounter the extended moral commentaries of the kind which are found in the writings of Basil, Ambrose, and Gregory. The *Hexameron* of St Ambrose is little more than a catalogue of the moral lessons to be learned from nature. 'Take care not to be bent over like cattle', he counsels, 'see that you do not incline – not so much physically as they do, but morally'. Similarly, of dogs: 'To dogs is given the ability to bark in defence of their masters and their homes. Thus you should learn to use your voice for the sake of Christ, when ravening wolves attack His sheepfold. Have the word ready on your lips, lest, like a silent watch-dog, you may appear because of your unfaithfulness to abandon the position entrusted to you.' Of fish: 'Fish are given to man for his use. They also constitute for us a pattern of the vices to be observed in our society. They serve, too, as an example to be avoided.' Of the vine: 'Would that, man, you could imitate the example of this species of plant, so that you may bear fruit for your own joy and delight. In yourself lies the sweetness of your charm, from you does it blossom, in you it sojourns, within you it rests, in your own self you must search for the jubilant quality of your conscience.'[40]

While the connexions between the characteristics of living things and their requisite moral lessons might at times appear rather strained, they were not merely arbitrary constructions of the Fathers' fertile imaginations. The upright posture of man in comparison to the animals, for example, had been noted by Plato and subsequent classical writers. The uniqueness of the human stance and its moral significance became a commonplace of antiquity and the Middle Ages.[41] On occasions, then,

---

[40] Ambrose, *Hexameron*, VI.3.10 (*FC* 42, 233); VI.iv.17 (pp. 236f.); v.v.13 (pp. 168f); III.xii.49 (pp. 103f.). Cf. Jerome, *Homilies* 21, 30, 58 (*FC* 48, 167; 225–8; 422f.)

[41] Plato, *Timaeus* 90a–92c; Aristotle, *Historia animalium*, 494a, *De partibus animalium*, 686a; Ovid, *Metamorphoses* 1.84–6, Cicero, *De natura deorum* II.56. Christian writers generally considered man's upright stance to be indicative of the image of God. See Justin Martyr, *Apologia* 1.50, Dionysius of Alexandria, *Exegetical Fragments*, II.14; Lactantius, *Divinae institutiones* II.i.15–18, Augustine, *De genesi contra Manicheos* I.xvii.28, *City of God* XXII.24; Aquinas, *ST* Ia. 91, 3; John Calvin *Institutes of the Christian Religion*, tr. Henry Beveridge, 2 vols. (London: Clarke, 1953), I.xv.3. Further references may be found in S. O. Dickerman, *De argumentis quibusdam e structura hominis et animalium petitis* (Halle, 1909), pp. 92f., and F. Robbins, *The Hexaemeral Literature* (University of Chicago Press, 1912), p. 10, n. 3. For a discussion of the history of this view, see C. A. Patrides, 'The Upright

the Fathers might therefore rely upon existing traditions about animals, plants, and other natural objects. However, a far more important key to the moral references of living things was scripture itself. In using the image of 'fishers of men' and in comparing the kingdom of heaven to a fishing net, Christ had not only authorised the general use of natural objects in moral edification, but he had shown that the comparison of man and fish is particularly apposite.[42] Similarly, in speaking of himself as 'the Vine', Christ had revealed something of the hidden moral purpose of the grape: the vine is designed 'for the instruction of our lives'. And further, like the vine, 'all species of trees have their utility'.[43] The hexaemeral writings of Ambrose and Basil, and later the *Moralia in Job* of Gregory the Great (540–604), were to serve as the models for numerous medieval imitations.[44]

While the moral significance of living things was well catered for in the hexaemeral literature, it fell to an anonymous contemporary of Origen, possibly one of his own disciples, to begin the task of disclosing allegorical meanings which lay hidden in the created world. The result was the *Physiologus*, a small but comprehensive work on animals, plants, and stones, the modest proportions of which belie its enormous influence.[45] 'Perhaps no book except the Bible', writes E. P. Evans, 'has ever been so widely diffused among so many people and for so many centuries as the *Physiologus*. It has been translated into Latin, Ethiopic, Arabic, Armenian, Syriac, Anglo-Saxon, Icelandic, Spanish, Italian,

Form of Man', *Premises and Motifs in Renaissance Thought and Literature* (Princeton University Press, 1982), pp. 83–9. Thomas Browne was eventually to point out that other creatures also stand erect. *Pseudodoxia Epidemica*, 2 vols., ed. Robin Robbins (Oxford: Clarendon, 1981) iv.i, (i, 291–4).

[42] Ambrose, *Hexameron*, v.v.13 (*FC* 42, 168f.); v.vi.15 (p. 170).

[43] *Ibid.*, iii.xii–xiii (*FC* 42, 106, 103f., 107). Cf. Basil, *Hexameron*, v.6 (*FC* 46, 76). In addition to these moral lessons the book of nature also taught specific theological doctrines. From his (unfortunately erroneous) observation that 'many kinds of birds do not need union with the males for conception', Basil concluded that the virgin birth was not 'impossible and contrary to nature'. Basil, *Hexameron*, viii.6 (*FC* 46, 128). Insect metamorphosis was similarly thought to show that changes involved in the resurrection of the body were not unprecedented in nature. Ambrose cited the metamorphosis of the silkworm in the hope that his listeners might 'be aroused by the force of such examples as these to a belief in the change that will be ours at the Resurrection'. Ambrose, *Hexameron*, v.xxiii.78 (FC 42, 219), Also Basil, *Hexameron*, viii.8 (*FC* 46, 132).

[44] Chenu, *Nature, Man and Society*, p. 122. For the medieval influence of Gregory, see Smalley, *The Study of the Bible*, 106–11.

[45] I have used an English translation of the Latin version, *Physiologus*, tr. Michael J. Curley, (Austin: University of Texas Press, 1979). Max Wellmann has argued that the work was written in Alexandria by a disciple of Origen, 'Der *Physiologus*, Eine Religions geschichtlich-Naturwissenschaftliche Untersuchung', *Philologus*, Supplementband 22, Heft 1 (1930), 1–116 (p. 13). For the background of this work, see F. Lauchert, *Geschichte des Physiologus* (Strassburg: Karl Trübner Verlag, 1889); for its medieval influence, see Carola Hicks, *Animals in Early Medieval Art* (Edinburgh: University of Edinburgh Press, 1993), pp. 106–11. Also see Helga Neumann, 'Tiersymbolik', *Evangelisches Kirchenlexicon*, 3rd edn, ed. Fahlbusch, Erwin et al., iv, 893–7.

Provençal, and all the principal dialects of the Germanic languages.'[46]
Another commentator has gone so far as to claim that 'the *Physiologus*
was responsible virtually single-handedly for blotting out the bright light
of Aristotelian science for nearly a thousand years'.[47] While the latter
assertion may be somewhat overstated, its remains true that for the
Middle Ages this repository of animal lore was easily to eclipse the
careful and systematic observations of the Greek natural historian. The
forty-odd chapters of the Greek text range over a variety of natural
objects, devoting a brief chapter to each, beginning with the lion, and
treating the serpent, the pelican, the phoenix, the agate-stone, the fig
tree, the unicorn, the magnet, and many others. The legends which are
recounted are drawn from a variety of sources, the most important of
which are Pliny and Aelian. But original to the *Physiologus* is the symbolic
import attributed to the stories. Consider, for example, how the
Physiologus treats the serpent and the pelican.

The serpent is said to have four natures, all of which indicate something of mystical import:

The first Nature is this: when he grows old, his eyes become dim and, if he
wants to become new again, he abstains and fasts for forty days until his skin
becomes loosened from his flesh. And if it does become loosened from fasting,
he goes and finds a narrow crack in the rock, and entering it he bruises himself
and contracts and throws off his old skin and becomes new again. We, too,
throw off for Christ the old man and his clothing through much abstinence and
tribulation. And you, seek out Christ the spiritual rock and the narrow crack.
"The gate is narrow and there is tribulation on the way which leads towards
life, and few are those who enter through it" [Matt. 7.14].[48]

Three further interpretations are given. Clearly the serpent, though a
natural enemy to mankind, symbolises a number of important spiritual
truths, and its existence is not allowed to count against the claim that
meaning pervades the whole of the created order. The serpent is, in the
words of St Ambrose, our 'tutor'. The pelican was one of the more
popular emblems expounded in the *Physiologus*:

If the Pelican brings forth young and the little ones grow, they take to striking
their parents in the face. The parents, however, hitting back kill their young

---

[46] E. P Evans, *Animal Symbolism in Ecclesiastical Architecture* (New York: Henry Holt, 1896), p. 41.
[47] B. E. Perry's view, paraphrased by Patricia Cox, 'The *Physiologus*: A *Poiesis* of Nature', *Church History* 52 (1983) 433–43 (433).
[48] *Physiologus*, xiii, (p. 16.) Actually the author says at outset that the serpent has three natures, but enumerates four. Cf. Aristostle, *History of Animals*, 5.17.549b; 8.17.600b; Pliny, *Natural History*. 8. 41; Aelian, *Characteristics of Animals*. IX.16; Plutarch, *Isis and Osiris*, 381b; Horapollo, *Hieroglyphica*, I, 2.

ones and then, moved by compassion, they weep over them for three days, lamenting over those whom they killed. On the third day, their mother strikes her side and spills her own blood over their dead bodies . . . and the blood itself awakens them from death.[49]

On the basis of this brief account, the pelican was to become an enduring symbol of Christ's atonement. This story, along with its accompanying interpretation, was rehearsed endlessly with minor variations in the medieval bestiaries, and the pelican became a central symbol in the iconography and sculpture of the Middle Ages. It survived in the emblem-books of the early modern period, and colours even sixteenth-century reports of animal behaviours. Dante refers to Christ as 'nostro pellicano', and Shakespeare's Lear refers to Regan and Goneril as 'those pelican daughters'. The pelican may still be seen on the lectern of Norwich Cathedral and perched on the top of the sixteenth-century sundial in the front quadrangle of Corpus Christi, Oxford.[50]

The general hermeneutical programme of Origen, which had been implemented by Basil, Ambrose, and the author of the *Physiologus*, was in the fifth century to receive the imprimatur of St Augustine. This most influential of the Doctors of the Church ensured the tenure of spiritual interpretation into the Middle Ages and beyond. In keeping with his thoroughly platonised Christianity, Augustine declared that mere observation of the sensible qualities of natural objects leads only to 'ignorance' and 'unintelligible discourses'. Similar misunderstandings would ensue if scripture were read in the wrong fashion. Augustine insisted that

---

[49] *Physiologus* vi (pp. 9f.) The account of the Pelican is more or less original to the *Physiologus*, but cf. Hermes Trismegistus, *Die Kyraniden*, ed. Dimitris Kaimakis, Beitrage der Klassischen Philologie, Heft 76 (Meisenheim am Glan: A Hain, 1976), 3.39; Horapollo, *Hieroglyphica*, 1.11, 54. It is recounted by Pseudo Jerome, *Epistola ad Praesidium*, 'De Cereo Paschali', (*PL* 30, 187); Isidore, *Etymologiae*, xii.vii; William of Normandy, *Le bestiare*, pp. 207–10; Albertus Magnus, *De animalibus*, xxiii.132 (Scanlon edn, p. 310), *The Book of Secrets* , ed. M. Best and F. Brightman, (Oxford: Clarendon, 1973) iii.14 (p. 56). Also see Louis Charbonneau-Lassay, *The Bestiary of Christ* (New York: Arkana, 1972), pp. 258–66; Victor Graham, 'The Pelican as Image and Symbol', *Revue de la littérature comparée* 36 (1962) 235–43.

[50] *The Book of Beasts*, tr. T. H. White, (London: Jonathan Cape, 1954), pp. 8, 132f. William of Normandy, *The Bestiary of Guillaume le Clerc*, tr. George Druce (Ashford: Headley Brothers, 1936), lines 521–614. Charbonneau-Lassay, *The Bestiary of Christ*, pp. 8f. Emile Mâle, *Religious Art in France: The Twelfth Century*, tr. Marthiel Mathews, (Princeton University Press, 1978), ch. 9. George Wither, *Choice Emblems, Divine and Moral* (London, 1681). 'Voyages and Discoveries of M. John Hawkins (1564)', Hakluyt, *Principal Navigations, Voyages and Discoveries of the English Nation* (London, 1589), p. 542. Allen Apsley, *Order and Disorder: or The World Made and Undone* (London, 1679), p. 21. For references in Dante and Shakespeare, see *Paradiso*, xxv. 113, *King Lear*, iii.iii.75. Thomas Browne deals with this account as a vulgar error. See *Pseudodoxia Epidemica*, iv.v (i, 366–9); also see the comprehensive commentary provided by Browne's editor (ii, 946–8).

all scripture was to do with faith or morals: 'whatever appears in the divine Word that does not literally pertain to virtuous behaviour or to the truth of faith, you must take to be figurative'.[51] Scriptural references to natural objects were not intended to provide information about the world. Indeed, knowledge of natural objects was only to be pursued in order to understand the similitudes of scripture: 'An ignorance of things makes figurative expressions obscure when we are ignorant of the natures of animals, or stones, or plants, or other things which are often used in the Scriptures for purposes of constructing similitudes.'[52] As an example, Augustine points to the account of the serpent found in the *Physiologus*, concluding that 'as a knowledge of the nature of serpents illuminates the many similitudes which Scripture frequently makes with that animal, an ignorance of many other animals which are also used for comparisons is a great impediment to the understanding.'[53] Profane learning might thus be granted a limited value, although profitable subjects for reading outside the scriptures were restricted by Augustine to 'explanations of whatever unfamiliar geographical locations, animals, herbs and trees, stones, and metals are mentioned in scripture', along with the rationale of 'those numbers mentioned in scripture'.[54] Generally, however, obtaining the requisite knowledge did not require resort to the study of nature as such, nor to pagan writings, for 'almost all' of this information could already be found in the writings of 'good and learned christians'.[55]

Specific guidelines for symbolic interpretations were set out in *De doctrina christiana*, the work in which the Middle Ages found its justification for symbolic interpretations. Here Origen's original three levels of interpretation were expanded to four – *historia, allegoria, analogia, aetiologia* – and specific rules were provided to guide higher levels of interpretation.[56] In the most common interpretative scheme of the Middle Ages, Augustine's *aetiologia* was replaced with *anagogia*. Together these four levels constituted the medieval *quadriga*, explained in the ancient verse:

[51] Augustine, *On Christian Doctrine*, III.x.14 (p. 88)
[52] *Ibid.*, II.xvi.24 (p. 50). See also Francesco Zambon, '*Figura bestialis*. Les fondements théoretiques du bestaire médiéval', in *Epopeé animale, fable, fabliau*, ed. G. Bianciotto and M. Salvat (Paris: Publications de l'Université de Rouen, 1984), pp. 709–19.   [53] *Ibid.*, II.xvi.24 (p. 51).
[54] *Ibid.*, II.xxxix.59 (p. 74).   [55] *Ibid.*
[56] *De Genesi ad litteram imperfectus liber* II (*PL* 34, 222); *On Christian Doctrine*, III.xxx–xxxvii (pp. 104–117). These rules were based largely on seven rules formulated by Tyconius. See *The Book of Rules of Tyconius*, ed. F. C. Burkitt (Cambridge University Press, 1894), pp. xviii–xxiv. Numerous medieval exegetes alluded specifically to these rules, including Isidore, *Libri sententiarum* I.xix.1–19 (*PL* 83, 581A–6A) and Hugh of St Victor, *Didascalicon* v.iv.

Littera gesta docet, quid credas allegoria,
Moralis quid agas, quid speres anagogia. ⟍ Faith
(The letter teaches the deed, the allegory what you believe,
The moral what you should do, the anagogue what you should strive for).[57]
live ⟍the end

In order to see how this four-fold hermeneutic might work in practice, consider the reading of Galatians 4.22–31 provided by ninth-century commentator Rabanus Maurus:

The 'historical' [i.e. literal] meaning embodies knowledge about a series of tangible events in the past. The Apostle describes it thus: 'It is written that Abraham begat two sons, one by a servant woman and one by his free wife. The son of the servant woman was born of the flesh, but the son of his free wife, on the other hand, was born by virtue of a promise.' It is what is to follow that contains the allegorical meaning. The apparent sequence of events can be described as portent of a mystery yet to come. 'For the two women represent two covenants. One of them comes from Mount Sinai and bears its children in slavery, and the model for this is in Agar. Mount Sinai is called Agar in Arabia and it corresponds to the present Jerusalem, which exists with its offspring in slavery.' The 'anagogic' meaning takes us upwards from spiritual mysteries to the highest and most holy secrets of Heaven. And the Apostle adds, 'But the Jerusalem which is above it is free, and she is our mother'. . . The 'tropological' meaning is the moral application, which is displayed in an improved life and in external actions. These four meanings can, if it is desired, combine with each other and the same Jerusalem can be understood in four different ways: Historically as the city of the Jews, allegorically as the Church of Christ, anagogically as the heavenly city, a mother for all of us, and tropologically as the soul of each individual, which is often reproached or praised in the Scriptures under this appellation.[58]

The *quadriga*, though clearly a modification of Origen's original scheme, thus retained his fundamental insight that the text of scripture could bear multiple meanings.

[57] For the more common four-fold system, see John Cassian, *Colationes*, xiv.8 (*PL* 49, 962–5); Gregory the Great, *Homilia in Ezechielem* 2.9.8 (*PL* 76, 1047B); Eucherius, *Liber Formularum spiritualis intelligentiae*, preface (*PL* 50, 727f.). On the verse see de Lubac, *Exégèse Médiéval*, 1.1, 23ff. For general references in Medieval literature to three- or four-fold interpretation see Guilbert of Nogent, *Quo ordine sermo fieri debet* (*PL* 156, 25D); Hugh of St Victor, *Didascalicon* v.2 (p. 120); Bonaventure, *De Reductione artium ad theologiam*, 5, in *Philosophy in the Middle Ages*, ed. Arthur Hyman and James Walsh (Indianapolis: Hackett, 1974), pp. 424f.; Aquinas, *ST*, 1a. 1, 10; 1a. 113, 7; 1a2ae. 102, 2.

[58] *Ennarationes in epistolas Pauli* 15.4 (*PL* 122, 331) qu. in Anders Piltz, *The World of Medieval Learning*, tr. David Johnes (Oxford: Blackwell, 1981), p. 30.

WORDS AND THINGS

Augustine did more than formalise Origen's system and add a fourth
level of interpretation to it. In addition, he provided an important new
theoretical foundation. While interpretative strategies of the Alexandrian school had been informed by Platonic conceptions of the world
and the person, Augustine, while remaining committed to these philosophical conceptions, linked the practice of interpretation to a theory of
signs.[59] According to Augustine, multiplicity of meaning is a function of
things, and not words. There exist different layers of meaning in scripture not because the *words* used are equivocal, but because the *things* to
which the words refer bear multiple meanings. Origen's scheme of
interpretation was thus recast: the literal sense of scripture is to be found
in the univocal meaning of the words; the spiritual sense, in the various
meanings of the objects to which the words refer.[60] This conception of
the multiple meanings of scripture was universally received in the
Middle Ages. As Aquinas was later to express it: 'These various readings
do not set up ambiguity or any other kind of mixture of meanings,
because, as we have explained, they are many, not because one term
may signify many things, but because the things signified by the terms
can themselves be the signs of other things.'[61] In the text expounded by
Rabanus Maurus, then, the word 'Jerusalem' unambiguously refers to
the actual city of Jerusalem, and nothing else. This is its literal or
historical sense. The object or place 'Jerusalem', however, may signify
any number of things, in this particular case, the Jews, the Church,
heaven, or the human soul.

It is difficult to overestimate the significance of this way of reading
texts. Because the mentality which informs allegorical meanings of texts
is so alien to the modern conception of the world, we have forgotten that
for its medieval practitioners allegory had actually become a way of
reading things, not words. Strictly, allegorical interpretation is not the
wresting of multiple meanings out of words which, properly considered,
are unequivocal. Multiple meanings emerge from allegorical readings of
texts because the things to which the words literally refer have themselves further multiple references. Thus while a word generally acts as

[59] R. A. Markus, 'St Augustine on Signs', and Darrell Jackson, 'The Theory of Signs in Augustine's
De Doctrina Christiana', both in *Augustine: A Collection of Critical Essays*, ed. R. A. Markus, (New York:
Doubleday, 1972) pp. 61–91, 92–147.
[60] Augustine, *On Christian Doctrine*, I.ii.2 (pp. 8f.). Also see Bruns, *Hermeneutics Ancient and Modern* (Yale
University Press, 1992), p. 141 and passim.
[61] Aquinas, *ST*, 1a, 1. 10 (1, 39). Cf. Hugh of St Victor, *Didascalicon* v.2–3 (pp. 120–1).

an arbitrary sign for one object, objects themselves might act as natural symbols for many other things. The multiplicity of meaning which arises out of allegorical readings is thus a function of the reader's view of the nature of objects. Tracing the fortunes of this enormously influential allegorical interpretation thus provides us with a window into the attitudes of readers to the things of nature. Changes in the way texts are read, and particularly such central texts as scripture, not only signal changes in an approach to the natural world, but may even inform and undergird such changes. When, in the sixteenth century, the Protestant reformers began to dismantle this fertile and fecund system of allegorical interpretation, they were unwittingly to precipitate a dramatic change in the way in which objects in the natural world were conceived.

Augustine's revised version of Alexandrian hermeneutics, in addition to making explicit the ontological implications of a symbolic approach to texts, also represents an attempt to control interpretation by forcing exegetes to occupy a middle ground between stark literalism and overimaginative allegorisation. Thus the literal sense of scripture was invested with new value, inasmuch as it identified the objects from which the various spiritual senses were to be derived. Yet readers were urged to look beyond the bare sign to what was being signified. 'He is a slave to a sign', said Augustine, 'who uses or worships a significant thing without knowing what it signifies. But he who uses or venerates a useful sign divinely instituted whose signifying force he understands does not venerate what he sees and what passes away, but rather that to which all such things are to be referred.'[62] Thus, the words of scripture refer unequivocally to polysemous objects. The meaning of these objects, however, is not a function of the unrestrained flights of allegorical imagination, but rather is controlled by scripture itself: the meaning of objects is 'divinely instituted'. Ambrose, as we have seen, cited scripture in order to legitimate his tropological readings of such objects as 'the vine' and 'fishes'. The pre-eminent example of a divine legitimation of the meaning of symbolic objects for Augustine and the Middle Ages was Christ's use of the symbols of bread and wine in the last supper. Augustine's theory of signs thus represents a subtle inversion of the priorities of Origen. For the latter, physical objects derived their significance from the intelligible forms of which they were copies. For Augustine, the meaning of things was given by scripture (generally in its literal sense). Origen, like Philo, allowed a conception of the nature of reality to

---

[62] Augustine, *On Christian Doctrine*, iii.ix.13, (pp. 86f.).

determine his approach to scripture. Augustine's theory of signs, together with the hermeneutical approach inherited from Origen, informed his conception of the nature of created objects.

That it had proven necessary for God to reveal in scripture the latent
meanings of created things did not weigh too heavily against the idea
that created objects bore some resemblance to the things which they
signified. The connexions between sign and signified to which scripture
pointed were not arbitrary ones, for natural signs were linked by a
likeness or similitude to the truths which they symbolised. As Origen
had pointed out: 'the things that are not seen are beheld through their
relationship and likeness to things seen'.[63] Yet these similitudes alone
had shown themselves to be insufficient to enable a carnally inclined
human race to determine the true meaning of things. Augustine's theory
of signs was thus a formal explanation of St Paul's observation that while
God's invisible nature was evident in the created things, his erring
creatures had frequently confused signs with the things signified, and
had resorted to worship of 'images resembling mortal man or birds or
animals or reptiles'.[64] On Augustine's analysis, the great sin of idolatry
was a confusion occasioned by too literal a reading of natural objects.[65]
The lesser sin of the pagan philosophers was simply to fail to see the
transcendental significance of the objects in the natural world. These
men possessed *scientia*, a knowledge of temporal things, but lacked
sapientia, the wisdom which comes through a knowledge of eternal
things.[66]

The legacy of Augustine to the medieval world was a systematic
hermeneutical method which attempted to balance the demands of
literal and spiritual readings, but which ultimately gave precedence to
the latter. Literal meaning was important, but subservient to spiritual
meaning. The natural world, for its part, was reduced to a catalogue of
naked signs, the true meaning of which was provided by scripture, the
reference of which lay beyond the physical world. To be concerned with
natural objects alone was to be 'a slave to the sign': it was to engage in an
idolatrous 'literalism' applied to objects. Thus the almost inevitable
consequence of the emphasis on 'spiritual' readings of scripture was the
devaluing of the surface meaning. As Eric Auerbach has expressed it:
'The total content of sacred writings was placed in an exegetic context
which removed the thing told very far away from its sensory base, in that

[63] Origen, *Song of Songs*, p. 218.   [64] Romans 1.18–23.
[65] Augustine, *On Christian Doctrine*, iii.vii (p. 85); Chrysostom, *Homilies on Genesis* vii.18 (*FC* 74, 102).
[66] Augustine, *The Trinity* xv.12.21–2 (*FC* 45, 480–2).

the reader was forced to turn his attention away from the sensory occurrence and toward its meaning. This implied the danger that the visual element of the occurrences might succumb under the dense texture of meanings.'[67] This was no less true for readings of nature. Those who would observe nature were encouraged to look beyond the sensory objects to the spiritual meanings with which they had been invested. The world was not to be read too literally. The conviction that spiritual truths were hidden beneath physical realities led in turn to the somewhat paradoxical consequence that physical objects themselves came increasingly to be obscured by those transcendental truths which they were supposed to represent. Augustine's verdict on the account of the pelican found in the *Physiologus* was that it was 'perhaps true, perhaps not': what counted in that context was not the literal truth, but the spiritual truth.[68] Again, attributing some fantastic trait to the eagle, he tells his reader not to be preoccupied with the accuracy of the report, but to consider its symbolic significance.[69] The things of nature, in their physical manifestations, were thus so burdened with spiritual meanings that they themselves tended to become completely transparent.

While this symbolist mentality endured, observation of the physical world would always be undervalued, or worse, be regarded as idolatrous. Augustine considered the material world to be a place of remarkable and bewitching beauty, yet it was not the place where God was to be found. 'People are moved to wonder by mountain peaks, by vast waves of the sea, by broad waterfalls on rivers, by the all-embracing extent of the ocean, by the revolutions of the stars', he wrote, 'but in themselves, they are uninterested.'[70] God was not to be found in the creatures that he had made, despite their compelling beauty, but in the innermost recesses of the human heart. Here, in the mind, was the gateway to the invisible world, and those who would know God were directed by Augustine to look inwards, rather than outwards. It was the counsel of the Oracle at Delphi – 'Know Thyself' – that was ultimately to issue in knowledge of the divine.[71] Augustine's theory of knowledge is thus, in one respect at least, thoroughly Platonic. 'We do not draw

---

[67] Eric Auerbach, *Mimesis*, (Princeton University Press, 1968), p. 48.

[68] 'Vos sic audite, ut si verum est, congruat; si falsum est, non teneat . . . Fortasse hoc verum, fortasse falsum sit; quaemodum illi congruat, qui nos vivicat sanguine suo, videte.' *Enarratio in Psalmum* 101, s. 1, 7–8 (*CCSL*, XL, 1431).   [69] *Enarratio in Psalmum* 100, s. 2.

[70] *Confessions* x.viii (p. 187). Cf. *Confessions* x.xxvii (p. 201).

[71] *Ibid.*, x.iii. Cf. Basil: 'Yet it is not possible for one, intelligently examining himself, to learn to know God better from the heavens and earth than from our own constitution.' *Hexameron* IX.6 (*FC* 46, 147); Plotinus, *Enneads*, v.iii.7.

images through our senses', he wrote, 'but discern them inwardly not
through images but as they really are and through the concepts themselves.'[72] Yet Augustine's disparagement of knowledge acquired through
the senses went beyond commitment to a particular theory of knowledge, for it was symptomatic of a larger moral concern. Scientific
curiosity about the material world was merely another species of sensual
temptation: 'Beside the lust of the flesh which inheres in the delight
given by all the pleasures of the senses . . . there exists in the soul,
through the medium of the same bodily sense, a cupidity which does not
take delight in carnal pleasure but in perceptions acquired through the
flesh.' Knowledge of the world is the fruit of this 'vain inquisitiveness',
which is 'dignified with the title of knowledge and science'. Thus 'when
people study the operations of nature which lie beyond our grasp', they
merely give reign to a 'diseased craving', a 'lust for experimenting and
knowing'.[73] Here was another reason for the spiritualising of those
passages of scripture which, on a cursory reading, seemed to present
scientific information. In the apparent cosmology of Genesis, for
example, plants and animals, the celestial spheres, geographical locations, historical events, all were mapped onto an internal world and
interpreted as features of the topography of the human psyche. Light
and darkness represented just and unjust souls, the lights in the firmament were spiritual gifts, herbs and fruit-bearing trees were good works,
and the wild beasts passions which needed to be brought under the
dominion of reason.[74] It was not the place of sacred scripture to satisfy
the idle curiosity of the carnal mind.

   The investigation of the sensory world was not only an idolatrous
pursuit, but it was a futile one as well, for if the meaning of nature was
determined by the meaning of scripture, the symbols which were to be
found in the physical world could not of themselves constitute any
intelligible pattern. Their ordering principles lay beyond them, embedded in the eternal truths of the spiritual or intelligible world. As Origen
insisted, 'The unseen and incorporeal things that are in heaven, then,
these are the true, but those that are visible and bodily on earth are said
to be patterns of the true, and not themselves true.'[75] This visible world,
said Chrysostom, is a world of 'shadows and dreams', inhabited by a
'people living in exile'.[76] The 'one system of really true philosophy',

[72] *Ibid.*, x.xi (p. 189).   [73] *Ibid.*, x.xxxv (p. 211); cf. *City of God*, xiv.28.
[74] *Ibid.*, xiii.xxx, xxxi, xxxvii, (pp. 291, 295f.); cf. v.v (pp. 76f.).
[75] Origen, *Commentary on Song of Songs*, p. 152, cf. p. 218.
[76] Chrysostom, *Homilies in Genesis* vii.20 (*FC* 74, 104).

Augustine agreed, is not of this world, 'but of the other intelligible world'.[77] Objects in the physical world were like the words of an inchoate language. The references of these objects were provided by scripture or exegetical convention, but 'syntactic' rules governing the relations between the objects themselves were completely absent. Indeed, the language of things was a makeshift language, necessitated by the human Fall.[78] Until such a syntax could be added to this language, nature could not even exist as a coherent entity, far less become an intelligible text. Not until the twelfth and thirteenth centuries were the symbols which constituted the physical world invested with their own syntax. Only then, could there be a book of nature.

[77] Augustine, *Against the Academics* III.19.42 (Ancient Christian Writers XII, 149).

[78] Augustine: 'These physical things have been produced to meet the needs of peoples estranged from your eternal truth'; 'the reason why all these utterances have to be physically spoken is the abyss of the world and the blindness of the flesh which cannot discern thoughts'. *Confessions* XIII.xxi, xxiii (pp. 289, 294).

CHAPTER 2

Sensible signs and spoken words

God has given us sensible signs and spoken words to show us
something of the divine.

Thomas Aquinas, *Summa theologiae*

All teaching is either about things or about signs.

Augustine, *De Doctrina Christiana*

Omnis mundi creatura,
Quasi liber, et pictura
Nobis est, et speculum

Alanus de Insulis, *Rhythmus de incarnatione Christi*

When we see all things in God, and refer all things to him, we read
in common matters superior expressions of meaning.

William James, *The Varieties of Religious Experience*

THE ASCENDENCY OF THE PHYSICAL

Augustine died in the year 430, making his own journey from the visible
to the invisible world. At the time of his death, vandal forces were laying
siege to Hippo Regius, the North African city in which he had spent the
last thirty-nine years of his life, most of them as bishop. Other regions of
Europe were beset by similar difficulties, for the disintegration of the
Western Empire was well in train. Rome, the eternal city, had fallen to
Alaric the Goth in 410, and in what was virtually a formality, the rule of
the last Western emperor, Romulus Augustulus, came to end in 476.
With the fall of the empire and triumph of the barbarians, the Dark
Ages ensued. Thereafter, virtually until the eleventh century, the fires of
Western civilisation were kept burning in isolated monastic communi-
ties. In cloister and cell, Catholic Christianity was preserved and nur-
tured, and along with it those vestiges of Platonic philosophy which had
been fortuitously incorporated in the body of Christian faith. The
monasteries, while undoubtedly playing an invaluable role in the preservation of learning and literacy, remained steadfastly scriptural in orien-

tation, conservative in approach, and Augustinian in general outlook. Their concern was with 'the philosophy of the other world', and their intellectual life centred on the sacred page, the commentaries of the Fathers and Doctors, and the fanciful fictions of the *Physiologus*. The dawn of the second millennium was to see the beginnings of a radical shift in these intellectual priorities.

The period 1050 to 1250 witnessed a considerable improvement in the material conditions of life, evident in the growth of towns and the more efficient organisation of labour. By this time the barbarians had ceased their wanderings, internecine conflicts within Christendom had all but ceased, and whatever residual warring tendencies remained within the Holy Empire were channelled outwards to spend their force in actions against the growing menace of Islam. With the establishment of new trade routes, the widespread cultivation of virgin land, and the more efficient organisation of labour, came surplus production. Such were the foundations which made possible the rise of the towns, and with them, new urban centres of learning. The intellectual ferment which accompanied these changes, along with its implications for the study of nature, is the subject of this chapter. In the most general terms, this revival of learning amounted to a rediscovery of the natural world, and a renewed fascination with all things physical, for as is so often the case in those periods of history which enjoy a degree of social stability and economic prosperity, attention was redirected towards this world rather than the next. In the eleventh and twelfth centuries we see the beginnings of the ascendency of the visible world, and the development of new prospects for its study.

The re-emergence of the physical world manifested itself in numerous ways. Anthropological speculations gave new positive appraisals of the human body. As it was graphically expressed by the first great woman theologian, Hildegard of Bingen (1098–1179), 'the spirit without the bloody matter of the body is not the living person'.[1] Allan of Lille (d. 1203) similarly insisted that it was the nature of human being to be united with the material. The embodiment of human souls was not, as Plato had thought, the imprisonment of an essentially spiritual being in a corporeal body, but was rather part of God's original design for humanity.[2] These affirmations of the corporeal nature of human exist-

[1] Hildegard, *Scivias* iii.vii.8 (*PL* 197, 648B).
[2] Allan of Lille, *Contra haereticos* i.14 (*PL* 210, 319); Hugh of St Victor, *On the Sacraments of the Christian Faith*, tr. Roy Deferrari (Cambridge, Mass.: Mediaeval Academy of America, 1951) i.vi.1–3 (pp. 94–6). Also see Chenu, '*Cur homo?* Le sous-sol d'une controverse au xiie siècle', *Mélanges de science religieuse*, 10 (1953) 197–204.

ence were to be firmly established in Western thought by Thomas Aquinas (c.1225–1274), who reasserted the Aristotelian view, though not without qualification, that the human person is form and matter, soul *and* body. The individual was not to be identified with the incorporeal soul, but was a substantial union of spirit and matter. Even in the next world the integrity of persons required that souls be embodied. Resurrection of the body for the first time became philosophically as well as theologically necessary.[3] Medieval ascetic practices were also informed by these new appraisals of the body. Fasting in the Middle Ages, commonly misinterpreted as a pathological attempt to liberate the spirit and punish the body, is actually symptomatic of quite a different concern.[4] 'Ascetics' of the Middle Ages sought to identify with the corporeal sufferings of Christ. Their efforts were a recognition that redemption is to be accomplished not in spite of the flesh, but by embracing it in its frailty and fallibility. Fasting, observes Caroline Bynum, was 'not a flight *from* but *into* physicality'.[5] Thus, paradoxically, feasting and fasting both evidence similar concerns.

The body of Christ also came to take on new significance in a variety of ways. The forensic theory of atonement set out by Anselm of Canterbury (c.1033–1109) emphasised anew the necessity for Christ to have been fully embodied. In *Cur deus homo* (1098), the work which was to become for the Middle Ages the standard theological text on the atonement, Anselm established a new setting for the drama of redemption. The reconciliation of man with God was no longer the consequence of a distant cosmic transaction between God and Satan. The cross was not to satisfy a debt owed by one supernatural being to another. Anselm's theory of atonement reasserted the centrality of Christ's incarnation in which Deity puts on human flesh, and equally importantly, shifted the venue for human redemption into the sphere of the mundane.[6] As the body is sanctified by Christ's full participation in

---

[3] Aquinas, *ST* 1a. 75, 4. Anthony Kenny, *Aquinas on Mind* (London: Routledge, 1993) pp. 136–9.

[4] The fathers had listed a number of reasons for fasting, chief among them the necessity to control the body from which come sinful desires. See Herbert Musurillo, 'The Problem of Ascetical Fasting in the Greek Patristic Writers', *Traditio* 12 (1956) 17.

[5] Caroline Bynam, *Holy Feast and Holy Fast* (University of California Press, 1988), p. 250.

[6] Anselm drew on traditional notions of the *person* of Christ, but redefined the *work* of Christ. In so doing he repudiated the theory of atonement current since the Greek fathers that the purpose of the cross was to satisfy a debt to the devil. Of course, Christ's full humanity had been a central tenet of Christian doctrine from the time of the Symbol of Chalcedon (451) and before. Anselm, however, provided a powerful reminder of the theological necessity of the God-man. For the significance of Anselm's theory of atonement for twelfth-century attitudes to the body and the physical world, see Sarah Beckwith, *Christ's Body: Identity, culture and society in late medieval writings* (London: Routledge, 1993), p. 47.

fleshly humanity, this physical world takes on a new positive light as the locus of divine redemptive activity. Anselm's explanation of the necessity of the incarnation signals the beginning of that important shift in medieval thinking in which, as Bynam puts it, 'physicality came to the forefront as a religious concern'.[7] This theological emphasis on Christ's body was also reflected in sacramental practice. In the mass, the centrepiece of medieval religion, priests were to rehearse the process of incarnation by transforming the matter of bread and wine into the very substance of God. The elements of the mass were not simply naked signs, significant for what they symbolised: now they were vested with intrinsic importance for what they literally were – the body and blood of Christ. Participants in the eucharist saw themselves as 'eating God.' Official recognition of this new emphasis came at the Lateran council of 1215, when transubstantiation became official Catholic dogma, and with the observation of the feast of Corpus Christi, commanded by Urban IV in 1264. The eucharist, writes Miri Rubin, 'was refigured in the eleventh and twelfth centuries to create a new structure of relations, thus modifying the symbolic order, and the social relations and political claims which could be attached to it'.[8]

If the physical world and its material elements came to be elevated in importance, the means by which these things were known – the senses – were also granted a new status. Knowledge of things was now thought to be mediated, not through ideas placed in the mind and illuminated by God, but through bodily organs. Hildegard of Bingen declared that 'we are strengthened and brought to our souls' salvation by the five senses'. More specifically, 'we can know the whole world through our sight, understand through our hearing, distinguish it by our sense of smell . . . dominate by our touch, and in this way come to know the true God, author of all creation'.[9] Her contemporary, Bernard of Clairvaux (1090–1153), agreed, insisting that 'there is no access open to us, except through the body, to those things whereby we live in happiness. . . The spiritual creature, therefore, which we are, must necessarily have a body, without which, indeed, it can by no means obtain that knowledge which is the only means of attaining to those things, to know which constitutes blessedness.'[10] With the arrival of Aristotelian texts and the

---

[7] Bynam, *Holy Feast and Holy Fast*, p. 251. Cf. Le Goff, *The Medieval Imagination*, pp. 14f., 83f.

[8] Miri Rubin, *Corpus Christi: The Eucharist in Late Medieval Culture* (Cambridge University Press, 1991), pp. 176–81, 348.   [9] *De operatione Dei* v.2; *Liber divinorum operum* i.iv.97 (*PL* 197, 876C–D).

[10] Sermo v, *Cantica canticorum: Eighty Six Sermans on the Song of Solomon*, tr. S.J. Eales, (London: Elliot Stock, 1895), qu. in Beckwith, *Christ's Body*, p. 49.

digestion of their contents, this orientation towards the world of the
senses became even more pronounced. Albert the Great (c.1200–1280),
sounding rather like an eighteenth-century British empiricist, announced that all universal knowledge arises out of sense experience.[11]
His famous protégé Thomas Aquinas agreed that 'all our knowledge
takes its rise from sensation', and that 'it is the knowledge we have of
creatures that enables us to use words to refer to God'.[12] Knowledge of
nature, therefore, conveys knowledge of God, and legitimates theological language, used analogously of God. This stance represents a complete reversal of the Augustinian view according to which our ability to
apply words to things is only possible through the activity of God
working directly in the human mind. For Augustine, it is God who
makes possible our knowledge of the world: for Aquinas, it is the world
which makes possible our knowledge of God.[13] Thus it was increasingly
recognised that something of the Deity could be seen by looking at the
world, rather than through it. The new breed of scholars came to regard
the empirical world as a coherent entity which could be systematically
investigated by the senses. In what they believed to be an essentially
religious endeavour, they also sought to explicate the relationship between human beings and the physical world of which they had now
become an integral part. In seeing the world again as a single corporeal
entity, medieval thinkers were to rediscover nature.[14]

[11] Albertus Magnus, *Summae de creat.*, II, 55, 3, *Opera Omnia*, 38 vols., (ed. Augustus Borgnet) XXXV,
456a.
[12] Aquinas, *ST* Ia. 1, 9–10; *ST* Ia. 13, 1 (III, 49). Cf. John Scotus Eriugena: 'As through sense
perception one comes to a concept, so through the creature one comes back to God.' *De divisione
naturae* III.XXXV (*PL* 122, 723).
[13] It is in this light that we are to understand Thomas's rejection of Anselm's celebrated *a priori*
proof of God's existence in the *Proslogion*. Anselm proceeds from the conception of God in our
minds, and goes on to establish his existence in reality, relying on a 'vertical' resemblance of our
conceptions to some transcendental truth. For Aquinas this path cannot be taken, for all our
knowledge must proceed by way of the world. We can know the sensible world because in
certain ways we resemble it. Only from knowledge of the world can we proceed by way of
analogy to knowledge of the Deity. It is our likeness to the world which makes possible
knowledge of God, not our likeness to the Deity. Aquinas, *ST* Ia. 2. Thomas proceeds on the
Aristotelian assumption that there must be an essential likeness between the knower and the
known. Anselm's epistemology is more Augustinian: knowledge depends on divine illumination.
God places the idea of himself in our minds and illuminates it: 'Now I understand by thy light
what I formerly believed by thy gift.' *Proslogion*, 2.
[14] On the 'discovery of nature', see Chenu, *Man Nature and Society*, pp. 4–18; Richard Dales, 'A
Twelfth-Century Concept of Natural Order', *Viator* 9 (1978) 179–92; G. B. Ladner, 'Erneuerung',
in *Reallexicon für Antike und Christentum* 6 (1964) 246–7; G. Post, 'The Naturalness of Society and
State', in *Studies in Medieval Legal Thought*, ed. G. Post, (Princeton University Press, 1964) 494–561.
More specifically on the role of William of Conches and the Chartres school in this discovery, see
Tullio Gregory, *Anima mundi: la filosophia di Guglielmo di Conches e la scuola di Chartres* (Florence, 1955)
pp. 175–246.

THE DISCOVERY OF NATURE

The discovery of nature was more than just a challenge to the priorities established by Augustine. It was not enough simply to attribute value to physical things to assert the importance of the physical world. The idea of nature is that of a particular ordering of natural objects, and the study of nature the systematic investigation of that order. These, in turn, required new theoretical conceptions, absent from the intellectual tradition which the eleventh century had inherited from late antiquity. Such conceptions were the products of new schools and new books.

The eleventh-century schools are the direct ancestors of our modern universities, or perhaps I should say, of some of our modern universities. Their establishment was an integral part of the story of the rise of towns and the formation of guilds. Most often they were associated with ecclesiastical centres, such as Chartres or Rheims, and they provided an alternative to education within the confines of the cloister. Scholars who taught there came to form a professional class of their own, similar in conception to the guilds of the craftsmen, independent of monastic orders, and relatively free from ecclesiastical control.[15] These men had become impatient with more traditional texts and had begun to study, in addition to the standard canon, other texts, generally Platonic or Neoplatonic in origin – translations of Pseudo-Dionysius, Plato's *Timaeus*, Macrobius, or various Hermetic writings.

In the ninth century, the Irish monk John Scotus Eriugena translated *The Celestial Hierarchy* of Pseudo-Dionysius. At this time it was thought that Dionysius was the convert of St Paul, the one great success of the apostle's otherwise disappointing foray into philosophical disputation at the Areopagus in Athens. This tradition conferred upon the author of *The Celestial Hierarchy* an almost apostolic status, and his blend of Christian mysticism and neoplatonic philosophy – to Luther's jaundiced eye he was 'more of a Platonist than a Christian' – came to exert a profound influence throughout the Middle Ages.[16] The notion that the cosmos was ordered into a graded hierarchy of beings made possible the

---

[15] For an account of the rise of the universities, see H. Rashdall, *The Universities of Europe in the Middle Ages*, 2nd edn, 3 vols. (Oxford: Clarendon, 1936); A. Kenny and J. Pinborg, 'Medieval Philosophical Literature', *CHLMP*, 11–42. The role played by these institutions in the development of science has generally been underestimated. Toby Huff has recently argued that the establishment of the urban schools was, 'from the point of view of the rise of modern science, the most significant event' of this period. *The Rise of Early Modern Science* (Cambridge University Press, 1993) p. 335.

[16] Martin Luther, *Babylonian Captivity of the Church*, in *Three Treatises* (Philadelphia: Fortress Press, 1970), pp. 240f.

establishment of new connexions between all living things. Pride of place was given to the human race, with man located at the very centre of a great chain of being, part-animal, part-angel. The further effect of this influential conception was a mitigation of the stark dualism of the Platonic tradition. There may be two worlds, but the human being is an inhabitant of both, and thus serves as a bridge between them.

To the diffuse and pervasive influence of Pseudo-Dionysius we must add what for the Middle Ages was the greatest of Plato's works - the *Timaeus*. The study of the *Timaeus* at Chartres during the twelfth century was to have a dramatic impact on cosmological speculations. The aim of this dialogue, in Plato's own words, was 'to discourse of the nature of the universe, how created or how existing without creation'.[17] While it is true that the answer which Plato was to give to this question stood as a challenge to the Christian doctrine of creation *ex nihilo* and problemati-cally asserted the existence of a world soul (*anima mundi*), it nonetheless provoked new readings of Genesis and galvanised a new interest in the phenomena of nature.[18] Nature was ordered, according to the Platonic conception, by a world soul, and while Christian writers were ultimately to reject this notion, they were happy enough to accept the implication that the world was organised like a living creature, and that profitable knowledge could be had of the world by conceiving of it as a macrocosm of the human animal. Plato had also suggested that the world was patterned on ideas in the mind of God, the physical world being 'the sensible God, who is the image of the intellectual'.[19] By implication, some knowledge of God might be gleaned through familiarity with patterns in nature. Such conceptions were reinforced by the *Commentary on the Dream of Scipio* and various hermetic writings, all of which had attracted renewed interest as a result of their parallels with the doctrines of the *Timaeus*. In the *Corpus Hermeticum*, the universe is described as 'a great and perfect living thing', and an entity which 'is rightly called a "cosmos" or "arrangement"'. In the *Asclepius* we find the corresponding statement that the sensible world is the image of God.[20] 'If you consider *the whole*', Asclepius is counselled, 'you will learn that the sensible world

[17] *Timaeus*, 27c.
[18] Chenu, *Nature, Man and Society*, pp. 20–2. R. D. Crouse, '*Intentio Moysi*', John van Engen, *Rupert of Deutz* (University of California Press, 1983), pp. 85f.; G. R. Evans, *Philosophy and Theology in the Middle Ages* (London: Routledge, 1993), p. 70f.   [19] *Timaeus*, 92c.
[20] *Corpus Hermeticum* XI.4, IX.6 (Copenhaver edn pp. 38, 29), *Asclepius* 8, 31 (Copenhaver edn. pp. 71, 86). For the influence of hermetic writings in the Middle Ages see B. P. Copenhaver, *Hermetica*, xiv–xlvii. The Greek κόσμος (cosmos/world/universe) has connotations of both 'adornment' and 'order' which are lacking in the Latin *mundus* (world/universe).

itself and all it contains are in truth covered by that higher world as if by a garment.'[21]

The impact of such works on the thought of the twelfth century can be detected in new usages of particular words and phrases which denote the totality of created things as a unified whole. Père Chenu has argued convincingly that in the use of the term '*universitas*' we can discern a whole new conception of the created order.[22] In writings of the period, the 'universe' is variously described as 'the ordered disposition of things', an 'intricate contrivance of heaven and earth'. It is 'bonded together with an indissoluble knot, eternally tied within the divine mind'. 'Nothing in the universe fails to participate in the Highest Good.'[23] In addition to this single term '*universitas*' we encounter in writings of the twelfth and thirteenth centuries a range of new metaphors which attempt to capture the essence of the new entity, 'nature'. The world is a machine, a harmonious musical instrument or a body politic, a fine hymn sung in harmony by all the creatures; the elements of nature are organised 'like the members of a great body';[24] nature is a great lady, the 'child of God and Mother of things'. The world is modelled after the likeness of a human being, or it is written like a book.[25] Nature, so conceived, is no longer simply a catalogue of religious symbols, each of which teaches some religious truth. Now, while ma-

---

[21] *Asclepius* 34 (Copenhaver edn pp. 88f.) my emphasis.

[22] Chenu, *Man, Nature and Society*, pp. 5–7. Also see Hugh of St Victor's discussion of the term, *Didascalicon*, I.x (pp. 56f.).

[23] Hugh of St. Victor, *De Sacramentis* I.ii.2 (*PL* 176, 206); Ps. Hugh of St Victor, *Quaest. in Ep. Pauli,* ad. Rom. q. 34 (*PL* 175, 440); Arnold of Bonneval, *De operibus sex dierum* (*PL* 189, 1516A); Hugh of St. Victor, *Expos. in Hier. coel.* III (*PL* 175, 980). Also see Chenu, *Nature, Man and Society*, p. 7.

[24] Hugh of St Victor: 'The visible world is this machine', *De arca Noe morali* IV.7 (*PL* 176, 672D). Honorius Augustodunensis: 'The supreme craftsman constructed the universe like a great zither, placing on it strings to yield a variety of sounds' *Elucidarium* I.12 (*PL* 172, 1179B); for Honorius the world was also a 'dei republica', *Hexaemeron* III (*PL* 172, 259A), cf. Eriugena, *De divisione naturae.* V (*PL* 122, 969D). William of Auvergne: 'If you look at the beauty and magnificence of the universe, you will discover that the universe is like a very fine hymn and the creatures, by their variety, sing in unison and make a harmony of a supreme beauty.' Qu. in Le Goff, *Medieval Civilization*, p. 348. Arnold of Bonneval: 'God ordered the things of nature like the members of a great body', *De operibus sex dierum*, prologue (*PL* 189, 1515D–16A).

[25] Alan of Lille described nature as the 'child of God and Mother of things', *De planctu naturae* (*PL* 210,447). Bernardus Silvestris, in *Cosmographia*, and Alan of Lille, in his *De planctu naturae*, depict nature as a woman. On this theme, see Chenu, *Nature, Man and Society*, pp.18–24; Winthrop Wetherbee, 'Some Implications of Nature's Femininity in Medieval Poetry', in L. Roberts, *Approaches to Nature in the Middle Ages* (New York: Medieval and Renaissance Texts and Studies, 16, 1982) pp. 47–61. Such conceptions of nature prompted controversial speculations about a world-soul. See L. Ott, 'Die platonische Weltseele in der Frühscholastik', in *Parousia: Studien zur Philosophie Platons und zur Problemgeschichte des Platonismus* (Frankfurt, 1965), pp. 307–31; Gilson, *History of Christian Philosophy in the Middle Ages*, p. 256; McEvoy, 'Microcosm and Macrocosm in the Writings of St. Bonaventure', p. 311, n. 6.

terial things still signify transcendental realities, they have a new significance which arises out of their relatedness to other things. The meaning of individual elements only emerges as the whole is known; it becomes apparent from context, not from consultation of the lexicon of scripture. Thus, the relations between objects, their arrangement, their order, their pattern – these connexions take on a new kind of religious significance. In the words of William of Auvergne, sometime Bishop of Paris, and last great theologian of the twelfth century:

> Knowledge of the universe may be interpreted in two ways, the first of which is the philosophy composed of the aggregation of all the philosophical sciences; and in this way the universe is regarded as the aggregate of all the things which exist, and their totality *is nothing other than the collection of all these same things.* . . But according to the other way, knowledge of the universe is knowledge of it by the mode in which it is universal, that is, knowledge of the things which exist, but according to this mode, that is, *insofar as it constitutes a universe.*[26]

necessity It was the discovery of nature which made possible this 'other way'.

At the most basic level, the new relationships now perceived to obtain between natural objects resided in resemblances or 'similitudes'. Up until now resemblances had served in the main to connect material entities with eternal verities. They had extended in a single direction, from visible things out to the boundary of the physical world and beyond to the realm of the intelligible. The visible world, all the while, had been but a shimmering patina of appearances, deriving whatever significance it had from the reflected glory of the intelligible world beyond. Now, for the first time in the Christian era, this world was to be invested with its own patterns of order, patterns which were based on similitudes perceived to exist amongst material things themselves. Indeed, the 'discovery' of nature is constituted by this recognition of a new sphere of resemblances. The twelfth century is the formative period in which those networks of 'similitudes' which determine the character of pre-modern knowledge of nature begin their most fruitful development.[27]

---

[26] William of Auvergne, *De universo* I.1 prooemium, *Opera Ominia*, 2 tom., (Parisiis, 1674) I, 593. Compare this passage in Aristotle's *Metaphysics*: 'We must consider in which sense the nature of the universe contains the good and the supreme good; whether as something separate or independent, or as the orderly arrangement of its parts . . . All things, both fishes and birds and plants, are ordered together in some way . . . and the system is not such that there is no relation between one thing and another. Everything is ordered together to one end.' (XI, ix. 1075a, *LCL* II, 167). Echoes of this sentiment may be found in Aquinas,' *ST* 1a. 47, 3 (VIII, 103). Also see *Corpus Hermicticum* IX.6. William of Auvergne's dates (ca. 1180–1249), incidentally, place him in the thirteenth century, but this thought is clearly that of the late twelfth. [27] Foucault, *The Order of Things*, ch. 2.

In the Platonic philosophy of the first centuries of the Christian era, 'similitude' (*similitudo*) had provided the basis of the relationship between the intelligible and the corporeal, between ideas and those physical objects which were brought into existence as imitations of those ideas. Both the creation of the world and the construction of artifacts by human craftsmen relied upon similitude. A thing is made, said Philo, 'in due similitude . . . that it might be an imitation perceptible by the outward senses of an archetypal sketch and pattern, appreciable only by the intellect'.[28] As we have seen, Origen appropriated this insight for the purposes of biblical exegesis, arguing that the spiritual and literal senses of scripture bear the same relation to each other as the intelligible and visible worlds.[29] Viewed in this light, the *quadriga* which the Fathers bequeathed to the Middle Ages is nothing but a guide to reading in which similitudes are categorised according to type. *Allegoria*, or 'prefiguring', relies upon resemblances between events separated in time (Moses lifts up the serpent in the wilderness to save the Israelites, Christ is crucified to save mankind); *Anagogia*, on resemblances between physical things and theological truths (e.g. the phoenix and resurrection); *Tropologia*, on resemblances between physical things and moral truths (e.g. the ant and the virtue of industry). Absent from these assumed connexions, with the exception of *tropologia*, is any sustained treatment of the resemblances which can found amongst physical things themselves. It is not that these are completely denied, for it was often the case that the connexions established by *allegoria*, *tropologia*, and *anagogia* were dependent upon physical similitudes. However, such resemblances were not explored for their own sakes, but used in an instrumental fashion to serve the purposes of theological or moral edification. Moreover, these resemblances, though conceded to have always been inherent in created things, were not overt, but were revealed in sacred scripture, or 'instituted' by scriptural authorities. Again, the important exception to this general principle was *tropologia*, for it could not be denied that there were pre-Christian traditions about the moral lessons which could be learnt from the natural world. However, while such resemblances might have been recognised by noble pagans, they fell far short of providing the complete knowledge which was to be discovered through the reading of scripture. Indeed the possibility for tropological readings of nature had served only to show that those beyond the pale of Christian revelation

---

[28] Philo, *De vita Mosis II*, xvi.76 (p. 497). Cf. *De opificio mundi* x.36 (p. 6); Aquinas, *ST* 1a. 12, 2.
[29] The same idea lies behind the notion of Christ as God incarnate. Jesus appeared 'in the likeness of sinful flesh' (Romans 8.3), was 'born in the likeness of Men' (Philippians 2.7).

had persistently ignored the lessons taught by nature, and could therefore be justly condemned.

In the twelfth century, then, 'nature' becomes a new locus for the play
of 'horizontal' resemblances, and the sphere of knowledge so constituted
is a necessary precursor to the emergence of natural science. By the
thirteenth century, Bonaventure was to able to identify two major
categories of resemblance: those *similitudines* which obtain among created things, and those which obtain between created things and God.[30]
Aquinas, likewise, pointed out that while God is the original exemplar of
all things, (and thus all the creatures have some transcendental referent),
'yet among created things some may be called exemplars of others
which are made to their likeness [*similitudinem*]'.[31] It is this last category
which is new, and which delineates the sphere of nature, establishing the
systematising principles upon which knowledge of the natural world is
based.

READING NATURE: THE WHOLE AND THE PARTS

All the familiar medieval images of nature – chain, mirror, machine,
musical instrument – bespeak something of the new-found intelligibility
of the visible world considered as a whole. At the same time, however,
discrete natural objects retain those meanings which had been attributed to them by the Fathers. 'Horizontal' similitudes, in other words,
did not displace, but rather supplemented 'vertical' similitudes. It was
this combination of the meaning and intelligibility of the cosmos which
led to the recognition that nature could be regarded as a book. Hugh of
St Victor thus declared that the whole of material creation consisted of
letters written 'by the finger of God', the meaning of which was hidden
from the unregenerate, but perspicuous to the spiritually literate.[32]
Vincent of Beauvais was to speak similarly of 'the book of creatures
given to us for reading'.[33] William of Conches regarded the elements
from which natural objects are formed as like letters, the indivisible parts
of syllables.[34] To Alan of Lille, every creature was a book.

[30] The distinction is explicitly stated by Bonaventure, *Quaestiones disputatae de scientia Christi*, q.2,
Opera Omnia, v. 9
[31] Aquinas, *ST* 1a, 44, 3 (VIII, 17). As Aquinas put it elsewhere, things 'have a relation to one
another, and to him [God]'. *ST* 1a. 47, 3 (VIII, 103).
[32] Hugh of St Victor, *De tribus diebus* 4, (*PL* 176, 814B). Also see Wanda Cizewski, 'Reading the
World as Scripture: Hugh of St Victor's *De tribus diebus*', *Florilegium* 9 (1987) 65–88.
[33] Vincent of Beauvais, *Libellus totius operis apologeticus*, version 1, ch. 5; Crouse, '*Intentio Moysi*'.
[34] William of Conches, *Philosophia mundi* 1.1–3, qu. in Stock, *The Implications of Literacy* (Princeton
University Press, 1983), p. 319.

The image of the 'book of nature' went considerably further than alternative metaphors which expressed the unity of the cosmos, for it implied firstly, that nature was to be read, expounded, investigated; that those meticulous labours which had hitherto been expended on the methodical investigation of that other book could now be directed towards the natural world. Indeed, those who expounded the book of nature were to bring to their new subject the habits of mind and techniques which they had employed in the investigation of scripture. Equally importantly, this metaphor implied that the world, like scripture, was a locus of divine revelation, and potentially both a source of knowledge of God and a means by which mankind might be reconciled to him. Nature was a new authority, an alternative text, a doorway to the divine which could stand alongside the sacred page. Honorius Augustodunensis could now write that there were two ways of knowing God: the contemplation of the created order, and knowledge of the sacred text. Together these provided a means of ascending to the very source of divine wisdom.[35] Study of the world took on a religious significance, and the exegesis of the book of nature became a vital concern.

To a large degree, the ways in which the book of nature was to be read were shaped by methods of scriptural interpretation. Indeed it is hardly surprising that the approach to this new book would take as its point of departure the only other systematic hermeneutical enterprise in existence at the time – the exposition of the sacred page. The search for patterns and connexions had up until now been solely the business of the biblical exegete. Now the world, too, had become a place where patterns could be discovered, and that impulse which had previously concerned itself with the harmonisation of various biblical texts, with the establishment of connexions between scriptural narratives, with seeking similitudes in scripture, was directed outwards to a new text – the book of nature. In order to see how the exegetical habits of mind might be transferred to their new subject, it is necessary to remind ourselves of the traditional methods of exposition of scripture. Moral and allegorical readings of scripture, while they may seem to the modern mind somewhat arbitrary and haphazard, were something of a

[35] Honorius follows Eriugena in linking these two forms of knowledge to the two-fold vestiture of the transfigured Christ. Honorius Augustodunensis, *De animae exsilio et patria*, xii (*PL* 172.1246A); Eriugena, *De divisione naturae* iii, 35 (*PL* 122, 723D); Bonaventure, *Breviloquium* ii. c.12; Crouse, 'Intentio Moysi', 155f. Also see Crouse, 'Honorius Augustodunensis: The Arts as *Via ad Patriam*', *Arts Libéraux et Philosophie au Moyen Age* (Paris: Vrin, 1969), pp. 531–9.

science, requiring of the exegete remarkable skill and ability. The task of the commentator was to set forth the truth of a particular passage by discerning links between it and other parts of scripture. Such links were constructed on the basis of resemblances between certain words or phrases, or even resemblances between the narrative 'shape' of passages. The one presupposition of this method was that scripture was a seamless text which formed a coherent whole and which bore witness to a single set of truths. The exposition of a passage would require of the exegete a knowledge of the whole of scripture and of the truths it contained, for only in the context of the whole could the meaning of the separate parts be known. Consider, for example, one small section of Augustine's exposition of Genesis 1.14 'Let there be lights in the firmament':

But you, the elect race (I Pet. 2:9), 'the weak of the world' (I Cor. 1:27), who have abandoned everything to follow the Lord (Matt. 19:27), go after him and 'confound the mighty' (I Cor. 1:27). Go after him, 'beautiful feet' (Isa. 52:7). Shine in the firmament so that the heavens may declare his glory (Ps. 18:2f.) . . . It is as if God says 'Let there be lights in the firmament of heaven' and 'suddenly there came a sound from heaven, as if a vehement wind blew, and tongues were seen split, like fire which sat on each of them' (Acts 2:2–3). And the lights, made in the firmament of heaven, have the word of life (Phil. 2:15–16). Run everywhere, holy fires, fires of beauty. Do not be under a bushel (Matt. 5:14–15). He to whom you have adhered is exalted, and he has exalted you. Run and make it known to all nations (Ps. 78:10).[36]

The meaning of this pastiche of scriptural references may escape the modern reader, and the fact that the passage has been removed from its original context is not helpful. Yet we should at least get a sense of how the meanings of various terms and phrases from different parts of scripture were associated. 'Lights', 'fires', 'firmament', 'heavens', every scriptural occurrence of these words is, for Augustine, like a recapitulation of some deeper meaning, which transcends its incidental appearance in the narrative. One word or phrase calls to mind another, and in the superficial resemblances which exist between the various parts of scripture a meaning emerges. For those schooled in this tradition of exegesis, the meaning of a particular passage lay in its interconnectedness with many other apparently disparate passages of scripture. The whole exegetical enterprise assumed that the sacred page constituted a coherent unity. Exegesis, in short, entailed relating parts to a whole, for

---

[36] Augustine, *Confessions* XIII.xix (pp. 287f.)

every passage of scripture was potentially a microcosm in which the meaning of the whole could be enfolded.

By the twelfth century, some of the intellectuals at the new schools had become impatient with this traditional way of reading texts. For one thing, the possibility of providing some kind of original exegesis of this kind was becoming increasingly difficult. Virtually every text was now burdened with layers of meaning, and there remained little scope for imaginative higher interpretation. The task of a traditional scholar had become one of preservation and transmission, rather than original exegesis. As we have witnessed in our own age, when the possibilities inherent in a traditional canon seem exhausted, both a new canon and new hermeneutical approaches are sought. Thierry of Chartres, before turning his attention to the book of nature, made the explicit complaint that the possibility for moral and allegorical readings of scripture had been exhausted by 'the holy expositors'.[37] His solution was twofold: to suggest a new way of reading scripture, and equally importantly, to find a new subject upon which to exercise his exegetical energies. So it was that interpretive skills which in previous generations would have been directed towards uncovering further connexions in the pages of sacred scripture, were turned outwards to a new text – the book of nature. The allegorical imagination was directed to the natural world, seeking patterns and similitudes in this new sphere. Through this reorientation nature was constructed as a coherent and meaningful text in its own right. Crucially, just as a determination of the meaning of separate elements of scripture required the conviction that the sacred page represented a single, coherent unity, so the interpretation of the material things was now made possible by the discovery of 'nature'.

The meaning of nature, then, like the meaning of scripture, was a matter of relating the parts to the whole. As a single passage of scripture might be made to bear the meaning of the whole, so discrete material objects were seen to be reflections of the whole. A speck of dust, observed Robert Grosseteste, 'is an image of the whole universe' and 'a mirror of the creator'.[38] The model which medieval thinkers were to rely

---

[37] 'Postea vero ad sensum litterae historealem exponendum veniam, ut et allegoricam et moralem lectionem, quas sancti expositores aperte executi sunt, ex toto praetermittam.' *Magistri Theoderici Carnotensis Tractatus* 1 (reproduced in N. Häring, 'The Creation and Creator of the World According to Thierry of Chartres and Clarenbaldus of Arras', *Archives d'Histoire Doctrinale et Littéraire du Moyen Age* 22 (1955) 184–200 (184).

[38] Qu. in S. Gieben, 'Traces of God in nature according to Robert Grosseteste, with the text of the *Dictum, Omnis creatura speculum est*', *Franciscan Studies*, 24 (1964) 144–58. Cf. R. W. Southern, *Robert Grosseteste: the Growth of an English Mind in Medieval Europe* (Oxford: Clarendon, 1986), pp. 216f.

upon to establish such connexions in nature was thus the ancient idea of microcosm-macrocosm, a conception employed in biblical exegesis, but one which, as Plato had intimated in the *Timaeus*, could also be applied to the world.[39] From very early in the Christian era, Plato's suggestion that the human frame mirrors the shape of the universe had been adapted to the business of biblical interpretation. In Philo's exegetical writings this link between the human being (the microcosm) and creation (the macrocosm) became a rich source of allegorical interpretations, with scriptural references to natural objects now being read as references to persons, or parts of persons.[40] The Fathers had followed his lead, utilising microcosm in the interpretation of scripture in a number a ways. Thereafter, microcosm-macrocosm was more or less restricted in its application to the enterprise of biblical hermeneutics.[41] Origen applied it in numerous allegorical interpretations and also used it to give an account of the notion of man as the image of God.[42] St Gregory, who in the Middle Ages was the chief patristic source for the idea of microcosm, relied upon it to explain a puzzling reference in Mark's gospel in which the disciples are enjoined to 'preach the gospel to every creature' (Mark 16.15). Casting about for reasons to avoid mounting what must have seemed a rather fruitless evangelistic enterprise, Gregory declared that it is actually man who is 'every creature' because he comprehends all creatures in himself.[43] St Ambrose noted that 'the body of man is constructed like the world itself', and that he is 'a summation of the universe'.[44] Our eyes are like the sun and moon, our hair like the trees, our eye-brows two-fold hedges or mountains, our nose a cavern.[45] For the most part, however, Ambrose was interested in how features of the world can represent human passions or affections, for it is these connexions which are required for tropological interpretation. If the world was to be a moral training ground for the human race, then stones, plants, animals and their behaviours, each would need to represent some aspect of human nature, some virtue to be emulated, some vice to be avoided.[46]

---

[39] Plato, *Timaeus*, 44d, 28d-30d (pp. 1173, 1163); cf. *Phaedrus*, 270c (p. 516). Aristotle, too, had made some perfunctory remarks to the effect that human anatomy is conformed to the architecture of the universe. *History of Animals* 494a; cf. *De resp.* 477a; *De caelo*, 284, *Physics*, 252b.

[40] 'Man is every kind of animal'; 'he resembled . . . both the world and God; and he represented in his soul the characteristics of the nature of each'. Philo, *De opificio mundi* LI.146, LIII. 151 (p. 21); Cf. *Legum allegoriae II*, vii.22f. (p. 40).

[41] Perhaps the single exception to this rule was Nemesius, *On the Nature of Man* I.2, 4, 10.

[42] *Homilies in Genesis* I.xi, xii (*FC* 71, 61f.). Cf. Philo, *On the Life of Moses II*, XII.65 (p. 496).

[43] Gregory, *Homiliae in Evangelium* 29 (*PL* 76, 1212); Cf. Nemesius, *The Nature of Man*, I.i-ii.

[44] Ambrose, *Hexameron*, VI.ix.54, 75 (pp. 268, 282).   [45] *Ibid.*, VI.ix.54–63 (pp. 268–74).

[46] *Ibid.*, VI.iii–iv (pp. 232–46).

The basis of tropological readings of the world was, in the words of Ambrose, that 'we cannot fully know ourselves without first knowing the nature of all living creatures'.[47]

Augustine had followed this trend, regarding the beasts as, amongst other things, allegorical representations of human passions. The true meaning of our original dominion over the animals is that through reason, the passions were once, and should again, be held under the sway of reason: 'then the wild animals are quiet and the beasts are tamed and the serpents are rendered harmless: in allegory they signify the affections of the soul . . . So in the "living soul" there will be beasts that have become good by the gentleness of their behaviour . . . For these animals serve reason when they are restrained from their deathly ways.'[48] Jerome, similarly, was to interpret scriptural references to certain beasts as Plato's 'irascible and concupiscible passions'. He was less trusting of reason, however, urging that the passions and reason alike be placed under the control of conscience (συνείδησις).[49] Gregory of Nyssa agreed that the dominion referred to in Genesis was the original freedom enjoyed by the human soul, before it succumbed to its lower nature – 'it owns no master, and is self-governed, ruled autocratically by its own will'.[50] Even John Chrysostom, generally not given to spiritual interpretations, spoke of 'bringing the beast under control' by 'banishing the flood of unworthy passions'.[51] This principle thus allowed entities in the material world to play their proper roles in the edification of the human soul. Things in the physical world derived their significance from their relatedness to the interior world. Moreover, notions of dominion which might otherwise have provided some motivation for engaging with the material world, were deflected by these 'spiritual' or psychological interpretations.

Medieval exegetes were thus familiar with the use of microcosm-macrocosm in the interpretation of texts. From their encounter with Plato's *Timaeus*, they now learnt that the microcosm-macrocosm relation could be redeployed in the natural world. Turned outwards upon

---

[47] *Ibid.*, vi.ii.3 (p. 229), The same idea is repeated by the author of the *Asclepius*, who wrote that 'on account of mankind's divine composition, it seems right to call him a well-ordered world. . . Mankind knows himself through the world'. *Asclepius*, 10 (Copenhaver edn p. 72).

[48] Augustine, *Confessions* XIII.xxi (p. 291).

[49] Jerome, *Commentariorum in Hiezechielem* 1.1.6/8 (*CCSL* LXXV, 11f.), and *Homilies* 7 (*FC* 48, 54); Cf. *Homilies* 30 (*FC* 48, 227).

[50] Gregory of Nyssa, *De hominis opificio*, 4.1 qu. in Pagels, *Adam, Eve, and the Serpent*, p. 98.

[51] Chrysostom, *Homilies on Genesis* VIII.14 (*FC* 74, 113). For animals as symbolising human passions, also see Philo, *De plantatione* XI.43 (p. 194b), Maximus, *Quaestiones ad Thalassium* 27 (*Corpus Christianorum series graeca* 7, 261, 53).

the book of nature, this conception became an all-encompassing paradigm, able to relate apparently disparate elements of the natural world in much the same way that it had previously served scripture. Whereas microcosm-macrocosm had enabled exegetes to establish the meaning of other living things, with creatures in the external world being interpreted as features of the inner spiritual and moral world, now this same principle posited man as a material being, embedded in a material world, and intimately connected with the whole creation. Now connexions were established between the human body and the world, and the resemblances upon which they were based posited sympathetic rather than semantic links. Microcosmic conceptions had formerly made known the meaning of the world, now they would hold out the possibility of its mastery. From being an interpretive principle, microcosm-macrocosm came to be an ordering conception by which the world could be known, and in theory, manipulated. References to objects in the world, in turn, could be mapped onto some interior element of the human soul.

The relation of the human being to the macrocosm was set out in various ways by medieval writers. At a simple level the body might be said to be a microcosm in that it is formed from all the elements of the universe.[52] Elaborations of this elemental microcosm depict the whole person as sharing in the material existence of inanimate objects, the life of plants, the sensation of animals, the reason of angels.[53] More specific structural correspondences between various parts of the world and parts of the human body were also common.[54] Hildegard of Bingen drew parallels between the human head and the firmament above the earth; between the movements of the blood and the flow of rivers; between bone and marrow, and rock and tree; between body and soul, and earth and sun.[55] Later, Robert Grosseteste was to write similarly that the head was the heavens, the eyes the moon and sun, the breath the winds, the belly the sea.[56] By the Renaissance, there were quite detailed accounts of

[52] Allers refers to this as 'elementaristic microcosm', pp. 321ff.

[53] Eriugena, *De divisione naturae* II.4 (*PL* 122. 530D); Alanus de Insulis, *Distinct. dict. theol.* (*PL* 210, 755a); Aquinas, *ST* 1a. 91, 1 (XIII, 19)

[54] Honorius Augustodunensis, *Elucidarium* I.11 (*PL* 172, 1116B-C). On microcosm in Eriugena, see *Jean Scot: Homélie sur le prologue de Jean* , ed. E. Jeauneau, (Paris, 1969), pp. 336–8; James McEvoy, 'Microcosm and Macrocosm in the Writings of Bonaventure', *S. Bonaventura II* (Roma: Padre di Editori di Quaracchi, 1974).

[55] Hildegard, *Liber divinorum operum*, I.iv.16, 97, 82, 81 (*PL* 197, 814D, 862D, 862C); *Subtilitates* II.3 (*PL* 197, 1212).

[56] Robert Grosseteste, 'Quod homo sit minor mundus', in L. Baur, 'Die Philosophie des Robert Grosseteste', *Beiträge zur Geschichte der Philosophie des Mittelalters* 9 (1912), 59. Cf. Isidore of Seville, *Differentiarum* II. 48f. (*PL* 83, 77f.).

the various correspondences which obtained between the human body
and the constitution of the universe. Sixteenth-century surgeon, Ambroise Pare, is typical:

Just as in the big world [i.e. the macrocosm] there are two great lights, to wit,
the sun and the moon, so there are in the human body two eyes which
illuminate it, which [microcosm] is composed of four elements, as in the big
world in which winds, thunder, earthquakes, rain, dew, vapors, exhalations,
hail, eclipses, floods, sterility, fertility, stones, mountains, fruits, and several
divers species of animals occur; the same thing also happens in the small world
which is the human body. An example of winds: they can be observed to be
enclosed in windy apostemas and in the bowels of those who have windy colic;
and similarly in some women whose belly one can hear rumbling in such a way
that it seems there is a colony of frogs there; the which [winds] upon issuing
from the seat make noises like cannons being fired. And although the artillery
piece is aimed towards the ground, nevertheless the cannon smoke always hits
the nose of the cannoneer and those who are near him.[57]

Pare goes on to give equally colourful examples of rains and floods,
fruits, mountains, stones, sterility and fertility, all of which could be
found in the microcosm.

The conviction that the superior realm governed the inferior persisted until well into the seventeenth century, and beyond. Cambridge
educated physician Nicholas Culpeper declared in his popular *Herbal*
(1653), that 'the admirable Harmony of the Creation is herein seen, in
the influence of Stars upon herbs and the Body of Man . . . one part of
the Creation is subservient to the other, and all for the use of Man,
whereby the infinite power and Wisdom of God is displayed'.[58] All but
the most sceptical of his contemporaries would have agreed. Indeed, the
theory of celestial influences provided an important justification for the
existence of heavenly bodies. In the words of Sir Walter Raleigh:

If we cannot deny but that God hath given virtue to springs and fountains, to
cold earth, to plants and stones, minerals and to the excremental parts of the
basest living creatures, why should we rob the beautiful stars of their working
powers? For, seeing they are many in number and of eminent beauty and
magnitude, we may not think that in the treasury of his wisdom who is infinite
there can be wanting, even for every star, a peculiar virtue and operation; as
every herb, plant, fruit, flower, adorning the face of the earth hath the like.[59]

---

[57] Amboise Pare, *On Monsters and Marvels*, tr. Janis Pallister (University of Chicago Press, 1982) pp.
53f.
[58] Nicolas Culpeper, *Complete Herbal and English Physician Enlarged* (Ware: Wordsworth, 1995), Epistle
to the Reader, p. vii.
[59] Qu. in Keith Thomas, *Religion and the Decline of Magic* (New York: Charles Scribner's Sons, 1971),
p. 333.

Natural objects inhabiting the heavens, no less than their terrestrial counterparts, played an intimate role in human affairs.

While the significant feature of the Medieval preoccupation with microcosm and macrocosm was the establishment of physical correspondences between human body and material world, the moral qualities and psychological faculties which had been the main interest of the Fathers were not completely neglected. Jacob ibn Zaddick (d. 1149), for example, wrote that 'There is nothing in the world which has not its correspondence in man. . . He is courageous like the lion, timorous like the hare, patient like the lamb, clever like the fox.'[60] Hildegard, too, wrote of the humours that course through the human body, sometimes raging fiercely, like the leopard, sometimes sluggishly as in the crab, at other times in ways analogous to the wolf, deer, bear, serpent, lamb, or lion.[61] Yet even these correspondences were now set out with a new intention. Jacob ibn Zaddick actually inverted the priorities of the Fathers, by proposing that self-knowledge will lead to a knowledge of the external world. His concern is not with the moral lessons which animals can teach us by virtue of their representing various passions, virtues, or vices; he is concerned rather with how the insight that man is a microcosm can be of assistance in gaining knowledge of the macrocosm. Hildegard seems to be making a veiled reference to the signs of the zodiac, and to how the movements of the heavenly bodies exert their influence on the souls of man and beast alike, although the implications of these astrological speculations are not developed here.[62]

The various structural correspondences made possible knowledge of the material world, based on the idea, as old as the presocratic philosophers, that 'like knows like'. As Empedocles had expressed it:

> For 'tis by Earth we see Earth, by Water Water,
> By Ether Ether, by Fire destructive Fire,
> By Love Love, and Hate by cruel Hate.[63]

Elemental microcosm thus provided the theoretical basis of universal knowledge, which was available uniquely to the microcosm. This is the meaning of Aristotle's remark in *De anima* that the human soul is, 'in a sense, everything'.[64] Aquinas, having established that 'man is called a

---

[60] Allers, 'Microcosmos', p. 246. The control of the passions by reason was thereby depicted as reflecting human dominion over the animals, lost at the fall. Cf. Philo, *De Plantatione*, xi.43 (p. 194).   [61] Hildegard, *Liber divinorum operum* (*PL* 197, 732f.); Cf. *HMES* ii, 150.

[62] As they are elsewhere. See *Causae et curae* (*PL* 197, 778); Cf. *HMES* ii, 150–3.

[63] Qu. in Aristotle, *De anima* 404b.   [64] Aristotle, *De anima* 431b.

little world or microcosm, because all parts of the created world are found in him in one way or another', points out the epistemological implications: 'it was proper for the human body to be made out of the four elements, in order to give man an affinity with lower bodies, as a sort of middle link between spiritual and bodily substances . . .'. This balance of the elements 'is necessary in man's constitution to ensure that he has a good sense of touch, which is the basis of the other senses'.[65] Because man is in a sense all things, he can know all things. The same idea is expressed in Andrew Marvell's couplet: 'The mind is that ocean where each kind / Does straight its own resemblance find.'[66] The knowledge of all things, in turn, held out the promise of the mastery of nature, for things linked by similitude were also linked causally on the basis of that likeness by sympathy. The principle 'like moves like' thus enabled the extension of knowledge based on the macrocosm to physic, meteorology, astrology, sympathetic cures, as well as the darker arts of divination and black magic. Terrestrial events could be accounted for by changes in the celestial spheres, while physiological changes in the human being relate to changes in the material world. Hildegard linked the flux and reflux of the tides, the flow of bloody menses, cycles of plague and pestilence, to the revolutions of the celestial spheres.[67] Likenesses, then, were not simply static resemblances, but were external signs of what we would regard as 'causal' principles. The active principle between entities which shared a likeness was 'sympathy'. Sympathetic connexions lay at the basis of medieval medicine, astronomy and astrology, natural magic.[68] Each of these arts was based on the manipulation of resemblances. Even knowledge of the future could be gleaned from the study of resemblances, for 'structural' analogies were accompanied by temporal analogies. As the firmament above resembles the earth below, as the world within resembles the world without, so the future resembles the past. This symmetry had always been implicit in figural readings of scripture, according to which historical events 'prefigured' what was yet to come. Now this temporal symmetry was to be read as well in the book of nature, primarily in the revolutions of the celestial spheres. Human destiny could be read from the movements of the corresponding celestial spheres, and equally, changes in the sublunary world were linked to the fortunes of human-

---

[65] Aquinas, *ST* 1a. 91, 1 (XIII, 19).   [66] Andrew Marvell, 'The Garden'.
[67] Hildegard, *Liber divinorum operum* 1.iv.98 (*PL* 197, 877A)
[68] Angus Fletcher thus speaks of 'allegorical causation', *Allegory: The Theory of a Symbolic Mode* (Cornell University Press, 1964), pp. 181–219.

ity.[69] And while there were those who still harboured suspicions about astrological prognostication, owing perhaps to the residual influence of Augustine's animus to the art, or to reservations about how the horoscope might be squared with free-will, practitioners of astrology could always point to the first chapter of Genesis, which tells how God placed lights in the firmament to serve for signs and for seasons, or to the story of the Magi, who had followed the star to Bethlehem.[70]

While some medieval accounts of microcosm make provision for other natural objects representing all the features of the universe in their structures, it was universally accepted that the human individual was the microcosm par excellence, owing to their pivotal position in the cosmos. William of Auvergne declared the human soul to be uniquely 'on the horizon of two worlds'.[71] Hildegard wrote that 'humanity stands in the centre of the structure of the world' and in consequence, 'is more important than all other creatures'.[72] To Honorius Augustodunensis, likewise, man was located at the very centre of the chain of being, between heaven and earth, between angels and the animals, constructed from spirit and matter, man the 'celestial animal' contains all things and

---

[69] Isidore of Seville (c. 560–636) was an important source for medieval ideas of medical astrology. He explicitly linked the conception of man as a microcosm to astrology, an art of which he whole-heartedly approved. *Etymologiae* IV.13–14. Also see J. Fontaine, 'Isidore de Séville et l'astrologie', *Revue des Études Latines* 31 (1953), 283–5; William Sharpe (ed. and tr.), *Isidore of Seville: The Medical Writings*. (Philadelphia: American Philosophical Society, 1964), pp. 25f.

[70] Isaiah 47.13–14, by way of contrast, condemns astrological prediction. For Augustine's opposition to astrology, see *Confessions* IV.iii.4, *De div. Quaest.* LXXXIII.xiv.1, *City of God* V.1–9; Cf. Aquinas, *Summa contra gentiles* III.82, 85–6. The embarrassing incident of the Magi was reckoned by Origen to be the final great moment of a now dead art. *Against Celsus*, II.60. Cf. Nemesius, *Of the Nature of Man* XXV.51 (Library of Christian Classics IV, 397). Astrological signs might also be imprinted on terrestrial things, such as stones, or the human body, and there serve as medium for the influence of the stars, planets, and constellations. The imprinting of zodiac signs on rocks is discussed by Albertus Magnus, *The Book of Minerals*, tr. Dorothy Wyckoff (Oxford: Clarendon, 1967), II.iii.5 'The meaning of the Images on Stones' (pp. 141–151). Later, signs on the human body were to provide the basis of physiognomy and cheiromancy (palm-reading). See, e.g., Jean d'Indagine, *Chiromance* (Lyon, 1549), Barthélemy Coclès, *Physiognomonia* (Strassbourg, 1533), Robert Fludd, *Utriusque cosmi historia* (Oppenheim, 1619).

[71] William of Auvergne, *De anima* VII.6, *Opera Omnia* II supp., 211. See S. Marrone, *William of Auvergne and Robert Grosseteste* (Princeton University Press, 1983), p. 34. Similar expressions, probably deriving from *Liber de causis* II, are to be found in Alanus de Insulis, Albertus Magnus, and Aquinas. See Allers, 'Microcosmus', p. 360; McEvoy, *The Philosophy of Robert Grosseteste*, p. 383. Cf. *Asclepius* 6 : 'man has been put in the happier place of middle status so that he might cherish those beneath him and be cherished by those above him. . . He is everything, and he is everywhere.' (Copenhaver edn, pp. 69f.).

[72] Hildegard, *Liber divinorum operum* I.ii.15 (*PL* 197.761B). Elsewhere: 'Man sits on the judgement seat of the world. He rules over the creation. Each creature is under his control and in his service. He is above all other creatures.' *Ibid.* I.iv.100 (*PL* 197.885C)

unites all things.[73] When combined with notion of man as the image and similitude of God, numerous implications followed for the unique relation of the human being to both Creator and the creation. 'Man' was the last-created, an exemplar, a *summa*, a resemblance of all things from the most lowly to God himself, image and likeness of God, lord of the creatures, and archetype of the universe. In the words of Robert Grosseteste:

In the last place the All-high established a product, man, who would be at once the exemplar of all [the grades] mentioned and drawn from them all, as one might do who wrote individual works containing his wisdom and then edited them into a *summa*. For man is on the same level as the angel in his soul, his sensibility relates him to the animals and he shares his organic level with all growing things, while certain parts of his body bear a likeness to other material things. In his physical aspect, therefore, he resembles the most lowly of things and so is imperfect, but his soul is the equal of the highest creature and hence most noble. Taken in all of what he is, however, he is the most worthy creature that exists. For I maintain that man resembles the Creator more than does any other thing made, for as all things stand in God as their cause, so too all shine forth in man as their effect, which is why he is called a tiny world. And since he is best of all, being equal to all together yet equalled by none, they commonly owe him natural obedience; so he is the image of God. The Lord said, 'let us make man in our image and likeness'. He gave him dominion over all things, for man had been conceived as the model of the whole universe.[74]

As the bearer of the dual images of the Deity and his creation, man had been given not only his place in the order of things, but also his destiny.

---

[73] 'Qui etiam et imaginem et similitudinem Dei creatus memoratur, ut coeleste animal intelligatur: dum ratione et intellectu c caiteris animantibus sequestratur. Et quia ei Dominus quandoque couniri disposuit, ei participium cum omni creatura tribuit: Scilicet discernere cum angelis, sentire cum animantibus, crescere cum herbis et arboris, esse cum lapidibus. Corpus ejus de quatuor elementis compegit, animam scientia replevit, et omni corporali creaturae praefecit.' Honorius Augustodunensis, *Hexaemeron* III (*PL* 172, 258C).

[74] Grosseteste, *De confessione*, pp. 240–1, qu. in McEvoy, *The Philosophy of Robert Grosseteste* p. 408. A similar passage occurs in Nemesius: 'In his own person, man joins mortal creatures with the immortals, and brings the rational beings into contact with the irrational. He bears about in his proper nature a reflex of the whole creation, and is therefore rightly called 'the world in little'. He is the creature for whom God thought worthy of such special providence that, for his sake, all creatures have their being, both those that are, and those that are yet to be. He is the creature for whose sake God became man, so that this creature might attain incorruption and escape corruption, might reign on high, being made after the image and likeness of God... Who, then, can fully express the pre-eminence of so singular a creature.' *Of the Nature of Man* I.10 (Library of Christian Classics IV. 254f.) In the thirteenth century, Bonaventure was to combine in a similar fashion the finality of man in the creation, and his relation to creation as microcosm. See McEvoy, 'Microcosm and Macrocosm', p. 315.

Man was to know the world, and to master it, and in doing so was to come to know God and be reconciled to him.

RESTORING LOST LIKENESSES

If the book of nature was to be read in conjunction with the book of scripture, it was no less true that the message to be read in the natural world was similar to that of scripture: nature provided knowledge of God and pointed the way to redemption. The possibility that God might be known through resemblances in the world was already familiar to readers of those Platonic works which had proved so influential in the twelfth century, all of which had stressed the immanence of God in the world. In the *Timaeus*, Plato asserted that the world is 'a sensible God who is the image of the intellectual'.[75] The *Asclepius* repeats this claim describing the cosmos as a god 'who can be seen and sensed'.[76] Macrobius further extended this conception, describing the visible world as the temple of God:

In order to show, therefore, that the omnipotence of the Supreme God can hardly ever be comprehended and never witnessed, he called whatever is visible to our eyes the temple of that God who is apprehended only in the mind, so that those who worship these visible objects as temples might still owe the greatest reverence to the Creator, and that whoever is inducted into the privileges of this temple might know that he had to live in the manner of a priest.[77]

Twelfth-century writers, while wary of the dangers of pantheism, were nonetheless influenced by these conceptions and came to stress in an unprecedented way the possibility of knowing God through his creatures. Hildegard, for example, tirelessly reminds us that 'all Creatures are an indication of God', that 'it is God whom human beings know in every creature'.[78] 'Wherever we look', agreed Grosseteste, 'we find vestiges of God.'[79] Hugh of St Victor was similarly enthusiastic about the prospects of a knowledge of God through nature: 'Every nature tells of God; every nature teaches man; every nature reproduces its essential

---

[75] Plato, *Timaeus*, 92c.

[76] *Asclepius* 8 (Copenhaver edn p. 71); Cf. *Corpus Hermeticum*: the cosmos is 'a great god and image of a greater' XII.15 (Copenhaver edn p. 46).

[77] Macrobius, *Commentary on the Dream of Scipio* XIV.1 (p. 142). In the seventeenth century, Robert Boyle was to cite this passage, and similar references in Philo, to support his claim that scientists were 'priests of nature'. *On the Excellency of Natural Philosophy* Part 1, Essay III, *Works* II, 31f.

[78] Hildegard, *Liber divinorum operum* 1.ii.15, 1.iv.105, 1.iv.97 (*PL* 197, 761B, 896B).

[79] Qu. in S. Gieben, 'Traces of God in Nature' p. 148.

form, and nothing in the universe is infecund.'[80] Indeed, of all twelfth-century writers, it was Hugh of St Victor who most explicitly set out the connexion between the reading of the two books.

Hugh's *Didascalicon*, subtitled *De studio legendi* (On the Study of Reading), was the twelfth-century equivalent of Augustine's *De doctrina christiana*. In it Hugh advances familiar platonic arguments: on the one hand, because the 'invisible things can only be known by visible things', the whole of theology must use visible demonstrations; on the other, 'worldly theology' never progressed beyond the appearances of things, was always marred by 'the stain of error'.[81] Hugh, like the majority of his contemporaries, also endorsed Augustine's view that in scripture 'things as well as words are significant'. Hugh's advance on Augustine comes in his conclusion that the study of things must therefore be a significant source of truth in its own right.[82] As it turned out, the curriculum of the medieval schools neatly matched this distinction between the study of words and things. The seven liberal arts were taught in order to serve the higher purpose of uncovering the meanings of the sacred page: the *Trivium* (grammar, rhetoric, and dialectic) illuminated the meanings of words; the *Quadrivium* (music, arithmetic, geometry, astronomy), the meanings of the things referred to by the words. Again, the reading of things was controlled by the now standard categories of tropology and allegory: tropological interpretation of things led to virtue, allegorical interpretation led to truth.[83] These two things, virtue and truth, together restore the divine likeness: 'Now there are two things which restore the divine likeness in man, namely the contemplation of truth and the practice of virtue.'[84] The contemplation of truth required knowledge of things of nature, and such knowledge was a means of restoring a lost divine likeness.

To know the world, then, is not merely to come to know God, it is to become *like* God: it is to restore a likeness which had been lost. For all

---

[80] Hugh of St Victor, *Didascalicon*, vi.v (p. 145). Hugh set out quite specific techniques for the interpretation of the text of nature, based on the general assumption that living things can be read as signs variously of God's power, wisdom and goodness: the power of God is seen in the immensity of creatures, his goodness in their usefulness, and his wisdom in their elegance. *De tribus diebus* 1, (*PL* 176, 812–13A).

[81] Hugh of St Victor, *Expositio in Hierarchiam coelestem* i.i (*PL* 125, 923–8).

[82] Hugh of St Victor, *On the Sacraments* i, prologue 5 (p. 5); *Didascalicon* v.3 (p. 121). Cf. Augustine, *On Christian Doctrine*, ii.iv.5 (p. 36).

[83] Hugh of St Victor, *On the Sacraments* i, prologue 6 (pp. 5f.).

[84] Hugh of St Victor, *Didascalicon*, i.viii; v.vi (pp. 54f., 127). Hugh reiterated the patristic justification for the existence of the material world: 'Men, because they had to advance to knowledge through intervals of time, had to be stimulated and instructed to knowledge of truth through the forms of the temporal and visible things without.' *On the Sacraments* i.vii.33 (p. 138).

that medieval thinkers were to place the human race at the very centre of the cosmos, theirs was no shallow optimism. They had read beyond the Idyll in Eden, to the Fall, the first homicide, and the sordid events which brought on the Deluge. Whatever pride might have resulted from the vision of man as a microcosm of the universe was thus muted by the sober recognition that human beings were fallen creatures, and that when the crown of creation had fallen, his dominions had fallen with him. The lustre of the luminous signs of divinity which had once shone out in the material world had now dimmed through that first human misadventure. Those similitudes which originally had borne witness to the spiritual origins of the world were now reduced to what Augustine and Grosseteste both termed 'vestiges'.[85] Other created things, too, lost their obvious similitude to those divine ideas which had been their original cause. Indeed, for those schooled in Platonism, the whole physical world become a place of *dis*similitude, for as Plato had observed in *The Statesman*, when creatures fall away from God, they enter 'the bottomless abyss of *unlikeness*'.[86] Plotinus had reiterated this sentiment, describing the fate of human souls in these terms: 'We are become dwellers in the Place of Unlikeness, where, fallen from all our resemblance to the Divine, we lie in gloom and mud.'[87] The idea that this fallen creation was a 'region of dissimilitude' (*regio dissimilitudis*) was adopted by Augustine, and like so many of his borrowings from Platonism, found its way into medieval thought.[88] Yet, whereas for Augustine the solution to our plight lay in retreat from this earthly region of dissimilitude to the more ordered world of the mind, for those progress-ive spirits of the twelfth century the lost similitudes of things could be re-established, and while such an ordering process was ultimately still to take place in the mind, it began with a knowledge of the sensory world. Empirical nature was to be re-ordered by human knowledge, and thus

---

[85] The loss of harmony was a two-fold loss – a loss of ordering knowledge on the part of Adam, as well as a loss of actual order amongst the creatures. The latter is clearly evident in observed antipathies between creatures, the former in the fact that man must now resort to a fragmentary sensory knowledge. Some intelligences, Grosseteste argued, have direct knowledge of universals and all particulars by illumination from the divine mind. Fallen man, who once had access to this knowledge, is now 'weighed down under the load of the corrupt body', and must have resort to the senses. Southern, *Robert Grosseteste*, p. 165.

[86] Plato, *The Statesman* 273d (Hamilton and Cairns edn, p. 1039).

[87] Plotinus, *Enneads*, I.viii.10 (p. 32).

[88] Augustine, *Confessions* VII.x, XIII.2; Pierre Courcelle, 'Tradition Néo-Platonicienne et Traditions Chrétiennes de la "Region de Dissemblance"', *Archives d'Histoire Doctrinale et Littéraire du Moyen Age* (1957) 5–33. Origen wrote, in a similar vein, that the diversity of living creatures was the consequence of a fall 'from that primeval unity and harmony in which they were at first created by God.' *De principiis*, II.

the human conception of the world, of 'nature', would be that same conception which had been in the mind of the Creator. In this manner the human mind would come to resemble the mind of God, and the human likeness to God would by this means be restored. Human beings stood in need of redemption, and indeed it is this necessity for their redemption, and the redemption of the world, which transformed what in antiquity had tended to be a static and sterile representation of their relation to the whole, into a dynamic programme. God's creatures must now embark upon that path which would result in the restoration of their former dignity, and that path would lead them to the attempt to know and master the world. Through knowledge, the world would be reunited, and both knower and known would be redeemed. The human being was to 'comprehend' all things in both ontological and epistemological senses of that term. The turn to the natural world was in some sense a turning away from the sacred page, but it could hardly be said that it was motivated by a secular, or non-theological impulse. On the contrary, acquisition of knowledge of the order of nature was enjoined on mankind as an integral part of the process of human redemption, and more specifically, a reversal of the losses incurred at the Fall.

In the emerging recognition that the goal of human life was to do with knowledge, mastery, and the regaining of an original perfection through a re-ordering of similitudes, there are again unmistakeable echoes of Plato. In the closing lines of the *Timaeus* Plato informs us that 'learning the harmonies and revolutions of the universe, should correct the courses of the head which were corrupted at our birth, and should assimilate the thinking being to the thought, renewing his original nature, so that having assimilated them he may attain to that best life which the gods have set before mankind.'[89] Knowledge of the harmonies and revolutions of the universe thus leads to a renewal of corrupted human nature. The study of nature was thus an essentially religious process. Similar themes can be found in the Hermetic writings: 'Learning the arts and sciences and using them preserves this earthly part of the world: god willed it that the world would be incomplete without them.'[90] In a more elaborate passage, the reader is given this counsel:

So you must think of god in this way, as having everything – the cosmos, himself, the universe – like thoughts within himself. Thus, unless you make

---

[89] Plato, *Timaeus* 90d (p. 1209).   [90] *Asclepius* 8 (Copenhaver edn p. 71).

yourself equal to god, you cannot understand god; like is understood by like . . . Having conceived that nothing is impossible to you, consider yourself immortal and able to understand everything, all art, all learning, the temper of every living thing. Go higher than every height and lower than every depth. Collect in yourself all the sensations of what has been made, of fire and water, dry and wet; be everywhere at once, on land, in the sea, in heaven; be not yet born, be in the womb be young, old, beyond, death. And when you have understood all these at once – times, places, things, qualities, quantities – then you can understand god.'[91]

The human, according to the *Corpus Hermeticum*, was created 'to be a working witness to nature; to increase the number of mankind; to master all things under heaven . . . and to discover every means of working skillfully with things that are good.'[92]

This analysis of the human quest as one involving the restoration of original similitudes is also a New Testament theme. St Paul wrote: 'And because for us there is no veil over the face, we all reflect as in a mirror the splendour of the Lord; thus we are transformed into his likeness.' Elsewhere, he was to speak of Christian life as being a new life 'which is being constantly renewed in the image of its creator'.[93] The means by which twelfth-century thinkers proposed this redemption take place however, was quite new, for the process of the restoration of the divine similitude in man required the similitudes between all created things to be restored. This was to take place in two ways: first, by knowing the world, the human mind would restore things to the original unity which they had possessed in the divine mind; second, by controlling and subduing the world, human beings would be restored to their original position as God's viceroy on earth, and harmony would be restored between those creatures within their constituency. The restoration of a lost likeness to God was thus to take place through imitation of God: of his power, by manipulating the world; of his wisdom, through coming to know it.[94] To know God, to become like God, to possess the knowledge

---

[91] *Corpus Hermeticum* XI.20 (Copenhaver edn p. 41).　　[92] *Ibid.*, III.13 (Copenhaver edn. p. 13)

[93] II Corinthians 3.18; Colossians 3.10.

[94] The standard view had been that it is through Christ that the divine likeness is restored. Irenaeus wrote that Christ became *like* us, that we might become *like* him. *Against Heresies* v.ii–iv. Chrysostom claimed that the 'image' of God possessed by the human race lay in the human control of the creatures: 'So "image" refers to the matter of control, not anything else, in other words God created the human being as having control of everything on earth, and nothing is greater than the human being, under whose authority everything falls.' *Homilies on Genesis* VIII, 9 (*FC* 74, 110), cf. IX.7 (74, 120). Does the world now replace Christ as a vehicle of redemption? Hugh of St Victor attempts to overcome this difficulty by suggesting that the divine Word became incarnate twice – in the creation of the world, and in the person of Jesus. 'Therefore,

of the mind of God, these were synonyms for the process of redemption. Redemption, in short, did not entail as it did for Augustine, flight from the material world, a mastery of the beasts within, and a mystical absorption into divine reality, but rather an ordered knowledge of the natural world.

The restoration to the human race of a lost similitude to God was thus seen to entail a restoration to creatures of their proper relations – relations which were to be established on the basis of similitude. For the human mind again to be godlike, it had to recapture the vision of nature as an ordered whole. The accumulation and systematisation of information about animals and plants was an ordering process, a rehearsal of that event in Eden, in which God had paraded the animals before Adam to be named – an event which, according to a long exegetical tradition, indicated Adam's perfect knowledge of the natural world. This knowledge had been lost as a result of the human Fall. Adam had penetrated to the true nature of things with the eye of reason, we now are forced back on sensory experience and 'grope our way' towards knowledge.[95] 'Through [the organs of sense] man looks upon all the creatures', wrote Hildegard, 'knowing them for what they are, distinguishing them, separating them, naming them'.[96] The Fall was the occasion of the loss of direct access to the spiritual world. Thereafter, knowledge of spiritual truths was mediated through material things.

This idea – that the accumulation of knowledge about the natural world would in some measure restore to man what had been lost at the Fall – is most commonly associated with Francis Bacon and the rise of modern science. Yet we can now see that the roots of this conception go back much further.[97] The imperative element which is incipient in the vision of man as the unique locus of two images becomes increasingly obvious in the writings of twelfth century. Hugh of St Victor (d.1142)

there was one book written once within, and twice without; first without, through the foundation of visible things, secondly without through the assumption of the flesh. *On the Sacraments* i.vi.5 (p. 98).

[95] Richard of St Victor, *Benjamin major* 2.4 (*PL* 196, 82CD). William of Auvergne shared this view. See Steven P. Marrone, *William of Auvergne and Robert Grosseteste* (Princeton University Press, 1983), pp. 67f.   [96] Hildegard, *Liber divinorum operum*, i.iv.14 (*PL* 197, 813D–814A).

[97] In fact, as early as the ninth century, the translator of Pseudo-Dionysius, John Scotus Eriugena, had suggested that a 'scientific' knowledge of the animals, derived from a literal reading of the natural world, is a means of unifying their diversity, and returning them to the original unity which they had once possessed, in the human mind, and in the divine plan. Eriugena, *De divisione natura*, 1.7 (*PL* 122, 446C–D); Cf. Arnold of Bonneval, *De operibus sex dierum*, prologue (*PL* 189, 1515f.). Also see R. D. Crouse, '*Intentio Moysi*', pp. 143f.

suggested that the chief depredation suffered by man at the Fall was a loss of knowledge.[98] Through study, the soul could rediscover the divine truths hidden behind the veil of the creatures and the literal words of scripture, and thereby be restored to its original dignity. In his *Didascalicon* Hugh explains that the aim of study is 'to restore within us the divine likeness' so that 'we are conformed to the divine nature' and 'there begins to shine forth again in us what has forever existed in the divine Idea or Pattern, coming and going in us but standing changeless in God'.[99] Similar ideas are expressed by Honorius Augustodunensis. Despite the Fall and the ills it brought upon the world, terrestrial reality remains the sphere of 'multiple divine appearances'. Man is the celestial animal in which God willed all things to be re-united.[100] The idea that man was a microcosm was thus at once indicative and imperative. All creatures were in a sense to be found in man, and in another, were to be re-united in him through an orderly knowledge of the natural world. In the thirteenth century, Bonaventure again stressed the role which the visible world was to play in the redemption of mankind. Man, 'in the state of innocence possessed knowledge of created things and was raised through their representation to God and to his praise, reverence, and love'. While this knowledge was lost through the misadventures of our first parents, its re-acquisition is still 'the goal of the creatures and the way in which they are led back to God'.[101] To accumulate systematic knowledge of created things was both to restore the knowledge of Adam, and approach knowledge of the very mind of God. Through the acquisition of knowledge came also the redemption of the world, for knowledge was assimilated or incorporated in the human mind, and thus redeemed along with it.

The twelfth and thirteenth centuries witness the end of the religious indifference, or even hostility, to the physical world which had been fostered by the Fathers. Augustine had believed that a person might be deficient in knowledge of nature, and yet have a robust faith. There is no shame in being 'ignorant of the position and nature of a physical creature', he wrote, provided that one 'does not believe something unworthy of you, Lord'.[102] Now the pendulum was beginning to swing

---

[98] Hugh of St Victor, *De arca Noe morali*, Prologus (*PL* 176, 619); *In ecclesiasten homiliae* (*PL* 174, 277D). Elsewhere Hugh speaks of a threefold depredation at the Fall: man's punishment was mortality of the body, concupiscence of the flesh, and ignorance of the mind. *On the Sacraments* I.viii.1 (p. 141).   [99] *Didascalicon* II.i (p. 61).

[100] Honorius, *Hexaemeron*, III (*PL* 172, 258D-259A); *De animae exsilio et patria* XIII (*PL* 172.1246B).

[101] Bonaventure, *Hexaemeron* 13 (*Opera Omnia*, V, 390). Qu. in McEvoy, 'Microcosm and Macrocosm', p. 330.   [102] Augustine, *Confessions* v.v (pp. 76f).

back, and an ordered knowledge of this world could not be so easily divorced from the knowledge of the other. Adelard of Bath observed that 'If anyone born or educated in the residence of this world neglects learning the plan underlying its marvellous beauty, upon attaining the age of discretion he is unworthy and, were it possible, deserves to be cast our of it.'[103] William of Conches likewise expressed contempt for those who would perpetuate the Augustinian indifference to science: 'Ignorant themselves of the forces of nature and wanting to have company in their ignorance, they don't want people to look into anything; they want us to believe like peasants and not to ask the reason behind things.'[104] With those who habitually invoked the direct activity of God in physical explanations he was equally impatient: 'You poor fools, God can make a cow out of a tree, but has he ever done so? Therefore show some reason why a thing is so, or cease to hold that it is so.'[105] This period thus witnesses the beginnings of the transformation of the study of nature into a thoroughly theological enterprise. Thereafter, in the schools natural philosophy was increasingly integrated into the Christian scholarly endeavour. In the renaissance of the twelfth century we see a religiously-motivated indifference to the natural world transformed into a religiously-motivated quest for knowledge. Alongside the words inscribed by God upon the human heart and on the sacred page of scripture, stands the book of nature. The search for truth required the diligent study of both books.

[103] Adelard of Bath, *Astrolabium*, praef. cited by C. H. Haskins, *Studies in the History of Medieval Science* (New York: Umgar, 1960) p. 29.
[104] William of Conches, *Philosophia mundi* 1.23 (*PL* 72.56) tr. by Chenu, p. 11 n.20.
[105] Qu. in *HMES* II, 58.

CHAPTER 3

The two reformations

That which was our Philosophy is made Philologie, from whence
we teach to dispute, not to live.

John Webster, *Academiarum Examen*

So in natural history, we see there hath not been that choice and
judgement used as ought to have been; as may appear in the
writings of Plinius, Cardanus, Albertus, and divers of the Arabians,
being fraught with much fabulous matter, a great part not only
untried, but notoriously untrue, to the great derogation of the
credit of natural philosophy with the grave and sober kind of wits.

Francis Bacon, *Of the Advancement of Learning*

. . . the *Church of England* will not only be safe amidst the consequences of a *Rational Age*, but amidst all the improvements of
Knowledge, and the subversion of old Opinions about *Nature*, and
introduction of new ways of Reasoning thereon. This will be
evident, when we behold the agreement that is between the present
Design of the *Royal Society*, and that of our *Church* in its beginning.
They both may lay equal claim to the word *Reformation*, the one
having compass'd it in *Religion*, the other purposing it in *Philosophy*.
They both have taken a like cours [sic] to bring this about; each of
them passing by the *corrupt Copies*, and referring themselves to the
perfect Originals for their instruction; the one to the *Scripture*, the other
to the large volume of the *Creatures*.

Thomas Sprat, *History of the Royal Society*

ARISTOTLE AND THE ENCYCLOPAEDIAS

'These are the effects - as observed in natural science [*experimenta physica*]
and tested by great men', wrote Albertus Magnus in his *Book of Minerals*:
'and I would have set forth the *Lapidary of Aristotle*', he continues, 'except
that the whole book had not come down to me, but only some excerpts
from it.'[1] For Albert the Great (1206–1280) and his contemporaries, the

---

[1] Albertus Magnus, *Book of Minerals*, ii.iii.6 (p. 151).

study of nature was very much a scholarly enterprise. Neither the new conception of a natural order, nor the elevation of knowledge derived from the senses, led medieval thinkers to a direct engagement with the empirical world, and the newly ideated 'nature' was constructed along the lines of metaphysical conceptions found within texts. Those animals and plants which inhabited nature were encountered, not in field and forest, but on the written page, for medieval intellectual culture was pre-eminently a culture of the book.[2] Thus the exploration of the physical world was carried out at one remove, as a scholarly investigation of those sources which had treated the subject of natural history. For the scholastics, nature existed primarily in books, and if from time to time they were to add glosses to the authorities on the basis of their own observations of the world, they nonetheless saw as their main task the preservation and transmission of a world which had already been closely observed by great minds in the past.

To give Albert his due, he was perhaps more progressive in this respect than those around him. His administrative duties as Provincial of the Teutonic province, combined with a Dominican Rule which prohibited any mode of transport other than the pedestrian, afforded him considerable scope for the first-hand observation of nature. Some of these observations were incorporated into his writings on stones, plants, and animals. In the twenty-six books of *De animalibus*, a work which is primarily a commentary on Aristotle's three treatises on animals, Albert took the opportunity to add his own remarks, to insert the opinions of other authorities, to describe animals unknown to Aristotle, and to note traditions which he considered doubtful.[3] He provides the first known account of whaling operations, for example, describing how whales were captured with harpoons launched from ballistas (a device like a large cross-bow). 'These facts about the nature of whales', he informs his reader, 'have been gleaned from experience. We have omitted what the ancients wrote because they do not accord with the practical knowledge of experienced fishermen.'[4] A number of fabulous beasts and marvellous behaviours are also treated with scepticism. The 'legendary exploits' of the pelican, he points out, 'have never been proved by methodical examination in a scientific manner'. The phoenix is more beloved of

---

[2] Of course, what did change in the twelfth century was the attitude to books, and the canon of books. As Le Goff has observed, 'the university book was quite different from the monastic book'. *Medieval Civilization*, p. 345. While the latter was a treasure, the former became a tool.

[3] Aristotle's translator, Michael Scot, had treated *History of Animals*, *Parts of Animals*, and *Generation of Animals* as a single corpus, numbering the books consecutively from one to nineteen.

[4] Albert, *De animalibus* xxiv.19 (Scanlan edn, pp. 340f.)

mystical writers than those devoted to the natural sciences. The winged dragon, self-mutilating beaver, and fire-dwelling salamander – all are said to be legendary.[5]

While Albert's keen personal observations of nature might distinguish him from his more sedentary contemporaries, he is far from being, as some have suggested, a harbinger of that empirical approach to nature which characterises the natural history of the seventeenth century. Albert's primary achievement lay in his recognition of the significance of the works of Aristotle, and in providing for them a central place in the study of natural history. His scepticism about the existence of certain creatures was not motivated by the desire to exclude the fabulous and fantastic from the study of nature. It was part and parcel of the business of commentary on the writings of the ancients. The account of the harpy in *De animalibus*, for example, reads in summary like this: a rapacious bird with hooked claws and a human face; lives near the Ionian sea, has a constant craving for rapine and is awesomely ferocious; sometimes kills humans; probably fabulous.[6] The criterion for inclusion in a work on birds, beasts, and serpents was not whether something existed in the world, but whether it existed in books. For medieval writers, real existence was simply another attribute. (It was this principle which, in another context, Anselm had famously exploited.) In many instances, Albert's scepticism about mythical creatures is merely a reflection of a scepticism which can be found in his sources. And in any case, relatively few fantastic creatures are treated with any degree of suspicion. Albert gives quite uncritical descriptions of the 'manticore' (a human-faced quadruped), the centaur, the winged horse, the 'lamia' (a monstrous woman), the satyr, and the pygmie, and informs his readers that 'many animals with composite forms exist in the world'.[7] By and large, then, Aristotle's detailed first-hand knowledge of nature did not inspire his thirteenth-century admirers to imitate his methods, but rather, in humility, to 'set forth' his findings. The chief activity of natural philosophers became, in the phrase of William Gilbert, to 'chew the cud of ancient opinion'.[8]

Part of the reason for the excessive bookishness and apparent deference to the ancient *auctores* was to do with the scholastic belief that the human race had at one time been in possession of a complete knowledge

---

[5] *Ibid.*, xxiii.132, 110, xxv.28, xxii.22, xxv.35f. (pp. 310, 288f., 404, 90, 410).
[6] *Ibid.*, xxiii.19 (p. 200).   [7] *Ibid.*, xxii. (p. 172)
[8] William Gilbert, *On the Loadstone and Magnetic Bodies and on the Great Magnet of the Earth*, tr. P. Fleury Mottelay, (Chicago: Encyclopaedia Brittanica, 1952), i.i (p. 4).

of the natural world. To be sure, this was a knowledge which had been corrupted and compromised by the Fall, but its vestiges had been preserved in oral traditions and in scripture, and indeed it had been in some measure restored through the efforts of earnest pagans of superior intellect, some of whom had enjoyed the advantage of familiarity with the scientific writings of Moses and Solomon. And if it were true, as a later writer expressed it, that 'Aristotle was but the rubbish of an Adam, and Athens but the rudiments of a paradise', Aristotle and Athens were, for all that, a good deal better than nothing.[9] Faced with the choice of beginning the whole process of a science of nature again by gathering and organising knowledge from the phenomena of the world, or re-building ancient knowledge from the textual monuments of antiquity, scholastics modestly opted for the latter course of action. Far better to reconstruct and present what could be gleaned from the sources of the Golden Age than rely upon the meagre and degenerated resources of atrophied human wit and dull organs of sense. The mastery of nature at which thirteenth and fourteenth century minds aimed, amounted to a reconstruction of a past body of knowledge, the ruins of which could be discovered in those texts of the ancients. So it was that recognition of the importance of observing nature manifested itself, somewhat paradoxically, in an elevation to authority of those past writers thought to have been the most acute observers of stones, plants, birds and beasts. The turn to nature as an entity in its own right was a turn to texts *about nature*, rather than a turn to that modern construct, the empirical world.

In the thirteenth century, texts written by approved authors fell into one of three broad categories. There were firstly the books of birds and beasts – the bestiaries – which were little more than various incarnations of the *Physiologus*. Second, were such early encyclopaedias as Isidore of Seville's seventh-century *Etymologiarum*, and Bede's eighth-century *De natura rerum*. The chief source for these works was Pliny. Finally, there were the newly translated works of Aristotle, Galen, Dioscorides and other writers from classical antiquity. In the second decade of the thirteenth century the biological writings of Aristotle – *Historia animalium, De partibus animalium, De generatione animalium* – were translated from Arabic into Latin. Along with *De plantis*, a compilation out of Aristotle and Theophrastus, these works brought a considerable improvement in the state of knowledge of the natural world, not only on account of their factual content, but because they represented natural history as a

[9] Robert South, *Sermons*, in *English Prose*, ed. W. Peacock, 5 vols. (Oxford University Press, 1949), II, 208.

discipline based on observation and systematic explanation. In turn, these works inspired the thirteenth-century encyclopaedias of Vincent of Beauvais, Bartholomew Anglicus, Albertus Magnus and others.[10]

The difference between the material contained in these sources cannot but have made an impression on thirteenth-century compilers of natural lore, for while the encyclopaedias of Bede and Isidore (and to a lesser extent the bestiaries) undoubtedly contained observations drawn from the empirical world, there is a vast gulf between the painstaking and systematically organised observations of Aristotle, and the fragmentary and often highly stylised accounts of living things which were to be found in Isidore, Bede, and the bestiaries. While the latter continued to be popular in the monasteries, playing an important role in teaching and moral instruction, the former found favour in the universities, where Aristotelian science was more welcome. Indeed, from this time, the universities tended to be Aristotelian in emphasis, nurturing an encyclopaedic approach to knowledge, and attempting to assemble and transmit all that could be known on various subjects. The openness to new ideas and willingness to be led by reason, so evident in the attitudes of such individuals as Adelard of Bath, William of Conches, and Peter Abelard, tended to be manifested in an openness to the learning of the ancients. Such was the nature of the scholastic method that discovery took place through exegesis and argument rather than by observation and experiment. The monasteries, for their part, remained anchored in the Augustinian-Platonic tradition, and persevered in their role as educators of the laity.[11] Symptomatic of these different directions is the fact that the circulation of Latin bestiaries began to wane after the thirteenth century, while bestiaries written in the vernacular continued to flourish into the late Middle Ages.[12]

The thirteenth-century encyclopaedias were undoubtedly more 'scientific' than the bestiaries and lapidaries which they tended to displace, simply because their sources were better informed. Yet they suffered from crucial limitations. In the first place, they were frequently

---

[10] Vincent of Beauvais, *Speculum naturale*, (1220–44), Thomas of Cantimpré, *De natura rerum* (c.1228–44), Albertus Magnus, *De vegetabilibus et plantis, De animalibus* (1258–62). On the encyclopaedias of Isidore and Vincent, see Jacques Fontaine, 'Isidore de Séville et la Mutation de l'Encyclopédisme Antique', *Cahiers D'Histoire Mondiale*, 9 (1966) 519–38, Michel Lemoine, 'L'oeuvre encyclopédique de Vincent de Beauvais', *Cahiers D'Histoire Mondiale* 9 (1966) 571–9. This whole number of the journal is devoted to the history of the encyclopaedia.

[11] Michel de Boüard, 'Encylopédies médiévales. Sur la 'connaissance de la nature et du monde' au moyen âge', *Revue des questions historiques*, series 3, 16 (1930) 258–304. (esp. p. 267 n. 2).

[12] Clark, *Book of Birds*, Introduction, p. 23.

based upon corrupted texts which had undergone translation from Greek, into Arabic, and again into Latin, with occasional detours into Syriac or Hebrew. Further, they were compiled using methods similar to those adopted by writers on theological topics. The standard theological text of the Middle Ages – Peter Lombard's *Sentences* – was so named because it consisted of an anthology of *dicta* or 'sentences' extracted from the Church Fathers, and arranged topically. Given the laborious nature of medieval book production and the relative scarcity of original sources, such collections of isolated quotations were the chief means by which scholars gained access to the writings of ancient authorities. As they were little more than collections of quotations removed from their original contexts, they were easily misinterpreted, and through the infidelities of copyists they became, over time, burdened with accumulated errors. As early as the twelfth century, Robert of Melun had pointed to the difficulty in distinguishing the work of the original authority from subsequent glosses, but he was a lone, and unheeded voice.[13] The botanical and zoological insights of the classical writers, when incorporated into the medieval encyclopaedias, tended to suffer a similar fate.

Thus, while it is true to say that nature was discovered in the twelfth century, up until the end of the sixteenth century it was a nature which for the most part was interpreted according to written authorities. All scholastic learning, be it theology, medicine, mathematics, or natural history, was based upon the dual principles of authority and reason. 'Authority' extended not only to ecclesiastical councils, the Doctors of the Church, and the deposit of scripture, but encompassed Aristotle, Galen, and other ancients. To a large extent, then, the secular writers of antiquity came to share the privileged status accorded to scripture and the Fathers. As the hapless Galileo was to discover, these combined authorities were to delimit the range of legitimate ways of reading the book of God's works, and together could present a formidable obstacle to novel interpretations of nature. It was inevitable, however, that written authorities would at times contradict each other, and it was at this point that reason would join with authority: it was the task of reason to reconcile contradictions, to consider opposing arguments, and to arrive at conclusions, relying upon the tools of logic and dialectic – tools now conveniently made available in Aristotle's *Organon*. Both the excesses of scholasticism and the remarkable intellectual achievements of this

---

[13] Le Goff, *Medieval Civilization*, p. 326.

period can be attributed to the workings of reason confined within the limits determined by textual authorities.

The greatest threat to this form of intellectual activity lay in the possibility of irreconcilable differences arising between written authorities, and in particular between those of pagan and those of Judaeo-Christian origin. Presentiments of this danger can be seen in the thirteenth-century misgivings about the place of Aristotle in the university curriculum. These earlier objections to Greek philosophy seemed to have been silenced for a time by the masterful synthesis of Thomas Aquinas. For various reasons, however, the sixteenth century was to witness the beginnings of an irrevocable breakdown of the concord which had existed between the traditional authorities, and along with that, the inevitable erosion of their prestige. Firstly, the development of textual criticism, the movement to return to the earliest and most accurate available texts, and the tendency to distinguish the work of original authors from subsequent interpreters were to bring to light many previously undetected errors in received texts and to challenge the presumed agreement amongst disparate authorities. Secondly, the adoption, particularly in the natural sciences, of the actual methods which the ancient authorities had used to acquire their knowledge came gradually to take precedence over the mere rehearsal of their findings. In time this was to make obsolete previously respected sources. Thirdly, and again in the natural sciences, voyages of discovery exposed enormous gaps in the ancients' knowledge of the natural world – gaps which could only be filled by first-hand investigation of nature. Fourthly, the move towards a literal, rather than allegorical, interpretation of sacred texts made it more difficult to gloss over inconsistencies between written sources. Finally, the re-emergence of the view, latent in Augustinian thought and revived again in the nominalism of fourteenth-century Oxonian William of Ockham, that Greek wisdom and biblical faith might be fundamentally opposed, was to drive a wedge between the classical authorities and scripture.

In the late fifteenth century the study of Aristotle was to enter a new phase. Humanist scholars embarked upon a comprehensive programme of editing and translating, producing new editions of the classical writings, along with Latin translations and commentaries. Whatever the relative merits of the encyclopaedias of the thirteenth century, they suffered from crucial limitations. Problems of textual corruption were compounded by the fact that the history of interpretation was often considered to be as important as what an authority might originally have meant to say. Neither readers nor copyists were overly concerned with fine distinctions between what was original and what was gloss, and as time passed it became increasingly difficult to distinguish the work of the author from the unsolicited contributions and egregious errors of generations of copyists. The botanical and zoological insights of the classical writers, when incorporated into the medieval encyclopaedias, were thus often buried beneath centuries-old layers of commentary, corruption and conflation.

In the fifteenth and sixteenth centuries, the encyclopaedic enterprises of the universities were taken over by secular scholars who brought to the task the new and powerful tools of humanist scholarship. Such figures as William Turner, Leonard Fuchs, and Konrad Gesner, quickly came to realise the superiority of older Greek texts of Aristotle, Theophrastus, and Dioscorides over the garbled and incestuous medieval catalogues based on second-hand compilations, often drawn from Latin writers. The earlier texts to which they now had access, moreover, were innocent of the glosses and additions of copyists. The task of these philologists, now in possession of more accurate texts, was to compare these with the later testimonies, and strip away the accumulated errors which had crept into the original natural histories. Ermolao Barbaro, for example, devoted his critical attention to the thirty-seven books of Pliny's natural history. The result was the *Castigationes plinianae* (1493), in which Pliny is taken to task for his many misrepresentations. The errors of Pliny, however, were exposed by comparing his descriptions with those of better authorities, not by consultation with nature itself. To consider but one example, the life span of the elephant, given by Pliny as two to three hundred years, was reduced to one hundred and twenty, the figure which Aristotle provided.[14] Philological techniques thus brought improvements to natural history without recourse to direct observation of the empirical world.

Encyclopaedias based upon Pliny were particularly vulnerable to textual criticism. Frequently, mistakes made in the process of compilation gave rise to new and monstrous creations because the descriptions of distinct creatures had been conflated. The attributes of a number of different animals might be telescoped together, giving rise to a single fictional hybrid. One of the more spectacular examples of this kind of confusion may found in the works of Thomas of Cantimpré, whose *De natura rerum* was one the principle sources of Albert the Great. In his

---

[14] Allan Debus, *Man and Nature in the Renaissance* (Cambridge University Press, 1978), p. 35.

Natural History, Pliny the Elder cites one of his authorities, Trebius Niger, on the characteristics of a marine gastropod: it is a foot long, the thickness of five fingers, can delay ships, and if preserved in salt, can recover gold which has fallen into a well. In the same place Pliny goes on to say that the white *maena* becomes darker in summer, and that the lamprey, which is the only sea-creature to lay its eggs in a nest, also changes colour. Led astray by minor grammatical and textual irregularities, combined with the fact that *niger* means 'black', Thomas combined the three descriptions, and applied them to Pliny's source. A subsequent reference in Pliny to Trebius Niger's description of the swordfish led Thomas, in the interests of consistency, to attribute to his 'black Trebius' the ability to sink ships with its sharp beak. Trebius Niger was thus destined to become known to posterity, not as an ancient authority on marine life, but as a black fish which lays eggs in a nest, is possessed of the power to extract gold from deep wells, and is capable of sinking ships. Albert the Great and subsequent writers repeated the error.[15] Similar scholarly mishaps led to equally remarkable mutations. Blue worms in the Ganges were transformed into creatures with enormous arms which could tear the trunks from elephants. Arabian villagers became gigantic sea-monsters with enormous jaws. The innocuous dolphin was accused of habitually devouring its young, the tuna equipped with twin udders and the ability to move on dry land, and the sea-urchin invested with the power to halt large ocean vessels.[16] These were the kinds of mistakes which could be detected by the tools of critical scholarship. The confusion which identified the sea-urchin with the ship-stopping remora occurred because of faulty transliterations of the respective Greek names *Echinus* (sea-urchin) and *Echineis* (remora). The mistake first appears in Thomas of Cantimpré, was copied by Albert the Great, eventually finding its way into Girolamo Cardano (1510–1576). This case of mistaken identity was finally corrected in Guillaume Rondelet's *De piscibus marinus* (1554): 'See how many errors he

---

[15] Pliny, *Natural History*, IX.41–2, XXXII.6 (*LCL* III, 215–17; VIII, 467–9); Thomas of Cantimpré, *De natura rerum*, vii.81. For this, and like conflations, see Pauline Aiken, 'The Animal History of Albertus Magnus and Thomas of Cantimpré', *Speculum* 22 (1947) 205–25. Here is Albert's description of 'trebius': 'TREBIUS is a black fish in summer, white in winter, according to Pliny. It grows largest in the Ocean; and by the time it is a foot long, it has a girth of five fingerbreadths. When preserved in salt, it draws gold from the waters, even though the gold has fallen into the deepest wells, and causes it to float to the bottom. This fish constructs its nest from seaweed and therein lays its eggs. When it reaches large size in the Ocean, it pierces boats with its extremely sharp beak.' *De animalibus* xxiv.58 (p. 376)

[16] Albertus Magnus, *De animalibus* xxiv.9, 60, 28, 57, 32 (pp. 367, 378, 349, 374f., 352). Also Aiken, 'Animal History of Albertus Magnus'.

[Cardano] has embraced in a few words. First he ascribes to Aristotle his conclusion from similarity of name and effect that the remora and torpedo are one . . . Next, he seems to put the torpedo in the genus of the *echinus* . . . Then, he calls the remora *echinus* when he ought to call it *echeneis*.'[17] Similar problems arose in the transmission of the information in the Herbals. *Ireos*, for example, is the genitive case of *Iris*, but because this was not recognised 'Ireos' came to be thought of as a separate species of Iris.[18] It is hardly surprising that John Gerarde wrote in his *Herbal* of 1517 that 'all the controversies of late time' were to be attributed to 'the carelessness of the middle times'.[19]

In this manner, philological research, even though it required no direct observation of the natural world itself, could lead to important advances. Edward Wotton's *De differentiis animalium* (1552) is markedly superior to the erroneous transliterations and equivocations of Albert the Great.[20] Rondelet's *De piscibus* (1554) exposes numerous errors in Cardan's work on fishes. William Turner's *Libellus de re herbaria novis* (1538) represents a considerable improvement on the medieval Herbal. At the pinnacle of humanist achievement in the field of natural history, however, were the works of Konrad Gesner and Ulisse Aldrovandi. The five folio volumes of Gesner's *Historiae animalium* (1551–1621) brought together all the known authorities on animals. Following the broad classifications of Aristotle, he provided a description of each creature, beginning with its nomenclature in Greek and Latin, followed by its names in numerous modern languages and dialects.[21] Then came descriptions of habitat, diseases, behaviours, use, diet. Aldrovandi compiled three folio volumes on birds and insects, a small portion of a far more comprehensive project which was interrupted by his death.[22] These works, in turn, provided the foundation for subsequent books of birds and beasts, serving the seventeenth century in much the same way that Pliny had served the thirteenth. Thus they tended to remain within the encyclopaedic tradition, correcting errors of translation and transliteration, seeking out the original sources, supplementing deficiencies, but

[17] Guillaume Rondelet, *Gulielmi Rondeletii doctoris medicinae in schola Monspeliensi professoris regii libri de piscibus marinus* (Lyon 1554), pp. 440–1. Qu. in Brian Copenhaver, 'A Tale of Two Fishes: Magical Objects in Natural History from Antiquity through the Scientific Revolution', *JHI* 52 (1991) 389.
[18] Jerry Stannard, 'Medieval Herbals and their Development', *Clio Medica* (1974) 23–33 (p. 27).
[19] Qu. in Grafton, *New Worlds, Ancient Texts*, pp. 164f.
[20] *Edoardi Wottoni Oxoniensis de differentiis animalium libri decem* (Paris, 1552), pp. 145–9; Copenhaver, 'Magical Objects', p. 384; F. D. and J. F. M. Hoeniger, *The Development of Natural History in Tudor England* (Charlottesville: University Press of Virginia, 1969), pp. 30–2.
[21] Gesner, *Historiae animalium*, 5 vols. (Tiguri, 1551–87); F. D. and J. F. M. Hoeniger, *Natural History*, p. 46.   [22] Debus, *Man and Nature*, p. 35.

only occasionally taking issue with the authorities. Rondelet, typically, could correct the mistake which had led to the conflation of the remora and sea-urchin, but having done so was happy to leave open the question of the remora's remarkable ship-stopping activities.

The textual bias of this humanist version of natural history is evident still in the seventeenth century, where it is conspicuous in the popular digests made by such writers as Topsell, Johnston, and Franzius. The description of the elephant which opens Wolfgang Franzius' *Historiae animalium* (1612) is drawn chiefly from scripture, with additional references to Aristotle, Virgil, and Aelian.[23] Franzius, a Professor of Divinity at Wittenberg, seems not to have seen an elephant, and if he had, did not see fit to add his own observations to those of the authorities. He informs the reader that he begins with the elephant because 'Job in his 40 th Chap : maketh this creature to be the beginning of the wayes of God, or the very first work of God.' The great size of the creature is inferred from its name (*Behema*), and from literary allusions to its tail, its thirst, its teeth, its footprints, and its 'nose'.[24]

It was not only exotic or rare species which were described from the works of others. Even the most familiar animals drew their being from the classics and from scripture. Johnston was a Scot who had made his home in Poland. In his *History of the Nature of Four-Footed Beasts* (1678) he pieced together a description of the horse from Porphyry, Xenophon, Vegetius, Nolanus, Aristotle, Pliny, Plutarch, Sertorius, Varro, and other authorities.[25] The compilation of a natural history thus afforded the writer the opportunity to display the extent of his learning. It was not the observation of animals and plants which counted, but whether all the relevant written sources had been consulted. This approach accounted for the inclusion in natural histories of many beasts the existence of which, to say the least, was doubtful. True, Isidore's dog-headed, one-eyed, one-legged, or headless men now rarely appeared.[26] But in the interests of comprehensiveness, zoological works commonly carried descriptions of such fantastic creatures as satyrs, unicorns, mermaids, manticores, dragons, lamias, and griffons. To neglect to mention any animal was failure of scholarship. From the point of view of the advocate of the new empirical science of the seventeenth century, such

---

[23] Franzius, *History of Brutes*, pp. 17–19. The only contemporary source cited is the chronologist Scaliger, whose first hand observation yielded the fact that an elephant may have tusks as big as a man.   [24] *Ibid.*, p. 19.
[25] Johnston [or Jonston], *Nature of Four-Footed Beasts* (Amsterdam, 1678), p. 2.
[26] Isidore, *Etymologiae* XI.iii.

writers of natural history were mere 'scoliasts and copyists' who 'to the end that their volumes might grow to the desired bulk, do write and copy all sorts about ever so many things of which they know naught for certain in the light of experience'.[27] The complaint seems justified, but is anachronistic. The encyclopaedists did not seek to provide naked descriptions of living things, based upon observations of nature, for they saw as an integral part of their task the location of living things within a broader literary context, a context in which physical description was merely one element amongst many. Their aim went beyond description to elucidation.

Natural history, we shall not be surprised to learn, remained closely associated with the interpretation of scripture. For many, the landscape in which the creature was to be encountered was still primarily the sacred page. Stephan Batman wrote in his prologue to the sixteenth-century translation of Bartholomew's *De proprietatibus rerum*, that 'All these properties of things be necessary and of great valew to them that will be desirous to understand the obscurities or darknesse of the holy Scriptures, which are given to us under figures, under parables & semblance or likelihood of things naturalls & artificialls.'[28] Wolfgang Franzius informed the readers of his *Historiae animalium* that the treatise should be of use and benefit 'not only to physicians, but also to all scholars, and more especially to Divines', who will find it to be 'very useful in sermons' (thus vindicating the view of a later writer that tomes of natural history 'serve for nothing else but for idle priests, to make their sermons more gaudy').[29] Edward Topsell had compiled his *Historie of Foure-Footed Beasts* (1607) out of Gesner with the laudable intention of acquainting his readers with all the animals referred to in scripture.[30] The *Herbal for the Bible* (1587) of Levinus Lemnius dealt with the 'Similitudes, Parables, and Metaphors, both in the olde Testament and the Newe, as are borrowed and taken from Herbs, Plants, Trees, Fruits, and Simples'.[31] One hundred years later, the *Historia vegetabilium sacra* (1695) of William Westmacott provided the same service to readers, discoursing rationally upon 'all the trees, shrubs, herbs, plants, flowers, fruits,

---

[27] Gilbert, *On the Loadstone*, pp. 1, 3. [28] *De proprietatibus rerum*, Prologue.

[29] Franzius, *History of Brutes*, pp. 1–2; John Hall, *An Humble Motion to the Parliament of England concerning the Advancement of Learning and the Reformation of the Universities* (London, 1649), p. 27.

[30] Topsell, (1607 edn) Epistle Dedicatory. Cf. F. D. and J. F. M. Hoeniger, *Natural History*, p. 49. Batman wrote in his preface to *De proprietatibus rerum* that the author 'studiously gathered this singular work, for the most part, of the properties of those things which he had found written in the Bible'.

[31] Levinus Lemnius, *An Herbal for the Bible*, tr. Thomas Newton (London, 1587), title page.

&c. mentioned in the Holy Bible', as if these plants were somehow possessed of a special status.[32] Such writers perpetuated the Augustinian tradition according to which the study of nature was undertaken primarily to assist in the interpretation of the sacred page.

Scripture also played an important role in the preservation of beasts which might otherwise have been consigned to oblivion. Those sceptical about the existence of pygmies, unicorns, griffons, the basilisk, and the phoenix needed only to consult the pages of scripture to have their doubts dismissed.[33] Additional corroboration often came from equally revered sources. 'The Hebrew names in Scripture prove Unicorns', declared Topsell, confident that this was sufficient to silence most sceptics.[34] Indeed, there are no fewer than eight separate references to unicorns in the Old Testament. A more extended argument appears in Franzius, who in his section on the unicorn asks first whether they exist, and second whether they might not be identified with the 'rhinoscerote'. On the first head he reasons in this fashion: 'the Scripture draweth many inferences from the nature of this beast, and doth apply them to good men and bad men, nay even to *Christ* himself, therefore it must necessarily follow that there are such creatures as *Unicorns*'. As to the second question, he concludes after an examination of the relevant Hebrew words that there are in fact two distinct creatures – the unicorn with a single horn, and the rhinoscerote with a large and a small horn. Franzius concludes his discussion of the unicorn by setting out a complicated stratagem for capturing them which involved, amongst other things, dressing a strong young man in women's clothes and dousing him liberally with perfume.[35]

---

[32] William Westmacott, *Historia vegetabilium sacra* (London, 1695), title page.

[33] Standard biblical references were as follows: Pygmies – Ezekiel 27.11; unicorns – Numbers 23.22; 24.8; Deuteronomy 33.17, Job 39.9f.; Psalms 22.21; 29.6; 92.10, Isaiah 34.7; griffon – Leviticus 11.13, Deuteronomy 14.12; the basilisk, Psalsm 91.13, Proverbs 23.32, Jeremiah 8.17, Isaiah 59.5 (Septuagint); the phoenix – Psalm 92.12.

[34] Topsell, *History of Four-Footed Beasts and Serpents* (London, 1653), p. 552. John Johnston similarly supported the existence of traditional unicorns, *An History of the Wonderful Things of Nature* (London, 1657), pp. 238f., *Nature of Four-Footed Beasts*, p. 19 and illustrations, Tables xi, xii. On the use of the unicorn as a symbol for Christ, see J. Schaper, 'The Unicorn in the Messianic Imagery of the Old Testament', *Journal of Theological Studies*, NS, 45 (1994) 117–36.

[35] Franzius, *History of Brutes*, pp. 79, 81. The stratagem was based on the tradition of the sympathy between virgins and unicorns, which tradition also accounts for the common medieval depictions of unicorns with young women. The bestiary of William of Normandy (BM MS Egerton b13) records both the link between Christ and the unicorn, and its method of capture: 'This wonderful beast, / Which has one horn on its head, / Signifies our lord, / Jesus Christ our saviour, / he is the spiritual unicorn / Who took up in the virgin his abode'. *The Bestiary*, lines 1375ff. An alternative, if more risky, method of capture involved a hunter standing in front of a tree. The unicorn was induced to charge, the hunter leapt aside at the last instant, and the

If Topsell and Franzius were to argue for the existence of unicorns on the basis of scriptural references, they needed to be sure that the relevant Hebrew words actually referred to the unicorn, and not to some other creature (such as the rhinoceros). At this point, the relevance of the study of the etymologies of Hebrew words, comparison of biblical texts, consideration of textual variations, and consultation of rabbinical writings becomes apparent. At times this would actually lead to the extinction of some fabulous creature rather than its preservation. Textual and philological studies could break the presumed corroboration between various ancient sources, or could show that a particular word had simply been mistranslated. This was particularly important in those instances in which scripture was presumed to lend support to ancient testimonies to the existence of mythical creatures. Thomas Browne's *Pseudodoxia Epidemica* (1646) contains a number of such analyses, many of which rely upon the previous work of Aldrovandi and Gesner. Browne thought it doubtful, for instance, that the men of Tyre had employed pygmies less than eighteen inches tall to guard their towers, as the book of Ezekiel seemed to suggest. (In the Latin of the Vulgate the relevant verse reads: '*Pigmaei erant in turribus tuis*'.) Not only would this have been a questionable military tactic, but as Browne points out, the Latin *pygmaei* commonly used to sanction their existence is a translation of the original Hebrew word *Gammadim*, which 'is very variously rendred [sic]'. After a consideration of various texts and translations, he concluded that scriptural evidence for pygmies is doubtful.[36] Similar analyses are given of biblical references to the griffin, the phoenix, and the unicorn.[37]

Initially, then, the recognition of such distortions in written authorities did not lead to an appeal to the empirical world. Instead, the correction of the errors came to be a special work of scholarship, in which texts were compared, their sources painstakingly identified. Special attention was paid to the translations of names, to the etymologies of words, and to likely sources of scribal infelicities. Only gradually did it dawn on scholars that the empirical world might serve as a standard by which textual accounts of living things should be judged.

unicorn, if everything went according to plan, would be caught with its horn embedded in the tree-trunk. See Anne Clark, *Beasts and Bawdy* (London: Dent, 1975), p. 46.

[36] Browne, *Pseudodoxia Epidemica* IV.xi (I, 331) Cf. Ezekiel, 27.11. Browne is possibly relying upon Hakewill. See *An Apologie*, (3rd edn) p. 10. The Septuagint speaks of 'watchmen'; modern translations, of 'men of Gamad'.

[37] Browne, *Pseudodoxia Epidemica*, pp. 199, 202–5, 256f. Cf. Hakewill, *An Apologie* (3rd edn) pp. 10–14. For a later discussion of the problems posed by the translation of Hebrew names for animals and plants in scripture, see John Edwards, *A Discourse concerning the Authority, Stile, and Perfection of the Books of the Old and New Testament*, 2 vols. (London, 1694), II, ch. 8.

For much of the sixteenth century this role was played instead by the elusive *Ur text* – the hypothetical autograph of the ancient author, the original text of which all extant copies were flawed variants.

TEXTS AND THE EMPIRICAL WORLD

The labours of Renaissance scholars were eventually to move beyond the simple provision of more accurate renderings of the fruits of ancient research. Almost inevitably, the work of textual criticism and translation led to a more active engagement with the empirical world. Thus, for example, when faced with an unknown Greek name, a scholar could either resort to the unsatisfactory practice of transliterating the name, as many of the Arab translators had done, or attempt to identify the species on the basis of the description. The first expedient had led to the very errors and confusions which the humanists sought to correct. Hence the only real option for the conscientious translator was to go into the field and match a known species with the description. In this way such scholars such as Konrad Gesner, whose original motivation was philological, found themselves developing an independent interest in the local flora and fauna.

Those working with the texts of herbals were in a similar situation. Up until the seventeenth century, botanical writings were used almost solely for the purpose of identifying plants which could be used in the practice of 'physick'. English theologian and naturalist William Turner came to the realisation that if English physicians were to apply the herbal remedies set down in the traditional medieval herbals, it was necessary for them to identify (from the Latin nomenclature) the relevant local plants. Existing herbals, he was later to say, were 'al full of unlearned cacographees and falselye naminge of herbes'.[38] His *Libellus de re herbaria novus* (1538) was an attempt to overcome the limitations and ambiguities of existing herbals, by listing alphabetically the Latin names of herbs, providing Greek and English equivalents for each, as well as Latin variants. Turner worked by identifying entries in the Greek texts from his fieldwork, and supplemented the catalogues with a large number of previously unrepresented local species. In 1568, the beauti-

---

[38] William Turner, *A New Herbal, wherein are conteyned the names of Herbes* (London, 1568) Preface. Also see F. D. and J. F. M. Hoeniger, *Natural History*, pp. 20–36. Turner was also a reformer in religious matters, and his anti-Catholic polemics cost him the Deanery at Wells. His periodic exiles to the Contintent brought him into contact with botanical developments there. See Charlotte Otten, *Environ'd with Eternity: God, Poems, and Plants in Sixteenth and Seventeenth Century England* (Lawrence: Coronado Press, 1985), pp. 26f.

fully presented folio edition of his *New Herbal* appeared in three parts, dedicated to Queen Elizabeth. The third part deals solely with herbs 'whereof is no mention is made nether of ẙ old Grecianes nor Latines'.[39] At the very least, then, nature itself needed to be consulted to remedy deficiencies in the ancients. When Turner came to compile a book on birds he again encountered the old difficulties. Only a small proportion of local species received mention in the classical texts, and such omissions could not be corrected without field work. On the Continent, meanwhile, Konrad Gesner, Leonard Fuchs and Hieronymous Bock were carrying out similar tasks with their own local varieties.[40] Thus it transpired that the most conscientious of the humanist scholars – Turner, Gesner, Fuchs, and Bock – found themselves forced to replicate the methods of the ancients, rather than merely reporting their findings. The result was a vast explosion of botanical data. By 1623, Karen Reeds estimates, the 600 plants described by the ancients had grown tenfold to 6,000.[41]

Perhaps the most spectacular success to result from the adoption of the methods of the ancients came in the field of anatomy. The vaunted 'new anatomy' of Vesalius which appeared in *De humani corporis fabrica* (1543) – coincidentally the same year as Copernicus' *De revolutionibus orbium coelestium* was published – had its origins in Renaissance scholarship. Up until the early sixteenth century, anatomists had relied upon corrupted and simplified texts of Galen, translated from Arabic. While Readers intoned lectures from these tomes, hapless surgeon-demonstrators found themselves in the unenviable position of having to identify all the anatomical features referred to by the ancient master – a number of which were unique to the animal cadavers which Galen had been forced to substitute for the genuine article. Galen's knives, Robert Boyle was later to observe, 'were more conversant with the bodies of apes, than with those of men'.[42] Ironically, it was through the adoption of Galen's own dissecting procedures set out in the new 1541 edition of the hitherto unknown *Anatomical Procedures* that Vesalius was able to surpass Galen.[43]

[39] Turner, *New Herbal*, Preface.

[40] Konrad Gesner, *Catalogus plantarum Latine, Graece, Germanice, et Gallice* (Tiguri, 1542); Leonard Fuchs, *De historia stirpium commentarii insignes* . . . (Basilae, 1542); Hieronymous Bock, *Hieronymi Tragi, De stirpium, maxime earum quae in Germania nostra* (Argentorati, 1552).

[41] Karen Reeds, 'Renaissance Humanism and Botany', *Annals of Science* 33 (1976), 540.

[42] Boyle, *Some Considerations touching the Usefullness of Experimental Naturall Philosophy*, in *Works*, II, 68.

[43] Stephen Pumfrey, 'The History of Science and the Renaissance Science of History', in *Science, Culture and Popular Belief in Renaissance Europe*, ed. Stephen Pumfrey, Paolo L. Rossi, and Maurice Slawinski, (Manchester University Press, 1991), p. 56; A. Rupert Hall, *The Revolution in Science* (London: Longman, 1983), ch. 2.

For all this, Vesalius still subscribed to the humanist programme, considering his mission to be the restoration of a lost discipline. It was his intention 'to restore from the world of the dead the knowledge of the parts of the human body that had died long ago', so that anatomy might once again be practised as it had 'of old in Alexandria'.[44] The supposed founder of modern anatomy was also reluctant to put into practice all of the procedures recommended by Galen. In the following century, William Harvey pointed out that his own controversial hypothesis of the circulation of the blood was supported by experiments recommended, but apparently not carried out, by both Galen and Vesalius. 'The experiment is spoken of by Vesalius, the celebrated anatomist; but neither Vesalius nor Galen says that he has tried the experiment, which, however, I did. Vesalius only prescribes it, and Galen advises it.'[45] Hardly surprising then, that Harvey should insist that anatomy be taken 'not from books, but from dissections'.[46] Yet through the efforts of anatomists like Vesalius the anatomy theatre was to become a venue in which a conflict between competing texts was played out: written texts of antiquity were pitted against the new text of the body, and increasingly the latter asserted its dominance.

Much of the prestige of the anatomical publications of Vesalius was owing to the lavish illustrations which accompanied his text. Indeed, the increasing use of drawings from nature also signals the beginning of the turn away from traditional representation to the natural world itself. In the past, depictions of creatures had been copied from an existing repertoire of types. These were often stylised images which had been designed to emphasise the symbolic meanings of animals and plants. 'During the middle ages', writes Kenneth Clarke, 'artists were for the most part unconcerned with appearances, concentrating upon the meaning of an image and therefore using a stylized vocabulary that conveyed the meaning most directly.'[47] This tradition was to persist throughout the seventeenth century in the form of emblem books, which reproduced a variety of images, explaining their tropological

---

[44] Qu. in Walter Pagel and P. Rattansi, 'Vesalius and Paracelsus', *Medical History* 8 (1964) 309–34.

[45] Harvey, *A Second Disquisition to John Riolan* (Chicago: Encyclopaedia Brittanica, 1951), p. 313.

[46] Harvey, *An Anatomical Disquisition on the Motion of the Heart and Blood in Animals*, ibid., Epistle Dedicatory, p. 268.

[47] Kenneth Clarke, *Animals and Men*, (London: Thames and Hudson, 1977), p. 104; Cf. Eisenstein, *The Printing Revolution*, pp. 193f. It is true, of course, that in the eleventh and twelfth centuries a new kind of realism enters the visual arts. This is most conspicuous in the sculpture and glass at Chartres, for example. Yet it is also true that the function of this art is largely symbolic.

meanings with accompanying text.[48] The new naturalism, however, is already apparent in Da Vinci and Dürer, whose works have been closely linked with Renaissance sciences.[49] The printing press, too, played an important role in changing the status of book illustration. Classical authorities had rightly discouraged the use of hand-copied pictures in the communication of botanical information, for they had realised that with the passage of time copies would deteriorate to such an extent that recognition of the original plant would become impossible.[50] The process of printing, however, when combined with the skills of artists and wood carvers, made replication of drawings from nature virtually error-free.[51]

The impact of more accurate illustration, along with the infallibility which the printing press conferred upon the process of reproducing images, was most apparent in the new botanical writings. Because the chief use of these works still lay in the provision of cures, the identification of plants was of considerable practical importance. The introduction of accurate drawings of new and local species thus provided an invaluable aid to the practitioners of physick, and to those whose task it was to gather the necessary cures. This practical application, in turn, served to ensure the accuracy of the drawings. The *Herbarum vivae eicones* (1530) of Otto Brunfels – 'living images of plants' – was the first printed herbal with illustrations drawn from nature.[52] Thereafter, such illustrations were to become an indispensable component of botanical works.

[48] On emblem books and natural history, see See Luce Giard, 'Remapping Knowledge, Reshaping Institutions', in Pumfrey et al. (eds.), *Science, Culture, and Belief*, pp. 28–32; Wolfgang Harms, 'On Natural History and Emblematics in the Sixteenth Century', in Allan Ellenius (ed.), *The Natural Sciences and the Arts* (Uppsala: Almqvist and Wiksell, 1985), pp. 67–83; D. Russell, 'Alcati's emblems in Renaissance Europe', *Renaissance Quarterly*, 34 (1981) 534–54; H. Diehl, 'Graven Images: Protestant Emblem Books in England', *Renaissance Quarterly*, 39 (1986), 49–66; M. Bath, 'Recent Developments in Emblem Studies', *Bulletin of the Society of Renaissance Studies*, 6 (1988), 15–20.

[49] Even Dürer at times, reverted to preconceptions in his art. Compare his remarkable 'Hare' with his equally remarkable 'Rhinoceros'. The latter bears his out his contention that he painted 'from the inner ideas of which Plato writes'. Qu. in E. Panofsky, *The Life and Art of Albrecht Dürer*, 4th edn (Princeton University Press, 1955), p. 280. The problem for illustrators, of course, was that their drawings were supposed to represent the general 'type' or 'species', and not some individual of the species. This accounts, I suspect, for Dürer's reference to Platonic types, and for the difference between his 'Hare' and his 'Rhinoceros'. The former is a particular hare, the latter representative of the type 'Rhinoceros'. Also see Ashworth, 'Natural History and the Emblematic World View'.

[50] Jerry Stannard, 'The Herbal as a Medical Document', *Bulletin of the History of Medicine* 43 (1969) 217. On medieval techniques for copying illustrations, see Samuel Ives and Helmut Lehman-Haupt, *An English 13th Century Bestiary: A New Discovery in the Technique of Medieval Illustration* (New York: Kraus, 1942). [51] Eisenstein, *The Printing Press*, II, 485–8.

[52] Stannard, 'Medieval Herbals', p. 31.

'Illustrations alone', writes Allan Debus, 'revolutionized the study of plant life.'[53] The practice of drawing from nature is perhaps the first tangible sign of the dawning realisation that things are more accurately represented in nature than they are in written sources.

(3)

NEW WORLDS

The discovery of the New World had also highlighted the limitations of Aristotle, Pliny, and Ptolemy, in the realms of both navigation and natural history. 'What else could I do, but laugh at Aristotle's philosophie', wrote Joseph d'Acosta, as he entered the tropics on a course for the shores of the Americas. Here was a new world, brimming with strange creatures and unfamiliar plants, none of which was represented in the natural history of the great philosopher.[54] Amerigo Verspucci wrote in his *Mundus novus* that 'Pliny did not touch upon a thousanth part of the species of parrots and other birds and the animals too which exist in those same regions.'[55] The ordinary seaman who travelled with Columbus, Robert Boyle pointed out, 'was able at his return to inform men of an hundred things that they could never have learned by Aristotle's philosophy'.[56] In more respectful tones, Bacon announced that 'by the distant voyages and travels which have become frequent in our times, many things have been laid open and discovered which may let in new light upon philosophy'.[57] The maps of Ptolemy, it was now universally recognised, were at best, half right. 'Grosse' was how George Hakewill characterised the knowledge of the ancients in matters of cosmography. 'Of the whole habitable world', he observed, 'hardly one halfe thereof was known to them'. Indeed, Augustine, as Hakewill went on to point out, had gone so far as to deny the Antipodes, while Lactantius had embarrassed himself further by stubbornly asserting, against the overwhelming opinion of his contemporaries, that the earth was flat.[58] George Ent, in his dedication of William Harvey's *Anatomical*

---

[53] Debus, *Man and Nature*, p. 44.
[54] Qu. in Prest, *The Garden of Eden*, p. 38.
[55] Qu. in Grafton, *New Worlds, Ancient Texts*, (Cambridge, Mass.: Harvard University Press, 1992) p. 84.   [56] Boyle, *The Christian Virtuoso*, in *Works*, v, 520.   [57] Bacon, *Novum Organum*, I. 84.
[58] Hakewill, *An Apologie* (3rd edn) pp. 28of. John Wilkins makes a similar observation. *The Discovery of a New World in the Moone* (London, 1638), pp. 6–12. Augustine, *City of God*, XVI.9. Lactantius, *Institutes*, l. 3, c. 24. Wilkins cites some of the reasons given by ancient authorities for denying the Antipodes. Lactantius thought it impossible that plants and trees grow downwards, and hail, rain and snow fall upwards. Procopius Gazaus thought that although the earth was spherical, because the Psalmist had written that 'he hath founded the earth upon the seas', the bottom half of the earth was 'sunk in the water'. Testatus reasoned that because Jesus' disciples had been enjoined to 'preach the Gospel to all nations' (Matthew 28.19), and had in fact done so without crossing the 'Equinoctiall', the Antipodes must be uninhabited.

Exercises on the Generation of Animals (1615), wrote of the ancients that 'as their knowledge of geography was limited by the boundaries of Greece, so neither did their knowledge of animals, vegetables, and other natural objects extend beyond the confines of their country'. By contrast, 'to us the whole earth lies open, and the zeal of our travellers had made us familiar not only with other countries and the manners and customs of their inhabitants, but also with the animals, vegetables, and minerals that are met with in each'. Knowledge, he concludes, was not 'exhausted by the first ages of the world'.[59]

Initially, these new discoveries were brought to bear on long-standing disputes between authorities themselves. Acosta might have laughed at Aristotle's opinion that the tropics were too hot to support habitation, but his disdain for Aristotle was matched by his admiration of Ptolemy and Avicenna, both of whom had 'believed that there were commodious habitable regions under the tropics'. Columbus, too, had rejected Ptolomy's calculations of the circumference of the earth in favour of those of the earlier geographer Marinus who had thought the globe to have been of more modest proportions. This misplaced faith in Marinus motivated Columbus to set out on a westward course to Asia, and a landfall in the 'Indies' had vindicated, in Columbus' eyes at least, the faulty reckoning of Marinus.[60] We should also recall that Copernicus found his champion in Heraclides of Pontus, an ancient advocate of the heliocentric view, and that Vesalius saw his mission as the revival of an uncorrupted Galenic anatomy.

As the sixteenth century progressed, the new knowledge of nature no longer simply adjudicated between conflicting written accounts, but also gave rise to challenges to the completeness and accuracy of the ancients. Aristotle's circumscribed world could yield up but a small fraction of what the enlarged globe had now to offer, and even if as legend had it he had enjoined upon his erstwhile pupil, Alexander the Great, the task of sending back to Greece biological specimens from newly conquered lands, these would still be as nothing compared to the riches of the flora and fauna of the New World. However accurate Aristotle's observations, the world was now a very different place. The Stagirite had trod but few pages of the book of nature, and the schools which championed his natural history had read, not trod. As each new land was discovered another page of the book of nature was turned, the limitations of the received version of natural history were further exposed.

The plants of the New World served not only to show the incomplete

[59] William Harvey, *Anatomical Exercises on the Generation of Animals*, tr. Robert Willis, Dedication, (Chicago: Encyclopaedia Brittanica, 1951), p. 329.   [60] Grafton, *New Worlds*, pp. 6, 77.

nature of the traditional herbals, but also held out the promise of many
new cures. Nicholas Monardes, in *Joyfull Newes out of the Newe Founde
Worlde* (1577), enthusiastically described the 'newe thynges and secretes'
which had been discovered in the Americas, setting forth 'the rare and
singular vertues of diuerse and sundrie Hearbes, Trees, Oyles, Plantes,
and Stones, with their applications as well for Physic as Chirurgerie'.[61]
Heading the list of these singular pharmaceuticals was 'tabaco', which
Monardes lauded for 'its marueillous Medicinable vertues'. This, the
wonder drug of the sixteenth-century, was to be prescribed for 'griefs' of
the head, the breast, stomach, and indeed any disease resulting from
cold causes. Its further uses included the treatment of wind, 'the evill of
the mother', bad breath, worms, toothache, chilblaines, poisoned
wounds, carbuncles, the bitings of venomous beasts, and as a dressing
for new wounds.[62] One hundred years later, John Swan was also to wax
eloquent over the 'Physical and Chirurgical' uses of tobacco, although
by this time enough was known of the drug for him to caution his
readers that 'they who have used themselves to it . . . know not well how
to leave it; neither on the suddain could they safely do it'.[63] Geographer
Peter Heylyn was less enthusiastic, granting that 'if moderately taken',
tobacco 'may be serviceable for physicke', but pointing out that 'besides
consumption of the purse, and impairing of our inward parts, the
immoderate , vaine, and phantasticall abuse of the hellish weed, corrup-
teth the naturall sweetnes of the breath, stupifieth the braine, and is . . .
prejudiciall to the generall esteeme of our country'.[64] With the benefit of
hindsight we may conclude that perhaps the most ill-advised prescrip-
tion of all is to be found in a lauditory verse by Castor Durante, which
concludes: 'For Breast and Lungs, when that we stand in need, / All
other herbs, *Tobacco* doth exceed.'[65]

---

[61] Nicholas Monardes, *Joyfull Newes out of the Newe Founde Worlde*, tr. John Frampton, (London, 1577),
title page, and fol. 34v. Similar works were published over the next 100 years. See, e.g., John
Josselyn, *New-Englands Rarities Discover'd . . . together with The Physical and Chyrurgical Remedies*
(London, 1672), and the series of *Observations* published by John Peachi between 1680 and 1695.

[62] Monardes, *Joyfull Newes*, Fols. 35r–37r. The properties of tobacco were ascribed to the fact that it
was 'hot and drie in the seconde degree' and 'hath vertue to heate and to dissolue'. Fol. 35v. Its
heat made it efficacious against maladies caused by cold.

[63] Swan, *Speculum mundi*, p. 224. Cf. John Hester, *The Pearle of Practise*, (London, 1598), pp. 76f.;
Culpeper, *Complete Herbal*, p. 250; Dunton (ed.) *Athenian Oracle* I, 334f., II, 546f. Pluche also
recommended tobacco as 'an excellent vulnerary'. It frees us 'from any redundant Humour' by
affecting the nerves 'with a kind of convulsive Motion'. *Spectacle de la Nature: or Nature Display'd*, 7
vols. (London, 1770). 5th edn revised and corrected, II, 202f. John Josselyn recommended it for
the cure of burns and scalds, *New-Englands Rarities*, p. 54.

[64] Peter Heylyn, *MIKROKOSMOS. A Little Description of the Great World* (Oxford, 1629), p. 792.

[65] The complete poem is given by Johnston, *Wonderful Things of Nature*, p. 160.

On the other side of the ledger, it must be said that voyagers to the New World brought back with them not only cures, but diseases as well. Through the ravages of syphilis, America wreaked a terrible revenge on its invaders. The 'French pox', as the malady was universally known (except in France, where it was referred to as 'the English disease' or 'the pox of Naples'), spread with alarming rapidity throughout Europe in the sixteenth century, giving pause to libertines and presenting practitioners of physick with perhaps their most difficult challenge. The revered writings of Galen and Hippocrates proved to be of limited assistance in the treatment of a disease completely unknown in the ancient world.[66] At the close of the century, John Hester, an advocate of medical innovation, pointed out the deficiencies of the classical writers in this regard: 'Now that the diseases of the French Pocks was neyther knowne to them, nor to theyr successors for many yeeres . . . is a matter so farre out of question, that it refuseth all shew of disputation, and therefore as this latter age of ours sustaineth the scourge thereof, a iust whyp of our lycentiousness, so let it (if there be any to be had) carry the credite of the cure, as some rewarde to some mens industries.'[67] The spread of this disfiguring disease gave added impetus to the contention of medical innovators, that 'the knowledge of True physicke . . . is deriued out of the light of nature, not out of the darke writings of the heathen'.[68] It was fortunate that new compartments were being discovered in nature's cabinet of medicines for another reason. Champions of the new physick, and Paracelsians in particular, suggested that the world had changed considerably since the times of those ancients who had been proficient in physick. Paracelsus claimed that ancient cures might now be ineffectual, or even harmful, for 'the world has become senescent, both microcosm and macrocosm have grown old'. Indeed it was commonly believed that the healing efficacy of medicinal plants was on the wane.[69] Accordingly, it was thought that the tired prescriptions of the ancients

---

[66] Some earlier writers, however, could not bring themselves to believe that the disease was unknown to the ancients. Niccolo Leoniceno, writing in 1497, denied 'the ancients had never known it', concluding that 'it is necessary to affirm that a similar illness, deriving from similar causes, had also infected preceding epochs'. N. Leoniceno, *Libellus de epidemica* (1497), qu. in Anna Foa, 'The New and the Old: The Spread of Syphilis (1495–1530)' in *Sex and Gender in Historical Perspective*, ed. Edward Muir and Guido Ruggiero (Johns Hopkins University Press, 1990), p. 29.

[67] Phillipus Hermanus, *An Excellent Treatise teaching howe to cure the French Pockes*, tr. John Hester (London, 1590), Epistle Dedicatory. As was to be expected, the cure for syphilis was sought in an American plant, in this instance, American guaiac, or pock wood. The alternative was treatment with a preparation of mercury. The latter was advocated by Paracelsus. See Pagel, *Paracelsus*, p. 24.

[68] Barnard Aquitanus, preface to Paracelsus, *A Hundred and Foureteene Experiments and Cures . . . collected by John Hester*, (London, 1596), Sig A3.r.   [69] Hakewill, *An Apologie* (3rd edn) p. 42.

needed to be adapted to suit the present condition of the world and its inhabitants.[70]

While new creatures were added to the inventory of known species, efforts to rid the zoological canon of fantastic creatures were redoubled. Moving beyond the scope of textual criticism alone, mythological creatures came to be identified with known, but unusual, species. Edward Tyson, in his *Philological Essay Concerning the Pygmies, the Cynocephali, the Satyrs and Sphinges of the Ancients,* established that these fabled animals in Homer, Pliny, Strabo, Aelian, were 'all either Apes or Monkeys; and not Men, as formerly pretended'.[71] Tyson had relied upon both philology and his own anatomical work on chimpanzees to arrive at this conclusion. George Hakewill and Abbé Pluche arrived at similar conclusions.[72] If fabulous creatures could not be even roughly matched with known creatures, they might simply be dismissed as never having existed, or as never having had the fantastic properties ascribed to them. As we have seen, the *echeneis* – a kind of pilot fish or remora – had been credited by Pliny with the power to stop ships.[73] The occult powers of the fish lent it a notoriety which ensured its appearance in many accounts of marine animals. Walter Charleton conceded that such a fish might exist, but thought it probable that its fabled effects were the result of ocean currents, the action of which coincided with the discovery of the attached fish.[74] John Johnston, however, made reference to contemporary witnesses, concluding that the remarkable ship-stopping capabilities of the remora 'hath been found true by examples of late'. The retarding mechanism he attributed to the cold virtues of the fish, which might cause the water around the rudder to freeze.[75] Jesuit Athanasius

---

[70] Paracelsus, *Contra calculum* IV. 1568d, cited in Walter Pagel, *Paracelsus: An Introduction to Philosophical Medicine in the Era of the Renaissance* (Basel: Karger, 1958), 252.

[71] Edward Tyson, *Philological Essay Concerning the Pygmies,* appended to *Orang-Outang, sive Homo Sylvestris, or the Anatomy of a Pygmie.* (London, 1699). Cf. Pluche, *Spectacle* I, 136. Ancient sources for Pygmies: Ezekiel, 27.11; *Iliad* iii.2–6; Herodotus, iii.37; Philostratus, *Vita Apollonii* iii, 47; Pliny *Natural History*, IV.11, V.29, VI.22, VII.2, X.30; Oppian, *Halieutica*, i.620–5; Isidore, *Etymologiae*, XI.iii. 26; Albertus Magnus, *De animalibus* VII.i.6 (*Opera Omnia*, Borgnet edn 1891, xi, 383). Augustine seems to have been sceptical of the existence of pygmies, and other mixed creatures, suggesting that they might have been monkeys. *City of God*, XVI.8. Jacob Bondt (1592–1631) seems also to have identified orang-outangs with satyrs. Debus, *Man and Nature*, p. 38.

[72] Hakewill, *Apologie* I.i.4 (1635, 1.10) (1628 edn p. 8); Pluche, *Spectacle*, I, 136.

[73] Pliny *Natural History*, XXXII.1–7.

[74] Walter Charleton, *Physiologia Epicuro-Gassendo-Charltoniana* (London, 1654), pp. 375–6.

[75] *Wonderful Things of Nature*, p. 301. It should not be concluded from this that Johnston was not a progressive natural historian. Johnston investigates this standard claim, and finds contemporary empirical evidence in support of it. On Johnston's contributions to natural history, see Ashworth, 'Natural History and the Emblematic World View', in Lindberg and Westman (eds.), *Reappraisals*, pp. 317f.

Kircher was (somewhat uncharacteristically) more sceptical, deciding that 'this small fish is simply a fable' and 'does not exist'.[76] More significant than these divergent conclusions concerning this little fish, however, is the means by which they were arrived at. Charleton, Johnston, and Kircher share a common commitment which goes beyond a clerical concern to record the opinions of previous authors. They also wanted to know if these opinions were true, and they tested them against available, non-textual, evidence.

Consigning animals to oblivion was all the more effective if a reasonable explanation of the origins of the mythology surrounding them could be provided. Thomas Browne, for example, suggested that the allegory of the pelican might have arisen from observations of the birds scratching their breasts during preening, and drawing blood.[77] The unicorn received a more extended treatment. This fabled creature, said Pluche, is 'entirely chimerical, or at least undiscovered by the Moderns', implying that reliable contemporary witnesses were the most important criterion for establishing the existence of a creature (quite the reverse of what Topsell had argued a century before). The myth of the unicorn, he explained, had been sustained by the displays of unicorn's 'horns' which in fact were nothing but the spiral tusks of a sea creature – the 'nerval' (narwhal).[78] Other writers accounted for the unicorn by equating it with the rhinoceros, as had Albertus Magnus.[79] Thomas Browne notes that some doubt the existence of the unicorn, but goes on to argue that there are in fact several 'unicorns': 'the Indian Oxe, the Indian Asse, the Rhinoceros, the Oryx, and that which is more eminently termed *Monoceros* or *Unicornis*, also amongst the fishes, and insects'. The animal, he concludes in something of an understatement, 'is not uniformly described'.[80]

Broadly speaking, then, the humanist endeavour progressed through two phases. From about the beginning of the sixteenth century we witness attempts to reconstruct past knowledge from the best available texts of ancient authorities. Frequently, in the interests of completeness, additions based on observations from nature were made to the observa-

---

[76] *Athanasii Kircheri Fuldensis Buchonii e Societate Iesu, Magnes seu de arte magnetica opus tripartitum*, (Rome, 1641), p. 759.

[77] Browne, *Pseudodoxia Epidemica*, v.i (p. 368). Others shared Browne's scepticism: Hakewill, *Apologie*, 1.i.5 (1627 edn p. 11); Franck, *Philosophical Treatise*, p 124.   [78] Pluche, *Spectacle* 1, 242.

[79] Albertus, *De animalibus* XXII.144 (p. 180).

[80] Browne, *Pseudodoxia epidemica* III.xxiii (pp. 256f.). The sceptics referred to by Browne appear to have been Aldrovandus, *De quadrupedibus solidipedibus* 6 (1623 edn p. 181), and Hakewill, *Apologie*, 1.i.5 (1635, i.14).

tions of the ancients. This stage, best represented by Gesner and Aldrovandi, had as its goal a comprehensive natural history which would encompass all available knowledge of animals and plants. This constructive period was followed by a phase of critical scholarship in which the writings of the ancients were not supplemented but were corrected. The ancients were found to be not merely incomplete, but often in error. Thomas Browne's *Pseudodoxia epidemica* and George Hakewill's *Apologie* are representative of this second phase. Even in this second phase, however, a textual hegemony remains in place. The empirical world does not yet unambiguously present itself as the unchallenged authority in natural history. Natural objects and their mutual relations are still viewed through the prism of traditional conceptions of the world, and such conceptions distort, or less pejoratively, inform, even the process of observation itself. Eye-witness reports of fantastic creatures continued to filter back to the home ports, increasing the tenure of a number of doubtful beasts. In Hakluyt's *Principal Navigations*, for example, a French Captain reported an encounter with 'a Serpent with 3 heads and 4 feete, of the bignesses of a great Spaniell'. Unfortunately, for 'want of weapon', he did not slay it, and no specimen could be conveyed back to the Europe.[81] Sightings of mermaids – often, admittedly, from men too long at sea – also continued to appear in the literature. John Johnston, as mentioned earlier, considered the occult powers of the remora to have been confirmed by contemporary witnesses. Even Albert the Great's amphibious and mammalian *Tygnus* (Tuna) reappears in a description of the fish of Jamaica, renamed the 'Manati': 'of strange shape, and nature: It brings forth her young alive, and nourishes them with milk from her teats, feeding upon grass in the field, but lives for the most part in the water: the hinder parts are like unto a Cow, and it eats like veal'.[82]

It must also be said that in an era in which new creatures were being discovered on a daily basis, scepticism about the veracity of written accounts of strange creatures was difficult to justify. To deny the existence of any animal, merely because one had no first-hand experience of it, was to elevate one's own limited experience over the testimonies of the most respected writers of the past. The fact that that there were few reliable contemporary witnesses to verify the existence of

---

[81] 'Voyages and Discoveries of M. John Hawkins (1564)', Richard Hakluyt, *Principal Navigations*, (London, 1589), p. 542.

[82] Clarke, *A Mirour or Looking Glass* , 4th edn (London, 1671), I, Section entitled *Examples of the Wonderful Works of God in the Creatures*, pp. 17f., 21, 23.

dragons, unicorns, and the like, caused little embarrassment to early modern compilers of animal lore. In his description of the dragon, Edward Topsell pointed out that 'the foolish world is apt to believe no more than they see', hence the need to adduce 'the testimonies of sundry learned men'.[83] Fossils, too, if accepted as the remains of living creatures, seemed to point to the existence of monstrous animals no longer observed, but presumably still extant, although it was allowed that such creatures might have perished in the Deluge.[84]

Logical deduction also played its part in determining what kinds of living things there must be. Paracelsus, avid supporter of experience and observation though he was, argued on *a priori* grounds for the existence of nymphs, sylphs, pygmies and salamanders, suggesting that there should be one of each of this kind of creature for each of the elements, water, air, earth, and fire.[85] Age-old patterns of microcosm and macrocosm, sympathy and antipathy also continued to play their part. The existence of both lions and unicorns in Florida was established by Elizabethan seafarer John Hawkins with this whimsical piece of reasoning:

The Floridians have pieces of Unicornes hornes, which they were about their neck whereof the Frenchmen have obtained many pieces. Of those Unicorns they haue many. . . But it is thought that there are many Lions and Tygers as well as Unicorns, Lions especially, if it bee true that is said of the enmity between them and the Unicorns. For there is no beast but hath its enemy, as the Cunny the Pollcat, a Sheepe the Wolfe, the Elephant the Rinoceros, and so of other beasts and the like: insomuch that whereas the one is the other cannot be missing.[86]

New plants and their virtues, too, were fitted into the old frameworks. Tobacco might have been unknown to the ancients, but its powers were explained in terms which they would have found familiar: 'hot and drie in the second degree, it hath vertue to heate and to dissolve'.[87] Thus could new data be accommodated within the traditional paradigms.

---

[83] Topsell, *The History of Four-Footed Beasts and Serpents* (1653), p. 707.
[84] Whiston, *Authentic Records*, pp. 901f.
[85] Paracelsus, *Ex libro nymphis, sylvanis, pygmaeis, salamandris, et gigantibus etc.* (1566) in *Four Treatises*.
[86] 'Voyages and Discoveries', Hakluyt, *Principal Navigations*, p. 542. Standard sympathetic pairings were: crow and heron, peacock and pigeon, lily and rose, vine and olive, rose and garlic, vine and elm, olive and fig, blackbird and thrush. Antipathetic to each other were man and serpent, lion and cock, elephant and ram, dragon and elephant, sheep and wolf, vine and colewort, hemlock and rue, rose and onion, vine and laurel. For complete lists, see Agrippa von Nettesheim, *Three Books of Occult Philosophy* (London,1651), IIxviii; Della Porta, *Natural Magick*, I.vii. Specific sympathies and antipathies were usually included in the descriptions of individual animals and plants. [87] Monardes, *Joyfull Newes*, fol. 34v.

Animals of the Americas were typically regarded as inferior versions of the more perfect originals of the first world.[88] The continent itself was variously a land which had wholly escaped the Deluge, a sodden continent only recently recovered from its inundation, or the New Atlantis of Plato's *Timaeus*. Its human occupants were fancifully thought to be descendants of the lost tribes of Israel, naked innocents who had escaped the fate of Noah's wicked generation, or degenerate savages who had wandered far from the site of Noah's disembarkation.[89] Chancellor Bacon reckoned the inhabitants of America to be 'a young people', a 'simple and savage people, (not like Noah and his sons, which was the chief family of the earth)'. Donne was to speak of 'That unripe side of the earth, the heavy clime / that gives us man up now, like *Adam's* time / before he ate'.[90]

Critical humanist scholarship, then, was at best parasitic on prevailing paradigms. An overarching ordering principle is conspicuously absent in critical and constructive humanist works on natural history. Browne's chapter headings from *Pseudodoxia epidemica*, to take an informative example, read as follows: 'I That an Elephant hath no joynts; II That an horse hath no Gall; III That a Pidgeon hath no Gall; IV That a Beaver to escape the hunter bites off his Testicles or stones; V That a Badger hath the legs of one side shorter then of the other; VI That a Bear brings forth her cubs informous or unshaped'.[91] Ironically, it is the errors of the past which dictate the structure of the work. Browne contributes no new shape to existing knowledge, proffering instead a modest list of errata. Physical collections of objects bear witness to the same taxonomic anarchy evident in scholarly collections of errors. Vast amounts of new data might have been accumulated, but in the absence of an alternative conception of natural order, these could not constitute a new science.[92] The early modern vogue for hoarding biological specimens thus gave rise to little more than haphazard collections of biological bric-a-brac. The empiricism of Bacon, Michael Hunter notes, clearly encouraged 'indiscriminate collecting of information relevant to no particular hypothesis'.[93] Seventeenth-century 'cabinets of curiosities'

[88] Gerbi, *The Dispute of the New World*, passim.

[89] On America as Atlantis, see Batman, *Batman vppon Bartholome*, p. 250r. Bacon, *New Atlantis*. On America and the lost tribes, see Manasseh ben Israel, *The Hope of Israel* (London, 1651); Thomas Thorowgood, *Jews in America: or probabilities that the Americans are of that race* (London, 1650). For links to the story of Noah, see D. C. Allen, *The Legend of Noah*, pp. 113–37.

[90] Bacon, *New Atlantis*, p. 227; Donne, 'To the Countess of Huntingdon', lines 1–2, *Complete English Poems*, p. 233.   [91] *Pseudodoxia Epidemica*, p. xii.

[92] In Thomas Kuhn's terminology, we are faced with facts in search of a paradigm. T. S. Kuhn, *The Structure of Scientific Revolutions*, 2nd edn (University of Chicago Press, 1970), p. 16.

[93] Michael Hunter, *Science and Society in Restoration England* (Cambridge University Press, 1981), p. 17.

seem more indicative of a compulsion to collect and a taste for the exotic than of an interest in nature *per se*. Robert Hubert's famous collection of fossils and other novelties, eventually purchased by the Royal Society for the sum of £100, thus included 'an ostrich whose young were always born alive; a herb which grew in the stomach of a thrush; and the skin of a moor, with the beard and hair white'.[94] In Paula Findlen's estimation, many such collections failed to dissolve the boundaries of the traditional world, and '"saved appearances" rather than unsettling ancient systems'. Museums were thus 'a reinvention of the old rather than the formation of the new'.[95] These practices embody what one historian has described as 'a crisis of Baconianism' which arose out of 'the problems of practising and defending natural philosophy without a theory, a metalanguage to negotiate between a fallen nature and its divine Creator'.[96]

Yet swelling collections of creatures and tomes of natural history bursting at the seams could not but place some pressures on the medieval understanding of the things of nature. Prior to the age of discovery, a symbolic world had existed in which a discrete set of natural objects had provided a ground for the composition of unlimited variations on eternal themes. The meanings of things were always accessible through reference to a rich literary tradition. Now, however, what had once been a coherent universal language was inundated by an influx of new and potentially unintelligible symbols. In this expanded lexicon of natural objects there existed signs for which the familiar symbolic associations were totally lacking. The literary allusions, the etymologies, the morals, the emblematic significance – all were absent.[97] A disturbing implication of this development was that the purportedly natural representative functions of living things were in fact merely conventional, that the things of nature bore no universal, God-given, significance, but instead had been arbitrarily allocated meanings by human agents. The logical terminus of this process is reached when allegorical interpretations are dismissed as fantasies of the reader, when allegory becomes a literary device rather than an approach to the world, when animal fables are invented rather than merely rehearsed. In the sixteenth century this is some way off. What we do find, however, is that critical humanists have begun to question the emblematic functions of natural objects. How could the pelican represent Christ if, as Thomas Browne

[94] Hunter, *Science and Society*, pp. 66f.
[95] Paula Findlen, *Possessing Nature: Museums, Collecting, and Scientific Culture in Early Modern Italy*, (Berkeley: University of California Press, 1995), pp. 4, 5.
[96] Markley, *Fallen Languages*, p. 10, cf. pp. 95–130.
[97] A point well made by William Ashworth, 'Natural History and the Emblematic World View', p. 318.

pointed out, it did not exhibit those behaviours on which the similitudes were based?[98] 'If naturally examined, and not hieroglyphically conceived' argued Browne, the account of the pelican is simply untrue. On the testimonies of the Fathers which seemed to support such behaviours, Browne observed that 'we may more safely conceive therein some Emblematicall then any real story'. Augustine, we recall, had been cognisant of possible discrepancies between 'natural' and 'hieroglyphical' ways of conceiving of objects. He differs from Browne giving prominence to the latter conceptions. Browne, despite his Platonic inclinations, thought the empirical world to be the real world, and saw possibilities for intelligibly ordering the things of nature in their observable properties, as opposed to their symbolic attributes as represented in written traditions.

To a degree, descriptions of new animals and plants made a contribution to the breakdown of the traditional systems of representation which had given meaning to the world. But even more important for the demise of this medieval world view were changes taking place in the literary sphere. The most direct challenge to the powerful symbolic universe was to come not from new discoveries in the empirical world, but from a new approach to the interpretation of texts, one which would lead to an irrevocable divide between the study of written texts and the observation of nature, between the humanities and the sciences, between words and things. The Protestant Reformation was the major force behind the new logocentric science of interpretation. If humanist scholarship had drawn attention to the importance of written texts and stressed the necessity of fidelity to original sources, the Protestant reformers were to apply this principle to the rectification of a religion which in their view was founded solely on the authority of canonical texts. The reformation of religion, as we are about to see, owed much to the textual criticism of previous generations of humanist scholars. On the foundations of the labours of the humanists the reformers constructed a new exegetical science which could find no place for the symbolic interpretation of the book of nature.

CORRUPT TEXTS AND REFORMED RELIGION

On the morning of 16 August, in the year 1513, a young professor of theology entered the lecture hall of the Augustinian house in Witten-

[98] Browne, *Pseudodoxia Epidemica*, I, pp. 367–9.

burg, and began to deliver the first of a series of lectures on the Psalms. The young teacher was Martin Luther. His lectures, we are reliably informed, began at 6.00 am, continuing twice weekly until 20 October, the following year. In the winter of that first year, in the course of his preparations, Luther had arranged for the university printer to prepare a text of the Psalter which was free of the glosses and commentaries of the Fathers and Doctors. The wide margins of this text, which in the normal course of events would have been reserved for the exegetical insights of past authorities, were left blank to enable students to record their own comments and observations.[99] This seemingly innocent event was to have far-reaching implications, and has not unfittingly been described as 'the symbolic moment of transition between ancient and modern hermeneutics'.[100] The Bible which had served as the text book in the medieval schools was not the bare words of the writers of the Old and New Testaments, but was the *Glossa Ordinaria* – an amplified Latin translation in which the original deposit of the scriptural writers was surrounded by the commentaries and notes of the Fathers. The text of scripture lay embedded in its own hermeneutical web in such a way that the words of the biblical authors were in practice not distinguished from the history of their interpretation. The *Glossa Ordinaria* thus provided not only the authoritative text of the words of scripture, but also provided the officially sanctioned meaning of those words. By extricating the original biblical text from what had become its natural setting – a thousand-year old tradition of gloss and commentary – Luther not only made possible novel ways of reading scripture, but also took the first step in distinguishing the authority of scripture from the tradition of the Church. He was later to write: 'Scripture without any glosses is the sun and the whole light from which all teachers receive their light, and not vice versa.'[101] It was his reading of this new text, and his insistence that it was the ultimate court of appeal on matters of Christian doctrine, which precipitated the Protestant Reformation.[102]

[99] Heinrich Boehmer, *Luthers erste Vorlesung* (Leipzig, 1924), p. 5.
[100] Bruns, *Hermeneutics*, p. 139. Cf. Ebeling, *Luther*, pp. 50f.
[101] *Answer to the Hyperchristian Book, Luther's Works*, 39, 164.
[102] Thus Bernt Moeller: 'Luther studies are today probably agreed, especially after the work of G. Ebeling, that Luther's theological breakthrough to the Reformation came about in direct connection with *the exposition of Scripture.*' 'Scripture, Tradition, and Sacrament in the Middle Ages and in Luther', in F. F. Bruce and E. G. Rupp, *Holy Book and Holy Tradition* (Manchester University Press, 1968), pp. 113–35 (p. 128). Cf. G. Ebeling, 'Die Anfänge von Luthers Hermeneutik', *Zeitschrift für Theologie und Kirche*, 48 (1951), 162–230; Karl Bauer, *Die Wittenberger Universitätstheologie und die Anfänge der Deutschen Reformation* (Tübingen, 1928); Alister McGrath, *The Intellectual Origins of the European Reformation* (Blackwell: Oxford, 1987) pp. 152–74.

For the first 1,500 years of the Church's history scripture did not exercise an authority which was independent of ecclesiastical tradition. Indeed, it was generally assumed that authority was vested in scripture by the councils of the Church. Taken together, the decisions of Church councils represented a tradition which had controlled firstly, the text of scripture, by declaring the 'Vulgate' (a late fourth-century Latin translation, for the most part the work of Jerome) to be the only official version of the biblical text; secondly, the canon of scripture, by determining which books were to be included in the Old and New Testaments and which were to be regarded as apocryphal; and thirdly, the meanings of those canonical texts, by providing authoritative interpretations. This general position was reasserted at the fourth session of the Council of Trent, which convened on 8 April 1546. Here the council specified the authoritative text of scripture, declaring that 'the said old and vulgate edition' is 'held as authentic; and that no one is to dare, or presume to reject it under any pretext whatever'. The canon of books which makes up the holy scriptures – that 'list of sacred books . . . that are received by this synod' – was also set out in full. And finally, the prerogative of the Church to determine which interpretations of scripture were to be regarded as authentic was asserted: 'no one, relying on his own skill, shall . . . wresting the sacred scripture to his own sense, presume to interpret the said sacred scripture contrary to that sense which holy mother Church, – whose it is to judge the true sense and interpretation of the holy Scriptures, – hath held and doth hold; or even contrary to the unanimous consent of the Fathers'.[103] This stance accounts for the vigour with which Roman authorities prosecuted those guilty of translating the Bible into the vernacular, for not only did such translations present a challenge to the supremacy of the Vulgate edition, but they gave licence to all individuals, on the condition of literacy, to come to their own understanding of the meaning of passages of scripture.[104]

The reformers had issued challenges to the Roman control of the Bible and its interpretation on all three points. Luther was to place the authority of scripture over the magisterium of the church, in the first place, by denying the superiority of the Latin Vulgate and by producing a German Bible based on more accurate texts. Luther's sources included the new editions of the Greek New Testament – fruits of the

1546

---

[103] 'Canons and Decrees of the Council of Trent, AD 1563', IV, in Schaff (ed.), *Creeds of Christendom* II, 80–3.
[104] On the impact of the English Bible, see Christopher Hill, *The English Bible and the Seventeenth-Century Revolution* (Ringwood: Penguin, 1994).

labours of that most talented of humanists, Erasmus of Rotterdam. Luther also questioned the canonical status of certain scriptural books. *appendix* The Letter of James, for example, was dismissed as 'an epistle of straw', which Luther did not want included in his Bible.[105] While Luther grudgingly came to accept that James should take its place with the other, more worthy books of scripture, he was able to exercise his editorial ambitions on the so-called apocryphal writings, works which are omitted from Protestant bibles to this day. Finally, Luther insisted that the individual, with the aid of the Holy Spirit, could come to a legitimate understanding of the meaning of the words of scripture without having to refer to the sanctioned interpretations of the Roman authorities.[106] Such individual readings were further facilitated by the printing and circulation of Bibles translated for the first time into the vernacular. John Calvin likewise sought to loosen the control which the Roman hierarchy exercised over the meanings of scripture. 'A most pernicious error has very generally prevailed', he wrote in the *Institutes* (1536), 'that Scripture is of importance only in so far as conceded to it by the suffrage of the Church.' These 'ravings' are refuted by St Paul, who 'testifies that the Church "is built on the foundation of the apostles and prophets" (Eph. ii.20)'.[107] The authority of the Church, according to Calvin, derives from the authority of scripture, and not the reverse.

Some of the more obvious parallels between the reformation of religion and the reformation of natural history should be apparent. David Norton writes that 'a major aspect of the Reformation is that it changed the basis of religion not only, to speak in extremes, from the accumulated tradition of the Church to private intercourse with the text of the Bible but also from biblical lore to the Bible text'.[108] Christianity came to be regarded by the Protestant reformers as a religion whose essence was most faithfully represented in a canon of ancient texts – texts whose meaning had been systematically corrupted in the Middle Ages, owing to 'the pestilent and *Heretical* Glosses of *Rome*', as one seventeenth-century writer put it.[109] The Catholic corruption of the very texts upon which Christianity had been founded, whether through negligence or fraud, was a constant complaint of the Protestants. Miles Coverdale, who produced the first complete English translation of the

[105] P. Althaus, *The Theology of Martin Luther* (Philadelphia: Fortress Press, 1966), pp. 83–5.
[106] Martin Luther, *To the Christian Nobility*, in *Three Treatises*, pp. 18–22. Cf. *The Freedom of a Christian*, *Ibid.*, p. 312; Ebeling, *Luther*, pp. 45f., 108f.; Althaus, *Theology of Martin Luther*, pp. 3–8, 76–8.
[107] John Calvin, *Institutes* I, 68f.   [108] Norton, *History of the Bible*, p. 53.
[109] Benjamin Keach, *TROPOSCHMALOGIA: Tropes and Figures* (London, 1692), Epistle to the Reader.

Bible in 1535, complained of the misleading 'glosses of our sophistical doctors'. William Fulke, who had helped revive the study of Hebrew at Cambridge in the middle decades of the sixteenth century, also spoke of the papists' 'adjoined unsavoury silly annotations'. The text of the Bible, wrote the keeper of the Royal Library in 1583, should be received 'nakedly' without 'corrupt notes and blasphemous glosses'.[110] And it was not merely additions to sacred text made over the centuries which had rendered it corrupt. The very translation itself was considered to be degenerate. Andrew Willet opened his popular treatise on the errors of papistry, *Synopsis Papismi* (1592) with a comprehensive critique of the attitude of Catholics to scripture. On the text of the Bible, he wrote that 'there are many & great errors in the vulgate translation, and contrarie to the originall'.[111] The Vulgate, agreed Thomas James, first keeper of Bodley's library, 'is a faulty, and corrupt, and depraved translation', with errors numbering in excess of 8,000.[112] Dryden wrote of 'How *Jewish, Popish* Interests have prevail'd', and of errors made 'Both in the *Copiers* and *Translators Trade*'.[113] Editor of the 'Polyglott Bible' (1653–7), Brian Walton, claimed in the prospectus to have produced an edition which was free 'from the negligence of scribes, the injury of times, the wilful corruption of sectaries and heretics'.[114] Even some Catholic scholars were now reluctant to rely on their own official translation. Neo-classicist William Lindanus (b.1525), to the delight of the Protestants, spoke frankly of 'the errors, vices, corruptions, additions, detractions, mutations, uncertainties, obscurities, pollutions, barbarianisms and solecisms of the vulgar Latin translation', and of his desire to reform the text.[115] Yet, when Catholics eventually produced their own vernacular

---

[110] Miles Coverdale, *Remains of Miles Coverdale*, ed. George Pearson, (Cambridge University Press, 1846), p. 19; Fulke, *The Text of the New Testament*, Preface; Anthony Marten, *The Commonplaces of . . . Peter Martyr* (London, 1583), Sig. A2v, qu. in Norton, *History of the Bible*, p. 136.

[111] Willet, *Synopsis Papismi, that is, A General View of Papistry* (London, 1592), p. 15. Willet identified seven points of difference: 1. The canon of scripture; 2. The authentic edition of scripture; 3. Whether the scriptures ought to be translated into vulgar tongues; 4. Whether the scriptures drew their authority from the Church; 5. Concerning the 'perspicuitie and playnnes' of the scripture; 6. Whether the scripture admits diverse senses, who should it expound it and how; 7. Concerning the perfection and sufficiency of scripture. (pp. 1–2). On Willet and the impact of the *Synopsis*, see Anthony Milton, *Catholic and Reformed: The Roman and Protestant Churches in English Protestant Thought 1600–1640* (Cambridge University Press, 1995), pp. 13–15.

[112] Thomas James, *A Manuduction, or Introduction unto Divinitie* (London, 1625), p. 12.

[113] *Religio Laici*, lines 249–50.

[114] Cited by Donald Hendricks, 'Profitless Printing: Publication of the Polyglots', *The Journal of Library History* 2 (1967) 98–115.

[115] Qu. in Norton, *History of the Bible*, p. 132. Later in the century, Jesuit biblical scholars were to turn the corruption of scripture argument back onto the Protestants. On account of the imperfections of the extant versions of the scriptures, religious authority ought to be vested in

translations, whether motivated by a concern to counter the influence of the new Protestant Bibles, or out of a genuine desire to produce a better version of scripture, they still attracted trenchant criticism. The general tenor of William Fulke's celebrated attack on the Rheims-Douai Bible (1582, 1609) – an English translation which was largely the work of exiled Catholic scholar Gregory Martin – is clear enough from the subtitle: *A Confutation of the Rhemists' Translation, Glosses, and Annotations on the New Testament, so far as they contain manifest impieties, heresies, idolatries, superstitions, profanness, treasons, slanders, absurdities, falsehoods and other evils* (1617).[116]

The writings of the Fathers were similarly regarded as having been corrupted. 'The workes of the most auncient', Thomas James complained, 'are daily depraued by this sinfull and deceitfull Romish brood'.[117] His *Treatise of the Corruption of Scripture* (1612) parallels those works of humanist critical scholarship in the field of natural history, in rooting out errors which had crept into texts of the scripture and the Fathers – errors which had been used, according to James, to sustain false Romish doctrines. William Crashawe's *Romish Forgeries and Falsifications* (1606) is a similarly conceived catalogue of 'filthy forgeries' of the Papists.[118] The Reformation was an attempt to reconstruct Christian religion from its origins, and those origins were to be discovered in the New Testament. Because the authority of Christianity was now to be located, not in the total history of the Church, but in that short period in which the apostles lived, taught, and wrote, historical criticism of the biblical texts took on an unprecedented importance. The enterprise of natural history, during its constructive phase at least, was similarly the reconstruction or restoration of a past discipline which had been created by Aristotle, Theophrastus, Dioscorides, and to a lesser extent, Pliny. The reformers thus shared the historical sense of those humanist scholars who sought to correct errors in the Aristotelian encyclopaedia by returning to the original sources and original languages. A theologian, Richard Bernard wrote in 1607, must also be a philologist.[119] The same, of course, had been true of naturalists.

If the new philology enabled the excision of many of the corruptions

the Church, not scripture. See Gerard Reedy, *The Bible and Reason: Anglicans and Scripture in Late Seventeenth-Century England* (Philadelphia: University of Pennsylvania Press, 1985), p. 104.

[116] Fulke, *The Text of the New Testament. With a Confutation* (London, 1617).

[117] James, *A Treatise of the Corruption of Scripture, Councels, and Fathers, by the Prelates, Pastors, and Pillars of the Church of Rome* (London, 1611), Epistle Dedicatory. Cf. Bernard, *Faithfull Shepheard* (London, 1607), p. 41

[118] William Crashawe, *Falsificationvm Romanarvm / Romish Forgeries and Falsifications* (London, 1606). Cf. William Whitaker, *Disputatio de sacra Scriptura* (Cantabrigiae, 1588).

[119] Bernard, *The Faithfull Shepheard*, p. 35.

which had marred the texts of natural history, the changes which the methods of humanist criticism, applied to the text of scripture, were to bring to Christianity were, if anything, even more far-reaching. Luther, for example, identified a number of doubtful renditions in the New Testament which had served to support Catholic doctrines or practices which he regarded as spurious. The Greek word μετανοία – to repent – appears in the Latin vulgate as *poenitentia* – to do penance.[120] This simple mistranslation could thus legitimise the whole unwieldy sacramental system of confession, penance, and ultimately, the traffic of indulgences to which Luther was so vehemently opposed, and which forms the main subject of the famous 'Ninety-Five Theses'. Biblical support for other Catholic dogmas similarly tended to vanish under the sustained pressure of Protestant biblical criticism. Francis De Neville thus argued that the biblical sanction for the practice of invocation of the saints and the doctrine of transubstantiation simply vanished when the relevant texts were read in their original languages.[121] In addition to calling into question traditional theological doctrines, the new scholarship also fuelled controversies concerning Church government. Pioneer Bible translator William Tyndale, who was eventually rewarded with martyrdom for his labours, attracted the criticism of the learned Thomas More for details of his translation relating to the nature of ecclesiastical officials. Tyndale had used 'Seniors' to translate the more customary 'priests', and had rendered 'Church' as 'congregation', innovations which More considered indications of a 'mischievous mind'.[122] If an ordained priesthood could find no sanction in scripture, if the New Testament spoke only of congregations but not a universal Church, then the necessity for Church reformation would be hard to deny. This particular discussion continued for over a century. Puritan scholars at the Westminster Assembly (1644) urged against their episcopal brethren that church leaders be elected rather than ordained. George Gillespie put the case that the Greek Χειροτονέω should be rendered 'choose'

---

[120] Gordon Rupp, *The Righteousness of God: Luther Studies* (London: Hodder and Stoughton, 1953), pp. 118f. The council of Trent finds numerous references in the New Testament to penance. Matthew 3.8, for example rendered 'bringing forth fruits of penance' (poenitentiae, μετανοία). Modern translations uniformly render the phrase 'fruits of repentance'. *Canons and Decrees of Trent*, XIV.xiii, in Schaff, *Creeds of Christendom*, II, 157.

[121] *The Christian and Catholike Veritie* (London, 1642) pp. 79, 103.

[122] Thomas More, *A Dyaloge of Syr Thomas More . . . wherein be treated dyuers matters* (London, 1529); Norton, *History of the Bible*, p. 100. Cf. Luther, *Answer to the Hyperchristian Book*, in *Luther's Works*, 39, 154.

rather than 'ordain'.[123] The relevant passage in Acts would read, in that case, 'And when they had *choosen* elders from every church' (14.13). Upon such apparently minor issues of translation depended weighty and potentially divisive issues of ecclesiastical polity. This reforming spirit was still alive in the great Isaac Newton, who in an unpublished manuscript entitled 'Two Notable Corruptions of Scripture', made the heretical claim that the biblical evidence for the doctrine of the Trinity rested chiefly upon Catholic corruptions. The author of the Vulgate, he charged, 'did insert ye testimony of the three in heaven'.[124] Newton believed that disinterested textual criticism would bring to light such emendations, and vindicate his unitarian view of the Deity. Thus, the tools of humanist scholarship, whether applied to religious or scientific texts, gave rise to a more accurate picture of what original authorities had actually written, and thus had the potential to revolutionise their respective spheres.

More generally, the Reformation stood as a challenge to authority as such, replacing the authority of the institution with that of scripture, or in the case of the more radical reformers, with that of the individual. In each instance, the pendulum swung away from institution to individual. This is evident first of all in the reformers' insistence that the individual be granted direct access to the book of God's word. The meaning of scripture, at whatever level it was interpreted, could be determined by the diligent reader without reference to the Fathers and Doctors, to councils and Popes. Ultimately, of course, the multiplicity of interpretations which this new freedom enabled was to undermine the authority of scripture, but this was to come later. In much the same way that the faithful were granted direct access to scripture, they were granted unmediated access to God himself. This is apparent both in attacks on the cult of the saints, and in the reduction in the number of sacraments.

---

[123] Hill, *English Bible*, pp. 51, 420. As it turns out, Gillespie was most probably mistaken. The customary meaning of Χειροτονέω is 'to choose, elect by raising of hands', but according to Bauer's *Greek-English Lexicon*, in this particular context the word is better rendered 'appoint, install'. Such debates about the biblical titles and manners of appointment of Church officials date back to Tyndale's earliest translations.

[124] Newton, *Correspondence*, III, 138f.; cf. Newton, 'Paradoxical Questions Concerning the Morals and Actions of Athanasius and his Followers', *Sir Isaac Newton's Theological Manuscripts*, ed. Herbert McLachlan, (Liverpool University Press, 1950), pp. 60–118. Also see Manuel, *Religion of Isaac Newton*, pp. 65–7; Markley, *Fallen Languages*, pp. 145–7; Richard Westfall, *The Life of Isaac Newton* (Cambridge University Press, 1994), pp. 122–5. Curiously enough, a book appeared a few years ago proposing the same general thesis. Bart Ehrman, *The Orthodox Corruption of Scripture* (Oxford University Press, 1992).

Prayer might now be directly addressed to the Deity, without priestly or saintly intercessors. Confessions, too, could be made directly to God, who in turn could dispense forgiveness independent of sacerdotal mediators. This tendency is also evident in the reformers' attitude to 'implicit faith', that conception of faith according to which individuals in the Church need not fully understand what it is they are to believe. This notion attracted sustained criticism from Luther and Calvin. The result of such a conception, said Calvin, is that that faithful come to 'understand nothing' merely submitting their convictions 'implicitly to the Church'. Individuals must not, he insisted, 'embrace every dictate of the Church as true, or leave to the Church the province of inquiring and determining'.[125] Luther's doctrine of 'the priesthood of all believers' – a doctrine of individualist anarchy according to Christopher Hill – made the same point.[126] All things considered, Cardinal Bellarmine had ample justification for his complaint against the reformers, that they made 'individual persons the judges in matters of faith, not only of the Fathers but also of the councils', leaving 'almost nothing to the common judgement of the Church'.[127]

This ideology which pitted individual against institution, and the ensuing religious controversies it was to generate, had the eventual effect of establishing as a general principle the liberty of the individual conscience.[128] 'We live in an Age of so much Light', wrote an anonymous translator in 1690. 'The Doctrine of Implicit Faith has lost its Vogue. Every Man will judge for himself in matters that concern himself so nearly as these do. And nothing is now admitted for Truth, that is not built upon the Foundation of Solid Reason.'[129] The first of the modern liberties was the freedom to read the Bible in the vernacular and make determinations for oneself about its meaning. That freedom could have pervasive social and political ramifications, as Christopher Hill has so

[125] Calvin, *Institutes* III.ii (I, 470).
[126] Luther, *To the Christian Nobility*, in *Three Treatises*, p. 14; Hill, *Collected Essays of Christopher Hill*, 3 vols. (Amherst: University of Massachusetts Press, 1986), II, 38.
[127] Bellarmine, *Disputations on the Controversies Over Christian Faith Against the Heretics of the Day*, I.iii.3, in Blackwell, *Galileo, Bellarmine, and the Bible*, appendix, III, p. 193.
[128] This does not mean that Protestants were any more tolerant of religious pluralism than Catholics. However, the repression of various religious groups in the sixteenth and seventeenth centuries was premised primarily on fears of political instability, rather than on the desire to enforce a religious uniformity *per se*. On the Reformation and liberty of conscience see Baylor, *Action and Person: Conscience in Scholasticism and the Young Luther* (Leiden: Brill, 1977); Huff, *Rise of Early Modern Science*, pp. 107–10; Klaaren, *Religious Origins of Modern Science*, pp. 91f., 108.
[129] Jean Le Clerc, *Five Letters concerning the Inspiration of the Holy Scriptures* (London, 1690), p. 7.

ably demonstrated with regard to the English Revolution.[130] The study of ancient texts could lead to modern revolutions, both intellectual and political. As an alarmed Dryden wrote in *Religio Laici* (1682): 'The Book thus put in every vulgar hand, / Which each presum'd he best cou'd understand, / the *Common Rule* was made the *common Prey*; / And at the mercy of the *Rabble* lay.'[131] Other applications of this liberty were equally far-reaching. In freeing persons to make determinations about the meaning of the book of scripture without deferring to authorities, the reformers had at the same time made room for individuals to make determinations about the book of nature, unfettered by the opinions of approved authors.[132] If the techniques of textual criticism pioneered by the humanists had played a role in precipitating a revolution in religious matters, now the Protestant Reformation, through its challenges to traditional authorities, was to assist in the reformation of learning.

It is sometimes difficult for modern minds to imagine the hold exercised by ancient authorities over institutions of formal education, and how reverence for authority was enforced with an almost religious zeal. When, for example, in 1559 English physician John Geynes ventured to suggest that Galen might not be infallible, he was excluded from the Royal College until he acknowledged the error of his ways and signed a recantation.[133] While the next century brought some improvements, up until about 1630 university statutes still prescribed penalties for infidelities to Aristotle. Robert Merton informs us that Bachelors and Masters of Arts 'were liable to a fine of five shillings for every point of divergence, or for every fault committed against the *Organon*'.[134] At times, institutional deference to the observations of the ancients was derided in the same terms which the reformers had used of subservience to the authority of Rome. John Hall urged his contemporaries, in 1649, to shake off the 'implicite faith' which bound them to the second-hand knowledge of written authorities.[135] As late as 1682, William Bacon, preaching innovations in medicine, pleaded of his listeners: 'Resolve to trust your own senses to inform your Reasons, and do not superstitiously adhere to the *Ipse dixit* of another.'[136] While the most progressive physicians of the age might have heeded such pleas, they were by no means

---

[130] Hill, *English Bible*, passim.   [131] Dryden, *Religio Laici*, ll. 400–4.

[132] See discussions in Eisenstein, *The Printing Press*, II, 657–60; Hooykaas, 'Science and the Reformation', in *The Protestant Ethic and Modernization*, ed. S. N. Eisenstadt (New York, 1968) 211–39.

[133] Debus, *The English Paracelsians*, p. 51.   [134] Merton, *Science, Technology, and Society*, p. 299.

[135] Hall, *An Humble Motion to the Parliament*, p. 41.

[136] Bacon, *A Key to Helmont* (London, 1682), p. 30.

in the majority. Indeed, the seventeenth-century education of physicians was based almost entirely on the writings of ancient authors, and
the recent innovations in anatomy and physiology had by this time
made little impact on the university curriculum.[137]

Religious reformers, too, launched attacks on the slavish adherence to
tradition evident in institutions of learning. Luther had long since
argued that the universities, 'where only that blind, heathen teacher
Aristotle rules', stood in need of 'a good, thorough reformation'.[138]
Various groups in seventeenth-century England echoed this concern.
Radicals and liberal puritans were particularly vocal in their demands
for reform: both groups reflected Baconian ideals.[139] In a series of
sermons delivered in 1653, appropriately to the army laying siege to
Oxford, radical preacher William Dell set out a catalogue of complaints
against the universities, chief of which was the fact that pagan authors
enjoyed 'more credit in the universities then Moses or Christ himself'.[140]
Milton, Hartlib, John Drury, Hugh Peter, and Noah Biggs added their
voices to the growing disquiet about the state of education in the land.[141]
Best known critic of all was John Webster, whose *Academiarum Examen*
appeared in 1654. The universities, in Webster's view, still slavishly
adhered to Aristotle: 'Neither is it fit that *Authority* (whether of *Aristotle* or
any other) should inchain us, but that there may be general freedom to
try all things . . . so there may be a *Philosophical* liberty to be bound to the
authority of none, but truth itself.' While Webster's complaints about
the universities generally met with a hostile reception, it was nonetheless
true that in such places as England the domination of the university
curriculum by Aristotle and Galen was to come to an end well before it
did in Catholic countries such as France. Indeed Thomas Hobbes had
shrewdly observed that the Aristotelian schools had originally been
established to serve the Romish religion, and despite the Reformation
which had ostensibly taken place in England, while universities con-

---

[137] Phyllis Allen, 'Medical Education in 17th-Century England', *Journal of the History of Medicine*, 1
(1946), 115–43. Also see Richard Greaves, *The Puritan Revolution and Educational Thought* (New
Brunswick: Rutgers University Press, 1969), pp. 11–15; Hugh Kearney, *Scholars and Gentlemen:
Universities and Society in pre-Industrial Britain, 1500–1700* (London: Faber and Faber, 1970), pp.
124–6.

[138] Luther, *To the Christian Nobility*, in *Three Treatises*, p. 92. Luther's pleas did not fall on totally deaf
ears. Gerhard Ebeling has remarked that the whole course of the Protestant Reformation 'was
accompanied by significant educational and university reforms.' *Luther: An Introduction to his
Thought* (London: Collins, 1970), p. 19.

[139] Greaves, *Puritan Revolution and Educational Thought*, pp. 1, 17–25, 28–35.

[140] Dell, *The Tryal of Spirits* (London: 1653), Appendix, p. 14, qu. in Webster, *Great Instauration*, p. 186;
Kearney, *Scholars and Gentlemen*, pp. 112f.   [141] Webster, *Great Instauration*, pp. 184–90.

tinued to support Aristotle, they were still in the business of perpetuating papism.[142]

Part of the problem which the Catholics faced was that since the time of Aquinas a considerable proportion of their dogma had been explicitly formulated in terms of Aristotelian philosophy. There is a degree of truth in Luther's description of the Roman establishment as 'the Aristotelian church'.[143] While the Protestants, with their emphasis on returning to the source of Christian ideas, had few problems jettisoning the Aristotelian framework of theology, Catholics, for whom the entire history of dogma was in a sense authoritative, could not as easily extricate themselves from their Aristotelian commitments.[144] The Catholic notion of transubstantiation, a popular target of Reformers, was couched quite explicitly in terms of Aristotelian ontology.[145] The Roman formulation of the doctrine of justification, a major point of contention during the Reformation, rested upon the principle of Aristotelian ethics that 'by doing right, one becomes righteous'. This 'Aristotelian' view was emphatically rejected by Luther.[146]

Throughout the course of the seventeenth century, many would-be reformers of natural philosophy drew attention to and attempted to exploit the apparent link between the two reformations. In 1605, Francis Bacon had observed that 'in the age of ourselves and our Fathers, when it pleased God to call the Church of Rome to account for their degenerate manners and ceremonies, and sundry doctrines obnoxious and framed to uphold the same abuses; at one and the same time it was ordained by the Divine Providence, that there should attend withal a renovation and a new spring of all other knowledges'.[147] Such a renova-

---

[142] Hobbes, *Leviathan*, ch. 46 (p. 482). Cf. Seth Ward's response, *Vindiciae Academiarum* (Oxford, 1654), pp. 51–61. Ward (and, in an epistle prefixed to the work, John Wilkins) was more concerned with Webster's criticisms, although there can be no doubt that despite their defensive posture, they themselves had actually introduced precisely the kinds of reforms advocated by Webster.   [143] Luther, *Babylonian Captivity*, in *Three Treatises*, p. 144.

[144] The doctrine of transubstantiation is an obvious example. Consider, too, the Tridentine statement of the doctrine of justification, which speaks of the final, formal, and instrumental causes of justification. *Canons and Decrees of Trent* XIII, 4; VI.vii, in Schaff, II, 131, 95. Also see Luther's criticisms, *Babylonian Captivity of the Church* in *Three Treatises*, pp. 148f.

[145] See Luther, *Babylonian Captivity*, in *Three Treatises*, pp. 144f.; Althaus, *Theology of Martin Luther*, p. 376, n. 2. For the problems generated for the doctrine by scientific conceptions of matter, see especially Keith Hutchison, 'Dormative Virtues, Scholastic Qualities, and the New Philosophies', *History of Science* 29 (1991) 245–78; Also Pietro Redondi, *Galileo: Heretic*, tr. Raymond Rosenthal (London: Penguin, 1987), pp. 203–26, 284f.; Rubin, *Corpus Christi*, pp. 350f.

[146] Ebeling, *Luther*, pp. 150–8.

[147] Bacon, *Advancement of Learning*, I.vi.15 (p. 42). Cf. George Hakewill: 'a soule shame then it were for us who professe a thorow reformation in matter of *doctrine*, to bee thought to grow worse in matter of *manners*, God forbid it should be so.' Hakewill, *An Apologie* (3rd edn) Sig. a4.v (Epistle Dedicatory).

tion, in Bacon's view, could only come about if the relevant authorities, respectively the books of scripture and nature, were consulted. The corruption of religion had resulted from the forsaking of scripture; the corruption of natural philosophy from the forsaking of nature. 'In the inquiry of divine truth' searchers were 'ever inclined to leave the oracles of God's word', so too, in the 'inquisition of nature they have ever left the oracles of God's works'.[148] This sentiment was echoed fifty years later during the inter-regnum. Thomas Culpeper wrote in 1655 that the dual reformations in religion and philosophy could only be fully accomplished when 'the pope in philosophy' (Aristotle) was dethroned along with the other Pope. In a petition to Parliament urging the reform of the universities, Milton's friend Samuel Hartlib argued that once religion had been established on its true course, the next step for the Christian commonwealth of England was the 'reformation and advancement of learning'. The 'reformation from Antichristianisme' was the source of 'all progressive Reformations', he pointed out.[149] Presbyterian Thomas Hall, despite his rejection of the central complaints of Webster's *Academiarum Examen*, petitioned Parliament on the same subject, describing the reformation of the universities as 'this last peece of Reformation'.[150] Thomas Sprat, perhaps sceptical about the prospects of progress in the universities, praised instead the Royal Society, of which he was an active member. Both reformed Churches and the Society, he observed, 'may lay equal claim to the word *Reformation*, the one having compass'd it in *Religion*, the other purposing it in *Philosophy*'. In each case, Sprat pointed out, the mechanism of reformation had been similar: 'They both have taken a like cours [sic] to bring this about; each of them passing by the *corrupt Copies*, and referring themselves to the *perfect Originals* for their instruction; the one to the *Scripture*, the other to the large volume of the *Creatures*.'[151] Supporters of tradition in the sphere of natural philosophy, Sprat thought, 'are more in love with their own *Commentaries*, then with the *Texts* of those, whom they seem to make their Oracles'. Champions

[148] Bacon, *The Interpretation of Nature*, in *Works*, III, 224 [ch. 1].

[149] Thomas Culpeper, *Morall Discourses and Essayes* (London, 1655), p. 63. Samuel Hartlib, Sheffield University Library, Hartlib Papers XLVIII 17, reproduced in Webster, *Great Instauration*, Appendix 1, pp. 524–8. Cf. Noah Biggs, *Mataeotechnia Medicinae Praxeos. The Vanity of the Craft of Physick* (London, 1651), To the Parliament. On Hartlib generally, see Mark Greengrass, Michael Leslie, and Timothy Raylor (eds.) *Samuel Hartlib and Universal Reformation* (Cambridge University Press, 1994).

[150] Thomas Hall, 'Histrio Mastyx, a whip for Webster', *Vindiciae Literarum. The Schools Guarded* (London, 1654).

[151] Sprat, *History of the Royal Society*, p. 371. Cf. James, *Treatise of the Corruptions of Scripture*, Epistle Dedicatory.

of the new science, by way of contrast, 'follow the most antient Author of all others, even *Nature* it self'.[152]

A sceptical reading of these various appeals might lead to the conclusion that comparisons of religious and philosophical reformations served a rhetorical purpose and little more. Certainly, while Bacon and Sprat had identified similar general principles at work in the respective reformations, they would have strenuously resisted any suggestion that religious and philosophical concerns were to be intermingled. On the other hand, the use of such rhetoric would prove ineffectual unless there were those who genuinely believed that religious reformation could legitimise reformation in the sphere of natural philosophy. In any case, as Charles Webster has argued, much of the discourse of general reformation in seventeenth-century England was owing more to a forward-looking millenarianism than a backward glance at the triumphs of Protestant Christianity. The reformation of religion was not so much the direct cause, nor even the occasion of a reformation of learning, but part of that great instauration which according to scripture would precede the last things. It was a sign of the approaching millennium and was appealed to as a catalyst to enlist support for the utilitarian, educational, or ecumenical projects advanced by Bacon, and later Hartlib, Drury, and Comenius.[153]

Some contemporary commentators, however, clearly regarded the 'two reformations' as parts of the same historical process. The followers of Paracelsus, in particular, regarded the movement back to the books of scripture and nature as part of a single revival of learning which would overturn the unholy alliance of Aristotle and the Church. Aristotle was as great an enemy to religion as to science, and his writings were not only 'heathnish', but what was worse, 'Romish'. 'The naturall Philosophie of *Aristotle* doth differ from the trueth of Gods worde', alleged paracelsian controversialist Robert Bostocke, 'and is iniurious to sounde doctrine.' Aristotle and the 'Ethnicks' were 'Idolaters and ignorant of the trueth'. To follow their teaching was to embrace both a heretical religion and a false science. Galen, too, was implicated in this ungodly science. Bostocke argued that 'the heathnish Physicke of Galen doth

---

[152] *Ibid.*, pp. 49, 47f. Also see the discussion in Brooke, *Science and Religion*, pp. 99–109.
[153] Webster, *Great Instauration*, ch. 1; Margaret Jacob, 'Millennarianism and Science in the late Seventeenth Century" *JHI* 37 (1976), 335–41; James Jacob, 'Boyle's Circle in the Protectorate: Revelation, Politics and the Millennium', *JHI* 38 (1977), 131–40. Cf. J. Henry, 'Atomism and Eschatology: Catholicism and Natural Philosophy in the Interregnum', *BJHS* 15 (1982), 211–46; Malcolm Oster, 'Millennarianism and the New Science: the Case of Robert Boyle', in Greengrass et al. (eds.) *Samuel Hartlib and Universal Reformation*, pp. 137–48

depende uppon that heathnish Philosophie and Aristotle . . . therefore is
that Physicke as false and iniurious to [God's] honour and glory as is the
Philosophie'. In contrast, the principles of 'auncient and true phisicke',
now revived by the Paracelsians, 'doe agree with the rule of Gods
worde, they depend upon the fountaine of trueth'.[154] The contemporary
practice of physick, like Roman religion, was 'mixed with impurities,
and standeth in outward ceremonies and traditions'. Copernicus and
Paracelsus, according to Bostocke, were the Luther and Calvin of
natural philosophy, charged with the sacred task of restoring it to its
'former puritie'.[155] Johannes Kepler, himself a victim of the religious
upheavals of Europe, had actually claimed for himself the designation
'the Luther of astrology'.[156] It was Kepler's laws of planetary motion
which were to provide the foundation upon which Newton could
complete the reformation in natural philosophy. In the following century, one of the last of the Renaissance men, Robert Fludd – whose
philosophy was a creative amalgam of alchemy, astrology, cabbalism
and Christian neoplatonism – was to put the argument in even stronger
terms: the philosophy of the 'Greekish philosophers' was 'terrene, animal, and diabolical'. It was 'founded upon the wisdom of the world'
which has as its source 'the Prince of darknesse'. Of the ancients, only
Plato was immune from criticism, usually on account of the fact that he
was thought to have 'read the Books of *Moses*'.[157] These sentiments were
endorsed by writers with more exclusively theological concerns as well.
We find in Luther's earliest marginal notes references to 'putrid philosophers', the '*fabulator* Aristotle', and to 'the shameless nonsense that
Aristotle does not disagree with the Catholic truth'. These adolescent
sentiments differ little from his mature judgement: 'Aristotle is related to
theology as darkness is to light.' 'We are now living in the dawn of the
future life', he wrote elsewhere, 'for we are now again beginning to have
the knowledge of the creatures which we lost at Adam's Fall. Now we
observe the creatures rightly, more than popery does.'[158] Calvin referred
to the 'absurd subtleties' and 'frigid doctrine of Aristotle' which had
prevented people from embracing spiritual truths.[159] Thomas James,
spoke of a time 'when blind superstition did so farre preuaile amongst

[154] Bostocke, *Auncient Phisicke* , Sig. Av.v, title page, Sig Bii.v. Cf. Fludd, *Mosaicall Philosophy*, p. 29.
[155] *Ibid.*, Sigs. Cviii.v., Hvii.v. John Baptist van Helmont, although a Catholic and sometime
     opponent of the Paracelsians, lamented with them that 'the Art of healing was a meer juggle,
     brought in by the Greeks: till at length, the holy Scriptures better instructed me'. *Oriatrike*, p. 17.
[156] Webster, *From Paracelsus to Newton*, p. 4.   [157] Fludd, *Mosaicall Philosophy*, pp. 9, 13, 42.
[158] Qu. in G. Ebeling, *Luther: An Introduction to his Thought*, (London: Collins, 1970) pp. 86, 89; and in
     Bono, *Word of God*, p. 71.
[159] Calvin, *Institutes* I.v.5 (I, 53). Calvin, however, was not invariably opposed to the doctrines of
     Aristotle.

us, that there was no God amongst us but *Aristotle, no Diuinitie but drawn out the dregges of Philosophy*'. And as if this were not enough, 'a labryinth [sic] of humane traditions were found out, to amaze and perplex vs'. With the Reformation, however, 'the night is passed, the day is come . . . abstruse and hard quotations of Aristotle will not serue the turne: God's word alone is certaine.'[160]

These complex interactions between humanistic scholarship, the development of natural science, and the reformation of religion are highly suggestive, but by no means conclusive in establishing some strong link between the respective reformations in learning and religion which took place in the sixteenth and early seventeenth centuries. Much of this story is in any case a familiar one. There is nothing particularly novel about the general observation that dramatic changes in the religious landscape of Europe coincided with improvements in learning, that the reformations in religion and learning were somehow associated. As we have seen, this much was obvious to many contemporary figures themselves. Less obvious is the fact that the Protestant insistence on the primacy of scriptural authority demanded a new approach to the interpretation of scripture, and that this hermeneutical stance brought with it an alternative conception of the natural order – a conception which was the precondition for the emergence of natural science. A revolution in hermeneutics would make orphans of all natural objects, stripping them of all those associations from which they had derived their meanings, and abandoning them to that silent and unintelligible realm which was to become the subject of the modern science of nature.

THE LITERAL SENSE AND THE MATERIAL WORLD

Sola Scriptura – scripture alone – was the motto of the Reformation. The Bible as interpreted by the enlightened individual was promoted as the pre-eminent authority in religious matters. There remained, however,

---

[160] Thomas James, *A Manvdvction, or Introdvction vnto Divinitie*, p. 7. Other writers simply employed the rhetoric of reformation to the changes taking place in the field of natural philosophy. Paracelsus attracted the nickname 'the Sectarie', for having broken with medical tradition. John Hester, *The Pearle of Practice* (London, 1594), Epistle Dedicatory. 'Chemists', observed Thomas Moffett in *Theatrum Chemicum* (Argenterati, 1613), 'depart completely from the authority of the medical fathers' (p. 89). The anonymous writer of *Philiatros, or, The Copy of an Epistle . . . to a Young Student of Physicke*, (London, 1615), compared the Protestants, Papists, Brownists, Anabaptists and Familists to the Galenists, Arabians, and Paracelsians, pointing out that just as the Christian sects all claimed scripture as their authority, so medical sects all proclaim Hippocrates to be their master (Sig. A2r–A3v). In his preface to the English translation of Duchesne's *Practise of Chemicall and Hermeticall Physicke*, Thomas Tymme made a similar comparison, likening religious sectaries and schismatics to the various schools of philosophers and physicians.

the question of how it was to be interpreted. The major reformers – Martin Luther, John Calvin, Philipp Melanchthon, and Martin Bucer – shared a clear preference for the literal or natural sense of scripture, combined with a suspicion of allegory.[161] Luther argued that the scriptures should be understood 'in their simplest meaning as far as possible'. The literal sense was 'the highest, best, strongest, in short the whole substance nature and foundation of the holy scripture'.[162] Origen was singled out for particular censure because 'ignoring the grammatical sense, he turned trees and everything else . . . into allegories'. Allegorical studies, in Luther's final judgement, were for 'weak minds', and 'idle men'.[163] John Calvin, in his more prosaic fashion, also argued that 'allegories ought to be carried no further than Scripture expressly sanctions: so far are they from forming a sufficient basis to found doctrines upon'.[164] Philip Melanchthon, who took over the reins of the Reformation while Luther was confined in the Wartburg, regarded the whole history of the Church as little more than the story of its gradual defection from a simple gospel message. Again the chief culprit was Origen, whose allegorising had distracted readers of scripture from the plain message.[165] Melanchthon, a professor of Greek at Wittenburg, was more strongly influenced by humanism than any of the other major reformers, and incorporated many of its innovations into the study of the Bible. Martin Bucer, whose hermeneutics also bears clear signs of the influence of humanist scholarship, took up a position with respect to biblical interpretation similar to Melanchthon's. Following the later Erasmus, he abandoned allegorical interpretation completely, arguing that such a method permitted various meanings to be read into passages, at the cost of their true sense.[166] Indeed, of the major reformers, only Zwingli exhibited a lingering fondness for non-literal interpretation.[167] We can thus endorse Hans Frei's observation that 'the affirmation that the literal or grammatical sense is the Bible's true sense became programmatic for the traditions of Lutheran and Calvinistic interpretation'.[168]

The animus of the reformers to mystical interpretation carried over

---

[161] On the different approaches of the reformers, see McGrath, *Intellectual Origins*, ch. 6.

[162] *Answer to the Hyperchristian Book, Luther's Works*, 39, 177.

[163] Luther, *Babylonian Captivity*, in *Three Treatises*, pp. 146, 241. Cf. Ebeling, *Luther*, pp. 101–9.

[164] Calvin, *Institutes*, II.v (I, 291).

[165] McGrath, *Intellectual Origins*, p. 186; Peter Fraenkel, *Testimonia Patrum: The Function of the Patristic Argument in the Theology of Philip Melanchthon* (Geneva: Droz, 1961), pp. 70–93.

[166] McGrath, *Intellectual Origins*, p. 171.   [167] *Ibid.*, pp. 167–70.

[168] Hans Frei, *The Eclipse of Biblical Narrative*, (Yale University Press, 1974), p. 37; Cf. Jaraslov Pelikan, *The Reformation of the Bible, the Bible of the Reformation* (Yale University Press, 1996).

into mainstream seventeenth-century hermeneutics. John Donne wrote in his *Essayes in Divinity* (c.1615) that 'the word of God is not the word of God in any other sense then literall . . . and it is called literall, to distinguish it from the Morall, Allegoricall, and other sense; and is that which the Holy Ghost doth in that place principally intend'.[169] All things necessary for salvation, agreed Thomas James, 'are founded in the literall sense of Scripture'.[170] As the century progressed, the odium of allegorical interpretation spread to a range of undesirables – not only papists, but radicals, deists, Jews, and natural philosophers whose hypotheses seemed to contradict the literal sense of scripture. The Geneva-born biblical scholar Jean Le Clerc, discussing how Genesis had traditionally been interpreted, wrote that while Moses had expressed himself in the plainest manner imaginable, the Jews or 'Rabbins', 'rather than understand him so . . . chose to commit violence upon his words, and betake themselves to Allegory', a method which, in Le Clerc's view, 'wholly depends upon the Fancy of the Interpreter'.[171] Moses, William Nicholls insisted against the deists, 'was a plain unaffected writer'. The Fathers may have used allegory as an apologetic device, but 'Moses, having no such reason to put a mystical meaning upon his words, . . . must be supposed to have used them in the literal sense'.[172]

It is important to make clear what was innovative in this insistence on the priority of the literal sense. In the medieval West there had been signs of disenchantment with higher levels of interpretation and warnings had been sounded against the over-use of allegory to the exclusion of the literal sense.[173] In the twelfth century, for example, those scholars with 'scientific' interests claimed that Genesis contained a cosmogony, which had been overlooked in allegorical readings. Thierry of Chartres had set about expounding the early part of Genesis according to 'physical science' and 'the literal, historical sense of the text'.[174] In this he was not alone. Rupert of Deutz's commentary on Genesis (c.1112) similarly

---

[169] Donne, *Essayes in Divinity*, pp. 39f.
[170] James, *Introduction vnto Diuinitie*, p. 7. Cf. Willet, *Synopsis Papismi*, pp. 26–8; Charles Drelincourt, *A Collection of Texts of Scripture . . . Against the Principal Popish Errors* (London, 1686), pp. 1–3.
[171] Jean Le Clerc, *Twelve Dissertations out of Monsieur Le Clerc's Genesis*, tr. Mr Brown, (London, 1696), pp. 143f.   [172] William Nicholls, *A Conference with a Theist* (London, 1696), p. 252.
[173] Bruns, *Hermeneutics*, pp. 140f.; Smalley, *Study of the Bible*, pp. 46–66.
[174] 'De septem diebus et sex operum distinctionibus primam Geneseos partem secundum physicam et ad litteram ego expositurus, imprimis de intentione auctoris et de libri utilitate pauca praemittam. Postea vero ad sensum litterae historealum expondendum veniam, ut et allegoricam et moralem lectionem, quas sancti expositores aperte executi sunt, ex toto praetermittam.' *Magistri Theoderici Carnotensis Tractatus* 1 (reproduced in N. Häring, 'The Creation and Creator of the World According to Thierry of Chartres and Clarenbaldus of Arras', *Archives d'Histoire Doctrinale at Littéraire du Moyen Age* 22 (1955) 184–200 (184).

emphasises the literal and historical features of the account of creation. He insists that 'waters above the firmament' were real waters (and not 'solid water' or a symbolic representation of angels), that Paradise was a real place, and the Tree of Life, a real tree, and draws upon pagan geographic and botanical writings to support his case.[175] Rupert also includes the information that the heavens revolve at a fixed speed, that the sun is larger than the moon or earth and serves as a source of heat and warmth, all ideas which he seems to have derived from Macrobius.[176] Hugh of Amiens, Gilbert de la Porrée, William of Conches, (c.1080–c.1154), Bernard Sylvester, and other exegetes adopted a similar attitude.[177] But these individuals were not literalists in the way that the reformers were, for their concern was not to do away with allegory, but to insist that literal readings had an equal claim to legitimacy. It must also be conceded that the principle adopted by the reformers – that only the literal sense of scripture was of use in matters of theological disputation – had been a long-standing rule in the Roman Church, endorsed by both Augustine and Aquinas, and most advocates of four-fold interpretation still insisted the literal sense was foundational.[178] This insistence, however, was motivated by the recognition that the superstructure of allegory could not be erected unless the literal meaning had first established what objects the words of the text referred to. The priority accorded to this level of interpretation meant simply that the literal meaning was the first in order, but not necessarily in importance. The

[175] Rupert of Deutz, *Gen.* 1.22–5; 2.24–5; 3.29–30. In this connexion John Van Engen remarks that Rupert's commentary on Genesis 'appears to be the first commentary on Genesis to reflect a newly revived interest in nature and cosmology', *Rupert of Deutz*, p. 85. Attempts to account for 'waters above the firmament' provide evidence of the extent of a commentator's scientific commitment. Abelard, for example did not think it inappropriate to cite God as the immediate cause of events during the days of creation. Others, like Thierry and Rupert, thought that some naturalistic explanation ought to be attempted. See, for example, Abelard, *Hexaemeron* (*PL* 178, 749). The assertion that there were real waters above the firmament, incidentally, was at odds with the Aristotelian division between celestial and terrestrial regions, which implied that corruptible earthly waters could not be found in the heavens.

[176] Van Engen, *Rupert of Deutz*, p. 86.

[177] Häring, 'Commentary and Hermeneutics', p. 195; Crombie, *From Augustine to Galileo*, pp. 13–18; Stock, *Myth and Science in the Twelfth Century* (Princeton University Press, 1972) pp. 237–73; Richard Dales, 'A Twelfth-Century Concept of the Natural Order', *Viator* 9 (1978) 172–92. The specific complaint was levelled against William of Conches, that he 'interpreted in a physical sense' certain passages of Genesis, thus drawing ridicule upon the 'history of divine authority'. *HMES* ii, 60. Toby Huff writes correctly that 'the organised scepticism which we associate with the modern, present-day views of things . . . begins not later than the biblical criticism of the twelfth and thirteenth centuries'. *The Rise of Early Modern Science*, p. 336. But Huff is mistaken when he identifies this 'biblical criticism' with the triumph of 'rational demonstration' over 'biblical literalism'. On the contrary, this critical tendency led to an insistence on primacy of the literal sense. The link between literalism and scientific concerns begins in the twelfth century.   [178] Aquinas, *ST* 1a.1.10.

medieval assertion that the literal sense was the foundation of all
interpretation was thus consistent with the view that biblical texts were
equivocal. Over all, evidence from medieval commentaries supports
Chenu's assertion that throughout the Middle Ages systematic allegorisation had universally destroyed the literal text of scripture.[179] By way of
contrast, when the reformers championed the literal sense their concern
was to deny the indeterminacy of meaning of canonical texts, and thus
to insist that each passage of scripture had but a single, fixed meaning.
Protestant exegetes were to use a variety of terms to express this
approach – literal sense, grammatical sense, historical sense, plain
sense.[180] It was always possible that such an approach would lead to a
situation where the single sense of some biblical passage was not, strictly,
its literal sense, as for example in the parables of Jesus, or the prophecies
of Revelation. Protestant 'literalism' thus needs to be broadly conceived
as an assertion of the determinacy of meaning of biblical texts, a
meaning which usually, though not invariably, will lie with the literal
sense.

It must also be recognised that Catholic deference to tradition, and in
particular, to the exegetical writings of the Fathers, always informed
contemporary readings. The history of interpretation thus remained an
inescapable fact for Catholic exegetes in a way that was less true for
Protestants, who might consult past authorities, but were not bound by
them. However much Catholic commentators might have wished to
elevate the literal sense of the text, as increasingly they did during the
seventeenth century, it was difficult for them to extricate themselves
from a ongoing history of interpretation which had burdened biblical
texts with meanings which went well beyond the literal.[181] So it was that
both figural and literal readings of various passages of scripture might be
ranged against theological opponents, or indeed, practitioners of the
new science. When Galileo reported the discovery of the moons of
Jupiter in his *Siderus nuncius* (1610), a young Tuscan named Francesco
Sizzi responded in a small work entitled *Dianoia astronomica*. Here he
argued that scripture teaches the existence of but seven celestial orbs
(sun, moon, and five visible planets), for the Fathers had agreed that the

---

[179] Chenu, *Nature, Man and Society*, p. 117; Moeller, 'Scripture, Tradition, and Sacrament', pp. 121–3.
[180] Thus Luther: '"Literal meaning" is not a good term . . . Those who call it "grammatical,
historical meaning" do better.' *Answer to a Hyperchristian Book, Luther's Works*, 39, 181. Cf. Paul
Noble, 'The *Sensus Literalis*', *Journal of Theological Studies*, (NS) 44 (1993), 1–23.
[181] Compare, for example, Calvin's treatment of the story of the Deluge, with that of the great
Catholic exegete Pererius. Calvin, *Commentary on Genesis*, pp. 257f.; Pererius, *Commentariorvm in
Genesin*, pp. 446–8.

seven lamps of the golden candelabra referred to in Exodus 25.37 and
Zechariah 4.2 symbolise these heavenly bodies.[182] Of course, literal
readings of various passages were also used against Galileo. One of the
most frequently cited references in this controversy was the episode in
which Joshua commanded the sun to stand still.[183] Francesco Ingoli
(1578–1649) in *De situ et quiete terrae contra copernici systema disputatio* put the
argument this way: 'Replies which assert that Scripture speaks according to our mode of understanding are not satisfactory: both because in
explaining the Sacred Writings the rule is always to preserve the literal
sense, when that is possible, as it is in this case; and also because all the
Fathers unanimously take this passage to mean that the sun which was
moving truly stopped at Joshua's request.'[184] Thus it was the patristic
interpretation of scripture, whether allegorical or literal, which told
against Galileo's views. Whether texts were taken literally or allegorically, the important feature of any permissible reading was whether it
had gained the past approval of the Fathers and the present sanction of
the Church. Catholic readings of scripture, however much they might
have been influenced by the tendency of the period to give priority to
the literal sense, had always to pass the final test of agreement with the
opinions of the Fathers. While hermeneutical innovation was limited by
the constraints of tradition, controversies between Protestants and advocates of the new science on the one hand, and Catholics on the other,
tended in the final analysis to amount to a conflict between some
innovation in science or religion based on reason or historical critical
method and some traditional position supported by authorities past or
present. The plight of the Catholic natural philosophers was well expressed by Kepler:

Let me say this about the authority of the sacred writings. To the opinions of the
saints about their nature, I reply with one word. In theology the influence of
authority should be present, but in philosophy it is the influence of reason that
should be present. St. Lactantius denied that the earth is round; St. Augustine
conceded its roundness but denied the antipodes; today the Holy Office
concedes the smallness of the earth but denies its motion. But for me the holy
truth has been demonstrated by philosophy, with due respect to the Doctors of

[182] Blackwell, *Galileo, Bellarmine, and the Bible*, p. 57. Stillman Drake, *Galileo at Work: His Scientific Biography* (University of Chicago Press, 1978) p. 467.
[183] Standard passages used against Galileo: Genesis 1.17, Joshua 12.10, I Chronicles 16.30, Psalm 104.5, Proverbs 8.25, 27.3, 30.3, Isaiah 40.12, Job 26.7, Ecclesiastes 1.5.
[184] Galileo, *Opere* v, 411, qu. in Blackwell, *Galileo, Bellarmine, and the Bible*, p. 63; Cf. Brooke, *Science and Religion*, pp. 97f.

the Church, that the earth is round, that its antipodes are inhabited, that it is quite despicably small, and finally that it moves through the stars.[185]

As Kepler identifies it, the chief impediment to improvements in natural philosophy lay not with the text of scripture, but with the decrees of the Holy Office and the opinions of the Doctors of the Church. For the Protestants, these same barriers had served to impede the reformation of religion. The fortunes of the Protestant Reformation and the scientific enterprise were linked in this way as well, for the downfall of an entrenched tradition would serve the purposes of each.

The reasons for the literal turn of the Protestant Reformers are not hard to identify. The quest for origins, which characterises humanism and Protestantism alike, arose out of a new historical consciousness, and with that, the realisation that texts have a history. In Protestant hermeneutics this awareness manifested itself not only in the quest for more accurate texts of authoritative documents, but also in the attempt to determine to exactly what ancient authorities had said or written. In fact, the humanist project which aimed at establishing more faithful texts was premised upon the belief that what an author originally wrote and intended, as opposed to what subsequent commentators thought about the text, was important. Hence the growing preference of Erasmus, as his career progressed, for literal rather than allegorical interpretation. With this new approach to texts, the focus shifted away from the process by which the written work could be aligned with some known truth, to what an author had originally written and meant to communicate. More importantly, however, if the Bible alone was to be the final court of appeal on matters of religious doctrine, it would need to be interpreted in a way which reduced ambiguities and multiple meanings. Only a literal method, or more strictly a method which allowed but a single meaning to be assigned to each passage of scripture, could serve this purpose. 'If you offer any Text to prove such or such a Doctrine', pointed out seventeenth-century Calvinist John Edwards, 'it will easily be evaded if the Letter may not be our Guide; for it is but saying, The Place is not meant as the Words sound, but must be taken figuratively and mystically.'[186] Finally, there was little point in translating the Bible into the vernacular if those for whom the translation was primarily intended could not easily

---

[185] Introduction to *Astronomia nova* (*Gesammelte Werke* III, 18–36) ET in *The Great Ideas Today 1983*, pp. 309–23.

[186] Edwards, *Discourse concerning the Old and New Testament, II*, 41f. 'If scripture is an obscure fog', Luther wrote to an opponent, 'how can you use it as a sharp weapon against me?' *Answer to a Hyperchristian Book, Luther's Works*, 39, 167.

grasp its meaning. For prospective new readers of the Bible, functional literacy was challenge enough without having to confront the complexities of tropology, anagogy and allegory. If the written word of scripture was to achieve the prominence in the Christian life which the Reformers desired, meaning, inevitably, had to reside in the plain sense. 'The Holy Spirit is the simplest writer and adviser in heaven and on earth', wrote Luther. 'That is why his words could have no more than the one simplest meaning which we call the written one or the literal meaning.'[187] Thomas Cranmer, one of the architects of the English Reformation, reiterated the sentiment in the preface to the Great Bible of 1540: 'The apostles and prophets wrote their books so that their special intent and purpose might be understanded and perceived by every reader.'[188]

The Protestant insistence on the literal sense of canonical texts had far-reaching, if unintended, consequences. As we have seen, the allegorical reading of scripture proceeded from a particular attitude to the world of things. The allegorical methods of interpretation pioneered by Philo and Origen were premised upon the notion that the things in the phenomenal world referred to by words in canonical texts actually represented, through resemblance, other things. To insist now that texts be read literally was to cut short a potentially endless chain of references in which words referred to things, and things in turn referred to other things. A literal reading of scripture was one in which the previously open-ended process of deriving a series of references from a single word was terminated once a word had performed its basic task of referring to a thing.[189] The assertion of the primacy of literal reading, in other words, entailed a new, non-symbolic conception of the nature of things. No longer were objects in the natural world linked to each other by sets of resemblances. As an inevitable consequence of this way of reading texts nature would lose its meaning, and the vacuum created by this loss of intelligibility was gradually to be occupied by alternative accounts of the significance of natural things – those explanations which we regard as scientific. In the new scheme of things, objects were related mathematically, mechanically, causally, or ordered and classified according to

---

[187] *Luther's Works*, 39, 178. Luther's literalism was also motivated by the belief that words retained some of the properties of the original language of Adam, being natural signs which expressed something of the true nature of things. The Holy Spirit's gift of tongues (Acts 2.4–11) reinforced this view of the nature of language. See Peter Meinhold, *Luthers Sprachphilosophie* (Berlin, 1958), pp. 32–44.

[188] Gerald Bray (ed.), *Documents of the English Reformation* (Cambridge: James Clarke, 1994), p. 237.

[189] On these implications of literalism, see Ferdinand de Escalante, *Clypevs concionatorvm versi dei* (Hispali, 1611), ch. 23, cols. 112–17; and Serarius, *Prolegomena biblica* (1612). Also see Madsen, *Shadowy Types*, pp. 18–53.

categories other than those of resemblance. John Ray, in the preface to the *Ornithology* might thus have implied that 'proper' natural history needed forcibly to displace an effete and impoverished humane science which had hitherto commanded the domain of natural things. In fact the things of nature had already been abandoned by the humane sciences, a state of affairs which finds its origin in the reading strategies of the Protestant reformers.

The process by which reference became the exclusive domain of words, while most evident in that approach to texts which was to become the standard mode of interpretation for the whole of the modern period, was reinforced by other features of reformed religion. It was not only natural objects which were denied signifying powers, but also those human artefacts which had been designed solely to exercise a symbolic function. The iconoclastic frenzy unleashed by the Reformation represents in a graphic, if unfortunate, way the desire to restrict to words those capabilities once shared with alternative modes of representation. Images painted onto canvas or plaster, constructed from pieces of stained glass or coloured tile, or carved into wood and stone, bore the brunt of the Reformers' iconoclastic zeal. The impact of these activities was devastating in another sense as well. Describing the effects of Protestant iconoclasm in sixteenth-century England, Eamon Duffy writes that 'for most of the first Elizabethan adult generation, Reformation was a stripping away of familiar and beloved observances, the destruction of a vast and resonant world of symbols'.[190] Iconoclasm, agrees Margaret Aston, 'affected the whole fabric of worship and the ways in which people believed'.[191]

The explicit ideological source of Protestant iconoclasm was the identification of various aspects of Catholic ritual as idolatry – the 'one religious error larger than all the others' according to Anthony Milton, and 'an error which made Rome's guild almost uniquely despicable'.[192] Whether the charge was true is somewhat moot, but this much is clear: If the things of nature, created by God, no longer resonate with symbolic potency, then those human artefacts which had once participated in that universe of meaning at one remove will be similarly mute. When the representative functions conventionally attributed to religious symbols are denied, a preoccupation with them is easily seen to be superstitious

---

[190] *Stripping of the Altars*, p. 591.
[191] Margaret Aston, *England's Iconoclasts*, vol. 1 (Oxford: Clarendon, 1988), p. 16; Cf. Ian Green, *The Christian's ABC: Catechisms and Catechising in England, c. 1530–1748* (Oxford: Clarendon, 1996), pp. 431–7. [192] Milton, *Catholic and Reformed*, p. 187; Aston, pp. 343f.

and idolatrous. In short, iconoclasm with respect to images directly parallels literalism with respect to texts. Denial of any level of meaning except the literal has the implication that objects do not refer. If objects do not refer, then their use as aids in worship is at best pointless, at worst idolatrous.

Protestant forms of worship thus helped shift the focus from symbol to word. Indeed the whole sensory context of worship – visual, spatial, auditory – was radically altered.[193] Rood lofts were dismantled, elaborately wrought screens defaced, niches which had once housed statues were bricked in, altars removed or reoriented. In reformed churches, services which previously had been centred upon the mass and its symbolic objects now tended to focus instead on the reading of scripture and its exposition. The catholic doctrine of transubstantiation, upon which much of significance of the mass had lain was now condemned as the paradigm case of idolatry, in which ordinary elements were blasphemously worshipped as the very being of God.[194] In fact the whole range of sacramental acts which had played a central role in the regulation of medieval lives from birth to death attracted Protestant censure. The term *sacramentum* had been used by the Fathers in the broad sense of 'figure', 'allegory', 'enigma' – the same categories used to interpret sacred scripture. Augustine's meaning of *sacramentum* had thus been 'inseparable from the spiritual interpretation of scripture itself'.[195] With the denial of the symbolic aspects of the interpretation of scripture, the sacramental emphasis of medieval piety was also reframed. Literalism also dealt a second, and more direct blow to the prevailing sacramental practice: of the seven Catholic sacraments, reformed churches were to retain only the two they considered to have been explicitly sanctioned by the literal words of scripture: baptism and eucharist. Even the eucharist, in many of the reformed liturgies, was reduced to a memorial meal. The change in the status of this rite was profound. Miri Rubin writes that 'in the Middle Ages the languages of religion provided a language of social relation and of a cosmic order; it described and explained the interweaving of natural and supernatural with human action, in a paradigm which from about 1100 was one of sacramentality, with the eucharist at its heart'.[196] By the end of the sixteenth century this world was in chaos, and its once potent vision of the cosmic order, of the deeper meanings of the material realm, of the interpenetration of natural and supernatural, was in irrevocable decline.

[193] Duffy, *Stripping of the Altars*, p. 472.   [194] Milton, *Catholic and Reformed*, pp. 196–205.
[195] Stock, *The Implications of Literacy*, pp. 241–59.   [196] Rubin, *Corpus Christi*, p. 1.

Its central rite was retained merely as a concession to the ignorant – in the dismissive pronouncement of the Augsburg Confession (1530): 'For therefore alone we have need of ceremonies, that they may teach the unlearned.'[197] The Protestant Reformation, by promoting the culture of the literal word, effected a dramatic contraction of the sphere of the sacred, forcibly stripping objects, natural and artificial, of the roles they had once played as bearers of meaning.

On a more positive note, Protestantism actively promoted its preferred system of representation, sponsoring the translation of the scriptures into the vernacular, and encouraging the reading of the Bible, the prayer book, sermons, and other devotional works. In places of worship, written versions of the ten commandments and the Lord's prayer came to replace coloured glass, carvings, and saints on pedestals.[198] On newly whitewashed walls, representations of the saints and apostles gave way to texts condemning the worship of graven images and idols.[199] Bibles in the vernacular were to be made available to the people, and the clergy were enjoined to 'expressly provoke, stir, and exhort every person' to read, or at least listen to, the word.[200] Books, it was generally thought, could more than adequately fulfil all of the previous functions of images with none of the attendant dangers. Even those not ill-disposed towards images now tended to regard them merely as a substitute for books. The final article of The Thirteen Articles (1538) explains: 'In so far as images of Christ and the saints can serve the illiterate instead of books, in instances where written books might remind them of their histories and deeds, we think they may be usefully set up.'[201] Edward Lee, Archbishop of York (d. 1544) allowed 'that images be suffered only as books, by which our hearts may be kindled to follow the holy steps and example of the saints represented by the same'.[202] Depictions of scenes of Christ, the saints and apostles might thus serve as devices to aid the memories of those denied access to the written word. Indeed, 'images', according to the Edwardian Injunctions (1547), 'serve for no other purpose but to be a remembrance'.[203] So it was that even justifications for the retention of images were couched in terms which implied the superiority of the written word. If words had once brought to mind objects and the transcendental truths which they signified, now the polarity of reference

---

[197] Bray, *Documents*, p. 625.

[198] David Cressy, *Literacy and the Social Order* (Cambridge University Press, 1980), p. 3.

[199] S. Brigden, *London and the Reformation* (Oxford: Clarendon, 1989), pp. 426f.

[200] 'The Second Henrician Injunctions' (1538), Bray, *Documents*, p. 179.

[201] Bray, *Documents*, p. 219.   [202] Duffy, *Stripping of the Altars*, p. 413.   [203] Bray, *Documents*, p. 249.

was reversed. Objects served merely as reminders of words, biblical texts, and doctrinal propositions.

A far preferable alternative to these concessions to ignorance was to read to the illiterate, or better still, teach them to read for themselves. Protestant clergy accordingly urged their flocks to avail themselves of the advantages of literacy. Puritan Nicholas Brownde recommended in 1595 'so many as can read, let them do it upon the Lord's day, and they that cannot, let them see the want of it to be so great in themselves that they bring up their children unto it'.[204] In the seventeenth century, the moderate puritan divine Richard Baxter repeated the plea: 'Let children be taught to read . . . or else you will deprive them of a singular help to their salvation.'[205] Whether this rhetoric was matched by educational reforms and increasing numbers of readers remains unclear. Certainly post-reformation Scotland and puritan New England enjoyed remarkable rates of literacy, in the latter case unsurpassed in the pre-industrial world. These advances have been plausibly linked to the influence of Protestantism.[206] It has also been claimed in this connexion that the Protestant Reformation owes much of its success to the printing press.[207] A culture of word rather than symbol would be difficult, if not impossible, to propagate in an environment which lacked cheap paper and moveable type, a fact not overlooked by the reformers themselves. John Foxe observed in his *Actes and Monumentes* (1563) that 'either the pope must abolish knowledge and printing, or printing must at length root him out'.[208] But it is equally true that the printing trade was one of the major beneficiaries of Protestant promotion of literacy. The publication of Protestant works in the sixteenth and seventeenth centuries helped establish printing as a major industry.[209] If the printing press had promoted the interests of the Reformation in its initial stages, Protestant religion was to return the favour with interest.[210]

It is perhaps worth mentioning that later in the sixteenth century even

[204] Qu. in Cressy, *Literacy and the Social Order*, p. 3.   [205] *Christian Directory*, p. 548.

[206] Kenneth Lockridge, *Literacy in Colonial New England* (New York, 1974), p. 12; Lawrence Stone, 'Literacy and Education in England, 1640–1900', *Past and Present* 42 (1969) 67–139 (80f.). Cf. Cressy, *Literacy and the Social Order* pp. 183 and passim; Charles Webster, 'Puritanism, Separatism, Science', in Lindberg and Numbers (eds.) *God and Nature*, pp. 192–217 (205f.).

[207] See Eisenstein, *The Printing Press*.

[208] *The Actes and Monumentes of John Foxe*, ed. G. Townsend and S. Cattley (London,1837–41) III, 720.

[209] Stone, 'Literacy and Education', p. 79; but cf. Duffy, *Stripping of the Altars*, pp. 77–87.

[210] On the market for books in seventeenth-century England, see Stone, 'Literacy and Education', p. 99, H. S. Bennett, *English Books and Readers, 1603–1640* (Cambridge University Press, 1970), pp. 78f.; Cressy, *Literacy and the Social Order*, pp. 45–52.

the minor mnemonic duties grudgingly allocated to images were challenged. Frenchman Peter Ramus, the most prominent educational reformer of his age, had proposed a new system of memory which eschewed the central feature of classical and renaissance models, the visual image. Memory, for Ramus and his followers, was a dialectical or logical operation, not an exercise of the imagination. In the words of Frances Yates:

No more will places in church or other buildings be vividly impressed on the imagination. And, above all, gone in the Ramist system are the images, the emotionally striking and stimulating images the use of which had come down through the centuries from the art of the classical rhetor. The 'natural stimulus' for memory is now not the emotionally exciting memory image; it is the abstract order of dialectical analysis which is yet, for Ramus, 'natural', since dialectical order is natural to the mind.[211]

The methods of Ramus enjoyed enormous vogue in Protestant Europe, his posthumous popularity boosted no doubt by his martyrdom as a Huguenot on the eve of the St Bartholomew's Day massacre, 1572.[212] However, it was his opposition to Aristotle and the incipient iconoclasm of his pedagogical techniques which most endeared him to those entrusted with the education of young Protestant minds. In England the system of Ramus was championed initially by the vigorously anti-Romanist divine, William Perkins, who during the 1580s directed a short series of tracts against a competing conception of memory which combined with the classical model elements of magic and hermeticism. After a brief hiatus, Ramism went on to further successes under the sponsorship of puritan educational reformers in the seventeenth century. More directly relevant to our present discussion, William Perkins, we will not be surprised to learn, also authored a work condemning the idolatry of popery, lamenting the fact that 'the remainders of poperie yet stick in the minds of many'. People still retained popish idols and images in their houses, rehearsing the excuse common to both papists and gentiles, 'that Images are Laiemens bookes'. This, however, was not a sufficient justification for their retention, for learning and recollection do not require the formation of mental images: 'So soone as the minde frames unto it selfe any forme of God . . . an idol is set up in the mind. . . .

[211] *The Art of Memory* (London: Pimlico, 1992), pp. 230f.
[212] On the fortunes of Ramism in Europe and England, see Howard Hotson, 'Philosophical Pedagogy in Reformed Central Europe between Ramus and Comenius: A Survey of the Continental Background of the Three Foreigners', in Greengrass et al. (eds.) *Samuel Hartlib*, pp. 29–50. On Ramism generally, W. J. Ong, *Ramus: Method and the Decay of Dialogue* (Cambridge, Mass: Harvard University Press, 1958).

A thing feigned in the mind by imagination is an idol.'[213] Thus in addition to the more conspicuous monuments of Roman idolatry, the residues of papism were still exemplified in certain habits of mind. These, too, demanded reformation.

The ideology of Protestantism and the material practices it propagated played a key role in that profound transition in which, as Lawrence Stone describes it, 'Europe moved decisively from an image culture to a word culture'.[214] The sacred rite which had lain at the heart of medieval culture was replaced by a text, symbolic objects gave way to words, ritual practices were eclipsed by propositional beliefs and dogmas. In the course of this process, that unified interpretive endeavour which had given meanings to both natural world and sacred text began to disintegrate. Meaning and intelligibility were ascribed to words and texts, but denied to living things and inanimate objects. The natural world, once the indispensable medium between words and eternal truths, lost its meanings, and became opaque to those hermeneutical procedures which had once elucidated it. It was left to an emerging natural science to reinvest the created order with intelligibility. Thus was one of the hallmarks of modernity, the triumph of the written text and the identification of its meaning with authorial intention, to give rise to another – that systematic, materialistic understanding of the world embodied in the privileged discourses of natural science.

[213] W. Perkins, *A Warning against the Idolatry of the Last Times*, in *Works* (Cambridge, 1603), pp. 811, 833, 830, 841. Qu. in Yates, *Art of Memory*, p. 270.

[214] Stone, 'Literacy and Education', p. 78.

negative theology

CHAPTER 4

Re-reading the two books

There is no part of true philosophy, no art of account, no kind of
science rightly so called, but the scripture must contain it.
Richard Hooker, *Laws of Ecclesiastical Polity*

All things here shew him heaven . . .
trees, herbs, flowers, all
Strive upwards stil, and point him the way home.
Henry Vaughan, 'The Tempest'

By the word of God heavens existed long ago, and an earth formed
out of water and by means of water, through which the world that
then existed was deluged with water and perished. But by the same
word the heavens and earth that now exist have been stored up for
fire, being kept until the day of judgement and destruction of
ungodly men. But do not ignore this one fact, beloved, that with the
Lord one day is as a thousand years, and a thousand years as one
day. . . . the day of the Lord will come like a thief, and then the
heavens will pass away with a loud noise, and the elements will be
dissolved with fire, and the earth and the works that are upon it will
be burned up. . . But according to his promise we wait for new
heavens and a new earth in which righteousness dwells.
II Peter 3. 5–13.

Moses must be so interpreted in the first Chapter of *Genesis*, as not to
interfere with himself in other parts of his History; nor to interfere
with S. *Peter*, or the Prophet *David*, or any other Sacred Authors,
when they treat of the same matter. Nor lastly, so as to be repug-
nant to clear and uncontested Science. For, in things that concern
the natural World, that must always be consulted.
Thomas Burnet, *A Review of the Theory of the Earth*

GENESIS AND HISTORY

One of the important foundations of the four-fold method of interpretation had been the assumption that scripture was a unitary text which

contained eternal truths which transcended time and place. The *quadriga* enabled exegetes to assign to every passage of scripture some present meaning. Medieval hermeneutics thus tended to blind readers to the historical nature of these texts – texts which for the modern reader have as their most obvious feature their historicity. These words, it is plain to us, were written in another time, about another time, addressed to an audience inhabiting a thought-world very different from our own. For the medieval reader, however, historical narratives were made contemporaneous through an application of the higher levels of interpretation. Allegory, tropology, and anagogy were vehicles which transported the sacred text through historical time into the present. Accounts of past events, as such, were simply unedifying. Only when relevant morals were drawn, only when theological truths became evident, did the texts speak to the present. With the new biblical literalism which followed in the wake of the Reformation, many portions of scripture were read for the first time as having, as their primary sense, history. The significance of narrative passages of the Bible now lay in the fact that they recounted things which had happened hundreds or thousands of years ago.[1] Whereas the accounts of creation in the book of Genesis had previously provided scope for the imaginations of exegetes given to allegory, now the significance of these stories was seen to lie in their literal truth as depicting past events. As a measure of this development, the status of Moses underwent a subtle change. From being a leading actor in the drama of the Exodus, he became 'the sacred historian', 'the father of history', an author and natural philosopher, an historical figure, who had written a factual account of the first ages of the earth, the significance of which was historical, not figurative or allegorical. The contents of the book of Genesis attracted new descriptions: 'the history of creation', 'mosaical history', 'scripture-history', the 'mosaick history of creation', 'the history recorded by Moses'.[2] At the same time, in a typically modern way, information about presumed authors and their intended audience came to be regarded as essential to a proper reading of the relevant text. In what was to become the standard pattern for

---

[1] Frei, *Eclipse of Biblical Narrative*, p.40.

[2] See, e.g., Simon Patrick, *A Commentary*, preface; George Walker, *History of Creation*; Robert Jenkin, *Reasonableness and Certainty*, p. x; William Nicholls, *A Conference*, pp. 169, 250–2; John Edwards, *Brief Remarks upon Mr. Whiston's New Theory of the Earth* (London, 1697), Epistle Dedicatory, p. 29; Keill, *An Examination*, pp. 11, 12; Whiston, *New Theory*, title page and passim; Stillingfleet, *Origines Sacrae*, 7th edn (Cambridge, 1702), p. 71; John Harris, *Remarks on Some Later Papers Relating to the Universal Deluge* (London, 1697), p. 63.

commentaries, George Hughes' *Analytical Exposition of the first Book of Moses* (1672) is prefaced by biographical information about its presumed author – his genealogy, place of birth, education, the time of his writing, the language in which he wrote, and the end or use of his work. Authorial intention was also seen as providing insight into the meaning of a text. 'The Design of the Writer', insisted Jean Le Clerc, 'is of great Importance towards the better understanding of his Writings.'[3] Most of this would have been quite foreign to those familiar with the allegorical interpretation of scripture. The Fathers had assumed that the intentions of the human author were subservient to the truth of the text. 'God has tempered the sacred books to the interpretations of many, who could come to see a diversity of truths', wrote Augustine.[4] In writing the book of Genesis, Moses might have 'had in mind perhaps only one out of the many true interpretations'.[5] According to the traditional Augustinian mode of interpretation, the truth of the sacred text transcended the merely human motivations of the writer.[6] The interpretation of a text had involved the alignment of its contents with truth, and this meant setting aside speculations about the intentions of the author and abandoning any notion that a text had a determinate meaning. The increasing visibility of authors was now to contribute to the process in which the sacred text came to be both anchored in historical time, and utilised as an historical source.

This new historical sense is reflected in a parallel transformation in the understanding of religious rites. In the medieval mass Christ was literally made contemporary with the participants: divine grace was present and efficacious. The mass was 'geared towards the present'.[7] In

---

[3] Le Clerc, *Twelve Dissertations*, p. 105; Cf. Francis Roberts, *Clavis Bibliorum. The Key of the Bible* (Edinburgh, 1649), pp. 36–9; Richard Bernard, *The Faithfull Shepheard*, p. 20; Boyle, *Considerations touching the style of the Holy Scriptures*, *Works* II, 260. The idea that author intention was the defining characteristic of literal sense had originally been suggested by William of Nottingham and Nicholas of Lyra. The latter is thought by some to have influenced Luther's hermeneutics. See Evans, *Language and Logic of the Bible*, p. 43f.   [4] *Confessions*, XII.xxxi (p. 271).

[5] *Ibid.* Cf. XII.xxiii–xxiv.

[6] Authors had already been given prominence in some of the twelfth-century schools. Peter Abelard opens his commentaries on Porphyry, Boethius, and Aristotle with such statements as: 'the intention [*intentio*] of Porphyry is . . . ', 'the intention, subject [*materia*] and purpose [*finalis causa*] of Aristotle is . . . ', 'the intention of Boethius is . . .'. See Nikolaus Häring, 'Commentary and Hermeneutics', in Robert Benson and Giles Constable (eds.) *Renaissance and Renewal in the Twelfth Century* (Cambridge, Mass.: Harvard University Press, 1982), 173–200 (185). Abelard also expresses an interest in Moses' intention. *Expositio in Hexameron* I (*PL* 178, 732D); cf. Honorius Augustodunensis, *Expositio in Cantica Canticorum* (*PL* 172, 347D). This does not prevent Abelard from engaging in allegorical interpretation, however. See *Expositio in hexaemeron* I (*PL* 178, 759–60).

[7] Rubin, *Corpus Christi*, p. 348

the early Church, by way of contrast, the sacrament had an eschatological, future orientation. For most Protestant confessions it was to become a memorial meal, and take on a backward-looking, commemorative aspect.[8] The Augsburg Confession declared that 'the mass has been instituted that faith in them which use the sacrament may remember what benefits it receiveth by Christ, and that it may raise and comfort the fearful conscience. For this is to remember Christ, to wit, to remember his benefits'.[9] Reading the words of the institution of this sacrament thus became, in the Protestant context, a reminder of an historical event, in Catholicism, it was a performative utterance. The Church of England, always somewhat ambivalent about the nature of the Eucharist and reluctant to deny the real presence, nonetheless asserted of lesser rites that their function was to link individuals to an historical past. According to the 'Ten Articles' of 1536, which codify the first official doctrine of Anglicanism, the sprinkling of holy water was 'to put us in remembrance of our baptism', holy bread 'to put us in remembrance of the sacrament of the altar', candles at Candlemass (2 February) to put us 'in memory of Christ the spiritual light'.[10] These ceremonies were significant not for their present potency, but as reminders of the past. Images of Christ and the saints, too, as we have seen, were allowed to serve only as reminders of their 'histories and deeds'.[11] Ritual acts thus tended to become subservient to the written record. The Bible provided the script for the acting out of those past events to which it presently bore witness.

The emphasis on the historicity of the biblical text, and on the circumstances of its human authors, had the inevitable consequence of reducing the gap between scripture and other writings. The procedure for the interpretation of scripture adopted by the puritans, wrote William Bradshaw at the turn of the seventeenth century, was 'to follow those rules onely that are followed in finding out the meaning of other writings, to wit, by waying the properties of the proprietie of the tongue wherein they are written, by waying the Circumstance of the place, by comparing one place with another, and by considerynge what is properly spoken, and what tropically or figuratively'.[12] Henry Hammond, one of the pioneers of English biblical criticism, also insisted that the Bible was to be understood by 'the use of ordinary means', and not through the 'extraordinary gift of the spirit'. By 'ordinary means', Hammond meant 'the use of learning, study, meditations, rational inference, colla-

---

[8] Moeller, 'Scripture, Tradition, and Sacrament', p. 123.   [9] Bray, *Documents*, p. 628.
[10] *Ibid.*, pp. 172f.   [11] Ten Articles; Edwardian Injunctions, *ibid.*, pp. 219, 249.
[12] William Bradshaw, *English Puritanisme* (London, 1605), p. 18.

tion of places, consulting of the original languages, and ancient copies and expositions of the Fathers of the church . . . and the like'.[13] The meaning of biblical writers was to 'be attained by the same means, or the like, by which other writings of men are expounded'.[14] Thus while in principle freedom to determine the meaning of the sacred text was given to individual readers of scripture, it was hoped at the same time that such readers would voluntarily submit themselves to a set of publicly available, rational, and universal canons of interpretation.

On account of the diminishing distance between scripture and other ancient writings the differences between them came to be regarded as more a matter of degree than kind. Scripture was no longer a magical text, the meanings of which somehow transcended the intentions of its human authors. Reading it had ceased to be a ritual act in which the reader was transported beyond the threshold of the present into a timeless eternity. Defenders of the inspiration of scripture now resorted to the argument that while the Bible might cover some of the same ground as writings of purely human origin, it was, in these areas, incomparably superior to profane works. The books of the Old Testament contained history, just like other chronologies: but the history recounted in scripture was uniquely reliable. 'In all other writings', wrote Bishop Stillingfleet, 'we have a *mixture* of *dross* and *gold*', but in scripture 'is nothing but *pure gold, Diamonds* without *flaws, Suns* without *spots*'.[15] Antiquarian Thomas Hearne insisted that the particular excellence of the Pentateuch lay in the fact that its author was of greater antiquity than such revered writers as Homer, Thales, and Pythagoras.[16] Moses' account of the creation and Deluge, John Arbuthnot asserted, 'surpasses all the accounts of Philosophers as much in Wisdom, as it doth in Authority'.[17] Newtonian Samuel Clarke, the most able English theologian of his age, wrote that 'Among the writings of all,

[13] Henry Hammond, 'A Postscript concerning New Light, or Divine Illumination', in *A Paraphrase and Annotations upon all the Books of the New Testament* 4 vols. (London, 1659) I, xix. Cf. Hammond, *A Paraphrase and Annotations upon the Books of the Psalms*, 2 vols., 1653, Preface; Bernard, *Faithfull Shepheard*, pp. 27–42; Le Clerc, *Twelve Dissertations*, passim; Boyle, Letter to John Mallet, Jan. 1652/3, *Works*, I, li. Also see Richard Kroll, *The Material World: Literate Culture in the Restoration and Early Eighteenth Century*, (Johns Hopkins University Press, 1991) pp. 253–60. Ironically, this would mean that the bare words of scripture, so painstakingly distilled from the *Glossa ordinaria* by Luther, were destined, almost from the start, to be enveloped in the glosses of new authorities. The Geneva Bible, so beloved of the puritans, was thus accompanied by extensive marginalia. The authority of these glosses, however, was derived not from the Church, but from a new and independent interpretive discipline which had emerged out of the labours of the humanists.
[14] Hammond, *Paraphrase of the New Testament*, Advertisement to the Reader.
[15] Stillingfleet, *Origines Sacrae*, (1662 edn) p. 613.
[16] Thomas Hearne, *Ductor Historicus* (London, 1698), pp. ii, 127.
[17] John Arbuthnot, *An Examination of Dr Woodward's Account of the Deluge* (London, 1697), p. 29.

even the most ancient and learned Nations, there are *None but* the books of the *Jews*, which [have] given any tolerable account in particular, of the *Formation* of *this our earth* into its present *habitable State*.'[18] David Collyer thought that Genesis alone contained 'all we know of the History of the World for above sixteen hundred years', while Timothy Nourse argued that the Bible's singular merit resulted from a number of factors – its antiquity, its plain and unadorned style, the lack of bias in its presentation, and the fact that it had been the source from which all other ancient chronologies had derived their information.[19] The Bible thus came to compete with secular writings on their own ground, although its superiority to all competitors was at this time widely granted.

The new status accorded scripture as a result of these developments meant that not every passage of holy writ could be read for its moral or theological message. Where the Bible was not obviously – that is at a literal level – conveying theological or moral information, it was thought to provide knowledge relating to history and geography, or the arts and sciences.[20] Indeed, allegory and tropology were now regarded as having for centuries blinded readers to the history and science which could be found in the scriptures. John Donne observed in this connexion that 'by the example of our late learned Reformers, I forbear this [allegorical] interpretation; the rather because we are utterly dis-provided of any history of the World's Creation, except we defend and maintain this Book of *Moses* to be Historical, and therefore literally to be interpreted'.[21] The import of Donne's claim becomes apparent when we consider more traditional readings of parts of the earlier chapters of Genesis. In the early modern period, the geography of paradise, to take one example, took on an unprecedented significance. Whereas for medieval and patristic exegetes the Garden of Eden had been a potent idea, laden with psychological or allegorical meanings – paradise was

---

[18] Clarke, *Evidences of Natural and Revealed Religion*, in *The Works of Samuel Clarke, DD*, 2 vols. (London, 1738), II, 705.

[19] David Collyer, *The Sacred Interpreter* (London, 1732); Timothy Nourse, *A Discourse of Natural and Reveal'd Religion* (London, 1691), pp. 178–84. On the superiority of scriptural history, also see Henry Smith, *God's Arrow against Atheists* (London, 1656), pp. 312f.; Hale, *Primitive Origination of Mankind*, p. 137.

[20] John Wilkins, in *Ecclesiastes, or, A Discourse concerning the Gift of Preaching* (London, 1647), provides lists of recommended reading for prospective preachers, so that they may familiarise themselves with 'Scripture Philosophy' and 'Scripture Geography or Topology'. (p. 26). Works recommended include Francisco Valés, *De sacra philosphia*, Levini Lemni, *De plantis sacrae*, Francisci Ruei, *De gemnis*, Wolfgang Franzius, *Historia animalium sacra*, Jo. Adamannus, *De situterre sanctae*, Christ. Adricomii, *Theatrum terrae sanctae*, David Chytraeus, *The Travels of the Patriarchs*.

[21] Donne, *Essayes in Divinity*, p. 18.

thus placed in the third heaven, the orb of the moon, or in the human mind – now considerable efforts were expended on attempts to identify the earthly location of Eden and in describing its physical features.[22] Marmaduke Carver complained, in *A Discourse of the Terrestrial Paradise* (1666), that the site of Adam's first introduction to the world was unknown, on account of 'the negligence of former times, in not making out the truth of it by the help of Geography, but blanching it over with Allegoricall or impertinant and ridiculous interpretations'.[23] In the seventeenth century, a steady stream of books issued from the presses attempting, with Mr Carver, to remedy this deficiency. These works situated the original home of Adam and Eve variously in Mesopotamia, Ethiopia, Palestine, beneath the tropics, 'near the mountains of America', and at the South Pole.[24] Additional information for the geographers of paradise came from voyages of discovery. Columbus himself had believed that the fresh waters of the Orinoco indicated the presence of a great southern land mass which he was almost certain was the earthly paradise.[25] By the end of the seventeenth century, however, the majority of sacred geographers had determined upon either Mesopotamia, between the Tigris and Euphrates, or Calvary as the most likely sites of Eden, thus conceding that paradise had long since disappeared.[26] As we shall see in the final chapter, this turn to literal readings of Eden and the Fall was to provide a crucial motivation for scientific enquiry.

Another tradition which received similar treatment was the story of

[22] For contemporary discussions of patristic and medieval readings of the location of paradise, see John Witty, *An Essay towards a Vindication of the Vulgar Exposition of the Mosaic History of the World*, 2 vols. (London, 1705), II, 31–57; Francis Walsh, *The Antediluvian World; or, A New Theory of the Earth* (Dublin, 1743), pp. 23–30, 194–219. This latter work was published posthumously.

[23] Carver, *A Discourse of the Terrestrial Paradise* (London, 1666), To the Reader. Cf. J. Salkeld, *A Treatise of Paradise* (London, 1617), p. 4.

[24] See, e.g., Thomas Malvenda, *De Paradiso* (Rome, 1605), pp. 11–20; H. Hare, *The Situation of Paradise Found Out* (London, 1683); John Hopkinson, *Synopsis paradisi* (Rotterdam, 1693); Alexander Ross, *An Exposition on the Fourteene first Chapters of Genesis* (London, 1626), pp. 40–2; Samuel Pordage, *Mundorum Explicatio* (London, 1661), pp. 28–30; Lancelot Andrewes, Ἀποσπασμάτια Sacra (London, 1657), pp. 157–9; Patrick Simon, *A Commentary on the First book of Moses called Genesis*, 2nd edn (London, 1698), pp. 42–9; Stephen Switzer, *The Nobleman, Gentleman, and Gardener's Recreation* (London, 1715), p. 3; Witty, *An Essay*, p. 51; Arthur Bedford, *The Scripture Chronology demonstrated by Astronomical Calculations* (London, 1730), p. 4. Bedford marks the location of paradise on a map, facing p. 774. Cf. Geneva Bible (1607 edn.) fol. IV, notes f, i. Also see Joseph E. Duncan's *Milton's Earthly Paradise: A Historical Study of Eden* (Minneapolis: University of Minnesota Press, 1972) chs. 7, 8; and his 'Paradise as the Whole Earth', *JHI* 30 (1969) 171–86 (p. 175).

[25] Stephen Greenblatt, *Marvellous Possessions*, pp. 78f.; Grafton, *New Worlds*, p. 82. Also see John Dunton (ed.), *The Athenian Oracle*, 3rd edn I, 19.

[26] On Eden and Calvary sharing the same site, see Donne's 'Hymne to God, My God, in My Sicknesse': 'We thinke that *Paradise* and *Calvarie* / *Christs* Crosse, and *Adam's* tree, stood in one place: / Looke, Lord, and find both Adams met in me' (26–8); Hare, *The Situation of Paradise*, p. 21.

Noah's Flood. John Chrysostom had written in the fourth century that 'the story of the Deluge was a sacrament, and its details a figure of things to come'. For the Fathers, the Ark was primarily a symbol of the Church, with those inside destined for salvation, and those without doomed to perish. The waters of the Flood represented a flood of passions which brought death and destruction, or the cleansing waters of baptism.[27] Even the dimensions of the Ark and its structure were given precise symbolic meanings. The three levels of the Ark variously signified earth, sky and abyss; the three stages in the development of the Church; faith, hope, and love; or Noah's three sons.[28] The Ark's physical proportions inspired similar interpretations: its breadth, fifty cubits, symbolised the fifty days of Pentecost; its height, thirty cubits, the thirty years of Jesus' life; its length, three hundred cubits (when broken into six lots of fifty cubits), the six ages of the earth.[29] Augustine and Ambrose claimed that the proportions of the Ark were the same as those of the body of man.[30] In the seventeenth century the details of the story of the Deluge which had been the occasion for much fruitful allegorising throughout the Middle Ages were now related to more mundane questions of science and logistics. Where did the waters come from, and where did they eventually go? What mutations of the earth took place as a result of the Deluge? How, wondered the moderns, could the great catalogue of creatures whose lives were to be preserved from the impending inundation be physically housed in a vessel of the specified dimensions?[31] And further, how was the craft constructed, how navigated, by what means did Noah assemble his cargo, where were the provisions stored, how were fox and fowl kept apart? True, some readers of scripture regarded such texts as having metaphorical refer-

---

[27] John Chrysostom, *PG* 48, 1037, qu. in Jack P. Lewis, *A Study of the Interpretation of Noah and the Flood in Jewish and Christian Literature* (Leiden: Brill, 1978), p. 157. Also see pp. 167f. Cyprian, *Ep.* 74.11; Jerome, *Ep.* xv.2; Augustine, *City of God*, xv.27; Origen, *Homilies on Genesis*, ii.5. Such readings were not completely unrepresented in the seventeenth-century literature. Catholic exegete Benedictus Pererius claimed that Noah stands for Christ, the Flood for baptism, the Ark for the Church, and so on. *Commentariorum in Genesin*, pp. 446–8. Allegorising of this particular story was popular because it was sanctioned by the writer of the Petrine epistles (I Peter 3.20). Matthew Mackaile also argued on the basis of analogies 'betwixt *Man*, and the *Earth*; and betwixt the *Spirituall condition of Man*, and the *naturall condition of the Earth*' that the Deluge was the baptism of the earth, and the final conflagration, its baptism by fire. *Terra Prodromus Theoricus* (Aberdeen, 1691), pp. 6f. Mackaile's reading relied upon the increasingly unfashionable notions of microcosm and analogy. [28] Origen, *Homilies on Genesis*, ii.3, 5; Augustine, *City of God*, xv.26.
[29] Augustine, *Contra Faustum*, xii.14. Also see Lewis, *The Interpretation of Noah*, pp. 161–7.
[30] Edwards, *A Demonstration of the Existence and Providence of God* (London, 1696), pt ii, p. 122.
[31] Wilkins, *Real Character*, pp. 164–6; Athanasius Kircher, *Arca Noë in tres libros digesta* (Amstelodami, 1675), pp. 108–10; Vossius, *Vossius de vera etat mundi*, 2nd edn, printed with *De Septuaginta interpretibus* (The Hague, 1661) pp. 283f. Cf. Cockburn, *An Enquiry*, p. 7. Cf. Hughes, *Analytical Exposition*, To the Reader; Ross, *An Exposition*, p. 107. Also see Allen, *Legend of Noah*, pp. 183–7.

ence to contemporary events. But for the more worldly and conservative seventeenth-century reader, these narratives came to have present significance because they provoked scientific and cosmological questions, or provided knowledge which could be categorised as 'science'.

MODIFICATIONS OF THE LITERAL: TYPOLOGY AND ACCOMMODATION

The recognition of the historicity of the biblical texts, combined with efforts to mine scripture for historical and scientific information, raised a number of questions about the religious functions of the Bible and the intentions of its authors. In the absence of tropological and allegorical readings of historical narratives, how was a record of past events to lead to the edification of a present generation of readers? Moreover, how could the 'scientific' information purportedly contained in the scriptures meet the needs of both the audience to whom it was originally addressed and a later scientific community, when each entertained profoundly different conceptions of the world? Finally, if the Bible contained information which accorded with the hypotheses of the new sciences, was it to be assumed that the biblical authors were privy to secrets of nature which had been withheld from their contemporaries?

Questions about the relevance of history, of course, are still with us. Seventeenth-century defenders of the utility of the discipline were to argue that God had revealed himself in past events, and that from the annals of history inferences about his providential activity might profitably be drawn. The sacred history set down in scripture, furthermore, was edifying because it was replete with 'types' – events and characters which were typical because they represented patterns or personalities which would recur in later times. The traditional use of typology had been to link the Old Testament with the New, a task which now assumed increasing importance as the history of the Israelite people could no longer be read allegorically as bearing witness to theological truths contained in the New Testament. In the key typological reading of scripture, Adam was a 'type' and Christ the 'antitype'. The first man thus foreshadowed the perfect man; as Adam was the original author of sin, Christ was the expiator of sin; as Adam was patriarch of Israel, Christ was the head of the Church, the 'new Israel'; and so on. In this manner the very first events recorded in scripture could be shown to be intimately linked with happenings of momentous import which had taken place thousands of years later.

Some Protestant exegetes were to take this process even further, linking biblical types and figures to contemporary events and personalities.[32] In the hands of the English radicals, the Bible, typologically interpreted, became a political manifesto which advocated the overthrow of princes and prelates, and the dispossession of land-owners and Lords. The Levellers, for example, took the wicked kings of the Old Testament – Nimrod, Saul, Ahab, Nebuchadnezzar, Absalom – to be figures or types of contemporary rulers. The grisly ends with which such figures frequently met at the hands of their own subjects lent authorisation to rebellion.[33] Not surprisingly, those of more conservative political persuasion took exception to such readings. 'The Scriptures of God are most extreamly perverted, abused, and misapplied' by such men, wrote Edward Symmons, for 'whatever judgement they read of (in Gods word) against any particular King . . . they most unjustly, and undutifully apply it against the *Lords Anointed*, their owne *Sovereign*'. How often, he complained, 'have they compared him to *Pharoah*, to *Saul*, to *Ahab*'.[34] Yet Symmons' grievance was not against typology as such, but against this particular application of it. The Kings of England, he implied, might equally be antitypes of the regal David, or the wise Solomon.[35] But whatever the disagreements about the identification of antitypes, typology or 'figural' interpretation served to bring to light the contemporary import of biblical history.

On the face of it, the popularity of typological readings in the seventeenth century may seem to run counter to the prevailing trend towards literal interpretation, but in fact the two developments are quite compatible. Certainly, biblical scholars of the time saw no incompatibility in asserting the vanity of allegory, while praising the virtues of typology. In one of the classic works on typological interpretation, *The Figures and Types of the Old Testament* (1683), Samuel Mather clearly distinguishes typology from allegory. While advocating the legitimacy of the former, he was to caution that 'men must not indulge their own Fancies, as the Popish writers use to do, with their Allegorical Senses'.[36] Typological interpretation was also justified, although less convincingly, by appealing to the literary forms of antiquity. Benjamin Keach noted

---

[32] Paul Korshin thus writes that: 'The Protestant reformers of the sixteenth century did not reject the Church's typological stratifications of scripture, but they did modify the direction of conventional typology significantly to embrace contemporary and future history.' *Typologies in England, 1650–1820* (Princeton University Press), p. 31.

[33] Hill, *English Bible*, pp. 103, 109–25; Cf. Hill, *World Turned Upside Down*, p. 143.

[34] Edward Symmons, *Scripture Vindicated* (Oxford, 1644), p. 84.

[35] For the various identifications of England's rulers with biblical types, see Korshin, *Typologies in England*, pp. 68f.   [36] Mather, *The Figures and Types of the Old Testament* (Dublin, 1683), p. 71.

that there were many tropes and figures in scripture 'peculiar to the sacred language'. Robert Jenkin agreed that 'The figurative expressions of the Prophets and their Types and Parables, were suitable to the customs of the places and times wherein they lived.'[37] The admission of typological readings for these exegetes was nothing more than an acknowledgement of the importance of locating authors within their historical context, and understanding their rhetorical techniques.[38]

However, the main reason for the compatibility of literal sense and typology is to do with the fact that typological reading is as much a way of understanding history as of interpreting texts. Just as allegory implied a certain symbolic view of natural objects, so typology carried with it a conviction about the nature of historical events: allegory is to do with things, typology with people and events. 'Types suppose still the verity of some history,' wrote James Durham in *Clavis Cantici* (1662), 'allegories again, have no such necessary supposition'. A typological reading, for Durham, was but another aspect of the literal sense. There were two literal senses, he insisted, one of which is 'proper and immediat', the other, 'figurative and mediat'.[39] Thus, one could consistently deny referential functions to the things of nature while retaining that view of history according to which the Deity had prefigured certain historical happenings and personages. Protestant literalism might have evacuated the spatial world of its symbolic significance, but it left the temporal world untouched. God might no longer be directly evidenced in the realm of nature, but his influence was ever-present in the realm of history. If the Bible no longer played a central role in the attribution of meaning to the things of nature, it retained, for a time at least, its part in the interpretation of history.

The history contained in scripture thus served to provide evidence of

[37] Keach, *Tropes and Figures*, Epistle to the Reader. Jenkin, *Reasonableness and Certainty*, p. 62.

[38] Such techniques were also imported into the seventeenth century. Andrew Willet, author of the anti-papist *Synopsis Papismi*, described his subjects in these unflattering terms: 'They have been from time to time, as prickes to our sides, and thornes in our eyes . . . they are the Foxes that destroy the Lord's vineyard, the progenie of the Pharisees, a generation of vipers, whose propertie it is to gnaw out the sides of their damme when they are brought forth . . . They are the serpent by the way, that byteth the horses heeles & causeth the writers to fall backward: that is, subtilly do vndermine and hinder the prosperous successe of religion. Of such prophecied Ezechiel, They do eate the good pasture, and tread downe the rest with their feete. . .' But despite his reliance on these types and tropes, Willet insists in the same work 'that of one place in scripture there can be but one sense, which we call the literall sense'. Andrew Willet, *Synopsis Papismi*, Sig. B1v, p. 26. (All of Willet's allusions are biblical, except the reference to the young vipers gnawing their way out of their mother's womb. This is to be found in the *Physiologus*, xii; Pliny, *Natural History*, x, 169; and Aelian, *Characteristics of Animals*, 1.24).

[39] See Durham, *Clavis Cantici: or, an Exposition of the Song of Solomon* (Edinburgh, 1662), pp 6,8.

divine participation in the ongoing human drama, or provided precedents for later events. The scientific content of the biblical writings was
another matter, complicated by the new insistence of the importance of
the author. The extent of Moses' own knowledge of the natural world
and its laws was a hotly debated topic, and had considerable bearing
upon the various natural philosophies which took Genesis as their point
of departure. Few doubted that Moses was possessed of a sophisticated
knowledge of the workings of the universe, but how much of this
knowledge could be found in his writings, and how much he had
intended to communicate to his contemporaries remained points of
serious contention.[40] Most seventeenth-century exegetes believed that it
was the primary intention of the scriptural writers to point out the path
to salvation. It was not Moses' design, said George Hughes, 'to make
men perfect in all natural and mathematical knowledge, but in that
which might make them wise for salvation.'[41] Richard Baxter pointed
out that the Bible is no 'perfect Rule of natural sciences, as Physicks,
Metaphysicks, &c', nor is it a rule for 'Medicine, Musick, Arithmetick,
Geometry, Astronomy; Grammar, Rhetorick, Logick; nor for Mechanicks, as Navigation, Architecture; and all the Trades and occupations
of Men; no not Husbandry by which we have our food'. What the Bible
did contain, however, was 'all the essentiall and integral parts of the
Christian Religion'.[42] Galileo's celebrated response to the question of
the purpose of scripture was expressed in similar terms: 'The intention
of the Holy Ghost is to teach us how one goes to heaven, not how
heaven goes.'[43] Indeed, this answer was in keeping with a long-standing
view that the primary intention of scripture is to lead erring human
beings to salvation. Augustine had declared that all scripture was to do
with faith or morals, adding, however, that 'whatever appears in the
divine Word *that does not literally pertain to virtuous behaviour or the truth of faith,
you must take to be figurative*'.[44] The difficulty faced by seventeenth-century
Protestant exegetes, however, was that the considerable proportion of
holy writ which was to do neither with virtue nor theological truth could
no longer so easily be invested with non-literal significance. Historical
narrative might be pored over in order to see anticipations of the New

[40] See, e.g., Pererius, *Commentariorum in Genesin*, p. 87; Hughes, *Analytical Exposition*, Epistle to the
   Reader.   [41] Hughes, *Analytical Exposition*, Epistle to the Reader.
[42] Baxter, *A Christian Directory*, 2nd edn (London, 1678), Pt III, p. 168.
[43] Galileo, *Letter to the Grand Duchess Christina*, in *Discoveries and Opinions*, p. 186. Galileo actually
   attributes the remark to Cardinal Baronius.
[44] Augustine, *On Christian Doctrine* III.x.14 (p. 88) my emphasis. For a comparison of the interpretive
   strategies of Augustine and Galileo, see Eileen Reeves, 'Augustine and Galileo on Reading the
   Heavens', *JHI* 52 (1991) 563–79.

Testament in the Old, or to link current anti-types with their biblical types, but a substantial residue remained. The book of Genesis, in particular, contained many narratives which when taken literally were not obviously to do with faith or morals, but appeared to be in the form of crude cosmology. One could therefore agree with Galileo that the scripture's main function was to teach salvation, but still be faced with the problem of the status of that material which seemed to present a kind of natural science. Were the Mosaic accounts of the creation and the Deluge, now no longer regarded as allegorical representations of theological truths, to be accepted as literal accounts of actual events? And if so, were they true in all their details? The conclusion which most exegetes wanted to avoid was one which suggested that Moses was expert in theological matters, but totally ignorant in the field of physical science, for this conclusion would impugn the whole authority of scripture.

A widely accepted compromise was the position which held on the one hand that scripture did not contain anything which contradicted known scientific truths, but conceded on the other that the science which was to be found in scripture was 'accommodated' to the mental capacities of its initial audience. Moses' account of the Deluge, for example, was generally thought to be accurate in its historical details, and this had important implications for cosmology. The events which Moses described had actually taken place, and they had taken place in the order set down by Moses. However, on those occasions when Moses had spoken of the physical mechanisms involved it was assumed that his explanations were couched in simple terms which could be readily understood by his audience.

The principle of accommodation was an elaboration of a long-standing hermeneutical principle *Scriptura humane loquitur* – scripture speaks in human language. In expounding the literal sense of Genesis, Augustine had claimed that the creation narratives were 'adapted to the sense of the unlearned'. In the Middle Ages both Jewish and Christian exegetes relied upon a similar principle when dealing with the literal sense.[45] For Protestants who were now unable to fall back upon higher levels of interpretation in order to reconcile scripture with natural

---

[45] Augustine, *De Genesi ad litteram* I,xxx.15, *Opera Omnia* III, 127; *Confessions* XII.xvii (p. 258); Aquinas, *ST*, 1a2ae. 98, 3 (XXIX, 15). Also see Funkenstein, *Theology and the Scientific Imagination*, pp. 213–21; Scott Mandelbrote, 'Isaac Newton and Thomas Burnet: Biblical Criticism and the Crisis of Late Seventeenth-Century England', in R. Popkin and J. Force (eds.), *The Books of Nature and Scripture*, pp. 149–78; *Historisches Wörtebuch der Philosophie*, ed. J. Ritter (Basel: Schwabe, 1971–), I; 'Akkomodation'; Stephen Benin, *The Footprints of God: Divine Accommodation in Jewish and Christian Thought* (Albany: SUNY Press, 1993); Madsen, *Shadowy Types*, pp. 54–84.

truths, accommodation became an increasingly indispensable component of biblical exegesis. Commenting on Genesis 1.16, in which Moses refers to the sun and moon as 'two great lights', Calvin, for example, argued that Moses is not explaining the true relation between sun and moon, and for this reason 'adapts his discourse to common usage'.[46] The Calvinist Lambert Daneau, who had attempted to write a natural science based on scripture, agreed. While the Bible might contain much 'generall naturall philosophie', it was also true that '*Moses* applyed himself to ỹ capacitie of our selves' and that his style was 'bare and simple'. Daneau hastened to add it can 'not bee proved that hee spake or wrote lyingly, falsely, and ignorantly of those things'.[47] Sir Thomas Browne expressed a similar view in *Religio Medici* when he claimed that certain teachings in the scriptures 'are often delivered in a vulgar and illustrative way, and being written unto man, are delivered, not as they truly are, but as they may be understood'.[48] Catholic scientists, too, had recourse to accommodation. Indeed, the most extended defence of the idea was made by Galileo in his *Letter to the Grand Duchess Christina concerning the Use of Biblical Quotations in Matters of Science* (1615).[49] While Moses was possessed of the true knowledge of the frame of the world, his intention in writing the book of Genesis was not to communicate this knowledge. The reason that scripture appears to contain propositions contrary to known facts was that some things 'were set down by the sacred scribes in order to accommodate them to the capacities of the common people, who are rude and unlearned'.[50] Galileo's arguments to this conclusion were cogent and persuasive, and frequently made reference to Augustine's commentaries on Genesis.

The principle of accommodation was not only a consequence of the assertion of the literal sense of scripture, but followed naturally from the Protestant view that access to scripture should not be denied to even the most ignorant reader. The first of the Lucasian Professors of mathematics at Cambridge, Isaac Barrow, pointed out that scripture, 'being not penned by Masters of humane art or science; nor directed to persons of more than ordinary capacities or improvements, doth not intend to use words otherwise than in the most plain and ordinary manner'.[51] Bishop

---

[46] Calvin, *Commentary on Genesis*, p. 87; cf. pp. 256f.; *Institutes*, i.xiv.3 (i, 143); Luther, *Table Talk* 119 (p. 58).

[47] Lambert Daneau, *The Wonderfull Woorkmanship of the World* (London, 1578) Fols. 9r–10v.

[48] Browne, *Religio Medici*, 1.45 (p. 48); Cf. *Pseudodoxia Epidemica*, i.ix.

[49] *Discoveries and Opinions of Galileo*, tr. Drake, pp. 175–216. Specifically on accommodation, see pp. 182, 199. Also see Brooke, *Science and Religion*, pp. 77–81.

[50] Galileo, *Letter to the Grand Duchess Christina*, in *Discoveries and Opinions*, p. 181.

Sanderson, thought that the holy scriptures are 'fitted to our capacity, speaketh of the things of God in such language, and under such notions, as best agree with our weak conceptions, but far below the dignity and majesty of the things themselves'.[52] William Derham remarked that many passages of scripture were 'spoken according to the appearance of things, and the vulgar notions and opinions which men have of them.'[53] Even the message of Christ himself was accommodated to vulgar understandings, according to Jean Le Clerc: 'the Apostles deliver'd the Doctrine of Christ . . . after their own way suitable to the People'.[54]

But it was the science of Moses to which the principle was most frequently applied. Thomas Burnet, whose ingenious sacred theory of the earth we shall consider shortly, wrote that Moses' description of the creation 'bears in it the evident marks of an accommodation and condescension to the vulgar notions concerning the form of the world'.[55] He is less delicate in the Latin *Archaeologiae philosophicae* (1692):

. . . the account given by Moses . . . is not true in it self, but only spoken popularly to comply with the dull Israelites, lately slavish brickmakers, and smelling strong of the garlic and onions of Egypt. To humour these ignorant blockheads that were newly broke loose from the Egyptian taskmasters, and had no sense nor reason in their thick skulls.[56]

Accommodation in this context thus meant that the details of cosmology and geology which Moses had included in his account, and which were acknowledged to be somewhat incidental to his chief purpose, were not false, but had been greatly simplified in order not to distract his listeners from matters of more immediate importance. As Isaac Newton expressed it in a letter to Thomas Burnet, the science of Moses was neither 'Philosophical' nor 'feigned'.[57]

It is frequently assumed that accommodation was a defensive strategy which preserved biblical authority by showing how particular passages

[51] Isaac Barrow, 'Of Justifying Faith', *Works*, II, 55. Cf. Benjamin Keach, *TROPOSCHMALOGIA: Tropes and Figures* (London, 1692), Epistle to the Reader; John Richardson, *Choice Observations and Explanations upon the Old Testament* (London, 1655) ch. 3; Daneau, *Wonderfull Woorkmanship*, fol. 9r.; John Harris, *Remarks on some Late Papers Relating to the Universal Deluge*, (London, 1697), p. 5; Stillingfleet, *Origines Sacrae*, (1664 edn) p. 615; Boyle, *Some Considerations*, *Works* II, 261.

[52] Robert Sanderson, *Thirty-Six Sermons* (London, 1689), p. 657.

[53] Derham, *Astro-Theology*, p. xxiv.   [54] Le Clerc, *Twelve Dissertations*, p. 40.

[55] Burnet, *A Review of the Theory*, (Centaur edn p. 407).

[56] Burnet, *Archaeologiae philosophicae* l.2 c. 7, 8, 9. Paraphrased translation is given in Edwards, *Discourse concerning the Old and New Testament*, II, 35. Edwards, while disagreeing with Burnet's approach to scripture nonetheless conceded that certain passages in Genesis are written 'in a manner of Speech adapted to the Capacity of the Vulgar'. (II, 51).

[57] Newton to Burnet, January 1680/1, *Correspondence of Isaac Newton*, II, 331.

of scripture could be reconciled with contemporary scientific theory: accommodation replaces allegory as a means of reconciling scripture to other authorities. From another perspective, however, it might be said that scientific theories could actually become a way of discerning hidden meanings of particular passages of scripture – meanings which had hitherto been obscured because the words which expressed them had been accommodated to the capacities of more primitive minds. Galileo proposed just such a procedure when he suggested that 'having arrived at certainties in physics, we ought to utilize these as the most appropriate aids in the true exposition of the Bible and in the investigation of those meanings which are necessarily contained therein'.[58] Bacon wrote that the book of nature was the key to an understanding of the book of God's written word.[59] Robert Boyle agreed: 'God has made some knowledge of his created book, both conducive to belief, and necessary to the understanding of his written one.'[60] Cambridge Platonist Henry More, whose exegetical writings on the Apocalypse so affected Isaac Newton, believed that the Copernican view of the solar system, Descartes' vortices, and the corpuscular philosophy of Boyle, could be discerned in the writings of Moses.[61] Richard Bentley, the most able classicist of his generation, repeated More's views in his Boyle Lectures, announcing that 'the mechanical or corpuscular philosophy, though peradventure the oldest as well as the best in the world, had lain buried beneath contempt and oblivion, till it was happily restored and cultivated anew by some excellent wits of the present age'.[62] The man who had nominated Bentley for the lectureship in 1691–2, Isaac Newton, also believed that the new discoveries in the sciences were in fact re-discoveries of ancient truths, traces of which could be found in a variety of texts, including scripture. The priest-scientists of antiquity had known of atomic theory, the existence of the vacuum, universal gravitation, and the inverse square law.[63] Advances in natural philosophy thus provided valuable assistance to biblical exegetes, enabling them to discern from hints in the biblical records what the original authors had actually

---

[58] Galileo, *Letter to the Grand Duchess Christina*, in *Discoveries and Opinions*, p. 183.
[59] Bacon, *Advancement of Learning*, I.vi.16 (p. 42).   [60] Boyle, *Some Considerations*, in *Works*, II, 19.
[61] More, *A Collection*, pp. xviii–xix. On More's relation to Newton, see Westfall, *Life of Isaac Newton*, p. 137.   [62] Bentley, *Works*, III, 74.
[63] Newton expressed this view in a manuscript version of his scholia to the *Principia*. Manuel, *Religion of Isaac Newton*, p. 23; J. E. McGuire and P. M. Rattansi, 'Newton and the Pipes of Pan', *Notes and Records of the Royal Society of London*, 21 (1966) 108–43. On Newton and the Bentley, see H. Guerlac and Margaret Jacob, 'Bentley, Newton, and Providence, *JHI* 30 (1969) 316; Jacob, *The Newtonians and the English Revolution*, p. 155.

believed. Moses, thought Thomas Burnet, could have provided an account of the creation according to scientific principles, but had refrained from doing so out of deference to his audience. Burnet had in fact written to Newton pointing out that 'if Moses had given ye Theory it would have been a thing altogether inaccommodate to ye people & a useless distracting amusemt'. Instead, Moses had given 'a short ideal draught of a terraqueous earth riseing from a Chaos'.[64] What Moses had really thought, however, could now be carefully reconstructed. As we shall see, a number of seventeenth-century writers attempted such reconstructions, re-reading Genesis in the light of Cartesian or Newtonian systems.

Scientists might thus see themselves, after the manner of the humanists, as attempting to arrive at a complete form of ancient knowledge. Adam had enjoyed a perfect knowledge of nature, and much of his knowledge had been transmitted to posterity. Some of this knowledge had been written down, some was passed on as oral tradition or cabbala. The legendary books of King Solomon were a part of this lost tradition. 'Salomens Bookes which were written copiously of the Nature of all thynges, are, through the negligence of men, perished', lamented Daneau. Andrew Willet thought that 'some books are now wanting, which were part of canonical Scripture, & yet that which remaineth is sufficient; as some of *Solomon's* bookes are perished, which he wrote of herbes & plants . . . the Lord sae that they were not so greatly necessary to saluation'. Bacon, Browne, Fludd, Boyle, and many others also lamented the loss of this ancient scriptural science.[65] But having now realised that crucial texts had been lost, and that in those writings which had survived to the present, authors' scientific knowledge was veiled by compromises made in the interest of their original audience, they concluded that empirical research was one way to fill in gaps left by missing texts, and to clarify that scientific knowledge now obscured by the accommodations made by original authors. This development thus represents a significant shift in the interpretive priorities of the medieval period: no longer was scripture to provide the key to the hidden religious

---

[64] Burnet to Newton, 13 January 1680/1, *Correspondence of Isaac Newton*, II, 323.
[65] Daneau, *Wonderfull Woorkmanship*, fol. 3v.; Willet, *Synopsis Papismi*, p. 36; Bacon, *Advancement of Learning*, I.vi.11 (p. 40); Browne, *Religio Medici* 1.24 (p. 37); Robert Fludd, *Apologia compendiaria*, in Huffman (ed.) *Robert Fludd: Essential Readings* (London: Harper Collins, 1992), p. 52; Boyle, *Some Considerations*, *Works*, II, 309; John Pettus, *Volatiles from the History of Adam and Eve* (London, 1674), p. 60; William Coles, *Adam in Eden: or, Natures Paradise* (London, 1657), To the Reader; Philip Barrough, *The Method of Physick* (London, 1652), Sig. A4r.

meanings of the natural world – instead, discoveries in the book of nature were to shed light on the neglected scientific treasures of the sacred text.

THE COSMOLOGY OF MOSES

The idea that the books of Moses contained scientific information, albeit in an accommodated form, gradually gained currency from the time of the Reformation. Calvin had made a number of passing remarks to the effect that scripture might confer upon its readers certain advantages in the sphere of natural philosophy, but had gone no further. Luther also had observed that one who did not understand God's word could hardly be expected to understand his works.[66] In Lambert Daneau's *Physice christiana* (1580), however, we have a systematic attempt to derive natural science from scripture. A product of Reformation Geneva, this work was premised upon the thesis that 'generall naturall Philosophie . . . is chiefly to bee learned out of holy Scripture'.[67] Daneau was prepared to concede that holy writ was often silent on specific details of the 'histories of living thynges, and of Plants', a failing which he attributed to the loss of the works of Solomon, yet he nonetheless insisted that the Old Testament was without peer in its descriptions of the formation of the earth.[68] As a contribution to natural philosophy, Daneau's book was something of a disappointment and did little more than reject the Aristotelian thesis of the eternity of the world and assert the Reformation principle that scripture and the Fathers were to be preferred over Aristotle and heathen philosophers. A similar project had been envisaged by Levinus Lemnius, who pointed out that the holy books of scripture were 'endited [sic] by the holie Ghost, and written by heauenly inspiration'. It followed that the biblical authors were 'most exquisitly also furnished with the entire knowledge of all things naturall: and not ignorant in anie kinde of learning or discipline'.[69] Hieronymous Zanchius took a slightly different tack, attempting to harmonise the Genesis account of the days of creation with Aristotle's *Physics*. This unlikely project set forth the rather general thesis that both books begin by

---

[66] Calvin, *Commentary on Genesis*, p. 63. Cf. *Institutes* I, xiv.1; vi.1. (1.141f.). Luther, *Table Talk*, tr. William Hazlitt (London: Harper Collins, 1995) 9 (p. 6).

[67] Published in English as *The Wonderfull Woorkmanship of the World* (London, 1578), fol. 7v.

[68] *Ibid.*, fol. 3v.   [69] *An Herbal for the Bible*, tr. Thomas Newton (London, 1587), p. 6.

discussing matter and move on to talk about form.[70] His efforts were not helped by the growing disenchantment with Aristotelianism.

Zanchius was one of the last commentators to seek agreement between the natural philosophy of scripture and the teachings of Aristotle. Increasingly, those who sought natural philosophy in the first chapters of Genesis were actually appealing to scripture against Aristotle. Robert Fludd, admittedly one of the more extreme proponents of a biblical natural science, insisted that 'the subject of true Philosophy is not to be found in *Aristotle's* works, but in the Book of truth and Wisdom, forasmuch as it is a copy of the revealed Word'. Neither was there any agreement to be found between Moses and the 'cavilling, brabling, heathenish Philosophy' of the Stagirite. Christians, counselled Fludd, ought not 'seek for the truth, where it is not to be found; I mean, in the workes of the pagan Philosophers, and that is made manifest, forasmuch as it contradicteth altogether the verity of the Scriptures.' Unlike Aristotle, Moses was 'a master of divine philosophy', who had possessed the key to both natural and supernatural knowledge. This wisdom, in turn, had been communicated to David, Solomon, Hermes Trismegistus, Plato, and others.[71] It was similarly claimed for the new prescriptions of the Paracelsians that 'they doe agree with the rule of God's worde, they depend on the fountain of truth', unlike the physick of Aristotle and Galen which appealed to the 'authoritie of men reprobate of God, and such as were idolaters and ignorant of the trueth'.[72] Henry More was less concerned with the content of pagan philosophy than with its ultimate source. The science of the book of Genesis, in one form or another, had been adopted by a number of Greek philosophers. Moses had written not only of 'the motion of earth, which is the famed opinion of Pythagoras, and which implies a Vortex about the Sun, but also the confessed Atomical Philosophy of Leucippus, Democritus, and Epicurus'. Genesis, in other words, contained the first articulations of the heliocentric theory of Copernicus, Cartesian vortices, and the corpuscular philosophy. More thus believed that his own interpretation of Genesis had brought 'that ancient and venerable Wisdom again to life', concluding that 'those truths were ever lodged in the tent of Moses and

---

[70] Hieronymous Zanchius, *De operibus Dei intro spacium sex dierum creatis* (1591), in *Perum Theologicorum* (Geneva, 1613) vol. III, 218–24. On Daneau and Zanchius see Sachiko Kusukawa, *The Transformation of Natural Philosophy: The Case of Philip Melanchthon* (Cambridge University Press, 1995), pp. 204–7.

[71] Robert Fludd, *Mosaicall Philosophy Grounded upon the Essential Truth or Eternal Sapience* (London, 1659), pp. 123, 28; *Essential Readings*, pp. 46, 229.   [72] Bostocke, *Auncient Phisicke*, Sig. Bii.v.

that no Philosopher has any the least pretence to magnifie himself against Religion and the Church of God, wherein such rich Theories have been ever treasured up, though men have not had, for these many Ages, the leisure or opportunity of unlocking them till now'.[73]

The idea that scripture could be used as a kind of scientific text-book was not accepted without qualification, however. Frequently it was associated with eccentric and erroneous science, or enthusiastic and heterodox religion. Francis Bacon criticised the 'extreme levity' of those Paracelsians who had attempted 'to found a system of natural philosophy on the first chapters of Genesis'.[74] Henry More himself took Henry Vaughan to task for basing his natural philosophy on scripture: 'What profane boldnesse is this to distort the high Majesty of the holy Scripture ... to decide the controversies of the World and of nature'.[75] Yet neither Bacon nor More were totally averse to the idea that scripture contained useful scientific information. Bacon wrote enthusiastically of 'that excellent book of Job', which was 'pregnant and swelling with natural philosophy'. Job taught the roundness of the earth, that it hung in space, and that the stars were fixed.[76] More's promotion of Mosaic science we have already noted. What was at issue between Bacon and the Paracelsians, and More and Vaughan was not so much whether scripture contained science, but how much. This in turn depended on the intentions and purposes of its authors. Had Moses intended to present a true account of the formation of the earth, or had he some other purpose in mind? And if the design of Moses had not been to set down a scientific account of the world, what was the status of the biblical accounts of the creation of the earth and its subsequent mutations?

Many natural scientists in the late seventeenth century entertained no

---

[73] More, *A Collection*, pp. xviii–xix; Cf. More, *Observations upon Anthroposophia Theomagica and Anima Magica Abscondita* (London, 1650), p. 65. For other advocates of a biblical science see Diodati, *Annotations upon the Holy Bible*, Sig. A3r.; Edwards, *A Demonstration*, Preface; Le Clerc, *Twelve Dissertations*, Sig. A3r, A4r. Also see Hill, *English Bible*, pp. 29, 373; Hooykaas, 'Science and Reformation', p. 235. One of the more extreme proponents of the scientific content of scripture came a generation after More. John Hutchinson wrote his *Moses's Principia* as 'a confirmation of the Natural History of the Bible'. It had been Moses' 'chief business', thought Hutchinson, to 'determine Natural Philosophy'. In England, Hutchinson's book excited considerable interest, enjoying a readership almost as wide as Newton's *Principia*, to which it had been a response. His ideas were developed and disseminated by a group of disciples who became known as the 'Hutchinsonians'. John Hutchinson, *Moses's Principia* (London, 1724–7), Pt II, ii. On Hutchinson, see Albert Kuhn, 'Glory or Gravity: Hutchinson vs. Newton', *JHI* 22 (1961) 303–22.

[74] Bacon, *Novum Organum*, I.65 (p. 45). Cf. *Advancement of Learning*, II.xxv.16 (pp. 207.). Bacon's primary target was most probably Paracelsus. Boehme also made extravagent claims for biblical science. See *Mysterium Magnum*, Epistle to the Reader

[75] Henry More, *Observations upon Anthroposophia Theomagica.*

[76] Bacon, *Advancement of Learning*, I.vi.10 (pp. 39f.).

doubts on this question. Whatever Moses had communicated, he had presented posterity with a true account of the earth's origins. It remained for contemporary commentors to interpret the Mosaic account with the help of prevailing scientific theories. Henry More was the first to grasp this opportunity, seeing the potential for a combination of Cartesian cosmogony and sacred history.[77] According to More, Moses and Descartes were in fundamental agreement over the physical mechanisms which had given rise to the formation of the earth: that suns and planets had been generated from the aetherial matter, that the earth was once a sun, that there existed only three elements – each of these features of Descartes' system could be discerned in the biblical text. The French philosopher, on account of his singular affinity with Moses, was lauded as the greatest philosopher of the Christian era.[78] When More turned his attention to the end of world, he discovered similar affinities. Discussing biblical references to the final conflagration of the world, More argued in his *Explanation of the Grand Mystery of Godliness* (1660), that beneath the earth's crust there lay 'in the hidden Mines of Providence such a provision of combustible matter as will serve for that universal Conflagration'. The end might eventually come about, More hypothesised, when the earth, growing old and exhausted, approaches too close to the sun, 'so that at last, what by its over-drieness and what by its approaching so near to the Fountains of heat, not only Forrests and Woods, which has happned [sic] already, but the subterraneous Mines of Sulphur and other combustible Matter will catch fire, and set the *Whole Earth* in a manner on burning'. The end of the world would thus take place 'according to the *Cartesian* Philosophy'.[79] More's remarks in this context rely on an implicit assumption that events traditionally attributed to the direct activity of the Deity might be explained nat-

[77] For an account of the reception of Cartesian cosmogony in England see Peter Harrison, 'The Influence of Cartesian Cosmology in England', in S. Gaukroger and J. Schuster (eds.), *Descartes' Natural Philosophy*, vol. 1 (Oxford University Press, forthcoming). On sacred histories of the earth generally, see Ernest Tuveson, 'Swift and the World Makers', *JHI* 11 (1950) 54–74; Jacques Roger, 'The Cartesian Model and Its Role in Eighteenth-Century "Theory of the Earth"', in *Problems of Cartesianism*, ed. T. Lennon, J. Nicholas, J. Davis (Kingston and Montreal: McGill-Queens University Press, 1982) pp. 95–112; Gordon Davies, *The Earth in Decay: A History of British Geomorphology 1578–1878* (London: Oldsbourne, 1969) pp. 1–94; Roy Porter, *The Making of Geology: Earth Science in Britain 1660–1815* (Cambridge University Press, 1977) pp. 1–90; Gabriel Gohau, *A History of Geology*, tr. A. and M. Carozzi (New Brunswick: Rutgers University Press, 1991), pp. 37–68.

[78] More, *Defence of the Threefold Cabbala*, pp. 80, 104, in *A Collection of Several Philosophical Writings of D. Henry More*, 2nd edn (London, 1662). For Descartes' cosmogony, see *Principles of Philosophy*, tr. V. Miller and R. Miller (Dordrecht: D. Reidel, 1983), pt III.

[79] More, *An Explanation of the Grand Mystery of Godliness*, (London,1660), pp. 231f., 240; Cf. *Annotations upon the Two Foregoing Treatises, Lux Orientalis . . . and The Discourse of Truth*, (London, 1682), p. 141.

urally, by contemporary scientific theories. This principle might apply not only to the Eschaton, but to the creation of the world, and indeed to any number of events presented in scripture as miracles. More, as it turned out, was not entirely comfortable with this possibility, and his last word on the subject of the fate of the earth is somewhat ambivalent: 'the earth will thus at the long run be burnt, *Either according to the course of Nature . . . or else by a more special and solemn appointment of Providence, the Period of her Conflagration shall be shortened*'.[80] A number of writers who came after More were far less circumspect, believing that biblical cosmology, as it related to both the beginning and end of the world, could be reconciled with Cartesian or Newtonian theories.

The most celebrated application of the interpretive principle first relied upon by More was Thomas Burnet's *Telluris Theoria Sacra*, a work which appeared in two parts, the first (1681) dealing with the Deluge and paradise, the second (1689) with the burning of the world and the production of the new heavens and new earth. English translations followed in 1684 and 1690. Burnet was friendly with members of the Cambridge Platonists, and corresponded with Newton on details of his cosmological theories. He brought to his labours a keen interest in contemporary scientific developments, a commitment to the historical veracity of the biblical accounts of the various mutations of the earth, and a masterful prose style. His theory regarding the formation of the world, in its barest details is as follows. The earth, when fresh-formed from the hand of God, had a perfectly smooth surface, like an egg. It was not pock-marked with mountains, nor riven with valleys. There were no surface waters, neither rivers nor seas. In Burnet's own poetic description, 'it had the beauty of Youth and blooming nature, fresh and fruitful, and not a wrinkle, scar or fracture in all its body; no Rocks nor Mountains, no hollow Caves, nor gaping Chanels'.[81] The earth's perfect crust enclosed the waters of the abyss, and a deep layer of water lay beneath the earth's surface. In time, the sun heated the earth's crust, penetrating to the waters beneath creating vapours and exhalations. These, in turn, destabilised the dessicated crust of the earth, causing it to crack and fall into the abyss. In this manner, the whole world was inundated with waters from beneath the crust. Eventually the waters became concentrated in specific places, and the dry land reappeared.

[80] More, *Grand Mystery of Godliness*, p. 240. More's hesitation possibly arises out of the biblical warning that no-one will know the exact timing of the last things: 'But of that day or that hour no one knows, not even the angels in heaven, nor the Son, but only the Father.' (Mark 13.32).
[81] Burnet, *Theory of the Earth*, p. 64.

This was how the world came to take on its post-diluvian form. Burnet concluded that the earth which is our present home is but the ruins and rubbish of a perfect first world; the original paradise in which Adam and Eve had dwelt was unmade by the Deluge. 'We still have the broken Materials of that first World, and walk upon its Ruines; while it stood, there was the Seat of paradise, and the Scenes of the *Golden Age*; when it fell, it made the Deluge; And this unshapen Earth we now inhabit, is the Form it was found in when the Waters had retir'd, and the dry land appeared.'[82]

Burnet believed that all of this could find support in scripture and nature. The psalmist had written that 'God hath founded the earth upon the seas', while the book of Proverbs adds that 'he drew an Orb [or sphere] over the surface of the abyss' (Psalms 24.2; 136.6; Proverbs 8.27). As for the dissolution of the earth's crust in the subterranean waters of the abyss, Moses had recorded that the Deluge began 'when the fountains of the abyss opened up' (Genesis 7.11). Rational considerations, too, played a role. Burnet reasoned that no amount of precipitation would provide enough water to inundate the whole earth, and that even if this were possible, there would be no place for the water to go once the Deluge was over. Of course it might be argued that both the inundation and the re-emergence of dry land were miraculous events which lay outside the normal course of nature. But it was precisely this kind of reasoning which Burnet wished to avoid – 'we must not fly to miracles, where Man and nature are sufficient'. Burnet's general approach, then, was 'to see those pieces of most ancient History, which have chiefly been preserv'd in Scripture, confirm'd anew, and by another Light, that of Nature and Philosophy'. The causes and manner of the final conflagration were likewise fixed 'according to the truest measures I could take from Scripture, and from Nature'.[83]

Burnet's theories attracted praise, imitation, and criticism. Isaac Newton seemed to have approved, in private at least, of the general direction of Burnet's theories: 'I think the main parts of your Hypothesis as probable as what I have here written, if not in some respects more probable', he wrote to Burnet in 1681.[84] Newton himself had thought that the theory of gravitation provided a ready explanation for the demise of the present world – irregularities in the solar system, owing to the mutual attractions of the various bodies, 'will be apt to increase, till

[82] *Ibid.*, Epistle Dedicatory.　　[83] *Ibid.*, pp. 6of., 281, 17, 233.

[84] Newton to Burnet, January 1680/1, *Correspondence of Isaac Newton*, II, 331

this system wants a Reformation'.[85] It was this view of the universe to which Leibniz took such exception, pointing out that it made God appear like an incompetent watchmaker, always having to mend his work.[86] It was Newton's belief, however, that the fate of the solar system predicted by his theory was nothing less than the destruction and renovation of the world prophesied in scripture.[87] So whereas More's scientific eschatology, which had set in train these physico-theological speculations, had been based upon Descartes' flawed cosmology, Newton thought that he had made possible more accurate predictions about the material circumstances of the world's eventual demise.

Newton's own theory of gravitation had yet to be pressed into the service of a biblical cosmology. This task fell to William Whiston, Newton's successor in the Lucasian chair of mathematics at Cambridge.[88] Whiston claimed for his *New Theory of the Earth* (1696), somewhat unfairly in view of Burnet's earlier efforts, that it represented 'the *First* attempt at an *Intire Theory*, or such an one as takes in *All* the great Mutations of the Earth'.[89] Whiston's cosmology was built around the newly discovered orbits of comets, and it was his belief that the Deluge had actually been caused by a comet whose path had come close to the earth. God 'praedisposed and praeordained the Orbits and Motions of both the Comet and the Earth, so that at that very time, the former shou'd pass close by the latter, and bring that dreadful punishment upon them'.[90] A comet, possibly the one responsible for the Deluge, would also serve as the instrument of the earth's final destruction by fire. Ancient astrologers, Whiston pointed out, were thus correct in their assumption that the conjunctions of heavenly bodies had a bearing on the fate of the earth and the fortunes of its human inhabitants, although their ignorance of the true causes of these conjunctions made the astrological art 'dark and unaccountable'.[91] In a later response to criticism, Whiston makes it clear that his theory had been given the imprimatur of both Newton and Richard Bentley.[92]

By the last decade of the seventeenth century, such accounts of the

---

[85] Newton, *Optics*, 4th edn (New York: Dover, 1952), p. 402.
[86] See *The Leibniz Correspondence*, ed. H. G. Alexander (Manchester University Press, 1976), pp. 11, 22f. Samuel Clarke quickly sprang to Newton's defence, and this correspondence with Leibniz resulted. [87] David Kubrin, 'Newton and the Cyclical Cosmos', *JHI* 28 (1967) 325–46.
[88] For a general account of Whiston, see James Force, *William Whiston: Honest Newtonian* (Cambridge University Press, 1985). [89] *New Theory of the Earth*, p. 103. [90] *Ibid.*, p. 359.
[91] *Ibid.*, p. 373. On the transition of cometology from astrology to astronomy see Simon Schaffer, 'Newton's Comets and the Transformation of Astrology' in Patrick Curry (ed.) *Astrology, Science and Society: Historical Essays* (Woodbridge: Boydell Press, 1987), pp. 219–43.
[92] Whiston, *A Vindication of the New Theory of the Earth* (London, 1698), Preface.

mutations of the earth became increasingly popular. Thomas Robinson's *New Observations of the Natural History of this World* appeared in 1696, shortly after Whiston's *New Theory*. Robinson agreed with his predecessors that 'the Schematical Account which Moses has given of the Creation' was 'Philosophical' as well as 'Historical' and that the earth was 'created in a Natural Way, by the Agency of Second Causes'.[93] While disagreeing with Burnet's hypothesis of a perfectly spherical earth, he allowed that Noah's Flood had partly been caused by a great 'subterranean damp' in which waters had risen from the deep. He also believed that the conflagration of the earth would take place when the central vault, filled with volatile matter, broke out, converting the earth into a fiery planet.[94] John Woodward set forth the view, in his *Essay toward a Natural History of the Earth* (1695), that 'the whole Terrestrial Globe was taken all to pieces and dissolved at the deluge', thus returning to its original chaos.[95] The strata of sedimentary rocks with their enclosed fossils all date from this time. It was part of his aim, 'to evince the Fidelity and exactness of the Mosaick Narrative of the Creation, and of the Deluge'.[96] Woodward seems to have drawn inspiration from the earlier work of Nicolaus Steno's *Prodromus* (ET. 1671) in which may be found a similar view. Steno also thought that the fire in the earth's centre heated the subterranean waters, forcing it up to flood the earth. Steno again professed his central concern to be 'the agreement of *Nature* with *Scripture*'.[97]

Not all were appreciative of these efforts to harmonise scripture and science, however. Miracles seemed to have been the first casualty of the theories of the earth, and it was frequently alleged against the theorists that they had claimed for events presented in the Old Testament as miracles that in reality they fell within the ordinary operations of nature. Inasmuch as a scientific explanation could be offered for an event, that event could not at the same time be regarded as miraculous. John Keill, another Newtonian, who had championed his mentor's priority in the discovery of calculus against Leibniz, complained that Whiston had deduced the history of the formation of the earth 'from natural causes, and the necessary Laws of Mechanism'. His concern was that God's direct activity could be so easily dispensed with. Keill also argued with

[93] Robinson, *New Observations of the Natural History of this World of Matter, and of this World of Life*, (London, 1696), Preliminary Postulata.   [94] *Ibid.*, pp. 31, 80, 177f.
[95] This view was later re-asserted by Hutchinson, in *Moses's Principia*.
[96] Woodward, *Essay*, Preface.
[97] Nicolaus Steno, *The Prodromus to a Dissertation concerning Solids Naturally contained with Solids* (London, 1671), pp. 104, 99

respect to the Deluge that it was impossible 'for Nature, not assisted with
extraordinary divine power, to bring so much water upon the earth' as
to drown the whole globe.[98] Many of Keill's contemporaries advanced
the same argument. The Flood, Jean Le Clerc insisted, 'could not have
been effected without a Miracle'.[99] The earth's inundation, agreed
Erasmus Warren, was 'a *Miracle* in good measure'.[100] Attacks on
miracles, of course, were attacks on the authenticity of the Christian
revelation, and while this was clearly not the design of Burnet and
Whiston, their more conservative colleagues were concerned lest these
theories be turned against the orthodox faith. Robert Jenkin thought
that while Whiston and Burnet 'have too much Philosophy to have no
Religion' they had nonetheless 'put dangerous Weapons into the Hands
of those who have neither the one nor the other'.[101] Keill shared his
concern, insisting that Whiston had 'set the *Atheists* and *Theists* in a
method of attacking our Religion'. Edwards agreed that the 'theists'
(those sceptical of miracles and of the Christian revelation generally)
should be 'deeply obliged' to Burnet and Whiston.[102]

It cannot be doubted that the works of Burnet and Whiston called
into question Old Testament miracles. Whiston candidly admitted that
'those Events or actions are in Holy Scripture attributed immediately to
the Power or Providence of God, which yet were to all outward appearance according to the constant course of things, and would, abstracted
from such Affirmation of the Holy Books, have been esteem'd no more
miraculous than the other common Effects of Nature'.[103] This denial of
at least some divine interventions recorded in scripture weakened the
apologetic argument based on miracles. It was miracles which justified
the Christian revelation against those who preached a simplified religion of nature. It was miracles, moreover, which demonstrated the
superiority of the Christian dispensation over the competing creeds of
Jew and Turk. But the losses sustained by Christian apologetics with the
weakening of the argument from miracles were more than compensated
for by the additional support given to the argument from prophecy.[104]
Theories of the earth were not only concerned with reconciling past
sacred history with contemporary science. The theorists, and Burnet

---

[98] Keill, *Examination of the Reflections*, p. 11; *Examination of Dr Burnet's Theory*, p. 30.

[99] Le Clerc, *Twelve Dissertations*, p. 168. Cf. John Edwards, *Brief Remarks*, pp. 26f.; John Beaumont,
Considerations on a book entituled The Theory of the Earth (London, 1693), pp. 44–6, 185.

[100] Warren, *Geologia: Or, A Discourse concerning the Earth before the Deluge* (London, 1690), p. 355.

[101] Jenkin, *Reasonableness and Certainty*, p. x.

[102] Keill, *An Examination of the Reflections on The Theory of the Earth* (Oxford, 1699), p. 12; Edwards, *Brief
Remarks*, p. 29.   [103] Whiston, *New Theory*, p. 218.   [104] See Harrison, 'Newtonian Science'.

and Whiston in particular, wished to demonstrate that events prophesied in scripture concerning the end of the world would come about at
the time and in the manner specified by the biblical authors. Reconciliation was to be effected not only between the accommodated science of
Genesis and geology, but also between the scripture prophecies and
contemporary cosmology.[105]

THE SCIENCE OF THE LAST THINGS

'The world that then existed was deluged with water and perished. But
by the same word the heavens and earth that now exist have been stored
up for fire, being kept until the day of judgement and destruction of
ungodly men.' These words from the second Epistle of Peter proved to
be a fruitful source for those given to speculation on the manner and
timing of the millennium. They link the Deluge with the day of judgement, state that the heavens and the earth will be dissolved by fire, and
look forward to a time when there will be a new heavens and a new
earth. The author goes on to remind his readers of the Psalmist's
observation that a thousand years is as a day with God – a formula
which throughout history has been employed in various ways by those
who wish to calculate a specific date for the day of judgement.[106] Burnet
turned his attention to these eschatological matters in the last two books
of his *Theory of the Earth*. Here he considered a range of possibilities as to
how the present world might come to an end – the earth's orbit
approaching too close to the sun, or the eruption of the earth's central
fire – before concluding that the conflagration would be caused by a
combination of volcanoes, flammable materials in the earth's core, and
fiery meteors.[107] More, as we have seen, adopted the 'Cartesian' view
that the earth would fall into the sun. Fellow Platonists Rust and
Glanvill both thought that the eruption of the earth's central fire would
initiate that final holocaust in which the wicked would be burnt and the
earth destroyed. Glanvill differed from More, however, in believing that
the earth would be catapulted out of its vortex to become a wandering
comet.[108] Whiston, of course, thought that a comet would be the cause
of the earth's final conflagration, rather than its eventual outcome.[109]

[105] Jacob, *Newtonians and the English Revolution*, pp. 110f.; Webster, *Paracelsus to Newton*, pp. 38f.
[106] II Peter 3.5–13. Cf. Matthew 24.37; Luke 17.22–37; Psalm 90.4.
[107] Burnet, *Theory of the Earth*, bk III, chs. vi, vii. Cf. Ray's discussion of the end of the world in *Three Physico-Theological Discourses*, 2nd edn (London, 1693), pp. 305–53.
[108] Rust, *Letter of Resolution*, p. 74; Glanvill, *Lux Orientalis*, pp. 136f., 141.
[109] Whiston, *New Theory*, pp. 360f.

The effect of these theories was to bring the Eschaton within the span of historical time. In its original form, Christian eschatology – teaching about the end-times – had posited a temporal dualism: the coming kingdom of God was not a future historical event, it was the end of history. It did not take place in time, but brought time to an end.[110] According to the theorists, however, the world would come to an end by natural means, and therefore of necessity within historical time. God's purposes are, by implication, visible in the workings of the cosmic machine, and the empirical basis of biblical prophecies – at least those regarding the destruction of the world – should become evident to scientific enquirers. According to Whiston, God enacts his purposes 'by a constant Course of Nature, and Chain of Mechanical Causes'. The first death of the world by water, no less than the second by fire, demonstrates that God 'can as well provide and praedispose natural Causes for those Mutations, Mercies, or Judgements before-hand; he can as easily put the Machin to such motions as he shall'. Thus, Whiston concluded, 'the state of the *Natural* is always accommodated to that of the *Moral* World'.[111] If the millennium were to take place within history, rather than bringing history to an end, there remained the possibility that 'the new earth' would proceed in time in much the same way as the old one had, and perhaps with similar inhabitants. Our present world, in short, might represent one phase in an ongoing cycle of destruction and regeneration. Such had been the view of the Stoics, a view which Origen had attempted to synthesise with Christian eschatology. This cyclical view of the cosmos is implied in the frontispiece to Burnet's sacred history, and More and Newton both seem to have at least flirted with the idea.[112]

The incorporation of eschatological events into historical time was accompanied by the appearance of eschatological sites in empirical space. An integral part of the confirmation of biblical chronology and eschatology was a discussion of the location and topography of heaven, hell, and purgatory. Poetic fancies about the psychological nature of

---

[110] The events of the English revolution are obviously important factors here. The millennial kingdom of the English radicals was a political, earthly kingdom. See Jacob, *Newtonians and the English Revolution*, pp. 100–7; William Lamont, *Godly Rule, Politics and Religion 1603–60* (London: Macmillan 1969).   [111] Whiston, *New Theory*, p. 360.

[112] Descartes to More, 15 April 1649, in *Philosophical Letters*, tr. and ed. A. Kenny (Oxford: Clarendon, 1970), pp. 249f. Kubrin, 'Newton and the Cyclical Cosmos'; Garry Trompf, 'On Newtonian History', p. 225, in Stephen Gaukroger (ed.) *The Uses of Antiquity* (Dordrecht: Kluwer, 1991) 213–49.

these places were replaced with scientific speculation. Milton had spoken of 'Paradise within', asserting that 'The mind is its own place, and in itself / Can make a heav'n of hell, a hell of heav'n.' 'To hav Blessings and to Prize them is to be in Heaven' wrote Traherne, 'To hav them, and not to prize then, is to be in Hell.' Robert Burton believed that hell was to be found 'in the melancholy mans heart'. The allegorising Thomas Browne had thought that heaven and hell were states of mind, or degrees of proximity to the Deity.[113] But in the latter half of the seventeenth century, in much the same way that geographers had concerned themselves with the location of an original paradise once thought to be an allegory, likely sites for heaven and hell were sought in the physical cosmos.

In casting about for the location of hell, the comet-obsessed Whiston found yet another use for his favourite celestial body. The biblical descriptions of hell, he observed, 'exactly agree with the Nature of a Comet, ascending from the Hot regions near the Sun, and going into the Cold Regions beyond *Saturn*'. Comets, he reasoned, might well provide that stage onto which 'the Devil and his Angels, with wicked Men their Companions . . . shall be cast for their utter *Perdition* or *second Death*; which will be indeed a terrible but a most useful Spectacle to God's rational creatures'.[114] Tobias Swinden suggested that the sun would provide an equally appropriate venue for hell, being large enough to accommodate legions of the damned, and hot enough to ensure their misery.[115] A more simple expedient than either of these elaborate schemes was to identify the burning earth with hell. Burnet described the death of the present world in these terms:

Here are Lakes of Fire and Brimstone: Rivers of melted Glowing matter: Ten thousand Volcanoes vomiting flames all at once. Thick darkness and pillars of smoke twisted about with wreaths of flame, like fiery Snakes. Mountains of Earth thrown up into the Air, and the heavens dropping down in lumps of fire

---

[113] Milton, *Paradise Lost*, XII.587, I, 254f.; Traherne, 'Centuries', 1.47; Burton, *The Anatomy of Melancholy*, Pt 1 Sec. 4 memb. 1, subs.1; Browne, *Works* I, 60. Louis Martz observes also that 'Milton's device of calling the roll of the fallen angels under the names of the later false gods has the effect of gradually dissolving our consciousness of Hell as any special place.' *The Paradise Within: Studies in Vaughan, Traherne, and Milton*, (New Haven: Yale University Press, 1964) p. 111, cf. Milton, *Paradise Lost* 1.392–411.

[114] Whiston, *Astronomical Principles of Religion, Natural and Reveal'd* (London, 1717), p. 156. Cf. Derham, *Astro-Theology*, pp. 218f. For Whiston's later views on the location of hell, see *The Eternity of Hell Torments Considered* (London, 1740), p. 110.

[115] Tobias Swinden, *An Enquiry into the Nature and Place of Hell* (London, 1727), pp. 145, 154; Cf. Derham, *Astro-Theology*, p. 219. Also see Almond, *Heaven and Hell*, pp. 125–30.

. . . It will be hard to find any part of the Universe, or any state of things, that answers to so many of the properties and characters of *Hell*, as that which is now before us.[116]

If none of these locations was considered unpleasant enough to have the desired effect on the damned, there remained the traditional view that the torments of the wicked would take place at the fiery centre of the earth.[117] Hell-hunting was more popular than attempting to fix the location of heaven, but there was also speculation about the future abode of the saints. Swinden predictably placed heaven at the furthest remove from his solar hell – the Empyreum. Burnet and Derham believed that the saints would spend eternity in the starry regions beyond the moon.[118]

These scientifically informed speculations about the mutations which heavenly bodies would undergo at the end-times were accompanied by theorising about the transformations of earthly bodies. If Cartesian and Newtonian philosophies were brought to bear on the mysteries of the earth's conflagration and regeneration, scientific explanations were also sought for the resurrection, purgation and apotheosis of human bodies. Three 'natural' processes suggested themselves as possible mechanisms for the post-mortem modifications to which the bodies of saints and sinners would be subjected: the transformation of base metals into gold, the germination of seeds, and the metamorphosis of insects.

Martin Luther had shown considerable enthusiasm for alchemy on this account: 'I like it [alchaemy] also for the sake of the allegory and secret signification, which is exceedingly fine, touching the resurrection of the dead at the last day'.[119] Amongst alchemists the transmutation of metals became a popular sign of human resurrection. Like base metals transformed into gold, said Thomas Vaughan, on the last day we shall be changed 'in a Moment, in the twinkling of an Eye'.[120] John Swan entertained the related idea that the refining of metals was a natural metaphor for the purging and restoration of the creatures in those trying

---

[116] Burnet, *Sacred Theory*, p. 305.

[117] Glanvill, *Lux Orientalis*, p. 136; Walsh, *The Antediluvian World*, p. 137. Cf. Swinden, *An Enquiry*, p. 188; Derham, *Astro-Theology*, p. 219;

[118] Swinden, *An Enquiry*, p. 145; Burnet, *Sacred Theory*, p. 315; Derham, *Astro-Theology*, pp. 227f. Also see Almond, *Heaven and Hell*, p. 123.

[119] Qu. in S. Linden, 'Alchemy and Eschatology in Seventeenth Century Poetry', *Ambix* 31 (1984) 102. Origen and Pseudo-Jerome had used similar metallurgical images of bodily transformation. See Peter Brown, *The Body and Society: Men, Women and Sexual Renunciation in Early Christianity* (London: Faber and Faber, 1990), pp. 167f., 441f.

[120] Vaughan, *Lumen de Lumine*, in *The Works of Thomas Vaughan*, ed. Alan Rudrum (Oxford: Clarendon, 1984), p. 357. Cf. Fludd, *Truth's Golden Harrow*, in *Essential Readings*, pp. 151–3.

times: 'As silver and Gold is changed by the fire, the drosse perisheth, but the substance remaineth; so shall these Creatures be changed in that day, when there shall be nothing unchangd, because all things shall be renewed, and each thing brought into a perfect state.'[121] Thomas Browne wrote that alchemy 'hath taught me a great deal of divinity, and instructed my belief how that immortal spirit and incorruptible substance of my soul may lie obscure, and sleep awhile within this house of flesh'.[122]

The world of insects and plants afforded further representations of resurrection. The germination of seeds, initially noted by St Paul, was thought very agreeable to the idea of resurrection: 'Do we not see', said Fludd, 'after the same example, how the very grain of wheat is so exalted in vertue, after it hath endured corruption, and hath been freed from the grosse elementary tie, that it would mount and soar upward towards the heaven.'[123] Said Magus Thomas Vaughan: 'You must *unite* them to a *new life*, and they will be *regenerated* by *Water* and the *Spirit*. These *two* are in all *things*, they are placed there by *God himself*, according to that speech of *Trismegistus, Unumquodque habet in se semen suae Regenerationis* [Everyone has in him the seed of his own regeneration]'.[124] The reappearence of plants in spring, according to Stephen Switzer, 'may well be taken Notice of, as the natural and instructive Hieroglyphicks of our Resurrection and Immortality'.[125] The metamorphosis of insects provided a related illustration of bodily resurrection. Abbé Pluche stated that insects change their form 'by a new kind of Resurrection, or Metamorphosis' which converts them 'into another set of living animals'. One 'real animal' dies to make way for a second, which is present within the body of the first. This 'appearance of Death, . . . is no more than it's [sic] Passage to a

---

[121] Swan, *Speculum Mundi*, p. 464. The principle behind alchemical aspirations was that metals, and indeed all material objects, differed not in their primary matter (*Materia prima*) but in their form. Thus if the form could be changed, metals might be transmuted. Boyle explicitly relied on this principle in arguing that resurrection is logically possible. *Physico-Theological Considerations* pp. 26f. By analogy, the resurrection was the imposition of a new form, on the existing primary matter.

[122] Browne, *Religio Medici*, 1.39, 48 (pp. 42, 51). The 'transmigrations' of silkworms, and the 'artificial resurrection and revivification of mercury' taught similar lessons.

[123] I Corinthians 15:35–50; Fludd, *Mosaicall Philosophy*, p. 76; cf. *A Philosophical Key* and *Truth's Golden Harrow*, both in *Essential Readings*, pp.115, 156, 169. Also see Boyle, *Physico-Theological Considerations*, p. 9; Nicasius le Fabure, *A Compleat Body of Chemistry* (London, 1664), Pt. 1, p. 14.

[124] Vaughan, *Lumen de Lumine*, 92, in *Works*, p. 356. I have been unable to locate this quotation in the hermetic literature. Vaughan's poet brother Henry saw in the succession of morning and evening a type of human resurrection: '*Mornings* are *Mysteries*; the first worlds *Youth*, / Mans *Resurrection*, and the futures *Bud*. . .' 'Rules and Lessons' in *Complete Poetry*, lines. 25–6.

[125] Stephen Switzer, *The Practical Husbandman or Planter*, 2 vols. (London, 1733), I, lxiv.

more amiable State'.[126] Such natural occurrences, said Pluche, illustrate
the fact that 'all Nature abounds with sensible Images of celestial
Things, and the sublimest Truths'.[127]

New analogies drawn from careful observation and experiment thus
came to replace the old. Fables of the phoenix and pelican, of unicorn
and salamander, now treated with considerable scepticism, were replaced by observations of nature which were based on a more certain
foundation.[128] The literature which contained these dubious relations
suffered a similar loss of status. Christian doctrines needed no longer to
find confirmation in the fictitious accounts of animals, plants, and stones
found in the *Physiologus*, in the Bestiaries, and more popular works of
natural history. Instead the industrious investigation of the world yielded up authentic resemblances of eternal truths. In addition, in the
latter half of the seventeenth century, these natural processes themselves
increasingly came to be regarded not as 'images' or 'hieroglyphics' of
primeval and eschatological events, but came instead to constitute the
actual mechanisms thought to be involved. Alchemical transmutations
were not just allegories of creation or resurrection, as Luther had
suggested: creation and resurrection were chemical processes. The
metamorphosis of insects was not merely 'a sensible image' of life in the
next world, but gave clues to the nature of the physical transformations
which the human body would undergo. The subtle shift is exemplified in
the conclusions drawn from an unusual experimental procedure, apparently successfully conducted by several seventeenth-century virtuosi.

In an address to the Society for Promoting Philosophical Knowledge
by Experiments, presented at Gresham College on 23 January, 1660, Sir
Kenelm Digby listed a number of experiments in which the ashes of
plants produced, under certain experimental conditions, latent images
of roots, stalks, leaves and flowers. He reasoned that the 'essential

---

[126] Pluche, *Spectacle*, I, 21.

[127] *Ibid.*, I, 34. Natural analogies for other stages of the Christian life were also sought. Salvation was
said to be like transmutation, repentance akin to distillation. Birth, baptism, death, and
purgation were also thought to be emblemised in nature. See, e.g., Thomas Vaughan, *Lumen de
Lumine* (1651), in *Works*, p. 357; Peter Sterry MS 291, p. 100, (Emmanuel College Library); R.
Franck, *A Philosophical Treatise of the Original and Production of Things* (London, 1687), p. 27;
Bostocke, *Auncient Phisicke*, Sig. Li. v-r. Also see Mulligan, 'Robert Boyle', p. 247; Philip Almond,
'The Contours of Hell in English Thought, 1660–1750', *Religion* 22 (1992) 297–311; Wayne
Shumaker, *The Occult Sciences in the Renaissance* (Berkeley: University of California Press, 1972) p.
189.

[128] Hakewill, for example, considers the phoenix to be 'but a fiction', despite the fact that 'sundry of
the Fathers have brought this narration to confirme the doctrine of the Resurrection'. The
pelican, he likewise observes, does not have a beak sharp enough to pierce its own breast.
Hakewill, *An Apologie*, (3rd edn), pp. 10, 14.

substance' of the plant somehow persisted after its apparent annihilation. This he referred to as 'a true *Palingenesis*' or 'a Resurrection of it after once it is destroyed'. Such experiments put Digby in mind 'of the Resurrection of humane bodies' and satisfied him that 'there is not impossibility nor contradiction in nature, against this great and amazing mystery'.[129] Digby was one of the last champions of Aristotelianism, and this, along with his famous 'weapon salve' – a powder which could heal wounds sympathetically at a distance – did not endear him to advocates of the new philosophy. Yet similar trials in which plants, having been completely incinerated, mysteriously regenerated themselves were reported in other sources. Thomas Browne had referred to an experiment apparently conducted by Robert Fludd in which a plant, reduced to ashes, was regrown. Robert Boyle also mentions the experiment in his *Physico-Theological Considerations about the Possibility of the Resurrection* (1675). Browne's observation was that: 'This is that mysticall Philosophy from whence no true scholar becomes an atheist, but, from the visible effects of nature, grows up a real divine, and beholds, not in a dream as Ezekiel, but in an ocular and visible object the types of his resurrection.'[130] Boyle, however, like Digby, spoke not of 'types' but rather of specific mechanisms, theorising that 'there may remain a Plastick Power inabling them to contrive disposed matter, so as to reproduce such a Body as was formerly destroyed'.[131] Thus while for Digby resurrection was a mystery, it was neither contrary to nature, nor wholly miraculous. These were not observations of natural processes which resembled resurrection, they were instances of resurrection. John Pettus also made a series of observations about of the revivication of various natural objects subjected to incineration, concluding like Digby that 'these Conclusions by *Fire* be pertinent to the manner of our *resurrection*'.[132] Pettus believed, in other words, that the phenomena which he observed did not symbolise resurrection, but cast light on the actual mechanisms involved in our future re-embodiment. Such interpretations went well beyond the more circumspect and modest claims made by previous investigators. Erasmus Warren had thought only that 'Nature shews the futurity of the Resurrection, while it prettily adumbrates and prefigures it to us, by various and lively Symbols and Resemblances'.[133] Boyle was careful to

---

[129] Kenelm Digby, *A Discourse Concerning the Vegetation of Plants* (London, 1661).
[130] *Religio Medici.*, 1.48 (p. 51).
[131] Boyle, *Some Physico-Theological Considerations about the Possibility of the Resurrection* (London, 1675), pp. 10f. Cf. D'Espagnet, *Enchyridion physicae*, p. 148.
[132] Pettus, *History of Adam and Eve*, pp. 183f.
[133] Warren, *Geologia*, p. 17.

point out that despite his scientific interest in the problem, resurrection
was to be effected 'not by or according to the ordinary course of nature,
but by his [God's] own Power'.[134] For researchers such as Digby and
Pettus however, such investigations shed light on the physical 'manner'
or mechanism of resurrection.

Some of the practitioners of alchemy also wished to claim much more
for their chemical experiments than that they merely signified Divine
activities or theological doctrines. Thomas Tymme, the English translator of Calvin's commentary on Genesis, believed that God had actually
used alchemical processes to create the world, bringing it forth from an
elemental chaos 'by his Halchemicall Extraction, Separation, Sublima-
tion, and Coniunction'.[135] Robert Fludd spoke of 'the separation of one
region from another' effected by 'The Spagericall or high Chymicall
virtue of the word'.[136] In his influential treatise on chemistry Nicholas Le
Fevre, apothecary to Charles I, wrote that 'Chymistry makes all natural
things, extracted by the omnipotent hand of God, in the Creation, out of
the Abysse of the Chaos.'[137] Jean van Helmont likewise thought the first
production of the heavens and earth to be best understood as chemistry
on a grand scale. The procedures carried out by the chemist in his
laboratory were thus re-enactments of the divine work of creation.[138] In
addition to the earth, the creatures, too, were said to have been brought
forth by chemical processes. 'Alchymy', writes Tymme, is 'God's created handmaid, to conceine [sic] and bring forth his Creatures'. In the
last days, the unmaking of the world would also occur through the
processes of alchemy:

in the fulnesse & last period of time (which approacheth fast on us) the 4
elements (whereof al creatures consist) . . . shall by Gods *Halchemie* be metamor-
phosed and changed. For the combustible hauing in them a corrupt stinking
feces, or drossie matter, which maketh them subiect to corruption, shal in that
great & generall refining day, be purged through fire; And then God wil make
new heauens and a new Earth, and bring all things to a christalline cleernes, &
wil also make the 4 Elements perfect . . .[139]

Jean d'Espagnet believed similarly that 'rarefaction and condensation
are the two instruments of nature, by which spirits are converted into

---

[134] Boyle, *Physico-Theological Considerations*, pp. 3, 29.
[135] Thomas Tymme, Epistle Dedicatory, in Joseph Duchesne, *The Practise of Chymicall, and Hermeticall Physicke*, tr. Thomas Tymme, (London, 1605); Cf. Timothy Willis, *The Search for Causes*
(London, 1616), pp. 8–11.   [136] Fludd, *Mosaicall Philosophy*, p. 175.
[137] le Fabure, *Compleat Body of Chemistry*, Pt I, p. 9.   [138] Debus, *English Paracelsians*, pp. 105f.
[139] Thomas Tymme, Epistle Dedicatory, in Joseph Duchesne, *The Practise of Chymicall, and Hermeticall Physicke*, p. 175.

bodies, and bodies into spirits, and also by which corporeal elements are changed into spiritual Beings, and spiritual into corporeal'.[140]

Some late seventeenth-century writers speculated that human bodies would also undergo chemical transmutations to change them into a form fit for the next life. Lady Anne Conway, in her *Principles of the Most Ancient and Modern Philosophy* (1692), set out a remarkable account of the physical transformations which humans and animals would undergo at death, attributing them all to transmutation, a process which Conway believed could be observed throughout nature.[141] 'Barley and wheat are convertible one into the other, worms change into flies, and the earth brings forth creatures without seed.'[142] In passing from this present life humans, too, would undergo a similar transmutation. 'And so there is a certain Justice in all these, as in all the Transmutation of Things from one *Species* into another. . . Is it not just and equable, if a Man on earth lived a pure and Holy Life, like unto the Heavenly Angels, that he should be exalted to an Angelical Dignity after Death . . . ?'[143] Resurrection, for Conway, is yet another natural transmutation. Conway's views are echoed in the early thought of Leibniz.[144] The German philosopher believed that 'it is incomparably more reasonable to think of the transformation of animated bodies than to conceive of the passage of souls from one body to another, which latter opinion, though very ancient, seems to be merely a form of transformation not well understood'.[145] Furthermore, if animal bodies undergo transformations, it follows that there is in the animal world no real death nor birth, and that all creatures:

---

[140] D'Espagnet, *Enchyridion Symbolorum*, p. 144.

[141] Anne Conway, *The Principles of the Most Ancient and Modern Philosophy* (London, 1692), pp. 64–6, 69. Cf. Bulstrode Whitelock, *An Essay in Defence of Pythagoras* (London, 1692), pp. 6, 13f.; Anon, *Seder Olam* (London, 1694), pp. 12f.; Fludd, *Truth's Golden Harrow*, in *Essential Readings*, p. 169.

[142] *Ibid.*, 64f. [143] *Ibid.*, pp. 69f.

[144] Indeed, so alike are the theories of transmutation of Leibniz and Conway that some degree of mutual influence seems likely. There is, however, no direct evidence of such influence and, in any case, given the circle in which both thinkers moved – a circle which included both More and van Helmont – it is not surprising that in working upon similar problems from similar premises they would have converging views. It is possible that Conway exerted some influence on the thought of Leibniz through the medium of F. M. van Helmont, but there is no clear evidence of this. It is clear from his correspondence with Arnauld that Leibniz was developing his ideas about animal transformations in the 1680s. For discussions of the influence of the More/Conway/van Helmont circle on Leibniz, see: Stuart Brown, 'Leibniz and More's Cabbalistic Circle', in Sarah Hutton (ed.), *Henry More (1614–1678) Tercentenary Studies* (Dordrecht: Kluwer, 1990) pp. 77–95; Nicholson (ed.) *Conway Letters*, 454–6.

[145] Leibniz to Arnauld, April 30, 1687, in *Discourse on Metaphysics, Correspondence with Arnauld, and Monadology*, tr. George Montgomery, (Chicago: Open Court, 1902), pp. 229f.

have been living from the very creation of the world, and that they will live to its end, and that birth being apparently only a change consisting in growth, so death is only a change or diminution which causes this animal to re-enter into the engulfing of a world of minute creatures, where perceptions are very limited until the command comes calling them to return to the theatre of action. The ancients made the mistake of introducing the transmigration of souls, in place of the transformation of the same animal which always preserves the same soul. They put metempsychoses in place of metaschematismi.[146]

For Leibniz the resurrection of human bodies was a special case of the progression of all living things towards perfection. This progression involved the natural transformation of bodies: 'Things progress of themselves toward grace along natural lines.'[147] Each of the substances which makes up living things, Leibniz says elsewhere, 'contains in its nature the law of the continuous progression of its own workings'.[148] Resurrection, then, is merely another kind of natural process. It is also significant that Leibniz and Conway both reject the Platonic dualism upon which the symbolic view of nature was premised. Material transformations cannot mirror spiritual ones, for they are ultimately one and the same.

In the main, Conway had relied upon alchemy to provide the mechanism of biological and spiritual transformation. Leibniz, influenced by microscopic discoveries in the late seventeenth century, seized upon the processes of animal generation as the key to an understanding of the spiritual mutations of living things. The notion that a seed from the old body would provide a foothold for the new – a view supported by the various experiments in which plants were regenerated from their ashes – was to mesh neatly with the related theories of embryological preformation and insect metamorphosis which were dominant in the second half of the seventeenth century. Jan Swammerdam, Bernard Niewentydt, and numerous others held the view that the reproduction of living things did not entail the creation of a new life, but the development from a seed or even a complete miniature organism which could be found within one of the parents prior to conception.[149] The

---

[146] *Ibid.*, p. 195. Also see n. 43 above. Leibniz believed that the microscope provides us glimpses of what conceivably could happen after the 'death' of animals – namely that they continue *in this world* in another form.   [147] *Monadology*, 88.

[148] Leibniz to Arnauld, March 1690, *Correspondence with Arnauld*, p. 244.

[149] Malebranche, *Father Malebranche his Treatise Concerning the Search After Truth*, 2nd edn, tr. T. Taylor, (London, 1700), p. 54 ; Swammerdam, *Historia insectorum generalis* (Utrecht, 1669), pt II, 29f.; Whiston, *New Theory*, p. 224; Bentley, *Works*, III, 83; le Fabure, *Compleat Body of Chemistry*, p. 14; Pluche, *Spectacle*, I, 11f., 250, 275; Ray, *Three Physico-Theological Discourses*, pp. 46–50, 60f.; van Helmont, *A Cabbalistic Dialogue* (London, 1682), pp. 135, 153; George Cheyne, *Philosophical*

process of generation, according to this view, was not the miraculous coming into being of a new creature, but the augmentation of one already existing.[150] One version of the theory extended to the claim that all the creatures that have ever lived, and ever shall live, had existed in microscopic form, each encased within its parent, from the time of the creation. Malebranche thought 'that there are infinite Trees conceal'd in a single Cicatricle; since it not only contains the future Tree wherefor it is the seed, but also abundance of other seeds, which may include in them new Trees still, and new Seeds of Trees'. On the same principle, 'we ought to think, That all the bodies of Men and of Beasts, which should be born or produc'd till the *End* of the World, were possibly created from the *Beginning* of it'.[151] This was a kind of material equivalent to the notion of pre-existing souls espoused by Origen, in this new form, as we have already seen, adopted by Leibniz. It also meshed neatly with the idea of original sin: in Adam, all men sinned because all men were physically present in Adam when he sinned, albeit in microscopic form. Adam did not symbolise the human race, he literally was the human race. Boyle lecturer George Cheyne thought it 'highly probable that we are all deriv'd from one *Seed*, and were once all actually in the Loynes of our first Parent, and have been ever since, growing to our present estate'. In this manner, human beings, and indeed all living creatures, possess 'an active and permanent principle of *Immortality* (so to speak) which is communicated to them from the Divine Nature, as being his

---

Principles of Religion: Natural and Revealed, 2nd edn (London, 1714), p. 168; Derham, *Physico-Theology,* p. 246. On theories of embryological pre-existence, see Jacques Roger, *Les Sciences de la Vie dans la Pensée Française du XVIIIe Siècle,* 2nd edn (Paris: Armand Colin, 1971), ch. 3; Peter Bowler, 'Preformation and Pre-existence in the Seventeenth Century', *JHB* 4 (1971) 221–44; Edward Ruestow, 'Piety and the defence of natural order: Swammerdam on generation', in Margaret Osler and Paul Farber (eds.) *Religion, Science, and Worldview* (Cambridge University Press, 1985).

[150] Strictly, Swammerdam's version of pre-existence involved what Peter Bowler has described as 'a pre-existent design, in the form of a material system "programmed" to develop into the living organism'. Bowler, 'Preformation and Pre-existence', p. 237. Ruestow adds that Swammerdam's pre-existing design 'bore within it not only the blueprint for the construction of the animal, but the pattern for the unfolding of both the behaviour and the physical changes of its specific life cycle as well'. 'Swammerdam on generation', p. 241.

[151] Malebranche, *Search after Truth,* pp. 54, 14, cf. p. 57. Centuries before, Augustine proposed that at the time of creation God had pre-formed the seeds [*semina*] of all living things – animal and vegetable – which were ever to exist. *De Gen ad lit* v.4.9–11; v.7.20; vi.6.10. Also see Ettiene Gilson, *The Christian Philosophy of Saint Augustine* (London: Victor Gollancz, 1961), 197–209; Michael McKough, *The Meaning of the Rationes Seminales in St Augustine* (Washington: Catholic University of America, 1926). Contemporary discussions of instantaneous creation, or creation of seminal forms, can be found in d'Espagnet, *Enchyridion physicae restitutae,* p. 109; Henry More, *Antidote,* 2nd edn, pp. 53, 79f.; van Helmont, *Oriatrike,* p. 31; Anon., *Two Remarkable Paradoxes*; Anon., *Seder Olam,* pp. 15f.; John Ray, *Three Physico-Theological Discourses,* 2nd edn (London, 1693), pp. 46–60; Thomas Robinson, *The Anatomy of the Earth* (London, 1694), p. 2.

Images and Emanations from him'.[152] The theory of emboitement, then, was as Pluche put it, 'most conformable to Reason and Experience, to the Omnipotence of God, and to the sacred Writings'.[153]

The initial impetus for this version of pre-existence came from Jan Swammerdam's observations of insect metamorphosis. Swammerdam noted that the new creature – say, a butterfly – can be observed *in toto* in the body of the old – the caterpillar. The theory of preformation of germs was seen by some to provide a link between the process of generation and *re*generation. In the words of Thomas Vaughan: 'The *Laws* of the *Resurrection* are founded upon *those* of the *Creation*, and those of *regeneration* upon those of *Generation*.'[154] The sphere of nature was thus seen to be linked to the sphere of grace: the physical process of generation, newly discovered, was posited as a likely mechanism for the resurrection of the body. George Cheyne thus observed that 'the Production of a Plant from its *Miniature* in the Seed; and of an *animal* from an *Animalcule*, is an astonishing Representation of the Resurrection of the Body'.[155] In the next century, speculations of this kind reached their peak in Charles Bonnet's theory of 'palingenesis'. In *Palingénésie philosophique* Bonnet argues that this present creation is but one stage in a cosmic succession of worlds.[156] In the initial creation, each soul was encased in a number of germs – one for each re-creation of the world. As successive worlds are born and die, human souls progress through the various germs, eventually reaching the highest form of perfection.[157] Animals, too, are promoted through the revolutions of the worlds. There may be latent Newtons amongst the present day apes, Perraults amongst the beavers. In future worlds, carnivores will cease to prey on their fellow creatures, plants will be animals, even microbes will be transformed into something more worthy.[158] Bonnet thus completes the naturalisation of eschatology begun by the English theorists, makes

---

[152] Cheyne, *Philosophical Principles*, I, 323, 192   [153] Pluche, *Spectacle*, I, 11f.

[154] Vaughan, *Magia Adamica* (1650), in *Works*, p. 185.   [155] Cheyne, *Philosophical Principles*, II, 130.

[156] Lovejoy, *Great Chain of Being*, p. 285. Bonnet's 'palingenesis' from the Greek παλιγγενεσία - rebirth, regeneration, resurrection. Cf. Matt. 19.28.

[157] 'To be transported from place to place with a speed equal to the speed of light; to be sustained by the force of nature without the help of any created being, to be absolutely exempt from every sort of alteration; to possess the power to move celestial bodies, or change the course of nature; to be endowed with the most exquisite and extensive awareness; to have distinct perceptions of all attributes of matter and all its modifications; to discover effects in their causes; to rise on the swiftest wing to the most general of principles . . .' and so on. *Contemplation*, I, 24f. It is not entirely clear, however, that Bonnet accepted the fully-blown theory of emboitement. Faced with the example of Trembley's budding polyp, he was to speak of a 'preordination' or 'the primordial foundation' which formed the basis of the new creature ('La palingénésie', pt VII, ch. iv).

[158] Bonnet, 'La palingénésie', *Oeuvres*, 16, 136, 73–5, 110–1.

explicit their tentative speculations about successions of worlds, and anticipates the dynamic evolution of Darwin. 'Perhaps', he mused, 'there will be a continued progress, more or less slow, of all species towards a higher perfection.'[159]

Posterity has not looked favourably upon these physico-theological accounts of the mutations of the earth and its inhabitants. In the eighteenth century, Count Louis Buffon passed harsh judgement on the previous generation's attempt to harmonise the books of scripture and nature. Burnet's theory was an 'elegant romance', and the man himself 'a heterodox divine, whose brain was so fully impregnated with poetical illusions that he imagined he had seen the universe created'. Whiston's hypothesis was 'extravagant and fantastical', a 'medley of strange notions'. The most remarkable feature of Whiston's book, in Buffon's view, was that he had managed to make it all sound plausible. All in all, the English theorists 'mistook passages of holy writ for physical facts', and their combined work merely represented 'the dark clouds of physical theology'.[160] Alchemy, too, became a totally discredited activity, an occult art, the direct antithesis of genuine chemistry. A discipline in disgrace, it could hardly function as an appropriate model for creation and resurrection. The mechanisms of insect metamorphosis were also better understood in the eighteenth century, and the preformation theory became simply another casualty of a progressive natural science. The imaginative thesis of human metamorphosis could no longer be sustained when the insect model on which it was based proved to be fatally flawed. These failed syntheses nonetheless represent an important phase in the history of the relationship between biblical hermeneutics and the natural sciences, a phase during which the literal truths of scripture and the theoretical truths of the new science were believed to coincide exactly. The two books were held to be in complete accord, and as the knowledge of nature could aid in the interpretation of scripture, so knowledge of scripture could assist in the understanding of nature. Scripture had provided a rudimentary sketch of the various mutations of the earth. Cartesian, and subsequently Newtonian, science

---

[159] *Ibid.*, III.iii, p. 149, qu. in Bentley Glass, 'Heredity and Variation in the Eighteenth Century Concept of the Species', p. 168. Also see Lorin Anderson, *Charles Bonnet and the Order of the Known* (Dordrecht: Reidel, 1982), pp. 7f., 26.

[160] Buffon, *Natural History*, I, 113, III, 101, 109, 131. Jean Le Clerc had earlier made similar remarks, chastising his contemporaries for mixing their chaff with the wheat of the biblical authors: 'What a monstrous Mosaick dress have we in Whiston's Theory with a train of Comets at his Tail; in Woodward's Essay with all the Mountains down about his Heels; in Nicholl's Conference with multitudes of Arks . . . and his Lyons in Greenland. Le Clerc, *Twelve Dissertations*, Sig. A3r, A4r.

had filled in the details. Whiston and Burnet thus utilised scientific theories as a novel hermeneutical principle which enabled them to read the sacred history of Moses in a new light and for the first time to discern the real meaning behind the accommodated message of the sacred historian. Scripture had also made reference to the future renovation of human bodies, the likelihood of which seemed to be greatly enhanced by the observations of Swammerdam and Niewentydt. The theory of embryonic preformation confirmed, for its adherents, scriptural claims about original sin and bodily resurrection.

The focus on eschatological concerns, however, is perhaps the most interesting feature of these accounts. Here we see the Christian doctrine of the last things divested of its metaphorical elements and imported virtually intact into the realm of nature. The timetable of the last days was explained in terms of cosmological theories, the resurrection of bodies accounted for within the ordinary operations of nature, physical locations were provided for heaven and hell, a geological account given of the formation of the new earth: even the purging of sin and torments of the damned were explained in physical terms. The genre of *physica sacra* thus exemplifies the collapse of a number of related dualisms. Spiritual readings of scripture are reduced to a single literal sense, the ontological dualism of Plato is replaced by monism, the distinction between the natural and supernatural becomes blurred as the realms of nature and grace merge, and the temporal dualism of the Judaeo-Christian apocalyptic tradition is accommodated within the single dimension of historical or geological time.

CHAPTER 5

The purpose of nature

So that clearly we must suppose . . . that plants exist for the sake of animals and the other animals for the good of man, the domestic species both for his service and his food, and if not at all events most of the wild ones for the sake of his food and of his supplies of other kinds, in order that they may furnish him both with clothing and with other appliances. If therefore nature makes nothing without purpose or in vain, it follows that nature has made all the animals for the sake of man.

Aristotle, Politics

> For us the windes do blow,
> The earth doth rest, heav'n move, and fountains flow;
> Nothing we see but means our good,
> As our delight or as our treasure;
> The whole is either our cupboard of food
> Or cabinet of pleasure.

George Herbert, 'Man'.

Let man then contemplate the whole of nature in her full and lofty majesty, let him behold the dazzling light set like an eternal lamp to light up the universe, let him see the earth as a mere speck compared to the vast orbit described by this star, and let him marvel at finding this vast orbit itself to be no more than the tiniest point compared to that described by the stars revolving in the firmament. . .

The eternal silence of these infinite spaces fills me with dread.

Pascal, Pensées

THE ENDS OF THE CREATION

With the collapse of the sacramental view of the cosmos, those questions which had previously found solutions in the symbolic character of natural objects posed themselves anew. The shrinkage of the symbolic world of the Middle Ages brought with it an increasing emphasis on the utility of natural things, and in the absence of some obvious application to human needs, provided motivation for natural philosophers to seek out the divine purposes hidden in the things of nature. In this way it now became incumbent upon students of nature to investigate the undiscovered utilities of those things whose usefulness had previously been found only at a symbolic level. As animals, plants, stones, and celestial bodies ceased to function as signs, the order of the natural world could only be maintained if alternative purposes could be found for them. The seventeenth century witnesses the change from a world which is ordered symbolically by resemblances to one which is ordered according to structural similarities, or abstract mathematical relations, and always, at a higher level, divine purposes. A clear indication of the new, non-symbolic status of living creatures is provided by the re-emergence of the problem of useless or hostile animals and plants. Indeed, in the seventeenth century the more general problem of evil reasserts itself in an acute way, signalling the disintegration of those epistemic structures which had given meaning to nature. No longer could it be confidently asserted with the Fathers that apparently purposeless features of the created world actually represented higher things of considerable import. If the natural world was again to make sense, some new account of innumerable creatures which served no obvious purpose had to be found.

A number of seventeenth-century writers fell back upon those alternative explanations which had always been part of the Christian tradition. Wild or vicious creatures, for example, might be regarded as instruments of divine justice. Harmful animals existed 'for punishment and reuenge against man', 'to chastise and correct', or to put God's people 'in remembrance of their sinfulnesse and corruption'.[1] Wild animals, Abbé Pluche thought, 'chastise Mortals when they grow impious and abandoned'. Worms and flies, similarly, 'are employed by the Almighty to humble the Pride of Men'.[2] Scottish preacher John Cockburn declared that locusts and caterpillars 'are a Party of the Army of the Lord of Hosts, which he sends out at his Pleasure, to chastise the Pride, Wantonness, Ingratitude, and Forgetfulness of man, who is the only disorderly Part of the Creation'.[3] 'Noxious Creatures', agreed William Derham, echoing Basil the Great, 'serve as Rods and Scourges to chastise us'.[4]

[1] Daneau, *Wonderfull Woorkmanship*, fol. 84v.; Walker, *History of the Creation*, p. 151.
[2] Pluche, *Spectacle*, I, 204, 28.
[3] Cockburn, *An Enquiry*, p. 40; Cf. Edwards, *A Demonstration*, pt 1, p. 241.
[4] Derham, *Physico-Theology*, pp. 55f.

Others adopted the principle of plenitude as set out by Augustine, and before him, Plotinus: *Non essent omnia, si essent aequalia* – if all things were equal, all things could not exist. If there is to be a variety of things in the creation, then things must vary in perfection.[5] Less perfect creatures are just that – creatures which if more perfect would actually be something else. Considered together, all things have beauty and each individual thing is beautifully adjusted to the rest of creation, and contributes to the whole as to a commonwealth.[6] God, Lactantius had pointed out, 'wished to display His providence and power by a wonderful variety of many things'.[7] Seventeenth-century proponents of the great chain of being regarded noxious creatures as necessarily occupying levels of being which would otherwise be vacant. 'It was necessary that there shou'd be a variety of Natures, and different Degrees of Life and Perfection', wrote Thomas Robinson. Thus 'every Creature even of the lowest Degree of Life, is Good and Perfect in its Kind'.[8] Cockburn agreed that God created 'an Infinite Variety of Beings, endued with all Degrees of Perfection'.[9] With 'greater Variety, the greater Art is seen', observed Derham.[10] The idea of the great chain of being was to play a central role in more general seventeenth- and eighteenth-century explanations of the imperfections of the natural world. The influential theodicies of Archbishop William King and Leibniz were both grounded on the Neoplatonic conception.[11] Augustine's aesthetic solution to the existence of problematic beings was also given a new hearing.[12] Henry More thought that animals of 'an *hateful* aspect . . . are byt like *Discords* in Musick, to make the succeeding chord goe off more pleasantly'.[13] Pluche borrowed Augustine's original image of the degrees of light and shade in a painting: 'neither are the most uncultivated

---

[5] *City of God*, xi.22. Elsewhere, Augustine was more explicit: 'The order of creatures proceeds from top to bottom by just grades, so that it is the remark of envy to say: That creature should not exist, and equally to say: *That* one should be different. It is wrong to wish that anything should be like another thing higher in the scale, for it has its own being, perfect in its degree, and nothing ought to be added to it'. *On Free Will*, iii, ix, 24, in *Augustine: Earlier Writings* tr. John Burleigh, (London: SCM, 1953), p. 185.   [6] *City of God* xi.22. Cf. *Confessions* vii.13; Plotinus, *Enneads*, i.viii.12.

[7] Lactantius, *On the Workmanship of God*, v (*ANF* vii, 6).

[8] Robinson, *New Observations*, pp. 139f., cf. p. 12; Cockburn, *An Enquiry*, p. 42; Edwards, *A Demonstration*, pt i, p. 233; More, *Antidote*, p. 53; Daneau, *Wonderfull Woorkmanship*, fol. 86r.

[9] Cockburn, *An Enquiry*, p. 42.   [10] Derham, *Physico-Theology*, p. 55.

[11] William King *De origine mali* (London, 1702); Leibniz, *Essais de Théodicée* , 2 vols. (Amsterdam, 1734). Also see Hick, *Evil and the God of Love*, ch. vii.

[12] Augustine, *Confessions* vii.xiii. The aesthetic view also had numerous medieval supporters. See Wanda Cizewski, 'Reading the World as Scripture', p. 75, 'Beauty and the Beasts: Allegorical Zoology in the Twelfth-Century Hexaemeral Literature, in H. J.Westra (ed.), *From Athens to Chartres: Neoplatonism and Medieval Thought* (Leiden: Brill, 1992), pp. 289–300.

[13] More, *Antidote*, p. 65. Cf. Daneau, *Wonderfull Woorkmanship*, fol. 86v–r.

Heaths, and barren Deserts, without their Usefulness: They are like
Shades in a Picture; they give more Life and Strength to the other
Parts'.[14] Thomas Robinson adopted the same metaphor, arguing that
those creatures which are 'less Beautiful and Lovely set off the Beauty of
the rest, as shadows set off the more lively colours'.[15] Edwards stated
simply that the hurtful things of nature 'are appointed by God to be a
Foil to the rest'. Snails and snakes are 'as beautiful in their kind in the
Universe as Angels and Cherubims'.[16]

The notion of Irenaeus, that human beings need to experience
adversity in this world if they are to be fit to enter the next, attracted
support amongst early modern writers. Lambert Daneau argued that
less friendly parts of the created order were there in order 'to proove,
tempt, and exercise Man'.[17] Henry More submitted that 'even those
stinking *Weeds* and *poisonous Plants* have their use. For first, the Industry
of Man is exercised by them to weed them out where they are hurtful'.
In addition, 'those *Herbs* that the rude and ignorant would call *Weeds* are
the Materials of very sovereign Medicines'. More concludes by observing that 'if humane Industry had nothing to conflict and struggle with,
the fire of mans Spirit would be half extinguish'd in the flesh'.[18] Derham
thought that venomous animals and plants acted 'as means to excite our
Wisdom, Care, and Industry', while John Edwards pointed out that
these creatures offer the individual 'a frequent opportunity of exercising
his Patience, or arming himself with Contentment and Humble resigna-
tion, or exerting his Fortitude and Self-denial'.[19]

It was also frequently claimed with respect to venomous animals and
plants that things might have been far worse, or that the evils of which
creatures were capable were always mitigated or limited in some way.
Edward Reynolds spoke of 'the strange instinct that God hath put into
some hurtfull Creatures to feare man, as the Serpent; into others to
come abroad at such times only when man stayeth in'.[20] Tame beasts,
others pointed out, 'seem disposed by Nature to be Domestic Animals
and live among us' whereas wild beasts 'delight to dwell in the Woods
and solitary Desarts, and of their own accord seem to avoid the Company of Men'.[21] Noxious animals, moreover, give warning. Here Will-

---

[14] Pluche, *Spectacle*, III, 113.
[15] Robinson, *New Observations*, p. 141; Cf. Cockburn, *An Enquiry*, p. 61.
[16] Edwards, *A Demonstration*, pt I, p. 232, 188–9.   [17] Daneau, *Wonderfull Woorkmanship*, fol. 84v.
[18] More, *Antidote*, pp. 55f.
[19] Derham, *Physico-Theology*, p. 56; Edwards, *A Demonstration*, pt I, p. 240.
[20] Reynolds, *Treatise of the Passions*, p. 433. Cf. Psalm 104.20–23.
[21] Bernard Niewentydt, *The Religious Philosopher*, 3 vols. (London, 1718), II, 629. Cf. Pluche, *Spectacle*,

iam Derham refers us to the shark and rattle-snake. The shark, apparently, turns on its back the instant before it attacks; the rattlesnake, more obligingly, warns potential victims while they are yet some distance away.[22] Poisonous plants, according to Daneau, are repositories for poison which they have filtered from the earth. Without them, wholesome plants would be polluted. Henry More agreed, suggesting that poisonous plants might remove poison from the soil as 'vulgarly is phancied concerning *Toads* and other poisonous *Serpents*, that they lick the venome from off the Earth'.[23] This latter opinion – that toads and serpents were only venomous because they purged the earth of poison – still attracted writers who could not justifiably be numbered amongst the ranks of the vulgar. Archbishop William King maintained that serpents, 'tho a Race hateful to us', 'gather Poison out of the Earth', rendering it more habitable.[24] William Derham, Thomas Robinson, and John Edwards concurred, with Robinson and Edwards adding that flies purify the air in a similar manner (which explains why they are always to found in the vicinity of 'any thing that is putrid and corrupt').[25]

For those who accepted the doctrines of Paracelsus, poisons, in small doses, made excellent medicines. 'Why then should poison be rejected and despised', wrote Paracelsus, 'For what has God created that is not blessed with a great gift for the good of man.'[26] Also in mitigation of the evils of venomous creatures was the widely held view that all noxious animals and plants carried an antidote. 'Ev'n poysons praise Thee', wrote George Herbert, for where there is poison, is always found the antidote.[27] John Edwards agreed that 'there is no Venomous Creature but carries its *Antidote* with it'.[28] Derham advanced the opinion that 'many, if not most of our European venomous animals carry their Cure, as well as Poison in their own Bodies. The Oil, and I doubt it not, the Body of *Scorpions* too, is a certain Remedy against its stroke'. He went on to explain that crushed bees, wasps and hornets act against their stings, and the flesh and heads of vipers act as antidotes to their poisons.[29] Sir

---

I, 204, II, 21, 294; Cockburn, *An Enquiry*, p. 39.

[22] Derham, *Physico-Theology*, p. 56 n.4.

[23] Daneau, *Wonderfull Woorkmanship*, Sig. 84v. More, *Antidote*, p.56.

[24] King, *Origin of Evil*, 134. Also 'Poison,' E. Chamber's *Cyclopedia*, 2 vols. (London, 1728). This claim was also made in Henry of Langenstein, *Lecturae super prologum et Genesim* I:90ra.

[25] Derham, *Physico-Theology*, bk 2, ch. 6; Robinson, *Anatomy of the Earth*, p. 5; Edwards, *A Demonstration*, pt I, pp. 237f.   [26] Paracelsus, *Four Treatises*, p. 21.

[27] George Herbert, 'Providence' lines 85–8.

[28] Edwards, *A Demonstration*, pt I, p. 239. Cf. Daneau, *Wonderfull Woorkmanship*, fol. 83r.; E. Chambers, *Cyclopaedia*, (London, 1728), 2 vols. sv. 'Poison', (II, 844b).

[29] Derham, *Physico-Theology*, p. 56, n.4.

Thomas Browne noted that animals which eat poisons can be used as antidotes for those poisons. 'Animalls that can innoxiously digest these poisons become antidotall unto the poyson digested. . . The bloud or flesh of Storks against the venome of Serpents, the Quaile against Hellebore, and the Dyet of Starlings against the draught of Socrates [hemlock].'[30]

Finally, not inconsistent with any of these explanations, and in a sense reinforcing them all, was the idea that apparently useless or hostile things existed as a spur to human industry. Most seventeenth-century natural philosophers shared a commitment to the principle that God had made everything with a purpose, and that it was human destiny to seek out that purpose. Things apparently useless and hostile did not, therefore, impugn the providence of God, but were rather living indictments of human idleness.[31] John Ray chided his dilatory peers for their indifference to the natural world: 'Some Reproach methinks it is to Learned Men, that there should be so many Animals still in the World, whose outward shape is not yet taken notice of, much less their way of Generation, Food, Manners, Uses observed.'[32] Scottish divine John Cockburn insisted that 'we cannot without Rashness conclude that a thing is without Contrivance, because we cannot find it out, nor is intended for any use, because we cannot perceive it. Our knowledge is very much limited, and it is impossible for us to comprehend all that God doth'.[33] William Derham pointed to the lessons of history – that 'what both seemed useless in one Age, hath been revered in another: as all the new Discoveries in Physick, and all the Alterations in Diet do sufficiently witness'.[34] Robert Boyle provided examples: Opium, formerly looked upon as a poison, 'is now imploy'd as a noble remedy'; the silk worm, sugar cane, and cocheneal, once despised or ignored, had each now found a purpose.[35]

---

[30] Browne, *Pseudodoxia Epidemica*, VII. xvii (I, 597).

[31] According to Augustine, in the puzzling and painful elements of creation there is 'a hidden utility' which we have as yet failed to discover. These mysteries serve at once as a spur to 'investigate their utility with care' and as a levelling of our pride. Cf. Plotinus, who states that 'the animal, too, exists of necessity, and is serviceable in many ways, some obvious and many progressively discovered. . .' *Enneads*, III.ii.9.

[32] Ray, *Wisdom of God*, p. 130; Cf. Pluche, *Spectacle*, I, 241.

[33] Cockburn, *An Enquiry*, p. 60; Cf. Edwards, *A Demonstration*, pt 1, p. 230; Robinson, *New Observations*, p. 142.

[34] Derham, *Physico-Theology*, p. 58. Cf. More's comment that knowledge of the uses of the creatures would always be incomplete so that 'succeeding Ages may ever have something left to gratifie themselves in their own discoveries'. *Antidote*, p. 56.

[35] Boyle, *A Disquisition about the Final Causes of Natural Things* (London, 1688), pp. 82, 91–3. It was also pointed out that things not useful to man may be useful to other creatures. Derham, *Physico-Theology*, p. 59; Cf. Edwards, *A Demonstration*, pt 1, p. 234.

Seventeenth-century natural history, then, imposes order on the world not through a passive reading which yields up meanings, but by an active investigation of things which uncovers their material utility. Such investigation remains a religious duty. Again, Bacon had set the tone: 'the Psalms and other scriptures do often invite us to consider and magnify the great and wonderful works of God, so if we should rest only in the contemplation of the exterior of them as they first offer themselves to our sense, we should do a like injury unto the majesty of God'.[36] The worship of God in nature thus went well beyond the offering of platitudinous remarks about the beauty of sunsets, the starry firmament, or the contrivance of complex creatures. Thomas Browne observed that the 'wisdom of God receives small honour from those vulgar heads, that rudely stare about, and with a grosse rusticity admire his workes; those highly magnify him whose judicious enquiry into his acts, and deliberate research into his creatures, returne the duty of a devout and learned admiration'.[37] Scripture not only commends God's works, William Derham reminded his readers, but also those 'curious and ingenious Enquirers that *Seek them out,* or *pry into them*'.[38]

The book of nature might thus have been open to all, but its investigation required more than a cursory reading. Nature was, as Shakespeare's soothsayer put it, 'an infinite book of secrecy'.[39] Galileo and Hooke, both of whom had emphasised the equivocal nature of the book of scripture, conceded that the book of the creature, if not ambiguous, was in many places obscure and difficult. Galileo wrote that nature does not care 'a whit whether her abstruse reasons and methods of operation are understandable to men'. Robert Hooke agreed that 'the footsteps of Nature are to be trac'd, not only in her ordinary course, but when she seems to be put to her shifts, to make many doublings and turnings, and to use som kind of art in indeavouring to avoid our discovery'.[40] Bacon, of course, had already made the same point: 'the secrets of nature reveal themselves more readily under the vexations of art than when they go their own way'.[41] The easy assumption of nature's accessiblity had been the major flaw of Aristotelianism. The philosopher had too readily assumed that nature was an open book, and his philosophy was based upon common-sense deductions from ordinary experiences. It was for this reason that he had failed to gain genuine insights into the phenom-

---

[36] Bacon, *Advancement of Learning*, i.vi.16 (p. 42).   [37] Browne, *Religio Medici*, i.13 (p. 14).
[38] Derham, *Physico-Theology*, p. 466.   [39] Shakespeare, *Antony and Cleopatra*, i.ii.8.
[40] Galileo, *Letter to the Grand Duchess Christina* in *Discoveries and Opinions*, tr. Drake, p. 183. Cf. pp. 187, 199; Hooke, *Micrographia* (London, 1665), Preface.   [41] Bacon, *Novum Organum* 1.98 (p. 69).

ena of inertia and motion, and had overlooked the connexion between the circular motions of the heavenly spheres and the linear motions of terrestrial bodies.

Fortunately God had equipped the human race, or some of them at any rate, with acute minds and senses, capable of discovering nature's hidden treasures. Indeed in the exercise of human wit natural philosophers were fulfilling the purposes for which God had created rational beings. The aim of the study of nature, according to Derham, was 'to answer the Ends for which God bestowed so much Art, Wisdom and Power about them, as well as given us Senses to view and survey them, and an Understanding and Curiosity to search into them'.[42] More, Hakewill, Ray, and Cockburn had expressed similar views. 'The Theatre of the world is an exercise of Mans wit', wrote More, 'therefore all things are in some measure obscure and intricate, that the sedulity of that divine Spark, the Soul of Man, may have matter of conquest and triumph, when he has done bravely by a superadvenient assistance of God.'[43] Human faculties were designed to be employed in the investigation of the things of nature. Hakewill observed that the capacity of mankind 'answeres to the universality of things to bee knowne'.[44] From our God-given capacity for knowledge we can infer that an important part of our earthly activities is the diligent pursuit of the sciences. John Cockburn declared that 'God keeps from us the ends and Purposes of his Providences, that he may oblige us to use our Reason', for, he continues: 'Our business in this world, is to cultivate our Reason'.[45] The creatures have been given to us, agreed Ray, 'to exercise our Wits and Understandings, in considering and contemplating them'.[46]

The study of the natural world thus became, as it had been for the discoverers of nature in the twelfth century, a religious activity, albeit in a new sense. Nature no longer comprised a vast array of symbols which pointed to a transcendent realm beyond: instead, the way in which the things of nature were ordered and disposed came to represent a logical premise from which God's wisdom and providence could be inferred. Of equal importance was the emergence of the conviction that God's purposes in the creation could only be realised when the functions of those things originally designed for human use were discovered. Interpreting the book of the creatures became a matter of discerning the intention of its author. In much the same way as the true meaning of a

---

[42] Derham, *Physico-Theology*, p. 466.　　[43] More, *Antidote*, p. 56.
[44] Hakewill, *An Apologie*, (3rd edn) Sig a3.r (Epistle Dedicatory).
[45] Cockburn, *An Enquiry*, p. 185.　　[46] Ray, *Wisdom of God*, p. 129.

written text came to be identified with the designs of the writer, so legitimate meanings of the book of nature were sought in the purposes for which God had designed its living contents.

DIVINE DESIGNS AND HUMAN UTILITIES

While it has been maintained that teleological explanations hindered the progress of the natural sciences, in reality, the search for the 'ends' of natural things proceeded on the very practical assumption that everything in nature was in some way useful. The motivation to study and explore all aspects of the natural world thus sprang, in part at least, from teleology. And while over the course of the seventeenth century criticism of the use of final causes in scientific explanation mounted, numerous writers in the field of natural history were happy to conflate Aristotle's final causes with the 'divine purposes' of Judaeo-Christian tradition. 'Final cause' thus came to be understood not as a *telos* immanent in the natural object, but rather the purpose for which God had designed the thing.[47]

There was no shortage of writers, particularly in England, wishing to justify explanation in terms of 'ends' as the only legitimate mode of knowledge of the natural world. George Walker wrote that 'knowledge of things, without knowledge of the end and use of them, is a vaine notion swimming in the brain'. The principal knowledge of things which we ought then to seek 'is to know and understand the special use of them'.[48] John Webster argued two uses for natural philosophy: that we might come to know the Creator through his creatures; and that we might gain knowledge of causes and effects in order 'to make use of them for the general good and benefit of mankind, especially for the conservations and restauration of the health of man'.[49] Members of the Royal Society also believed themselves to be involved in a quest for the uses of natural things: the new philosophy, Thomas Sprat announced, 'shall impart to us the uses of all the *Creatures*'.[50] Such uses, moreover, could be more easily discovered than the hidden essences and occult qualities of the old Aristotelianism. According to Pluche: 'In the Study of natural Things true philosophy is never limited to the Contemplation of their Mechanism, but extends its curiosity to the benefits they produce.'

---

[47] For a recent discussion of this change, see Margaret Osler, 'From Immanent Natures to Nature as Artifice: The Reinterpretation of Final Causes in Seventeenth-Century Natural Philosophy', *The Monist* 79 (1996), 388–407.   [48] Walker, *History of the Creation*, p. 35.
[49] Webster, *Academiarum Examen*, p. 19.   [50] Sprat, *History of the Royal Society*, p. 438.

Aristotelian science had foundered because it sought the essences and
qualities of things. God, said Pluche, 'has given us Abilities and Powers
to discern clearly the Use and Fitness of things' but 'he has cast a veil
over their essences'. It was not God's intention, he continues, 'to satisfy
our Curiosity . . . but to affect our Minds with the Sense of His
Benefits'.[51] Investigators who sought such ends concerned themselves
with such varied tasks as determining 'The End and Design of this
constant and regular Motion of the Seas', the 'uses' of the moon, of the
central fire at the core of the earth, or the 'natural causes and uses' of the
gross geological features of the earth's surface.[52] Still others enquired
after the 'advantages' of rivers and mountains, the 'end and design' of
clouds, 'the usefulness of tides', 'the benefit of volcanos', and the 'use of
sands'.[53] Details of human anatomy and physiology were described in
similar terms. Walter Charleton, sometime physician to Charles I, spoke
of 'the Uses of the Blood', 'The *Final Cause*, or *Use of Respiration*', '*the Use of
the Muscles*'.[54]

While not all writers were to identify these final causes with divine
purposes, most did. 'We see in Nature every thing is serving a *Rational*
End', wrote Matthew Barker in *Natural Theology* (1674). Discernment of
this end constitutes a complete explanation:

As the *Sun* enlightens the World, which else would be but one great *Dungeon*,
and unfit for habitation. The *Clouds* and *Rain* serve an *end*, which is to cool and
moisten the Earth, which else would be dry and barren. The Winds do serve an
end, which is to purge and purifie the Air, that for want of *motion* it might not
corrupt and putrifie. And the earth is endued with a *Seminal* vertue to bring
forth Herbs and Fruits of several kind for the use of Man and Beast . . . and as all
things in Nature serve an *End*, so they are wonderfully fitted to their several *ends*.
Now whence is this but from some wise *Agent* that fitted things to their *end*.[55]

For such writers the investigation of nature had as its goal the determination of ends or purposes, which in turn would lead to both the praise
of the Deity and the advancement of humanity. In the seventeenth and
eighteenth centuries God came to be understood as a technician, whose
intricate designs were everywhere to be investigated, admired, and put
to use. As author of creation, God had crafted the things of nature with a

[51] Pluche, *Spectacle*, ii, 22, iii, 322, 349.
[52] Robinson, *Anatomy of the Earth*, pp. 14, 20; *Natural History*, p. 35.
[53] Pluche, *Spectacle*, iii, 47, 84, 116, 123, 166, 226.
[54] Walter Charleton, *Natural History of Nutrition, Life, and Voluntary Motion* (London, 1659).
[55] Barker, *Natural Theology*, pp. 21f. Cf. Edwards, *A Demonstration*, pt i, p. 4. Also Pluche: 'We are
     endeavouring to discover the Original, the Structure, and Use of every Thing we see'. *Spectacle*, i,
     307.

purpose rather than a meaning. The investigation of nature could again lead to knowledge of the mind of God, not, as was the case in the Middle Ages, through a knowledge of the exemplary forms of natural objects, but through an acquaintance with God's designs in the world which he had made. This knowledge also led to a direct acting upon the world, for it entailed putting to use those things for which God's purposes had now been discerned.

The combination of Aristotle's final causes and the Christian belief in the divine purposes of all natural things gave rise to a new category of literature – physico-theology. This enterprise amounted to a detailed elaboration of the design argument for God's existence, based on the systematic elaboration of divine purposes in the natural world. A tradition dominated by the English, whose clergymen seemed to have the time to devote to natural history, it began with Henry More's *Antidote Against Atheism* (1653), reached its acme in the Boyle Lectures, and enjoyed its last hurrah in the Bridgewater Treatises (1833–40).[56] More's *Antidote* ranges over numerous natural phenomena, discerning in them all the providential purposes of the Deity. The 'exquisite contrivance' of the parts of animals 'is an undeniable Demonstration that they are the effects of Wisdome, not the results of Fortune or fermented Matter'. The tilting of the earth's axis is part of a divine design. The 'rudely scattered Mountains' are 'Nature's *Stillatories*'; rivers are '*Quarries of Stone*'. The magnet is a help to navigation, which activity is further facilitated by the fact that wood floats upon water. Vegetables have '*Form* and *Beauty*' and are of 'great *Use* as well for *Medicine* as *Sustenance*'. Animals have numerous uses. The silkworm 'seems to come into the world for no other purpose than to furnish man with more costly cloathing'. The life of fishes is 'but for Salt, to keep them sweet till we shall have need to eat them'. The camel has humps 'that they may be in stead of a *Pack-saddle* to receive the burthen' and his four knees and the protrubancy under his breast that he 'might with ease *kneel* down, and so might the more gainly be loaden'. The structure of the human body also affords '*Unavoydable Arguments for divine Providence*'. The eyes are protected by the brow and the nose, 'the *sweat* of the Forehead is fenced off by those two wreaths of haire which we call the *eye-brows*; and the *eye-lids* are fortified with little *bristles* as with *Palisadoes*, against the assault of Flyes and Gnats'; the

---

[56] On Physico-theology generally, see Webster, *Great Instauration*, pp. 150–1, 507–10; C. E. Raven, *Natural Religion and Christian Theology* (Cambridge University Press, 1953); Neal Gillespie, 'Natural History, Natural Theology, and Social Order: John Ray and the "Newtonian Ideology"', *JHB* 20 (1987) 1–49.

upper lid is a fence, or 'a *Portcullis* against the importunity of the Enemy'. In addition, 'Nature has made the *hind-most parts* of our body which wee sit upon most fleshy . . . making us a natural Cushion as well as for instruments of motion for our *Thighes* and *Legges*'. All in all, 'Nothing is done foolishly nor in vaine', for 'there is a divine *Providence* that orders all things'.[57]

More's *Antidote* spawned numerous imitations, notable amongst them a number of the sermons delivered under the auspices of the Boyle Lectureship. At his death in 1691, Robert Boyle left the sum of fifty pounds in his will for an annual series of eight lectures to be delivered in London Churches and directed against unbelievers. The 'Boyle Lectures' became the premier venue for the presentation of physico-theological arguments for the existence of God, and proofs of his wisdom and providence. The best known of the series are Richard Bentley's *The Folly and Unreasonableness of Atheism* (1692), Samuel Clarke's *Demonstration of the Being and Attributes of God* and *Discourse Concerning the Unchangeable Obligations of Natural Religion and the Truth and Certainty of the Christian Revelation* (1704–5), and William Derham's *Physico-Theology: or A Demonstration of the Being and Attributes of God from the Works of Creation* (1711–12).[58] To this list we must also add John Ray's classic *The Wisdom of God Manifested in the Works of Creation* (1691). Although he was overlooked for the Boyle Lectureship, Ray's piece has long been considered the most representative example of the genre. In France, Noël Antoine Pluche introduced the genre of physico-theology to the Continent with his *Spectacle de la Nature* (1732).

There was scarcely a feature of the natural world which physico-theologians found an unsuitable subject upon which to discourse. However, as was the case with moralising naturalists, it was the smallest of creatures which most attracted their attentions. While the expansion of the universe made possible by the telescope threw up a number of obstacles in the path of the physico-theologians, the microscope was able to show that even the most modest of creatures had been designed with a remarkable precision. Serious students of nature had previously tended to consider the lower animals – gathered together under the broad designation 'insect' – as improper objects of investigation. That there might be microscopic animals and plants had at times even been denied *a priori*. Aquinas had declared that no living creatures could exist

[57] More, *Antidote*, pp. 5, 41, 48, 52, 55, 63, 72, 93f., 97. Cf. Edwards, *A Demonstration*, pt 1, p. 186.
[58] A list of Boyle Lectures for the years 1692–1714 appears in an appendix to Jacob, *Newtonians and the English Revolution*.

beyond the boundaries of the unaided senses. 'It is not possible', he announced in his commentary on Aristotle's *Physics*, 'that there should be certain parts of flesh and bone which are non-sensible because of smallness'.[59] Part of the prejudice against such creatures was owing to widespread belief that they had not been part of the original creation, and were bred from dung and corruption.[60] Virtuoso John Woodward was thus lampooned as one who had 'abandoned the acquaintance and Society of Man for that of Insects, Worms, Grubbs, Maggots, Fleas'.[61] William Harvey spoke of those 'who scoff at and deride the introduction of frogs and serpents, flies, and other of the lower animals upon the scene, as a piece of peurile levity'.[62] In time, disdain gave way to enchantment, and the world of minute creatures came to exercise a unique fascination over seventeenth-century minds. Harvey chastised the despisers of imperfect creatures, asserting that 'the great and Almighty Father is sometimes most visible in His lesser, and to the eye least inconsiderable works'.[63] Aristotle, as had become customary, was also taken to task for his sins of omission. 'Were Aristotle now alive', and in possession of the 'dioptrical advantages' of the moderns, wrote Henry Power in 1664, 'he might write a new History of Animals; for the first Tome of Zoography is still wanting.'[64] Thomas Sprat agreed that both the voyages of discovery and the invention of various glasses had greatly increased the scope of natural history, and thus opportunities for praising the powers of the Creator: 'It is not to be doubted, but still there may be an infinit number of *Creatures*, over our heads, round about us, and under our Feet, in the large space of the *Air*, in the Caverns of the *Earth*, in the Bowels of the *Mountains*, in the bottoms of the *Seas*, and in the shades of *Forests*; which have hitherto escap'd all *Mortal Senses*. In this the *Microscope* alone is enough to silence all opposers.'[65] This hitherto unsuspected fecundity of the natural world thus gave modern writers occasion both to chastise the limitations of the ancients and laud the powers of the Creator.

Those who made the study of the once despised 'insects' their specialty – men such as Moffett, Swammerdam, Réaumur – repeatedly

[59] Aquinas, *Commentary on Aristotle's Physics*, tr. R. Blackwell et al. (London: Routledge and Kegan Paul, 1963), p. 34, qu. in Keith Hutchison, 'What Happened to Occult Qualities in the Scientific Revolution?', *Isis* 73 (1982) 233–53 (236). Hutchison provides a useful discussion of the theological implications of this assumption.

[60] Godfrey Goodman thought that flies and worms were 'mixt imperfect creatures . . . the marks of corruption'. *The Fall of Man* (London, 1616), p. 19; Cf. Hughes, *Analytical Exposition*, p. 9.

[61] Joseph M. Levine, *Dr Woodward's Shield: History, Science, and Satire in Augustan England* (Cornell University Press, 1991), p. 125.   [62] Harvey, *A Second Disquisition to John Riolan*, p. 313.

[63] *Ibid.*   [64] Power, *Experimental Philosophy*, Preface.   [65] Sprat, *History of the Royal Society*, p. 384

drew their readers' attention to the intricate designs of these small creatures. Dutch naturalist Jan Swammerdam (1637–80) was particularly enthusiastic about the structures of minute creatures: 'Herewith I offer you the Omnipotent Finger of god in the anatomy of a louse: wherein you will find miracles heaped upon miracles and will see the wisdom of God clearly manifested in a minute point.'[66] Réné Réaumur, who divided his studies between metallurgy and entomology, thought likewise that from the natural history of insects we can demonstrate the existence of God.[67] Robert Hooke, pioneer and populariser of microscopy, observed that the more we magnify objects, 'the more we discover the imperfections of our senses, and the Omnipotency and Infinite perfections of the great Creatour'.[68] The discoveries of these pioneers of entomology were quickly to become grist to the mill of more general writers whose theme was God's providential design. 'The most despicable and disregarded pieces of decayed nature are so curiously wrought and adorned with such eminent signatures of Divine Wisdome', marvelled Joseph Glanvill.[69] John Edwards thought that 'an insect is an Argument of the Divine Wisdom, as well as an animal of the first magnitude'.[70] Malebranche enthused that 'One insect is more in touch with Divine wisdom than the whole of Greek and Roman history'.[71] God had taken special care with creatures of modest proportions, compensating them by adorning their structures with the most lavish ornamentation: 'they have Crowns, Helmets and other Curiosities on their Heads which outdo the most luxuriant Fancies of Men'.[72] John Ray quoted John Wilkins to the same effect: 'The works of Nature the better Lights and Glasses you use, the more clever and exactly formed they [insects] appear.'[73] Even the young Diderot was to agree: The best proofs of God, he once remarked, are 'a butterfly's wing, a flesh-worms' eye'.[74] Robert Hooke argued that the smallest creatures could be favourably compared with the largest, for God had expended as much 'care and providence' in the production of the most lowly creature, as he had

---

[66] *The Letters of Jan Swammerdam to Melchisidec Thévenot*, tr. G.A. Lindeboom (Amsterdam: Smuts and Zeitlinger, 1975), Letter 19a, April, 1678, (p. 105).

[67] Réaumur, *Memoirs pour servir a l'histoire des Insectes*, 6 vols. (Paris, 1734–42) I, 4.

[68] Hooke, *Micrographia*, p. 8. On Hooke and the argument from design see John Harwood, 'Rhetoric and graphics in *Micrographia*', in *Robert Hooke: New Studies* ed. Michael Hunter and Simon Schaffer (Woodbridge: Boydell, 1989) pp. 119–48.

[69] Joseph Glanvill, *Scepsis Scientifica* (London, 1665), p. 3.

[70] Edwards, *A Demonstration*, pt 1, p. 220.

[71] Malebranche, *Eloge du P. Malebranche, Oeuvres*, v, 461.

[72] Cited by Edwards, *A Demonstration*, pt 1, pp. 204f.   [73] Ray, *Wisdom of God*, p. 41.

[74] Diderot, *Philosophical Thoughts*, xx (p. 38).

in the largest.[75] The great natural historians of the past, wrote Henry Power, 'have regardlessly pass'd by the Insectile Automata, (those living-exiguities) with only a bare mention of their names, whereas in these prety Engines (by an incomparable Stenography of Providence) are lodged all the perfections of the largest Animals'.[76] 'The Eye of a Flie', in the judgement of John Edwards, was 'a more curious piece of Workmanship than the Sun it self'.[77] Cockburn wrote that 'there is Use and design to be seen in every Creature, nay, even in Insects and creeping Things, which we look upon with so much contempt'.[78] If God had thought it worth the trouble to make insects, Pluche argued, we ought not think it beneath our dignity to study them: 'the minutest Things in Nature were appointed to some End and Purpose; and . . . the Deity is as conspicuous in the structure of a Fly's paw, as he is in the bright Globe of the Sun himself'.[79]

While it is true that the rhetoric of physico-theology which led to the search for practical applications and evidence of design in nature was a crucial motivating factor in early modern natural history, it must also be conceded that at times the search for benevolent adaptations in nature degenerated into an armchair exercise which produced little of practical value. Some teleological accounts of things became laboured, transparently making virtues out of necessity. Again, it was the smallest creatures, many of which on the face of it we could afford to be without, which exercised the ingenuities of the physico-theologians. Pluche, for example, explained that the woodworm, which eats the hulls of ships, actually contributes to harmonious international relations, for it provides opportunities for some countries to sell to others pitch with which to protect ships' hulls: 'Thus does this little Animal, which we so much complain of as being troublesome and injurious to us, become the very Cement which unites these distant Nations in one common Interest.'[80] Discussions of the functions of human pests and parasites were similarly far-fetched. 'Vermine', declared John Hutchinson, 'prevent that hoard-

---

[75] Hooke, *Micrographia*, p. 195. Cf. Boyle, *The Usefulness of Natural Philosophy, Works* II, 12. Also see Edward Davis, '"Parcere nominibus": Boyle, Hooke and the Rhetorical Interpretation of Descartes', in Michael Hunter (ed.) *Robert Boyle Reconsidered* (Cambridge University Press, 1994), pp. 157–75.   [76] Power, *Experimental Philosophy*, Preface.

[77] Edwards, *A Demonstration*, pt I, p.205. Edwards is actually quoting Boyle. See Davis, 'Parcere nominibus', pp. 160, 170.   [78] Cockburn, *An Enquiry*, p. 40.

[79] Pluche, *Spectacle*, I, 1, 34. This was almost an exact echo of John Edwards. When Pluche speaks of God making insects he is obviously rejecting the common view that insects were spontaneously generated out of corrupt earth. 'Every insect', he had argued earlier, 'is generated, like other animals, from a seed' (I, 10). The rejection of spontaneous generation was thus an important factor in the new status of insects.   [80] Pluche, *Spectacle*, III, 318.

ing which is prejudicial to society'. He also pointed out that as a consequence of the unwanted attentions of body parasites, 'Men and other animals are induced to cleanliness'. Indeed, in Hutchinson's view, 'invisible or small agents' make a vital contribution of social cohesion, for 'they jointly labour to distress men when out of society, to force them in, to raise in them a detestation of filth and greediness, to find them employment, to prey upon what they do not need'.[81] On the same theme, John Edwards suggested that fleas may bleed the poor, 'and thus save them the Charges of A *Lancet*, and clear them of their Blood gratis'. This is why fleas conveniently infest the lower classes in greater numbers than the rich.[82] Bernardin de Saint-Pierre thought that fleas offered further economic benefits to the disadvantaged in that they afforded opportunity for the poor to work for the rich to keep them clean. The poor, moreover, were assisted in their work by the fact that fleas were black and hence could be more easily be seen against white skin.[83]

More astute students of nature avoided these extremes, being content to discover what they could. 'Our knowledge is very much limited', admitted John Cockburn, 'and it is impossible for us to comprehend all that God doth.'[84] Robert Boyle also thought it presumptuous to claim to know all of God's purposes for the natural world, yet insisted that it was our 'duty' to discover as many as we could.[85] In one sense, then, every aspect of the creation serves human beings, by affording scope for their investigative powers, even if the definitive application could not be found. Henry More also cautioned against an impatient quest for omniscience, pointing out that the uses of some natural objects would be discovered by future generations. Our present relative ignorance is necessary in order that 'succeeding ages may ever have something left to gratifie themselves in their own discoveries'.[86]

---

[81] Hutchinson, *An Abstract from the Works of John Hutchinson* (Edinburgh, 1753), pp. 419, 420, 421. William Kirby was to rehearse the cleanliness thesis almost one hundred years later. The human louse, he argued, provided a gentle reminder to those with a relaxed attitude to personal hygiene that cleanliness was next to godliness. *On the Power, Wisdom and Goodness of God as manifested in the Creation of Animals* (1835) II, 316.   [82] Edwards, *A Demonstration*, pt I, p. 237.

[83] Bernardin de Saint-Pierre, *Etudes de la Nature* (1784), qu. in Leonora Rosenfield, *From Beast-Machine to Man-Machine* (New York: Octagon, 1968), p. 186.

[84] Cockburn, *An Enquiry*, p. 60; Cf. Edwards, *A Demonstration*, pt I, p. 230.

[85] Boyle, *Disquisition*, pp. 15, 10.

[86] More, *Antidote*, p. 56. Cf. Bacon: 'There is therefore much ground for hoping that there are still laid up in the womb of nature many secrets of excellent use . . . which have not yet been found out'. *Novum Organum*, I.109 (p. 74). Paracelsus followed Origen in holding that only at the end of time would we come into a complete knowledge of nature: 'many things are still hidden from us till times to come, when the Saviour will come (for there is a saviour for the arts just as there is one in other respects)'. *Von der Kranheiten, so die Vernufft berauben*, in *Four Treatises*, pp. 198f. Cf. Origen, *De principiis*, II.xi.5.

THE CENTRE OF THE UNIVERSE

The general drift of teleological accounts of features of the natural world was inevitably anthropocentric. Natural things were found to have purposes which, in one way or another, related to the human race and its welfare. While the anthropocentrism which has characterised the Western approach to nature has commonly been thought to have originated in the Judaeo-Christian tradition, the view that nature has been designed to serve human ends may be found in Aristotle, and appears later as a basic tenet of Stoicism.[87] In a well-known passage in the *Politics* Aristotle had stated 'that nature has made all the animals for the sake of man'.[88] This principle was subsequently enshrined in Stoic philosophy. 'Everything in the world which we enjoy', announced Cicero's Stoic spokesman Balbus, 'was made and ordered for our sake.' Chrysippus even went so far as to say that the life in a pig is merely 'the salt which preserves it until it finds its way onto the table'.[89] The paradigm which was to provide the basis of medieval anthropocentrism, man the microcosm, also derived from the Greek tradition. Having said this, it is certainly true that during the Christian era the anthropocentric view of the Stoics was easily grafted onto the biblical tradition according to which man had been granted dominion over all living creatures.[90] The Church Fathers Origen, Methodius, Lactantius and Augustine all set forth the Stoic position with little or no modification.[91] Man, declared Augustine, 'is a rational animal, and consequently more excellent than all other animals of the earth'. Beasts, 'lacking a rational soul, [are] not related to us by a common nature. Accordingly, the Creator decreed that the beasts in 'both their life and death are subject to our use'.[92] In

[87] Indeed, certain strands of Old Testament wisdom literature suggest that there is more to animal creation than mere servitude to human masters. The behemoth which 'ranks first among the works of God', and the leviathan which is 'king over all that are proud' epitomise the power and independence of the wild animals, and serve some more obscure purpose in creation, one not directly related to the human destiny. The writer of Job suggests that as the justice of God is inscrutable, so too, are his creative purposes. The destiny of the animals is not irrevocably bound up with human ends. Job, chs. 38–41. Cf. Psalm 104, Hosea 2.18. Plutarch was an outspoken critic of Stoic anthropocentrism, and wrote a number of works extolling the intelligence, skill, and beauty of the creatures. Nature, he insisted had not simply produced animals for our use, as Aristotle suggested, but 'for the sake of their beauty and grace', *De essu carnum*, 994B. Neoplatonic writers, such as Celsus and Porphyry also criticised anthropocentric views which they associated with both Christianity and Stoicism.   [88] Aristotle, *Politics*, 1256b 15–23.

[89] Cicero, *De natura deorum*, II. 154, 156 (pp.185, 187); More, *Antidote*, p. 63.

[90] Genesis 1.26–30, 9.1–3; Psalm 8.6–8; Cf. Cicero, *De natura deorum*, II.158.

[91] Origen, *Divine Institutes*, IV.lxxiv ; Methodius, *From the Discourse on the Resurrection* I.x; Lactantius, *Divine Institutes*, VII.iv. Cf. Philo, *Quaestiones in Genesin*. I, 94. (p. 811)

[92] Augustine, *City of God.*, XXII.24 (p.851); *The Catholic and Manichean Ways of Life*, XVII(FC 56, 102, 105).

the Middle Ages, Aquinas and Bonaventure both endorsed the now
standard view, Bonaventure stating that 'we are the end of all things that
exist,' and that 'all corporeal beings are made for the service of man'.[93]
Even the sixteenth-century reformers tended towards this view, Luther
remarking that 'the animals are subjected to man as to a tyrant who has
absolute power over life and death'.[94] Seventeenth-century thinkers
were divided on this issue however. Some confidently reasserted the
centrality of human beings with regard to final causes. Derham wrote
that the great variety of things in the world 'is a most wise Provision for
all the Uses of the World in all Ages, and in all Places. Some for Food,
some for Physick, some for Habitation, some for Utensils, some for
Tools and Instruments of Work, and some for Recreation and Pleasure'.[95] Pluche agreed: 'All nature is link'd together by one universal Law
of Harmony and Agreement: and as the Whole Earth declares itself to
be the Work of one only all-wise Creator, so it is no less evident that the
Good of Man was the only chief End and Design of his forming it.'[96]
Others entertained serious reservations.

The major threat to such easy assumptions of the primary position of
the human race was posed by the expansion of the universe which had
taken place as a result of the invention of the telescope. If the microscopic world had served as a fresh source of arguments for proponents of
teleological views, the telescope had placed obstacles in their path.
Perhaps the most difficult challenge presented to champions of anthropocentric teleology by the new sciences was the heliocentric theory
of the solar system. The Copernican model, which gained increasing
acceptance during the course of the seventeenth century, had dethroned
the earth from its accustomed position at the centre of the universe.
Telescopes had added weight to the theory that the terrestrial globe was
an unremarkable planet, rotating about one of innumerable suns, in a
giant cosmos. In the words of Donne:

> The new Philosophy cals all in doubt,
> The Element of fire is quite put out;
> The Sun is lost, and th'earth, and no mans wit
> Can well direct him, where to looke for it.[97]

Others were not so resigned, resisting not only the implications of the
heliocentric view, but the thesis itself. Those who had dislodged our

---

[93] *Breviloquium* 2.4. Aquinas, *Sancti Thomas Aquinatis in Aristotlelis Librum de Anima Commentarium*, ed. M.
Pirotta (Turin, 1925), paras 255, 260, 279; *ST*, 1a.78, 1.   [94] *Luther's Works*, II, 132f.
[95] Derham, *Physico-Theology*, pp. 57f.   [96] Pluche, *Spectacle*, III, 112.
[97] Donne, 'The First Anniversary', lines 205–8.

planetary home from its rightful place at the centre of the universe, rued Edward Howard, have made the earth 'a diminutive Brat'. This seemed to him sufficient grounds for retaining its privileged position. That other late champion of the geocentric theory, John Edwards, agreed that if the Copernicans were correct, then 'this terrestrial Globe is a despicable Spot, a Speck, a Point in comparison of the Vast and Spacious Conjeries of the Sun and Fixed Lights'.[98] Less reactionary advocates of physico-theology found themselves asking what possible use there might be for the countless stars which were not even visible to the naked eye. In what manner could these be said to serve the human race? The fixed stars, admittedly, could be used as aids to navigation, or might provide man with grounds to admire the workmanship of the Deity.[99] But it was extravagant to claim that these were the only ends of the myriad celestial bodies. The decline of astrological prognostication and the related conception of the celestial influences – long-standing explanations of the significance of the stars – made the problem more acute. The dread which filled Pascal as he contemplated the vastness of space and the innumerable stellar bodies is attributable to the fact that the infinite heavens were now 'silent'.[100] The firmament was no longer a book of harmonious discourses, as Augustine had believed, but another prob-lematic element in a universe which threatened to defy explanation in human terms.[101]

Many thinkers, hard pressed by the enormity of space, resorted to the hypothesis of extraterrestrial life: the heavenly bodies were worlds, or systems of worlds, designed as habitations for other beings.[102] As a rule, these musings were not concerned with how the requisite conditions for life might have eventuated in space, but were informed instead by

[98] Edward Howard, *Remarks on the New Philosophy of Descartes* (London, 1700), p. 207; Edwards, *Brief Remarks*, Epistle Dedicatory, pp. 23–6. Edwards considered the Copernican hypothesis to be nothing more than a passing fad. On the connection between final causes and cosmology also see John Witty, *An Essay towards a Vindication of the Vulgar Exposition of the Mosaic History of the World*, 2 vols. (London, 1705) I, 105, 108f. [99] Boyle, *Disquistion*, p. 98.
[100] Pascal, *Pensées*, para. 201. [101] Augustine, *Confessions*, XIII.15.
[102] Pierre Borel, *A New Treatise Proving a Multiplicity of Worlds* (London, 1658); Burnet, *Sacred Theory*, II.ii (p. 220); Whiston, *New Theory*, p. 102; Robert Burton, *The Anatomy of Melancholy*, (1676 edn) p. 161; Cockburn, *An Enquiry*, p. 45; Cudworth, *True Intellectual System*, v.i (II, 601); d'Espagnet, *Enchiridion physicae restitutae*, p. 165; Charron, *Of Wisdom*, (London, 1697), p. 367; Bernard Fontenelle, *Conversations on the Plurality of Worlds* (Dublin, 1687); Joseph Glanvill, 'The Usefulness of Real Philosophy to Religion', p. 37, in *Essays on Several Important Subjects in Philosophy and Religion*, (London, 1676); Matthew Hale, *Primitive Origination of Mankind*, p. 7; Henry More, *Divine Dialogues*, 2 vols. (London, 1668), I, 525, 533, *Democritus Platonissans; or, An Essay upon the Infinity of Worlds out of Platonic Principles* (Cambridge, 1646), p. 51, *An Explanation of the Grand Mystery of Godliness*, pp. 244f. in *Theological Works* (London, 1708). Cf. Joseph Addison, *The Spectator*, no. 519 (October 25, 1712).

platonic notions of plenitude, with the neoplatonic scale of being, and with classical arguments about a plurality of worlds. But these ancient conceptions were now overlaid with physico-theology. Those who sought design in all the things of nature were to speak of the 'use' of these new heavenly worlds to other beings. John Ray wrote in 1691 of the 'now received hypothesis' that every star is a sun with planets 'in all likelyhood furnished with as great a variety of corporeal Creatures animate and inanimate as the Earth is'.[103] Derham, in his *Astro-Theology* (1715), and Whiston, in his *Astronomical Principles of Religion* (1717), both argued that other worlds had their uses as places of habitation for other beings.[104] Cheyne concurred: 'I shall proceed in supposing, the *Planets* to be inhabited, and that the *fix'd Stars* have their *Planets* and Inhabitants.'[105] Fellow Boyle Lecturer, Richard Bentley, arrived at the same solution with this argument: 'since the earth was principally designed for the being and service and contemplation of men, why may not all other planets be created for the like uses, each for their own inhabitants which have life and understanding'.[106] Bentley thought that even Mars or the Moon might be inhabited by rational creatures. These extraterrestrials might be more or less perfect than human souls, for God 'may have made unnumerable orders and classes of rational minds'.[107] Few speculated on the exact forms of inhabitants of other planets, however, conceding with Derham that it was beyond human wit to know.[108]

More novel uses of the stars were also suggested. Robert Boyle thought that the bodies in deep space might cater to the needs of angels, or that the stars might be used by human souls.[109] Samuel Clarke was said to have remarked that the souls of brute beasts, post-mortem, might be lodged in Mars, or Saturn, or one of the other planets.[110] As we saw in the previous chapter, Burnet believed that the starry regions beyond the moon would provide a commodious home for the saints after the general resurrection. Here in their 'sublime Station, remote from the

---

[103] Ray, *Wisdom of God*, p. 2.
[104] Derham, *Astro-Theology*, p. xlixf. Whiston, *Astronomical Principles*, pp. 149–50.
[105] Cheyne, *Philosophical Principles*, pt. 1, p. 210.   [106] Bentley, *Works*, III, 175.
[107] *Ibid.*, III, 176. Such speculation brought with it the issue of the soteriological status of these alien beings, and called into question the uniqueness of the Christian revelation. Bishop Wilkins, e.g., enquired of men in the moon 'whether they are of the seed of *Adam*, whether they are there in blessed estate, or else what means there may be for their Salvation?' *Discovery of the New World*, 5th edn, p. 125. This had further implications for terrestrial events, for if alien beings had not inherited original sin from Adam, or were able to avail themselves of some alternative means of redemption, it was possible that similar considerations might apply to earthly creatures – such as the Americans. See Harrison, *'Religion' and the Religions*, pp. 126–9.
[108] Derham, *Astro-theology*, p. lvi.   [109] Boyle, *Disquisition*, pp. 113, 84f.
[110] Thomas, *Man and the Natural World*, p. 139

earth', the elect would enjoy the prospect of the heavens for all eternity. William Derham later entertained the same thought, believing that after death the blessed would together share the joys of the astronomer: 'With what pleasure then, shall departed happy souls survey the most distant regions of the Universe, and view all those glorious Globes thereof.'[111] Whiston, of course, believed comets to be instruments of divine judgement, and very likely venues for the accommodation of the damned. This strange view was to have a tenure which extended until well into the eighteenth century. Derham, too, thought comets 'to be destined . . . for a place of torment'. Richard Turner agreed that these heavenly bodies could well be 'habitations of the damned'. James Ferguson, one of Newton's eighteenth-century popularisers, speculated that comets served as the scattered sites of a celestial purgatory, being 'peopled with guilty Creatures reclaimable by Sufferings'.[112] Ferguson and Turner also took seriously the other purposes which Whiston had found for cometary bodies. According to Ferguson, comets might cause 'Deluges and Conflagrations for the Correction and Punishment of Vice' in other world systems, thus implying not only that there were other inhabited worlds, but also that their inhabitants, like those of our own planet, were liable to divine judgement through the instrumentality of celestial objects. Turner thought that comets, most probably, are 'the Executioners of God's vengeance on sinful Worlds; by scattering their Baneful Influences on the Inhabitants, or dashing the Planet to Pieces, and reducing it to its chaotic State again'. [113]

The new astronomy could thus be accommodated by the teleological tradition. But it was an accommodation which spelt the end of *anthropocentric* teleology. With the earth displaced from the centre of the universe, no longer could its inhabitants claim to be the sole end of the created order. Other beings had legitimate claims.[114] It is 'vulgarly received', wrote John Ray, that 'all this visible world was created for

[111] Almond, *Heaven and Hell*, p. 123; Derham, *Astro-Theology*, pp. 227f. Cf. Ray, *Miscellaneous Discourses*, pp. 197f.

[112] Derham, *Astro-Theology*, pp. 218f.; James Ferguson, *An Idea of the Material Universe, Deduced from a Survey of the Solar System* (London, 1754), p. 27; Richard Turner, *A View of the Heavens*, 2nd edn (London, 1783), p. 20. On Ferguson and Turner, see Patrick Curry, *Prophecy and Power: Astrology in Early Modern England* (Princeton Unversity Press, 1989) pp. 149f.

[113] Ferguson, *Idea of the Material Universe*, p. 27; Turner, *View of the Heavens*, p. 20.

[114] This same development saw the demise of the notion of man the microcosm – a conception, which like the Ptolemaic, tended to place man squarely in the centre of the universe. Thus Timothy Willis: man was 'the *Epitome* and Abridgement of the whole Creation; and therefore rightly called *Microcosmus*, a little world: for whose vse and seruice all other things were created'. *The Search for Causes*, p. 20.

Man; that man is the end of creation . . . yet Wise Men now think otherwise'.[115] Jean d'Espagnet had expressed the matter more bluntly: 'They which believe that an almost innumerable multitude of heavenly bodies, were created for the commoditie of the globe of the Earth, and for her inhabitants, as to their proper end, are deceived.'[116] Thomas Burnet was equally critical of the view that the universe had been created chiefly for 'the meanest of all the Intelligent Creatures'. Such thoughts were 'groundless and unreasonable in themselves', and 'derogatory to the infinite Power, Wisdom, and Goodness of the First Cause'.[117] Most other proponents of the heliocentric view agreed. The opinion that man was the sole end of creation was characterised as 'an extravagant imagination' (Pierre Charron), '*false* Principle' (Henry More), 'an opinion with 'inextricable difficulties' (Archbishop King), an 'old vulgar opinion' (Derham), or simply, 'erroneous' (Boyle).[118] And it is not insignificant that John Edwards, one of the few of his era to argue for the old, exclusively anthropocentric view of the cosmos, also rejected the Copernican system as 'contrary to the Verdict of our Senses'.[119]

For some, the denial of anthropocentric teleology did not go far enough. Bacon, Descartes, and Hobbes had each decried the use of teleological explanation *per se* in the natural sciences. 'True knowledge', declared Bacon, 'is knowledge by causes.' Bacon even allowed the Aristotelian division of causes, but he vehemently denied Aristotle's own priority, according to which the final cause was the most important: 'And causes again are not improperly distributed into four kinds: the material, the formal, the efficient, and the final. But of these, the final cause rather corrupts than advances the sciences, except such as have to do with human action.'[120] Bacon listed precisely the kinds of explanations which were to become favourites of the physico-theologians as examples of the dangers of teleological explanation. To say that '"the leaves of trees are for protecting of the fruit"; or that "the clouds are for watering of the earth"; or that "the solidness of the earth is for the

---

[115] Ray, *Wisdom of God*, pp. 127f. Ray gives as his reasons invisible celestial objects, and animals which have no obvious utility.   [116] d'Espagnet, *Enchyridion physicae restitutae*, p. 162.

[117] Burnet, *Sacred Theory*, ii.xi (p. 218).

[118] Charron, *Of Wisdom*, pp. 365f.; More, *Antidote against Atheism*, appendix, p. 178; King, *Essay on the Origin of Evil*, p. 91; Derham, *Astro-Theology*, p. 39; Boyle, *Disquisition*, p. 10.

[119] Edwards, *A Demonstration*, pt i, p. 12; cf. pt i, pp. 28, 42.

[120] Bacon, *Novum Organum*, ii.2. (p. 88). Bacon thought that the formal cause was the most important for science. Seventeenth-century logic texts repeated the view of Aristotle, thus Pierre Du Moulin: The final cause is 'the best, and the most excellent; because all the others tend to that, and serve that'; it is 'the last in execution . . . the first in the intention'; it is 'the noblest, because it can be demonstrated no further'. *The Elements of Logick* (Oxford, 1647), pp. 52, 137.

station and mansion of living creatures", and the like, is well inquired and collected in metaphysic, but in physic they are impertinent'. Explanation by reference to final causes Bacon concludes, 'hath intercepted the severe and diligent inquiry of all real and physical causes, and given men the occasion to stay upon these unsatisfactory and specious causes, to the great prejudice of further discovery'.[121]

It was Descartes and Hobbes, however, who saw more clearly than Bacon the psychological origin of teleology. Hobbes wrote in a discussion of the recently discovered laws of motion that 'men measure, not only other men, but all other things, by themselves; and because they find themselves subject after motion to pain, and lassitude, think every thing else grows weary of motion and seeks repose of its own accord'. For this reason, said Hobbes, we intuitively reject the suggestion that 'when a thing is in motion, it will eternally be in motion, unless somewhat else stay it'.[122] Descartes offered a similar analysis of arguments from analogy in the opening lines of the *Regulae*: 'Whenever people notice some similarity between two things, they are in the habit of ascribing to one what they find true of the other, even when the two are not in that respect similar.'[123] Classical and Medieval thinkers had placed souls in celestial spheres, in the world and in its animals and plant inhabitants. All such notions, in Descartes' view, were premised on a false analogy from human actions and motivations. Our awareness of our own conscious plans and purposes and how they issue in actions leads us to the false assumption that all events in the universe are so motivated. Our ideas about divine purposes in the world also arise out the erroneous belief that God's designs are to some degree analogous to our own.

There is a sense in which both sides of the debate about the place of final causes in the natural sciences have their origins in the demise of the symbolically-ordered medieval world. As we saw at the beginning of this chapter, explanations of natural objects in terms of their practical purpose were introduced to make sense out of those objects which in a previous era had derived their primary significance by functioning as symbols. The rise of teleological explanation thus accompanies the collapse of a previous symbolic natural order. Critics of teleology, by the

---

[121] Bacon, *Advancement of Learning*, ii.vii.7 (p. 94). Cf. *Novum Organum*, 1.48, 65.
[122] Hobbes, *Leviathan* 1.2, in *Works*, ed. William Molesworth (Aalen: Scientia, 1962) iii, 3f.
[123] *The Philosophical Writings of Descartes*, tr. J. Cottingham, R. Stoothoff, and Douglas Murdoch (Cambridge University Press, 1984–), i, 9. For Descartes' application of this to mechanics, see *Principles of Philosophy*, 2.37. As applied to the actions of animals, see 'Letter to Reneri, April 1638, *Philosophical Letters*, p. 53.

same token, wished to exorcise the ghosts of previous modes of explanation by denying a place in the new sciences to knowledge based upon analogies or surface similitudes. Their complaint was that while previous assumptions of the centrality of man in the cosmos – the epitome of which was the paradigm of microcosm-macrocosm – had been discarded, such assumptions had been replaced by an anthropocentrism which was almost as flawed. Teleological explanation, however, played a vital role in the development of the modern science of nature. On the one hand, it can readily be acknowledged that Matthew Barker's explanations of physical phenomena – 'The *Clouds* and *Rain* serve an *end*, which is to cool and *moisten* the Earth, which else would be dry and barren' – are not ultimately very helpful in providing what we would regard as a 'scientific' account of the phenomena of clouds and rain.[124] On the other hand, that questing after final causes is an impediment to the investigation of the world, as Chancellor Bacon had urged, is by no means clear either. While Bacon might have been correct in asserting that the search for teleological explanations prejudices the progress of natural philosophy, nonetheless, the assumption that everything in nature has a use, was, and still is, though now divorced from its theological underpinnings, a powerful motivating force in the investigation of nature. The claim that God had ordained some human purpose for every element of the creation might well be completely false, or at best unknowable, but the search for such purposes, if not conflated with enquiry into the (efficient) causes of things, far from impeding natural philosophy, was one of its primary justifications in the seventeenth century. Boyle, in his lengthy discussion of the relative merits of final versus efficient causes pointed this out: 'I judge it erroneous to say in the strictest sense, that every thing in the Visible World, was made for the Use of man; yet I think 'tis more erroneous to deny, that any thing was made for ends Investigable by Man.'[125] The search for divine purposes in the natural order provided a clear religious warrant for a pursuit which might otherwise have been regarded as the accumulation of vain and futile knowledge, little different from the bookish and unprofitable endeavours of the encylopaedists. The scientific achievements of men such as Robert Boyle and John Ray give the lie to Bacon's assertion of the baleful influence of final causes.

[124] Barker, *Natural Theology*, p. 21.
[125] Boyle, *A Disquisition about the Final Causes of Natural Things* (London, 1688), p. 10, cf. pp. 230f.

THE NATURAL WORLD AND THE MORAL ORDER

The denial of symbolic functions to natural objects at once motivated a search for new utilities and brought to an end the allegorical reading of the natural world. Yet this removal of referential functions from the things of nature did not effect so dramatic a decline in tropological or moral readings of the world. The uses sought for the things of nature were thus not restricted to material comforts, and the quest for moral lessons in the natural world continued alongside the more exploitative investigation of things for practical purposes. Prior to the modern period, moral readings of the natural world had relied to a considerable degree upon the notion that man was a microcosm. The reason that animals could serve as moral tutors to their erstwhile sovereign was that the human being was an epitome of all the animals. Birds and beasts could thus symbolise distinct passions, virtues and vices. By the time of the Renaissance there existed a general consensus about which moral qualities various animals represented. In Spenser's *Faerie Queen* the peacock appears as a symbol of pride, the lion of wrath, the wolf of envy, the goat of lust, the pig of gluttony, the ass of sloth.[126] Owing largely to the efforts of the Paracelsians, Alchemists, and Boehmenists, the arcane idea of the microcosm persisted until well into the seventeenth century, and with it, the associated idea that animals could teach their human cousins important moral lessons.[127] Boehme, for example, wrote that man was 'a *Beast* of all beasts'. There were, he thought, 'various properties in man; as one a Fox, Wolfe, Beare, Lion, Dogg, Bull, Cat, Horse, Cock, Toad, Serpent; and in briefe as many kindes of creatures are upon the earth, so many and *Various* properties likewise there are in the earthly man'.[128] His English disciple Edward Taylor observed similarly

---

[126] *Faerie Queen*, 1.4.17–36. Helga Neumann provides a comprehensive list of the virtues and vices represented by various animals. 'Tiersymbolik', Fahlbusch, Erwin et al. (eds.), *Evangelisches Kirchenlexicon*, 3rd edn, 4 vols. (Göttingen: Vandenhoeck & Ruprecht, 1986–96), IV, 893–7. Cf. Diane McColley, *A Gust for Paradise: Milton's Eden and the Visual Arts* (Urbana: University of Illinois Press, 1993), pp. 82f.; A. Lytton Sells, *Animal Poetry in French and English Literature and the Greek Tradition* (London: Thames and Hudson, 1957), p. 117; G. C. Taylor, 'Shakespeare's Use of the Idea of the Beast in Man', *Studies in Philology*, 62 (1945) 531–2; A. Yoder, *Animal Analogy in Shakespeare's Character Portrayal* (New York, 1947). Impetus for such identifications might have been provided by the recovery of Horapollo's *Hieroglyphyphica* (date unknown) which is essentially a dictionary of symbols. See Ashworth, 'Natural History and the Emblematic World View'.

[127] Bacon complained that the idea of microcosm 'hath been fantastically strained by Paracelsus and the alchemists'. *Advancement of Learning*, II.x.2 (p. 105).

[128] Boehme, *Mysterium Magnum*, p. 93. Cf. *Signature Rerum*, Sig. A2r; Joseph Duchesne, *Chymicall and Hermeticall Physicke*, Sig. K3r; Charron, *Of Wisdom*, p. 16; d'Espagnet, *Enchyridion Symbolorum*, pp. 99, 107; Franck, *A Philosophical Treatise of the Origional and Production of Things* (London, 1687), pp. 6, 12; Pettus, *History of Adam and Eve*, p. 188.

that 'men see themselves in the brute creatures'. Unregenerate men are represented 'by the Haughty proud Beasts . . . or by envious Reptiles . . . or by the cruel wrathful ones'.[129] As we might expect, with the waning influence of these microcosmic conceptions and the dismantling of the symbolic order of the natural world, these standard justifications for regarding aspects of living nature as moral authorities began to collapse. However, this was not to mean that with the introduction of the empirical approach to nature, its moral authority ebbed away. On the contrary, in much the same way that fanciful symbolic representations of theological truths in the natural world were replaced by literal representations established by observation and experiment, nature was to retain a portion of its moral authority, an authority which now rested on the basis of observations of animal behaviours rather than on such dubious principles as the microcosm-macrocosm relation. As physiologists and anatomists saw as their task the discovery of evidence of design in nature, students of animal behaviour came to consider their labours fruitful to the extent that they illustrated universal moral laws implanted in the created order by the Deity. Learning the moral lessons of nature now required careful scrutiny of the actual habits and activities of living creatures.

The origins of this new conception of nature's moral authority can be traced to rise of Neostoicism with its emphasis on the living in accordance with nature.[130] In the sixteenth century, French essayist Montaigne revived a number of the arguments of the ancients to the effect that animals ought to be our moral exemplars.[131] Montaigne insisted that nature be our chief guide in matters of morals. 'We cannot erre in following nature', he argued, 'and the sovereign document is, for a man to conforme himself to her.' Because animals more perfectly follow the dictates of nature, Montaigne reasoned that 'our wisdome should learn of the beasts, the most profitable documents'.[132] In the seventeenth century this line of thought was pursued with some vigour by Pierre Charron and Marin Cureau de la Chambre.[133] Montaigne's chief dis-

---

[129] Taylor, *Jacob Behmen's Theosophick Philosophy Unfolded* (London, 1692), p. 75.

[130] Anthony Levi, *French Moralists* (Oxford: Clarendon, 1964).

[131] Montaigne was particularly indebted to Plutarch, *De sollertia animalium*, esp. 968F–969C; 971B–972F. For general accounts of animals as moral exemplars, see George Boas, *The Happy Beast in the French Thought of the Seventeenth Century* (New York: Octagon, 1966); Hester Hastings, *Man and Beast in French Thought of the Eighteenth Century* (Johns Hopkins University Press, 1936).

[132] Montaigne, *The Essayes of Michael Lord of Montaigne*, tr. John Florio 3 vols (Oxford University Press, 1951), III, 316, 305.

[133] Other disciples of Montaigne who propagated animal sagacity and virtue were Estienne Pasquier, *Les Lettres d'Estienne Pasquier* (Paris, 1586), esp. pp. 289–303; La Mothe le Vayer, *Politique*

ciple was Charron, who seemed even more convinced of the moral and intellectual superiority of animals than was his mentor. The beasts, he argued, enjoy many advantages over men, including health, moderation, and innocence; they are exempt from 'infinite Vices and Exorbitances', and they are not burdened with superstition, ambition, avarice, envy, and fancy.[134] Charron also defended Montaigne's view that the goal of life was to live in conformity with nature, and that animals seemed much better at this than humans: 'If we regard the living in agreement with Nature, and in conformity with what she dictates and requires from us, Beasts seem to excel us in this respect very much; for they lead a Life of more Freedom, more Ease and Security, more Moderation and Contentedness, than Men do.' From this Charron concluded 'that Man is deservedly reputed *Wise*, who makes *them* his Pattern, and his Lesson, and reaps Profit by *their* Example; by reforming himself to that Innocence, Simplicity, Liberty, Meekness, and Gentleness of Temper, which Nature had originally implanted both in us and Them'.[135]

Montaigne and Charron, curiously enough, seemed to hold that animals were genuine moral agents. To read moral lessons in nature, however, did not require such an extreme position. Many naturalists, more sceptical of the putative moral purity of the beasts, nonetheless regarded them as providing important moral lessons for their human observers. Edward Topsell pointed out in his *History of Four-Footed Beasts and Serpents* that in scripture animals were said to have three 'holy uses' – sacrifices, visions, and reproof and instruction.[136] With sacrifices and divination no longer as popular as they used to be, moral edification became an important justification for accumulating knowledge of the natural world. This accounts for Topsell's enthusiastic descriptions of the virtues of various creatures:

How great is the love & faithfulness of Dogs, the meekness of Elephants, the modesty of shamelessness of the adulterous Lioness, the neatness and politure of the Cat and Peacock, the justice of the Bee, which gathereth from all flowers that which serveth their turn and destroyeth not the flower; the care of the Nightingale to make her voice pleasant, the chastity of the Turtle, the canonical voice and watchfulness of a Cock, and to conclude, the utility of a Sheep? All these and ten thousand more I could recite, to shew what the knowledge of the nature of brutish creatures doth work or teach the minds of men . . .[137]

du Prince, *Petits traites ou lettres*, Lettre LIV, *Opuscule ou Petit Traite sceptique sur sette commmune facon de parler, N'avoir pas le sens commun*, in *Oeuvres* (Paris, 1654). Also see Boas, *The Happy Beast*, pp. 52–63.
[134] Charron, *Of Wisdom*, pp. 247f.   [135] *Ibid.*, p. 263.
[136] Topsell, *History of Four-Footed Beasts and Serpents*, (1653), Epistle Dedicatory.   [137] *Ibid.*

Horses and elephants were frequently singled out for special praise. John Johnston claimed that horses demonstrate love, fidelity, chastity, and courage. They exhibit, in addition, wit, teachableness, and 'faithfulnesse towards their masters'.[138] Philip Sidney relates in *An Apology for Poetry* how his instructor at an Italian riding school so praised the virtues of horses, that had he 'not been a piece of a logician' he might nearly have been persuaded to wish himself a horse.[139] Wolfgang Franzius agreed that animals have 'shadows of virtues', but thought Elephants far more worthy of our attention than horses.[140] Elephants are mild and gentle towards others and their own; they live quietly together; they do not eat the flesh of other animals; they delight in music and singing; they never gorge themselves by overeating, they never couple with strange elephants, coming together only for the purpose of generation, (and then in private); they never neglect their young and are always ready to defend them; they 'shew a great deal of piety' towards their dead brethren.[141] In addition to these qualities, and despite his denial of reason to animals, Franzius states that elephants can comprehend the language of their country, and can be taught to make letters of the alphabet with their trunks. Johnston, on the other hand, considered the linguistic abilities of elephants to be a fiction, but allowed that elephants worship the sun and the new moon, would set a wandering man back on the right path, and will 'watch adulterers, and murderers and reveale them'.[142]

The peculiar piety of elephants had been noted by a number of seventeenth-century writers. Montaigne, Franzius, and More all repeated the tradition, found in Pliny and Aelian, that elephants (and possibly apes as well) worshipped the sun and moon.[143] A sixteenth-century edition of Bartholomew's encyclopaedia records that 'among beasts ye Elephant is most of vertue'. Elephants, the author goes on to say, 'when they be sicke, they gather good hearbs, and ere they use the hearbs, they heave up the head and looke towarde heaven & pray for help of God in a certaine Religion'.[144] Notwithstanding the conviction of Latin Father, Lactantius, that religion was the unique property of the human race,

---

[138] Johnston, *Nature of Four-Footed Beasts*, p. 4. Franzius, *History of Brutes*, pp. 89–95.
[139] Philip Sidney, *An Apology for Poetry* 1595, in *English Critical Essays* ed. E. Jones (Oxford University Press, 1963) p. 1   [140] Franzius, *History of Brutes*, p. 12.   [141] *Ibid.*, pp. 21–5.
[142] Johnston, *Nature of Four-Footed Beasts*, p. 18.
[143] Montaigne, 'An Apology for Raymond Sebond', *Essayes*, tr. John Florio (Oxford University Press, 1951), II, p. 180; Franzius, *History of Brutes*, p. 25; More, *Grand Mystery of Godliness*, p. 50. Pliny, *Natural History*, x.41; Aelian, *Characteristics of Animals*, IV.10, VII. 44. Cf. John Smith, *Select Discourses* (London, 1660), p. 375.   [144] *Batman vppon Bartholome*, fol. 363v.

Godfrey Goodman had actually produced a complete work on the religious sentiments of animals, entitled *The Creatvres Praysing God: or The Religion of Dumbe Creatures* (1622). Goodman ventured the thesis 'that the dumbe Creatures haue likewise their proper kinde of religion as well as men, and that they are very deuout, godly, zealous, strict and most religious in their owne kinde'.[145] He went on to show that animals acknowledge one God (albeit implicitly), immutable, eternal, good, simple, wise, free, powerful, and providential.[146] The piety of animals was defended even in the eighteenth century, by one Richard Dean, Curate of Middleton, who declared that 'it is notorious to the World, that numbers of them [animals] make as great a Point of attending at Church on public Service day, as the most rigid pietists do'.[147] We would do well, the curate implied, to follow their example.

While the largest of beasts was undoubtedly one of the most popular moral exemplars, the smallest also attracted their share of attention. Indeed, the formerly despised insects, particularly ants and bees, were destined to become the firm favourites of the early modern moralists.[148] 'Every Particle of an Insect', wrote Thomas Pope Blount, 'carries with it the Impress of Ethicks or Divinity.'[149] Edward Tyson, translator of Swammerdam's *Ephemera vita*, pointed out that the history and anatomy of the 'ephemeron' (a fly that lives but five hours) is a natural guide to divinity.[150] The poet Guido concurred '*The smallest* Ant *does* Providence *Teach / Does* Foresight *to the Sluggard Preach, / And here in this* Ephemeron *we see / An Embleme both of Change, and of* Mortality'.[151] The hive, said Pluche, 'is a School to which Numbers of People ought to be sent; Prudence, Industry, and Benevolence, Publick-Spiritedness and Diligence, Oeconomy, Neatness, and Temperance, are all visible among the Bees . . . they read us Lectures upon them'. Ants, too, were 'very instructive'.[152] John Edwards thought that bees exhibit 'great industry' and 'sagacity' and,

---

[145] Goodman, *The Creatvres Praysing God*, (London, 1622), pp. 4f. Cf. Lactantius, *Divine Institutes*, II.iii, x; *A Treatise on the Anger of God*, VII.

[146] *Ibid.*, pp. 9–12. On animal prayers, see also Abbot, *An Exposition on the Prophet Ionah*, (London, 1600), p. 471. Other writers denied that animals were religious. Pluche says that animals possess 'not the least Shadow of Religion'. *Spectacle*, V, 8.

[147] Richard Dean, *An Essay on the Future Life of Brutes, Introduced with Observations upon Evil, its nature, and Origin*, 2 vols. (Manchester, 1767), II, 71.

[148] As they had been of the ancients and the Fathers. See, e.g., Aelian, *Characteristics of Animals*, I.22, II.25, VI.50; Pliny, *Natural History*, XXXVI.30; Basil, *Hexameron*, VIII.4; IX.3. Amongst the moderns, see Charron, *Of Wisdom*, p. 252.   [149] Blount, *A Natural History* (London, 1693), Preface.

[150] Jan Swammerdam, *Ephemera vita or the Natural History and Anatomy of the Ephemeron* (London, 1681), preface.   [151] *Ibid.*

[152] Pluche, *Spectacle*, I, dialogues 7, 8 (106ff.). Cf. Edwards, *A Demonstration*, pt I, pp. 206–13.

perhaps less commendably, have a 'Female Monarchy'.[153] Bees, agreed French pioneer of entomology Réaumur, afford us 'useful instructions, and examples fit for imitation'. Their life, he concluded, 'is almost a treatise of morality'.[154] Thomas Moffet, who had taken time out of his medical studies at Cambridge to complete the editing of Gesner's *Historia Animalium,* wrote in his *Insectorum sive minimorum animalium theatrum* (1634) that ants were 'exemplary for their great piety, prudence, justice, valour, temperance, modesty, charity, friendship, frugality, perserverence, industry and art'.[155] Moffet's title is thus not without significance: the natural world was a theatre, human beings spectators, and other living things players to be observed, insignificant in themselves, useful for the roles which they mechanically played out.[156] The world, in the words of Du Bartas, was both a school and a stage, established not merely for the material sustenance of its human inhabitants, but serving for their moral edification as well.[157]

The encomiums which the moderns heaped upon the most modest of creatures seem at first reading to be all of a piece with the extreme praise of irrational creatures which we encounter in Aelian, Plutarch, and Pliny. Yet there is an increasing awareness in the seventeenth-century writers of the need to base moral lessons on what can actually be observed in nature, as opposed to what is reported to take place. The mark of the good natural historian, observed Edward Topsell, 'is to follow truth and not deceivable Fables'.[158] This was an admirable principle, but Topsell, writing in 1607 and collecting most of his material from Gesner, was unfortunately not well placed to make the distinction between fact and fiction, however much he might have stressed its importance. As we have seen, his works included many descriptions of fantastic beasts and their properties and behaviours. Much of John Edwards' admiration for the moral qualities of ants also resulted from his indiscriminate use of sources. To his credit, he does refer to Swam-

---

[153] Edwards, *A Demonstration,* pt I, pp. 206f.

[154] René Antoine Ferchault de Réaumur, *The Natural History of Bees* (London, 1744), p. 297.

[155] Thomas Moffet, *Insectorum sive minimorum animalium theatrum* (1634) ch. 16. Cf. Edwards, *A Demonstration,* pp. 210–13.

[156] Plants, too, were a part of this theatre, Cf. John Parkinson, *Theatrum Botanicum: The Theatre of Plantes* (London, 1640).

[157] 'The World's a Schoole, where (in a generall Storie) / God alwayes reades dumbe Lectures of his Glorie . . . / The World's a Stage, where Gods Omnipotence / His Justice, Knowledge, Love, and Providence, / Do act their parts; contending in their kindes / Above the Heav'ns to ravish dullest mindes'. Du Bartas, *Divine Weeks and Works,* i.vii, ll. 157f., 169–73. Henry More also uses the metaphor, *Antidote,* p. 56.

[158] Topsell, *Historie of Foure-Footed Beastes* (1607), Epistle Dedicatory.

merdam and Bochart, but these modern authorities were vastly out-numbered by the ancients: Aristotle, Pliny, Aelian, Plutarch, Horace, Virgil, Ovid, Tully, Epiphanius.[159] Réaumur, writing some hundred years after Topsell, was better placed to know what animal behaviours could be borne out by observation. While adhering to the principle that the study of the natural world disclosed a moral order which extended to the irrational creatures, he insisted that the facts related about the creatures be literally true. Writing on the natural history of ants, he observed:

> ... the attempt has been made to convert ants into little men, more perfect than the large ones to whom they have been proposed as models worthy of imitation. It is certainly permissible to regard the ants as small animals of even greater accomplishments if one have need of them in composition of a pretty and instructive fable, but ... it is not permitted to naturalists to represent them otherwise than Nature has made them, or rather such as we can observe them ...[160]

Réaumur thus allows that both fables and the direct observation of nature may serve the purposes of moral edification. But he insists that the two must not be confused. The relations of Pliny and Aelian according to which ants took holidays on one day of the month, or had market days, or practised funeral rites were not confirmed by observa-tion, and had no place in natural history.[161] Boyle made a similar point in his *Occasional Meditations*, 'It was doubtless a very great pleasure to Esop, that by his ingenious efforts he could, in a manner, lend reason and speech to lions, foxes, crows, and other animals, to whom nature had denied both', he observed. But while such fictions serve useful moral purposes, careful observation of 'all kinds of creatures in the world' will reveal them to be, in spite of themselves, 'not only teachers of ethics, but ... doctors of divinity'.[162] For both Boyle and Réaumur, there remained sufficiently well attested facts about all kinds of creatures for them to remain our moral mentors without resort to a confusion of fact with fable.

However, these concessions to fables – that they could as easily serve as moral purposes as authentic reports from nature – turned out to be highly significant. From about the beginning of the eighteenth century, the pressure on the natural world to serve as a moral teacher began to

---

[159] Edwards, *A Demonstration*, pt 1, pp. 208–14.
[160] Réaumur, *The Natural History of Ants*, tr. W. M. Wheeer (London: Knapp, 1926).
[161] *Ibid.*, preface. Aelian, *Characteristics of Animals*, 1.22; vi.50; Pliny, *Natural History*, xxxvi.30.
[162] Boyle, *A Discourse touching Occasional Meditations*, *Works*, ii, 340.

ease as explicitly fictional accounts of the exploits of animals began to take hold of the public imagination. Fables assumed the tropological burden previously borne by natural history.[163] While Johnston had attributed love, fidelity, chastity, and courage to horses, these equine virtues were transferred in Swift's *Gulliver's Travels*, to the fictional 'houyhnhnms'.[164] Here horses are imbued with 'temperance, industry, exercise and cleanliness' and comprise a society 'well united, naturally disposed to every virtue, wholly governed by Reason'.[165] Swift clearly assumed that the fact that his narrative was a complete concoction would not stand in the way of the moral task it had to perform. Cyrano de Bergerac had already done something similar with his *Story of the Birds*, in which a human being is tried by birds possessed of speech and reason for crimes committed against fellow creatures.[166] Animal fables thus emerge as a distinct literary genre, independent of the discipline of natural history.

To a lesser extent, something similar took place in the case of allegory. The use of allegory persisted until well into the seventeenth century and beyond, albeit in rather a different form than that which we encounter in the Middle Ages. Now allegory ceases to be a principle of interpretation and becomes primarily a device utilised by an author. Accordingly, allegorical interpretation is permitted only when it is has been established that an author has quite explicitly encoded the meaning of his writing allegorically. John Bunyan's *A Book for Boys and Girls* (1686), a popular work reprinted a number of times into the eighteenth century, employs allegory in this fashion. Here various animals are taken to be representative of particular human failings: 'The Frog by Nature, is both damp and cold / Her Mouth is large, her Belly much will hold . . . The Hyppocrite is like unto this Frog / As like as the Puppy to the Dog. . .'[167] Bunyan's more extended allegorical work, *Pilgrim's Progress* (1678, 1684), illustrates the same general point. One could easily argue that this work contained important truths without being thereby committed to the view that 'Pilgrim' and 'Giant Despair' were real persons, or that 'the valley of the Shadow' or 'the Palace Beautiful' could

---

[163] Hence the many editions of Aesop's fables to appear in the sixteenth and seventeenth centuries. Luther himself actually translated a number of Aesop's fables into German, supplementing them with his own. See Reinhard Dithmar (ed.), *Martin Luther's Fabeln and Sprichworter* (Darmstadt: Wissenschaftliche Buchgesellschaft, 1995).

[164] *Ibid.*, p. 4. It is not clear how these virtues stand given Johnston's earlier statement that horses are the most lustful of beasts.   [165] Jonathan Swift, *Gullivers Travels*, pt IV, (chs. 8, 9).

[166] *Cyrano de Bergerac's Voyages to the Moon and the Sun*, tr. John Aldington (London: Folio Society, 1991), pp. 161–209.   [167] John Bunyan, *A Book for Boys and Girls* (London, 1686), xxxvi. p. 46.

be given fixed geographical locations. Similarly Bunyan's *Book for Boys and Girls* was not confused with treatises on natural history. In such works, the legitimacy of an allegorical interpretation thus came to depend on the intention of the author. If the intended meaning lay in allegory, then well and good. Otherwise, the literal sense should prevail. Strong elements of medieval symbolism and allegory are also present in the poetry of George Herbert and Henry Vaughan.[168] In the metaphysical poets generally we witness the trend in which the symbolic mode of reading the world is displaced from hermeneutics and natural history to find a home in the composition of literature. Samuel Johnson observed that the metaphysical poets relied upon 'a combination of dissimilar images, or discovery of occult resemblances in things apparently unlike'. He continues: 'The most heterogeneous ideas are yoked by violence together; nature and art are ransacked for illustrations, comparisons and allusions.' Johnson apparently had little taste for the didactic aspects of metaphysical poetry, concluding that while 'their learning instructs . . . the reader commonly thinks his improvements dearly bought, and, though he sometimes admires, is seldom pleased'.[169] So it was that those similitudes which had provided the basis for the medieval conception of the order of nature became, in the modern period, literary devices which might be employed by writers. Allegory and tropology became ways of writing, and in those cases where legitimated by an author's intention, ways of reading; allegory and tropology were now to do with words and not things. Symbolism and similitudes were thus destined to be relocated from the book of nature to the writings of men and women.[170]

GOD AND THE BOOK OF NATURE

The rise of physico-theology in the seventeenth century ensured the survival of the medieval image of 'the book of nature'. While the things of nature do not give us access to a transcendental realm of eternal truths, nonetheless, certain attributes of God, the place of the human being in the cosmos, particular moral lessons, could still be discerned in the frame of nature and in the designs and behaviours of its living

---

[168] Rosemary Freeman, *English Emblem Books* (London: Chatto and Windus, 1967).

[169] Samuel Johnson, *Lives of the English Poets*, 2 vols. (London: Dent, 1950), 1, 11f. 'Dissimilar similitude', incidentally, was for Pseudo-Dionysius the basis of analogy.

[170] On the uses of allegory and typology in seventeenth- and eighteenth-century writing, see Korshin, *Typologies*, pp. 17, 37, and passim.

creatures. It is hardly surprising that the expression 'book of nature' is ubiquitous in works of theology and natural philosophy alike. Yet it is important to attend to the discontinuities between the medieval and early modern uses of the metaphor. The triumph of literalism contributed to a widening gap between the written text of God's word and the book of the creatures. For this reason 'book of nature' takes on a quite different meaning in the sixteenth and seventeenth centuries. Medieval uses of the image are more or less uniform: the idea that nature is a book underlines the fact that things act as signs just as words do. Nature and scripture must be read together for the meaning of words of scripture is given by the meanings of the natural objects to which they refer. The key to the meanings of natural objects, in turn, was provided by references to scripture. Hermeneutics was a dialectical enterprise which always entailed a knowledge of both books. In the early modern period, by way of contrast, the metaphor is used in a variety of ways. The general tendency now is to elevate nature over some alternative authority – such as scripture or the writings of Aristotle – or to contrast nature with written authorities by arguing that it has a different purpose, that it is to be interpreted by a different strategy, that it enjoys particular advantages over written texts.

Paracelsus took a lead in refashioning the medieval metaphor, contrasting the book of nature with both the scriptures and the writings of ancient authorities. In place of Galen, Avicenna, and Aristotle, Paracelsus set 'Nature' – that library of books which 'God himself wrote, made and bound'.[171] Every country, he insisted, is a page of nature's book: 'He who would explore her must tread her books with his feet. Scripture is explored through its letters; but nature from land to land. Every land is a leaf. Such is the *Codex Naturae*: thus must her leaves be turned.'[172] Numerous others followed Paracelsus in lauding the virtues of the book of nature over the books of human authors. John Webster, in his famous attack on the English universities, declared the macrocosm to be 'the great unsealed book of God, and every creature as a Capital letter or character'. Yet in the universities, 'Alas! we all study and read too much upon the dead paper rolls of creaturely invented letters but do not, nor cannot read the legible characters that are onely written and impressed by the finger of the Almighty.' In his opinion, the Aristotelian schools,

---

[171] For this and other references to the book metaphors of Paracelsus, see W. E. Peuckert, *Paracelsus, Die Geheimnisse. Ein Lesebuch aus seinen Schriften* (Stuttgart, 1941) 172–8.

[172] Paracelsus, *Seven Defensiones* (1564), in *Four Treatises of Theophrastus von Hohenheim called Paracelsus* tr. C. Lilian Temkin et al. (Johns Hopkins, 1941), p. 21.

with their 'paper idols', wished 'to open the cabinet of Natures rich treasure, without labour and pains, experiments and operations, tryals and observations'.[173] Seventeenth-century naturalists were to advocate the superiority of the book of nature in much the same way. The study of nature, wrote Edward Topsell, 'is to be preferred before the Chronicks and Records of all ages made by men', for nature is 'that Chronicale which was made by God himself, every living beast a word, every kind being a sentence, and all of them together, a large History'.[174] Robert Hooke thought that 'we might then, instead of studying Herbals (where so little is deliver'd of the virtues of a Plant, and less of truth) have recourse to the Book of Nature it self, and there find the most natural, usefull, and most effectual and specifick Medicines'.[175] 'Nature is the best and choicest Library', wrote Pluche, 'it is always open, and if we will use our Eyes, we shall be sure to find better Instruction there than we possibly can in Books.'[176]

More caution was required for the prosecution of the advantages of the book of nature over the book of scripture. One ground for superiority which suggested itself to seventeenth-century minds was that nature was a universal text which, unlike scripture, had been accessible at all times, in all places, to all peoples: nature was, in the words of Thomas Browne, 'a Universal and publick Manuscript'.[177] Long before written scriptures had been compiled, there was nature. Tertullian had written in the second century, at a time when the canon of scripture had yet to be settled, that 'God must first be known from *nature*, and afterwards authenticated by *instruction*: from nature, by His works; by instruction, through his revealed announcements'.[178] In the seventeenth century, when the true meaning of the canon had become the subject of controversy, Tertullian's priority was again asserted. 'God sent us the *Booke of Nature*, before he sent us the *Booke of the Scriptures*', pointed out Ralph Austen. 'The People of God in the beginning of the World were without the Scriptures for many yeares, and they read many things in the *Booke of the Creatures*.'[179] 'In matters of Fact', declared Thomas Sprat, 'we follow the most antient Author of all others, even *Nature* it self'.[180] Nature was a

---

[173] Webster, *Academiarum Examen* (London, 1654), pp. 28, 92.

[174] Topsell, *History of Four-Footed Beasts and Serpents*, (1653) Epistle Dedicatory.

[175] Hooke, *Micrographia*, p. 155.   [176] Pluche, *Spectacle*, III, 115.

[177] Browne, *Religio Medici* 1.16 (p. 16).

[178] Tertullian, *Against Marcion*, I.xviii (*ANF* III, 284) Galileo cited this reference to support his views about the relationship between the two books.

[179] Ralph Austen, *The Spiritual vse of an Orchard*, (Oxford, 1653), Preface.

[180] Sprat, *History of the Royal Society*, pp. 47f.

book, according to the Abbé Pluche, which 'never confines her Instructions ta any particular Language or People'; nature was 'our first
Revelation'.[181]

The vulgar and illiterate were also able to comprehend the theology
of the book of nature, while the subtleties of scriptural doctrines were
likely to escape them. 'Some Instructions lye obvious, and plaine to
every mans eye, an illiterate man may here read distinctly', wrote Ralph
Austen of the book of nature. 'They who cannot read a line in any
Printed Booke, may read many good lessons in the Booke of the
Creatures.'[182] 'The Prospect of Nature' said Pluche, 'is a kind of vulgar
Theology, in which all Men may learn those Truths which it is of the
highest Consequence and Importance for them to know.'[183] Du Bartas
devoted a numerous lines of his *Divine Weeks and Works* to this theme:

> To read this Booke, we neede not understand
> Each Strangers gibbrish; neither take in hand
> *Turkes* Caracters, nor *Hebrue* Points to seeke,
> *Nyle's Hieroglyphics*, nor the Notes of *Greeke.*
> The wandring *tartars*, the *Antartkes* wilde,
> Th' *Alarbies* fierce, the *Scithians* fell, the Childe
> Scarce seav'n yeare old, the bleared aged eye,
> Though void of Arte, read heere indifferently.[184]

An anonymous seventeenth-century English poet made the point somewhat more succinctly: 'In nature's book the weakest brain may
speed/Th' untaught may learn it, and th' unlettered read.'[185] In his
Boyle Lectures, William Derham pointed out that the works of God
show forth his nature 'especially to such as are unacquainted with the
Subtilties of Reasoning and Argumentation; as the greatest part of
, Mankind are'.[186] John Donne cited with approval the view of Raymond
of Sebonde, that 'the book of the creatures . . . teaches al [sic] things,
presupposes no other, is soon learned, cannot be forgotten, requires no
books, needs no witnesses, and in this, is safer than the Bible itself, that is
cannot be falsified by Hereticks'. Sebonde, he observes, had gone even
further, asserting that 'because his book is made according to the Order
of Creatures, which express fully the will of God, whosoever doth
according to his booke, fulfils the will of God'. In Donne's judgement,

---

[181] Pluche, *Spectacle*, i, viii; iii, 326.
[182] Austen, *Spiritual Use of an Orchard*, Epistle Dedicatory, Preface.   [183] Pluche, *Spectacle*, iii, 303.
[184] Du Bartas, *Divine Weeks and Works* i.i, lines 184–91.
[185] Anon. 1751, cited in John Prest, *The Garden of Eden: The Botanic Garden and the Re-Creation of Paradise*
(New Haven: Yale University Press, 1981), p. 55.   [186] Derham, *Physico-Theology*, pp. 2f.

however, Sebonde was 'too abundant in affirming, that *in libro creaturarum* there is enough to teach us all particularities of Christian religion'.[187]

Not only was the book of nature universally available and easily read by the illiterate, but it was also a book whose interpretation was relatively uncontroversial, particularly when compared to the interpretation of scripture. Passages of scripture, pointed out Galileo, 'may have some different meaning beneath their words', but 'Nature, on the other hand, is inexorable and immutable'.[188] Hooke argued that '*Rabbins* find out *Caballisms*, and *Enigmas* in the figure, and placing of Letters, where no such thing lies hid; whereas in *Natural* forms there are some so small, and so curious, and their design'd business so far removed from the reach of our sight, that the more we do magnify the object, the more excellencies and mysteries do appear'.[189] The book of nature may be read at many levels, while scripture has only one true sense. Caballists and allegorisers delude themselves when they seek multiple levels of meaning in the book of God's words. Pluche wrote of the book of nature that 'we neither find Errors nor different Opinions, nor Controversy, nor Prejudice, nor Contentions'.[190] The anonymous 'J.S'. argued in the introduction to one of Boehme's works that the language of nature 'doth show in every ones Mother tongue the Greatest Mysteries' while the meaning of scripture is 'vayled by Doubtfull Interpretations, Expositions, Inferences and Conclusions'.[191]

It is not insignificant that the language used to promote the virtues of the book of nature is redolent of that previously used in the justification of the use of images and the performance of sacramental rites: it provided a theology for the unlettered, the untaught, the vulgar, the weak-brained. Physico-theology does not only present itself as an alternative hermeneutics for interpreting the book of nature, but it moves to occupy the territory from which icon and sacrament had been so violently expelled. Those unable to understand abstruse theological

---

[187] John Donne, *Essayes in Divinity*, ed. Evelyn Simpson (Oxford: Clarendon, 1952) pp. 17f. The *Essayes* first appeared in 1651. Raymond of Sebonde was a fifteenth-century Spanish philosopher, best known in the early modern period as the thinker who inspired Montaigne's extended essay, 'Apologie pour Raymond de Sebonde'. Sebonde was condemned at Trent for having written: 'Scripturas sacras facile quis impia interpretatione subruere potest, sed nemo est tam execrandi dogmatis hereticus, qui naturae librum falsificare possit.' His *Liber naturae sive Creaturarum* was placed on the Index in 1595 for asserting the priority of the book of nature over scripture and tradition. See Curtius, *European Literature*, p. 320.

[188] Galileo, *Letter to the Grand Duchess Christina* in *Discoveries and Opinions*, tr. Drake, p. 183. Cf. pp. 187, 199. On nature as unequivocal compared to scripture, see Eugenio Garin, 'Alcune Osservazione Sul Libro Come Simbolo', in *Umanesimo e Simbolismo*, Archivio de Filosophia (Padua, 1958), pp. 93–102.   [189] Hooke, *Micrographia*, p. 8   [190] Pluche *Spectacle*, III, 115.

[191] Boehme, *The Second Booke*, Sig. A3r.

formulations, those poorly equipped to delve into the deep mysteries of the faith, those with no facility in the original languages of scripture, those who in previous ages were forced to resort to implicit faith, all could now be presented with the simple theology of nature. Natural philosophers, for their part, might also cast themselves in the role of priests – priests who had eschewed idolatrous rites and the preaching of unintelligible dogmas, demonstrating instead the divine power apparent in the natural order and humbly reading lessons from the book of nature. Kepler thus described astronomers as 'priests of the most high God, with respect to the book of nature'.[192] Reformers in religion and science alike were to insist that the true function of a priest was not the performance of ritual acts with symbolic objects, but the exposition of some authoritative text and the communication to others of information. The text given to students of nature to expound was the world itself. The image of natural philosophers as priests expounding a word-less text struck a chord with a number of seventeenth-century writers. Henry More spoke of the universe as 'the temple of God', and its human inhabitants priests, who ought to be 'invested as it were and adorned with the Knowledge of the Laws and Measures of the Creation'. Fellow Platonist John Smith agreed that the world was 'God's temple'.[193] Robert Boyle exploited the same image. 'I esteem the world a temple,' he wrote, and 'if the world be a temple, man sure must be the priest'. Natural philosophy, Boyle goes on to say, is 'reasonable worship (λογική λατρεία) of God . . . and discovering to others the perfections of God displayed in the creatures is a more acceptable act of religion, than the burning of sacrifices'. The study of nature, he concludes, is 'the first act of religion, and equally obliging in all religions'.[194] The book of nature

---

[192] Kepler, *Werke* VII (1953), 25. Kepler, Letter to Herwath von Hohenburg, March 26, 1598, *Werke* XIII (1945) 193.

[193] More, *A Collection*, p. v; *Antidote*, p. 103. John Smith, *Select Discourses*, pp. 433f., Cf. Bacon, *Novum Organum*, 1.120; Traherne, 'Centuries' 1.31; Joseph Addison, *The Spectator* 564, Friday 9 July, 1714 (p. 805). The Geneva Bible's annotations on Genesis also refer to 'this great tabernacle of the world'. (1607 edn, fol. 1r). In a variation on this theme, George Herbert declared that 'Man is the world's high priest', for man alone is able to articulate the praise of trees, birds and beasts. George Herbert, 'Providence', line 13. Poet Henry Vaughan used the same expression. 'Man is their high -priest, and should rise / To offer up the sacrifice'. 'Christ's Nativity', lines 11f. Pluche likewise observed that man is the priest of all the creatures, because by discovering their perfections, he articulates their 'Tribute of Praise to him who has formed them for his glory'. Pluche, *Spectacle*, 1, 390.

[194] Boyle, *Some Considerations*, in *Works*, II, pp. 32, 29, 63, 62; Cf. III, 627, V, 401. Also see H. Fisch, 'The Scientist as Priest: A Note on Robert Boyle's Natural Theology', *Isis* 44 (1953) 252–65. It is likely that Boyle found these ideas in ancient writers. Thus, Macrobius, *Commentary on the Dream of Scipio* XIV.1 (p. 142): the visible world is 'the temple of God' and 'whoever is inducted into the priviledges of this temple . . . had to live in the manner of a priest'. Philo, *On the Special Laws* 1.66: 'We ought to look upon the universal world as the highest and truest temple of God'. (*Works*, p.

and those natural philosophers who interpreted it thus assumed part of the role previously played by the sacraments and the ordained priesthood.

The book of nature, interpreted according to canons of physico-theology, thus came to represent a source of theological knowledge independent, to a degree, of the book of scripture. The investigation of the world was commended as a theological activity. John Johnston, explaining his motives in compiling *The Nature of Four-Footed Beasts*, refers his reader to 'Natures book, wherein we may behold the supreme power'. The study of nature, no less than the study of scripture leads us to God, for, as Johnston continues: 'the knowledge of God is the principall end of the sciences'. Thus, God 'is comprehended under the title of natural history'.[195] John Edwards declared that 'The Works of Creation' are 'Nature's Bible, wherein we plainly read a God'. 'Our skill in Natural History', he thought, 'must lead us to Theology'.[196] To Richard Franck the world was 'the Almighty's Commonplace Book, in which the elements and principles were 'marginal notes', the creatures 'the consonants and vowels'. Accordingly, we ought to 'read daily Lectures' in the 'glorious frontpiece' of the creation, for 'God assignes it our duty to study the Creation'.[197] The world could even be read as a devotional work. 'What an excellent Book is the visible world for the daily studies of a holy soul', wrote puritan divine Richard Baxter.[198] Even John Calvin, who was quite sceptical about the possibility that saving knowledge of God could be gleaned from nature, had nonetheless allowed that the world was 'the book of the unlearned', 'a school', and 'a mirror in which we ought to behold God'.[199]

The apparent advantages enjoyed by the book of nature led more daring thinkers towards the end of the seventeenth century to assert the superiority of 'nature', broadly conceived, as a religious authority superior to particular revelations. The religion which they proclaimed was a natural religion.[200] The brother of poet George Herbert – Edward,

---

540); Seneca: 'The whole world is the temple of the gods'. *De benificiis*, vii.7 (*Moral Essays*, *LCL*, iii, 473). Cf. Hebrews 8.4f., 9.24. These judgements confirm Marsilio Ficino's remark to the effect that true philosophy and true religion are one and the same thing. *Laus Philosophiae moralis*, *Opera*, 2 tom., (Basileae, 1576), i, 668.

[195] Johnston, *Wonderful Things of Nature*, Sig. a3v. Cf. R. Franck, *Philosophical Treatise*, Epistle Dedicatory. [196] Edwards, *A Demonstration*, pt i, Preface, p. 262.

[197] R. Franck, *A Philosophical Treatise*, Epistle to the Reader.

[198] Richard Baxter, *A Christian Directory*, 2nd edn, (London, 1678), Pt i, p. 125.

[199] Calvin, *Commentary on Genesis*, pp. 80, 60, 62.

[200] On natural religion see Peter Byrne, *Natural Religion and the Nature of Religion* (London: Routledge, 1989); Harrison, *'Religion' and the Religions*, pp. 28–34; Natural religion includes not only knowledge of God which can be inferred from the natural world, but that which is 'written on the human heart' as it were, or is able to be deduced *a priori*.

first Lord Herbert of Cherbury – thought that from reason and nature could be derived a religion which was both universal and sufficient, a religion which, in Herbert's words, 'comprehends all places and all men'. The tenets of this religion were simple: the worship of God, the practise of virtue, repentance for wrong-doing, and future rewards and punishments. Subscription to these beliefs was all that was required for membership in 'the only Catholic and uniform Church' and Herbert controversially asserted that 'it is only through this Church that salvation is possible'.[201] The so-called 'deists' who came after Herbert of Cherbury likewise preached a religion of nature, which they presumed to have been practised before there were written scriptures and imposing priests. Charles Blount believed that prior to the advent of revealed religion, 'there was no worship of God but in a rational way'. This rational religion consisted simply in 'Virtue and Piety'. 'Natural religion was easy first, and plain', wrote John Toland, 'Tales made it mystery, offrings made it gain'. Thomas Morgan agreed that in the 'first and purest Ages', natural religion consisted in leading a life of purity and temperance.[202] Natural religion, in short, would reflect the qualities of the book of nature: it would be open to all, easily understood, and it would not engender the kinds of vicious and bloody disputes which had plagued post-Reformation Europe. This latter feature of natural religion was for many its most appealing quality. 'Take Natures's path, and mad Opinions leave', counselled Pope, 'All States can reach it, and all heads conceive'.[203] To follow nature's path, in practical terms, was to adopt a tolerant and universal religion. It was with this in mind that naturalist Swammerdam wrote of his erstwhile friend Nicolaus Steno, the great Swedish polymath, who had forsaken his studies of nature in order to wear the scarlet: 'I wish he were still like he was when he sought God in the Bible of nature. Then he would not be so opinionated in his religion and he would love all men, though they might not bear the name of his religion'.[204] For the proponents of natural religion, the revelation contained in scripture was not universally available, and quarrels over its meaning had led to controversy, conflict and blood-

---

[201] Herbert of Cherbury, *A Dialogue between a Tutor and his Pupil* (London, 1768), p. 30.

[202] Charles Blount, 'Great is Diana of the Ephesians', p. 3, in *Miscellaneous Works* (London, 1695); John Toland, *Letters to Serena* (London, 1704), letter III; Thomas Morgan, *The Moral Philosopher*, 2nd edn, 3 vols., (London, 1738–40), III, 94.

[203] Alexander Pope, *An Essay on Man*, IV.29f, in *Poems*, Twickenham edn.

[204] Swammerdam, *Letters*, Letter 14, Jan. 1678, p. 84. Ironically, Swammerdam himself was soon to fall prey to the immoderate religion of Antoinette Bourignon, and he spent the last years of his short life embroiled in religious controversies.

shed. As Pluche pointed out, nature, by way of contrast, 'never confines her Instructions ta [sic] any particular Language or People' and her theology 'is constantly well-received because it is intelligible'.[205]

Such attempts to ground religion in the book of nature attracted sustained criticism, however, and the deist controversies of the late seventeenth and early eighteenth centuries were resolved in favour of the orthodox. The more numerous opponents of deism argued that for the purposes of salvation, knowledge of the divine image or the divine will was required, and such knowledge, on most accounts, could not be found in the natural world. The reformers, while they had grudgingly conceded that God could be known through his creation, had categorically denied that this information was in any way useful. Luther wrote: 'There is a vast difference between knowing that there is a God and knowing who or what God is. Nature knows the former . . . the latter is taught only by the Holy Spirit.'[206] Calvin declared that while 'God is manifested by the creation of the world', this manifestation has no further effect 'than to render us inexcusable'.[207] Both pointed to the damning words of St Paul: 'For the wrath of God is revealed from heaven against all ungodliness and wickedness of men who by their wickedness suppress the truth. For what can be known about God is plain to them . . . in the things that have been made. So they are without excuse' (Romans 1.18–20). This subsequently was to become the standard Protestant position, enshrined in the Thirty-Nine Articles and the Westminster Confession.[208] Even those with a more relaxed approach to salvation than the Calvinists tended to deny that saving knowledge could be found in nature. Latitudinarian Bishop Stillingfleet wrote that 'the large *volume* of the Creation, wherein *God* hath described so much of his *wisdom* and *power*, is yet too dark and obscure, too short and imperfect to set forth to us the *way* which leads to eternal happinesse'.[209]

Most of those who extolled the virtues of the book of nature were to adopt this standard Protestant line. The world, wrote Daneau, tells us of God's 'Power, wisdome, goodness'.[210] Pluche's list is slightly longer. The book of nature teaches us not only of the existence of God, but of 'His

---

[205] Pluche, *Spectacle*, 1, 34.   [206] *Luther's Works*, 19, 55.

[207] Calvin, *Institutes* I.v (1, 62). Calvin cites Romans 1.19 and Acts 17.27 for support.

[208] See e.g. 'The Westminster Confession' I.i (Schaff III, 600).

[209] Stillingfleet, *Origines sacrae*, 1662 edn p. 602. The Protestant emphasis on the possession of the right kind of knowledge was to lead to formation of the modern category 'religion', now conceived of as subscribing to a body of doctrines. See Wilfred Cantwell Smith, *The Meaning and End of Religion* (London: SPCK, 1978), pp. 40–1, Harrison, *'Religion' and the Religions*, pp. 24–8; J. Bossy, *Christianity in the West, 1400–1700* (Oxford University Press, 1985) pp. 170–1.

[210] Daneau, *Wonderfull Woorkmanship*, fol. 65v.

Unity, His Power, His Wisdom, His Independence, His Goodness, His Providence'.[211] Absent from both lists is reference to God's will, or to the knowledge which brings with it salvation. The pious Richard Baxter allowed that 'the world is Gods book, which he set man at first to read'.[212] Robert South, too, wrote of Adam, that 'He had no catechism but the creation, needed no study but reflection, read no book but the volume of the world.'[213] Yet, for neither of these writers was there any suggestion that nature was an adequate source of saving knowledge of God. On the contrary, it was the human failure to discern truths in the volume of nature which necessitated the more direct revelation now to be found in the pages of scripture. As South simply put it, 'It was not then, as it is now.'[214] Human sin brought a loss of the ability to penetrate the secrets of nature, and so, 'all those arts, rarities, and inventions, which vulgar minds gaze at, the ingenious pursue, and all admire, are but the relics of an intellect defaced with sin and time'.[215] Thomas Tymme agreed that 'If man had not sinned, the booke of Nature would have sufficed to have him always in the knowledge & obedience of God his Creator.'[216] Thomas Traherne, thought, conversely, that changes in the natural world itself had rendered its characters illegible: 'if nature were divested of its Corruption, the Natural Man . . . might by the light of Nature, be fitted to understand' those truths about God which were now hidden in the workings of nature.[217] The Fall had either distorted the characters of natural objects, rendering them unintelligible, or had dulled human wit, diminishing its capacity to interpret what had once been obvious: in either case, the vanity of symbolic readings of the cosmos which proposed to give propositional content to the created order was exposed. The baleful and pervasive consequences of human sin, given prominence in the Reformers' rehearsal of Augustinian pessimism, gave a theological justification for the failure of the medieval interpretation of nature. The book of nature could not be read like scripture, it did not yield knowledge leading to salvation or give indications of many other truths revealed in the scriptures. The book of nature could only be interpreted through arduous empirical investigation, and even then, it would yield only an indirect knowledge of the existence of the Deity, and a limited number of his attributes.

---

[211] Pluche, *Spectacle*, III, 304. [212] Baxter, *Christian Directory*, pt I, p. 253.
[213] South, *Sermons*, in *English Prose*, ed. Peacock, II, 208. [214] *Ibid.*
[215] *Ibid.* Cf. Walker, *History of the Creation*, p. 151.
[216] Thomas Tymme, *A Dialogue Philosophicall* (London, 1612), To the Reader.
[217] Thomas Traherne, *Christian Ethicks: or Divine Morality* (London, 1675), p. 101.

To a degree, this apparently harsh line of reasoning was yet another consequence of the fact that natural objects and processes had lost their representational powers. No longer could they symbolise the complex theological dogmas which they had in the past. God and his activities could not be directly read in nature: instead, a limited number of moral and theological truths could be inferred from the natural order. From the intricate mechanisms of nature, from the remarkable causal interactions of created things, from the providential adaptations of animals and plants to their various modes of life, we might deduce the Creator's wisdom and power: but we do not find vestiges of the divine image in the world, and we are not permitted to imagine similitudes of the divine nature in natural objects. As Bacon put it, the works of God 'show the omnipotency and wisdom of the maker, but not his image'.[218] Nature is no longer an autobiographical text, in which direct references to the author may be found. It is more like a mathematical treatise, which has no meaning as such, and does not speak directly of its author, but from which we can make inferences about certain of the qualities of the person who produced it. At best, the study of the book of nature was 'Preparative to Divinity', it was 'our first Revelation', 'a preparative to, or Proof, of the Second'.[219]

In the seventeenth century, then, natural objects were regarded as having been designed for their utility rather than their meaning: creatures were not symbols to be read, but objects to be used or investigated for potential applications. Those who studied the things of nature in order to determine their uses thus assisted God with the fulfilment of his designs. The Deity, for his part, was the source of all truths, sacred and scientific, and students of nature were his priests expounding for the benefit of their fellow human beings the significance of the wordless text of creation. In this new scheme of things physico-theology presents itself as the key to the interpretation of the book of nature. This theologically-motivated mode of enquiry reinvests the natural world with a purpose, a purpose which had been lost with the disintegration of the symbolic world view of the Middle Ages. Physico-theology thus attempts to mediate between the two books, providing a new, rational discourse to take the place of the old, symbolic order. As Robert Markley observes, 'physico-theology becomes the quest for a single system of representation that articulates its equally strong commitments to experimental philosophy and theology'. It seeks 'to perfect representational schemes

---

[218] Bacon, *Advancement of Learning* II.vi.I (p. 86); Cf. Boyle, *Some Motives to the Love of God, Works* I, 264.
[219] Ray, *Wisdom of God*, p. 127; Pluche, III, 326; Edwards, *A Demonstration*, pt I, 262.

capable of describing the phenomena of nature with new precision and of demonstrating the physical and metaphysical order of a divinely authored universe'.[220] This new work of exposition was to be no cloistered commentary which yielded no practical applications, however. As Bacon pointed out, 'the rule of religion, that a man should know his faith by his works, holds good in natural philosophy too'. Science and religion alike, according to Bacon, 'must be known by works'.[221] The fruits of the new hermeneutical approach were nothing other than the knowledge of nature, and the power which that knowledge could bring, for 'knowledge and human power are synonymous'.[222] Yet it was not only the spectacular failure of the interpretive strategies of the past which motivated the quest for a new way of ordering nature. The text of Genesis, read literally, afforded glimpses of how the human race had once been in the possession of a complete knowledge of the natural world, had exercised a dominion over all of its creatures, and had thought and spoken in a natural language perfectly able to capture the essences of all things. If the search for benevolent adaptations in nature provided the motivating force behind the new scientific enterprise, natural philosophers, as we shall see in the final chapter, were also drawn forward by the vision of a natural world which once again would meekly serve its human masters.

[220] Markley, *Fallen Languages*, p. 7.
[221] Bacon, *Redargio philosophiarum* (1608) qu. in B. Farington, *The Philosophy of Francis Bacon*, (Liverpool, 1964), pp. 92f.   [222] Bacon, *Novum Organum*, 1.3.

CHAPTER 6

Eden restored

Thou hast given him dominion over the works of thy hands;
Thou hast put all things under his feet,
all the sheep and oxen,
and also the beasts of the field,
the birds of the air, and the fish of the sea.

Psalm 8.6–8.

For man by the fall fell at the same time from this state of innocency
and from his dominion over creation. Both of these losses however
can even in this life be in some part repaired; the former by religion
and faith, the latter by arts and sciences.

Francis Bacon, *Novum Organum*

our businesse is to rectifie
Nature, to what she was
John Donne, 'To Sr Edward Herbert. At Julyers'

PARADISE WITHIN

The literal approach to texts which became increasingly dominant in
the sixteenth century had the consequence that objects in the natural
world could no longer be regarded as signs. As a result, those who
believed that the Deity had imposed a particular order on the cosmos
moved their attention away from the symbolic functions of objects and
focused instead on the ways in which the things of nature might play
some practical role in human welfare. As we saw in the previous
chapter, the scientific investigation of nature in the seventeenth century
was motivated to a large degree by the necessity to find uses for the
numerous objects which had hitherto derived their purpose and place in
the cosmos by acting as signs or symbols. The literalist mentality which
effected these transformations, it need hardly be said, also had important implications for the way in which the Bible was read. Certain
passages of scripture, when taken in their plain or historical sense, were

also to have a profound influence on the development of the scientific approach to the natural world. In particular, the literal reading of the first chapters of Genesis which accompanied the view that things in the world are not signs, provided this additional motivation by holding out a vision of Eden which was to do neither with moral imperatives nor theological verities, but represented an historical past which might be revisited through present human efforts.

Numerous writers have commented upon some supposed connexion between God's command to Adam and Eve in Genesis to 'fill the earth and subdue it, and have dominion over . . . every living thing' and the contemporary tendency to exploit the natural environment. Best known proponent of this view, Lynn White Jr., has argued that the typically Western propensity to exploit the earth and its living contents finds its ideological origins in 'the orthodox Christian arrogance toward nature'. This source of this attitude, in turn, is said to be the Christian doctrine of creation in general, and more particularly, the granting of dominion over nature to Adam.[1] More positively, perhaps, the thesis posits a link between the Judaeo-Christian tradition and the rise of science, suggesting that the quest for order in nature, and for mastery over it, was motivated by a characteristically Judeao-Christian vision of the nature and destiny of the human race. The fundamental inadequacy of this thesis, as it stands, is to do with timing. Why did the Genesis imperatives which grant dominion to the first man and his progeny only begin to take effect in the early-modern period? Why did science have its rise in the seventeenth century, and not before? Part of the answer to this question has already emerged. The Christian doctrine of creation had always held that the natural world had a purpose, a purpose related to human welfare. However, up until the modern period, that purpose had encompassed both spiritual and material aspects of human existence. When the world could no longer be interpreted for its transcendental meanings, it was actively exploited solely for its material utility. Equally

---

[1] Lyn White Jr., 'The Historical Roots of our Ecological Crisis', *Science*, 155/3767, March 1967, pp. 1203–7; For discussions of the thesis, see Ian Barbour (ed.), *Western Man and Environmental Ethics: Attitudes towards Nature and Technology* (Reading, Mass.: Addison-Wesley, 1973); Donald Gowan and Millard Shumaker, *Subduing the Earth: An Exchange of Views* (Kingston, Ont.: The United Church of Canada, 1980); Robin Attfield, *The Ethics of Environmental Concern* (Oxford: Blackwell, 1983); David and Eileen Spring (eds.), *Ecology and Religion in History* (New York: Harper and Row, 1974); Carl Mitcham and Jim Grote (eds.), *Theology and Technology: Essays in Christian Analysis and Exegesis* (New York: University Press of America, 1984); Elspeth Whitney, 'Lynn White, Ecotheology, and History', *Environmental Ethics* 15 (1993) 151–69; James Barr, 'The Ecological Controversy and the Old Testament', *Bulletin of the John Rylands Library* 55 (1972) 9–32; Lloyd H. Steffen, 'In Defence of Dominion', *Environmental Ethics* 14 (1992) 63–80.

importantly, however, the central canonical text of the Western tradition contains a narrative which, when interpreted in its historical sense, presents the image of a human individual who knows and controls nature, and who directly exercises a divine grant of dominion. The recognition that the paradise of knowledge enjoyed by our first parents was an historical reality, combined with the acceptance of the command 'have dominion' in its full literal sense, provided a vital impetus to the seventeenth-century quest to know and master the world.[2] Only when the story of creation was divested of its symbolic elements could God's commands to Adam be related to worldly activities. If the Garden of Eden were but a lofty allegory, as Philo, Origen, and later Hugh of St Victor, had suggested, there would be little point in attempting to re-establish a paradise on earth.[3] If God's command to Adam to tend the garden had primarily symbolic significance, as Augustine had believed, then the idea that man was to re-establish paradise through gardening and agriculture would simply not have presented itself so strongly to the seventeenth-century mind.[4] If dominion over the animals was thought to be an oblique reference to mastery of the passions, or the scholarly activity of collating an encyclopaedia, then Baconian notions of reproducing the effects of nature through knowledge of efficient causes would never have been allied with the necessary religious motivations.[5] If the command to 'be fruitful and multiply, and fill the earth'

---

[2] In Part v of *The Great Instauration*, Charles Webster has provided an exhaustive account of the Puritan mission to restore to the earth to its paradisal integrity. Here, Puritan scientific activity is related to 'the social ethic of Protestantism' (p. 335), and more significantly, to an eschatology which 'became an important determinant of scientific attitudes' (p. 505). Webster also notes that 'Puritans came to accept an extremely literal interpretation of the millennium' and that 'Biblicism was one of the most conspicuous elements in English puritanism' (p. 509). While I am in general agreement with this analysis it needs to be stressed that literalism is a precondition of the millennial vision of a paradise on earth which motivated scientific endeavours.

[3] 'And who is so silly as to believe that God, after the manner of a farmer, "planted a paradise eastward in Eden"', wrote Origen, 'these are figurative expressions which indicate certain mysteries through a semblance of history and not through actual events.' *On First Principles*, IV.iii.1; cf. Philo, *Legum allegoriae* I, 2 (p. 25). Origen's paradise was placed in the third heaven, and regarded as a symbol of the celestial paradise. Many medieval writers placed paradise above the moon's sphere, thus accounting for its incorruptibility. For typical medieval allegorical interpretations of paradise, see Bartholomew Anglicus, *De proprietatibus rerum* 15, 111, cf. 158; Alexander Neckham, *De naturis rerum*, 2. 49; Guibert of Nogent, *Moralium Geneseos* 1.1.21–4 (*PL* 156, 50–51); Bruno, *Expositio in Genesim* I (*PL* 164, 156). Also see discussion in Williams, *The Common Expositor*, p. 96; Cizewski, 'Beauty and the Beasts'; D. C. Greetham, 'Bartholomaeus Anglicus on Nature', *JHI* 41 (1980), 663–78 (674f.). J. Salkeld, writing in the seventeenth century, lists such allegorical readings of the nature of paradise, and rejects them. *Treatise of Paradise*, p. 4.

[4] Williams, *The Common Expositor*, p. 110.

[5] For examples of tropological readings of 'dominion' see Augustine, *Confessions* XIII.xxi, Chrysostom, *Homilies on Genesis* VIII.14, Philo, *De plantatione* XI.43, Gregory of Nyssa, *De hominis opificio* 4.1. Also see notes 10–13 below.

was taken to refer to the cultivation of virtues or 'fruits of the spirit', then there would be no onus on the human race to colonise under-utilised lands.[6] If the Fall were not an historical, but a cosmic event in which souls fell into bodies, then its consequences would be difficult to reverse in the present life.[7] Now that Genesis was regarded primarily as historical narrative, however, the divine imperatives it contained could be read unequivocally. The contemporary relevance of those early narratives of the book of Genesis – the Fall, the expulsion from the Garden, the Flood, the confusion of tongues – now lay in regarding them as past events which, through human endeavour, could in some measure be reversed. Human redemption could be achieved through the mastery of nature, and this was not a mastery which consisted, as twelfth-century visionaries had thought, in the passive reordering of the natural world in the human mind. The natural world was to be known and literally mastered, and in the process would be restored in some measure to its paradisal perfection. Literalism thus contributes to the emergence of natural science in two distinct ways: first, by evacuating nature of its symbolic significance; second, by restricting the possible meanings of the biblical narratives of creation and Fall, in that they cannot be read other than as enjoining upon the human race the necessity of re-establishing its dominion over nature. The impact of these literal readings of the creation story on the scientific endeavours of the seventeenth century is the subject of this final chapter.

The complicating factor in this equation is the fact that the demise of allegorical and tropological understandings of Eden was accompanied, somewhat paradoxically, by the last great resurgence of that Augustinian-Platonic conception of reality upon which symbolic readings of the two books were based. Paradise, Augustine had believed, was an idea lodged in the memory of every member of the human race. Through reminiscence it could be brought into consciousness. Every human being sought in the present world the bliss which Adam and Eve had once enjoyed in paradise. In a typically platonic move, Augustine explained that because we cannot desire that of which we have no direct

---

[6] Even when taken in its literal sense, in pre-modern interpretations the force of this apparent injunction was deflected. Jeremy Cohen in his comprehensive history of the interpretation of this passage in patristic and medieval periods, has ably demonstated that this apparent command was considered more an indicative than an imperative: 'The primary meaning of Gen. 1.28 during the period we have studied [i.e. pre-modern period, is] an assurance of divine commitment and election, and a corresponding challenge to overcome the ostensive contradiction between the terrestrial and the heavenly inherent in every human being.' *'Be Fertile and Increase, Fill the Earth and Master It': The Ancient and Medieval Career of a Biblical Text* (Ithaca: Cornell University Press, 1989), p. 313. [7] More, *Conjectura Cabbalistica*, p. 28, in *A Collection*.

knowledge, we must all have been present with Adam in paradise, and in our quest for earthly happiness are unwittingly seeking a return to the *beata vita* of our first parents.[8] For Augustine, the paradise to be restored is a paradise within. Augustine's contemporary, Gregory of Nyssa, further reinforced the notion of a psychological paradise as the goal of human life. It had been the task of Christ, he suggested, to transform the wilderness of the human soul into a perfect garden, 'by planting virtues and making it flourish with the pure and divine stream of solicitous instruction by means of the word'.[9] In a similar fashion, the dominion over the creatures which God had granted Adam was read by patristic exegetes as dominion over the passions of the soul. Origen, drawing upon the idea of the human microcosm, wrote that the various animals were nothing other than 'the dispositions of the soul', the 'thought of the heart', 'bodily desires' and 'motions of the flesh'. These had once served reason, but with the Fall had rebelled against their legitimate master. Now the natural order was subverted and 'the impulses of the flesh' have come to 'hold dominion over sinners'. [10] John Chrysostom agreed that certain impulses and ideas in the soul 'resemble brute beasts, others more ferocious and savage'. In the Christian life 'there is need to control them and submit them to the rule of reason'.[11] Ambrose wrote that through the exercise of self dominion, and with the assistance of the Holy Spirit, 'the madness of lions, the spots of leopards, the craftiness of foxes, the rapacity of wolves have passed from our affections'. Augustine, Gregory of Nyssa, and Jerome agreed that human dominion was primarily to be exercised over the beasts within.[12] Thus, for patristic exegetes and their medieval imitators, notions of a physical domination of the material world played a secondary role to moral and psychological interpretations of dominion. 'The superiority of our dominion', wrote Chrysostom, means that 'we live in self-command.'[13]

A number of seventeenth-century platonists found themselves attracted to the idea of the interior paradise, and to the internalised exercise of dominion over unruly, bestial inclinations. Oliver Cromwell's chaplain, Peter Sterry, explained that paradise had been 'in the midst of man',

[8] Augustine, *Confessions*, x.xx.
[9] Gregory of Nyssa, *In canticum canticorum* (*PG* 44, 1092D); George Williams, *Wilderness and Paradise in Christian Thought* (New York: Harper, 1962), p. 40.
[10] Origen, *Homilies on Genesis and Exodus*, 1.16f. (*FC* 71, p. 69f.).
[11] Chrysostom, *Homilies on Genesis* ix.7 (*FC* 74, 121f.), Cf. viii.14, xii.10; *Homilies on the Gospel of St John* ii (*NPNF* i, xiv, p. 9).
[12] Ambrose, *The Holy Spirit*, 10, 109 (*FC* 44, 134); Augustine, *Confessions* xiii.xxi (p. 291). Cf. Jerome, *Commentariorum in Hiezechielem*, 1.1.6/8 (*CCSL* 74, 11f.).
[13] Chrysostom, *Homilies on Philippians*, vii (*NPNF* i, xiii, p. 218).

and that it was not '*lost* or destroyed' but is 'hid beneath the ruins of the fall'. The knowledge of paradise is thus 'a *remembrance*, the Life of all good, an awakening by reason of the primitive image of pure Nature, raising it self by degrees, and sparkling through the *Rubbish*, the confusion of the present state'.[14] Sebastian Franck wrote that 'God alone and his omnipotent Word is our Paradise, the *Tree of* Life, and the Temple wherein we inhabit, walk, serve, pray &c.'[15] Poets Henry Vaughan and Thomas Traherne characterised paradise as the lost child-like innocence of the human race. Vaughan wrote in 'The Retreate' of a lost childhood: 'O how I long to travell back / And tread again that ancient track! / That I might once more reach that plaine, / Where first I left my glorious traine.'[16] The restoration of the paradisal state was not accomplished through external works, but through interior disciplines. 'Whosoever would enjoy the Happiness of Paradice', wrote Traherne, 'must put on the Charity of Paradice.' Pico, he believed, was correct to point out that 'Man by retiring from all Externals and withdrawing into Him self, in the centre of his own Unity, becometh most like unto God.'[17] The paradisal peace of the platonic soul, moreover, was forever in danger from anarchic animal passions. Human affections were 'beastly and sensual', 'wild beasts which are never tamed', 'serpents and basilisks', 'monsters and rebellious slaves'.[18] Bishop Lancelot Andrewes thus followed the patristic reading of 'dominion' stressing its moral sense: 'The bruitish affection of anger of the Lion must be covered with patience; the bruitish affection of lust of the Goat must be clothed with chastity.'[19] Only the religious life, agreed John Donne, can make that ravening Wolfe a Man, that licentious Goate a man, that insinuating Serpent a man.[20]

---

[14] Peter Sterry, *The Appearence of God to Man in the Gospel* (London, 1710), p. 463; *Discourse of the Freeedom of the Will* (London, 1675), p. 99. On the Augustinian conception of an interior paradise and its influence in seventeenth-century England, see Louis Martz, *Paradise Within*, passim.

[15] Sebastian Franck, *The Forbidden Fruit* (London?, 1640), p. 5.   [16] Vaughan, 'The Retreate'.

[17] Traherne, 'Centuries', 4.22; 4.81. Digger Gerrard Winstanley, while neither poet nor Platonist, also wrote of the individual soul as paradise: 'Adam himselfe, or that living flesh, mankinde, is a Garden which God hath made for his own delight, to dwell and walk in, wherein he has planted variety of Hearbs, and pleasant Plants, as love, joy, peace, humility, knowledge, obedience, delight, and purity of life.' Winstanley, *The Mysterie of God*, p. 2. The serpent, according to Winstanley, was nothing other than human pride, which was to turn the garden of the human soul into a wilderness. See Williams, *Wilderness and Paradise*, p. 80.

[18] Reynolds, *Treatise of the Passions*, p. 62; Senault, *Man becom Guilty*, (London, 1650), p. 203, *The Use of the Passions*, (London, 1674), Epistle Dedicatory; Thomas Wright, *The Passions of the Minde*, (London, 1601), p. 3.   [19] Andrewes, Αποσπασματια Sacra, pp. 332f.

[20] Donne, *Sermons*, IX, 58; Donne also considered the Ark to be an emblem of the human animal: 'Man is a lumpe, where all beasts kneaded be,/ Wisdome makes him an Arke where all agree; / our business is to rectify Nature to what she was'. 'To Sr. Edward Herbert. at Julyers', *Complete*

This interior paradise of poet and platonist, however, represents the last gasp of a dying world view.[21] As we have already seen, even as such verses were being penned, worldly contemporaries of the English platonists were speculating about the geographical location of the original paradise, and putting forward suggestions about its animals and plants, its soil and its climate. But more important still than these historical reconstructions of a past paradise were the efforts of those who sought to restore to the present human race the material blessings of that original paradise and who set about the business of restoring Eden in a conspicuously physical way.

THE FALL

In order to understand what was entailed in the recovery of those privileges which the human race had originally enjoyed, we need first to consider what seventeenth-century thinkers thought had been lost in those three successive setbacks, the Fall, the Flood, and the confusion of tongues; for as much, if not more, effort was directed towards the analysis of human ills in the light of the first chapters of Genesis, as was expended in determining the means by which those ills might be overcome. For those involved in the reformation of the sciences, the most tragic consequence of the Fall was that the human race lost a natural knowledge of the world and its operations. In *The History of the Creation*, George Walker declared that 'in the state of innocency in the first creation, *man had perfect naturall knowledge of* all naturall things, arising and springing immediately from his naturall soule'.[22] Robert South was equally generous in his estimation of Adam's abilities, scarcely stopping short of granting him omniscience:

He came into the world a philosopher, which sufficiently appeared by his writing the nature of things upon their names: he could view essences in themselves, and read forms with the comment of their respective properties; he could see consequents yet dormant in their principles, and effects yet unborn in their causes; his understanding could almost pierce into future contingents, his

---

English Poems, ed. C. A. Patrides (London: Dent, 1994), 200. This was a common patristic understanding of the Ark's significance. See Augustine, *Confessions* xiii.xxi; Chrysostom, *Homilies on Genesis* viii.14; Jerome, *Commentariorum in Hiezechielem* 1.1.6/8; cf. Philo, *De plantatione* xi.43.

[21] William Ayloffe, writing in 1700, thus describes as the 'poet's fancy' the notion that we encounter 'in the Person of every Man, the Malice of a Serpent, the Fury of the Tyger, the Choler of the Lyon, and the Lubricity of the Goat, and Demonstrate from hence, that Man alone had as many Passions as all the Beasts together.' *Government of the Passions*, p. 31.

[22] Walker, *History of the Creation*, p. 193.

conjectures improving even to prophecy, or the certainties of prediction; till his fall it was ignorant of nothing but of sin.[23]

Not all were as generous as South in granting such extensive knowledge to Adam, but it was generally agreed that his store of information was far superior to that of the moderns.[24]

There were a number of views of how Adam came by his knowledge. Some attributed it to superior organs of reason and sensation. Had Adam not fallen, lamented Edward Reynolds, 'there should have been in all men a greater facilitie to apprehend the misteryes of Nature, and to acquire knowledge'. Dryden spoke of 'Those Gyant Wits, in happyer Ages born'.[25] In addition to this dimming of the intellectual powers, the senses too were dulled. Joseph Glanvill wrote that in Eden, 'Even the senses, the Soul's windows, were without any spot or opacity.' He concluded that the first man's sensory apparatus 'must needs infinitely more transcend ours'.[26] Some commentators, ignoring active intellect and sensation, held that the knowledge of the first man was born with him. Innate ideas provided the basis of Adam's store of knowledge. Alexander Ross thus supposed that Adam had 'the knowledge of all things as soon as he was created'.[27] Still others believed that God had directly revealed to Adam the secrets of the universe.[28] In all such speculations, one thing at least was certain, Adam did not rely upon the modern methods of gaining knowledge. As South put it: 'Study was not then a duty, night watchings were needless', for it is 'the doom of fallen man, to labour in the fire, to seek truth *in profundo*, to exhaust his time and impair his health, and perhaps to spin out his days, and himself into one pitiful, controverted conclusion'.[29]

Whether, upon the occasion of the Fall, Adam lost his remarkable

---

[23] South, *Sermons*, in *English Prose*, ed. Peacock, II, 208. Cf. Bacon, *Advancement of Learning*, I, i.3 (p. 6); Salmon, *Clavis Alchymiae*, p. 180; Culpeper, *Complete Herbal*, p. vii; Witty, *An Essay*, pp. 178–80; Andrewes, Αποσπασματια Sacra, pp. 208–12; Salkeld, *Treatise of Paradise*, pp. 185–91.

[24] See Williams, *The Common Expositor*, pp. 80–4.

[25] Reynolds, *Treatise of the Passions*, pp. 6, 438; Dryden, *Religio Laici*, line 80. The general question of whether the ancients were more intelligent, and hence more knowledgeable, than the moderns was one of the points of contention between Godfrey Goodman and Hakewill. The former had argued in his *Fall of Man*, that contemporary knowledge was less than that of the first inhabitants of the earth on account of the earth's gradual decay. This view was rejected by Hakewill, who responded that 'If we come short of our *Ancestours* in *knowledge*, let us not cast it upon the deficiencie of our wits in regard of the *Worlds decay*, but upon our owne *sloth*.' *An Apologie*, (3rd edn.) Sig. A3v.

[26] Joseph Glanvill, *The Vanity of Dogmatising*, p. 4, in *Scepsis Scientifica* . Cf. Philo 'The first created men ... must also of necessity received more accurate sense, and, what is more excellent still, a power of examining into and hearing things in a philosophical manner.' *Quaestiones in Genesin*. 1. 32 (p. 797). [27] Ross, *An Exposition*, pp. 49f. [28] See, e.g., Bostocke, *Auncient Phisicke*, Sig. F4r.

[29] South, *Sermons*, in *English Prose*, ed. Peacock, II, 208.

abilities, whether he forgot what he once knew, how much he was able to pass on to his progeny, these remained open questions. However no-one doubted that his descendants, lacking perfect organs of reason and sensation, came to inherit only a fraction of their parent's once encyclopaedic knowledge. With the confusion of tongues (Genesis 11), their misfortunes multiplied. After Babel came the loss of the original language – if, indeed, it had remained in use that long – and along with it, the common medium for the transmission of what Adam had once known. Josephus thought that at least some of the knowledge of Adam might have been preserved by the actions of Seth, who had prudently inscribed what knowledge he could on two great pillars, one of brick, one of stone. These monuments had survived the Deluge, and served as the source for Moses' knowledge of the creation.[30] The longevity of the Patriarchs had preserved much of Adam's knowledge, and indeed it had been argued that their extended tenure was a divine gift intended to ensure that Adam's knowledge of the creation passed to Moses through as few intermediaries as possible.[31] The Fall, then, could be interpreted as having brought about a reliance upon authority and tradition – the very sources of knowledge which were under attack by reformers in matters of religion and natural philosophy.

The second curse which resulted from the Fall was old age and death, for the threat which had reinforced the injunction not to eat of the fruit of the forbidden tree – 'neither shall you touch it lest you die' (Genesis 3.3) – was usually taken to mean that had Adam not sinned, he might have enjoyed immortality. Admittedly, the severity of the sentence of death was mitigated somewhat by the fact that Adam lived for a further nine hundred and thirty years after his expulsion from the garden (Genesis 5.5), but this longevity was as nothing compared to the boon of immortality. For those with a fondness for Platonism, human mortality was related to embodiment, it being thought that only with the Fall did Adam become a truly material being, for all and only material entities were subject to corruption. 'Nor could he be clogg'd before he fell, with a *Dark Body* stuft with the Elements, and built upon Bones to bear it up', wrote Edward Taylor.[32] Henry More believed that after the Fall, '*Adam's* Soul descended into the prepared Matter of the earth', and he became

---

[30] Josephus, *Antiquities*, 1.70–1 (*Works*, p. 32); Cf. Du Bartas, *Divine Weeks and Works*, II.ii.4 (I, 467–88); Andrewes, Αποσπασματια Sacra, pp. 208, 212; Thomas Burnet, *De Originibus Rerum*, p. 104, in *Doctrina Antiqua de Rerum Originibus* tr. Mead and Foxton, (London, 1736), p. 104.
[31] Williams, *The Common Expositor*, p. 147. Cf. Hakewill, *An Apologie* (1635 edn), pp. 172f.
[32] Taylor, *Theosophick Philosophy*, p. 22.

'a down-right *Terrestrial Animal*'. This was the true meaning of the
passage which records that after his expulsion from the garden, Adam
was 'clothed in the skin of beasts' (Genesis 3.21).[33] As a result of the sin,
thought Jacob Boehme, the human body, 'was become earthly, and
must turne to Earth againe'.[34] Boehme's English disciple, Samuel Pordage, wrote that Adam's prelapsarian body was immortal and imperish-
able, and could move with equal ease through the air and sea: 'His body
which before could flye / Clog'd now with a load of flesh, doth lye /
Fin'd to this Orb.' Neither did Adam's original body gain sustenance in
the customary manner. Rather he ate 'magically, yet with mouth, lips,
and tongue'. Nothing passed into the body, or out of it; so 'nothing
could turn into excrement'.[35] It was also frequently suggested that had
Adam not fallen, he would never have suffered decreptitude and death,
but would have been translated to heaven in the manner of Enoch and
Elijah.[36] George Herbert wrote that before he knew sin, Adam might
have moved from paradise to heaven 'as from one room t'another'.[37]
Sickness and pain were accompaniments of mortality. Eve was forced to
suffer the pangs of childbirth (Genesis 3.16), but there was much more.
After the Fall the human body suffered 'the necessity of Pain, Sickness,
Want, continual Danger, transitory Mutations, Mortality and Putrifac-
tion'.[38] Adam 'lost his skill in Herbs when he needed it most', wrote the
anonymous 'R.I.', 'hence came pale grief, diseases, early death'.[39] Other
creatures, too, came to share in man's mortality: 'And for mans transgressions all things were made mortall, that is to saie, were by God
appointed unto miserie and destruction.'[40] Even plants had once enjoyed the gift of immortality, according to Milton, who wrote that in

---

[33] More, *Conjectura Cabbalistica*, p. 28, in *A Collection*. A more common reading was that this implied
permission to kill or at least to sacrifice animals. See, e.g., Andrewes, Αποσπασματια Sacra, p.
332–4; Simon, *A Commentary*, pp. 79–80. On 'the skins of beasts' in Patristic interpretation, see
Panayiotis Nellas, *Deification in Christ: Orthodox Perspectives on the Nature of the Human Person*
(Crestwood, NY.: Vladimir's Seminary Press, 1987), pp. 43–91.

[34] Boehme, *The Second Booke*, p. 216.

[35] Pordage, *Mundorum Explicatio*, pp. 59, 61, 62. These readings of More, Boehme, Taylor, and
Pordage all go well beyond the literal sense. The notion of a fall into a body relies upon an
allegorical interpretation of the consequences of Adam's sin, and stems ultimately from Origen's
platonic gloss on this event. For obvious reasons, it was seldom thought that such mishaps would
be reversed in the present life.

[36] Andrewes, Αποσπασματια Sacra, p. 214; Cf. Luther, *Table Talk* 106 (p. 53).

[37] George Herbert, 'The Holy Communion', lines 35f.

[38] Taylor, *Theosophick Philosophy*, p. 28; Bostocke, *Auncient Phisicke*, Authors obtestation, Sig Ci.v;
Milton, *Paradise Lost*, XI.23–6; Dunton, *Athenian Oracle* I, 416, 438.

[39] Stephens and Brown, *Catalogus Horti Botanici Oxoniensis*, Dedicatory poem.

[40] Bostocke, *Auncient Phisicke*, Authors obtestation. Cf. Willis, *The Search for Causes*, p.28.

paradise, Adam and Eve had enjoyed 'immortal Fruits'. Boehme thought similarly that fallen plants now suffered from 'transitory fading' so that they 'must now continually be planted againe'.[41]

Death was not the only certainty brought by the Fall. It was held in some quarters that Adam and Eve became sexual beings for the first time after they were expelled from the garden.[42] Eve, wrote John Richardson, 'fell a virgin'. This need not necessarily imply any fault with conjugal bliss as such. Richardson adopts the very common view that Adam and Eve fell on the same day that they were created, and implies that they simply may not have had time to move beyond the alimentary delights on offer in the garden.[43] More extreme was the view of Edward Taylor, who thought that 'The Propagation of *Adam's* Race should have been by *Adam* alone.' Taylor was particularly unhappy about the modifications to Adam's body necessitated by the new method of procreation. 'The hanging on him the Bestial Genitals is That whereof Nature it self (as depraved as it now is) is Ashamed of and Blusheth at: The Soul hideth it self all it can from This Monstrous filthy Brutish Deformity.' Thus fallen man came to possess 'a New Strange Heteful Image', and the law of circumcision 'shews God's displeasure at That New-gotten way, like the Bestial Propagation'.[44]

Taylor's grim assessment of human sexuality was not, of course, entirely original. Several of the Fathers had taught that Adam originally enjoyed a sexless state, and that his Fall was occasioned by his division into two beings – male and female.[45] The Fall was nothing other than the separation of Eve from Adam. Still others believed that the crime for which Adam and Eve were expelled from the garden was knowledge of the sexual kind.[46] Only after the expulsion from the garden is it recorded that 'Adam knew his wife, and she conceived and bore a son' (Genesis 4.1).[47] Julius Cassianus, a fifth-century ascetic, believed that Satan learned of the sexual act from his keen observations of animals, and from thence succeeded in persuading Adam and Eve to emulate the amorous activities of the beasts.[48] According to the Rabbinical writings, Eve's

[41] Milton, *Paradise Lost*, xi.285; Boehme, *The Second Booke*, p. 217.
[42] While this view has patristic precedents, its popularity in seventeenth-century England is partly owing to the influence of Cornelius Agrippa's *De originale peccato*. See *Opera Omnia* ii, 554–8.
[43] Richardson, *Choice Observations*, Sig. B3r.   [44] Taylor, *Theosophick Philosophy*, p. 23.
[45] Boas, pp. 43, 70. Cf. Philo, *De opificio mundi* 76 (p. 11); Plato, *Symposium* 189c–192a.
[46] Irenaeus, *Adversus Haereses* iii.xxviii.8; Clement of Alexandria, *Stromata*, iii.17.
[47] See, e.g., Simon Patrick, *A Commentary*, p. 85.
[48] Clement, *Stromata* iii.17. Also see Pagels, *Adam, Eve, and the Serpent*, ch. 1; Brown, *The Body and Society*, pp. 93–6, 399–403.

seduction by the serpent was a sexual one, and the offspring of this ill-fated union were Cain and his descendants.[49] Such traditions were current in the sixteenth and seventeenth centuries, and various aspects may be found in the writings of Paracelsus, Fludd, F.M. van Helmont, and Boehme.[50] Jacob Boehme had thought, for example, that God had intended human generation to take place 'without Beastiall impregnation, without a wife'.[51] Boehme had also thought that the fratricidal Cain was the offspring, not of Adam and Eve, but of Eve and the serpent.[52] Marvell wrote that in paradise 'man ther walk'd without a mate'. Taylor, as we might expect, also declared the sinless Adam to have been 'a Virgin of Purity, with both *Masculine and Feminine Tinctures*'.[53] The 'English Behmen', Samuel Pordage, expressed similar sentiments:

> (Such members as we have now he had none
> To propagate) . . .
> He should both Father be, and Mother then
> For *Male*, and *Female* God created Man:
> Both *Man*, and *Woman*, *Wife* and *Virgin* he
> Together was in State of purity.[54]

Certain 'virtuosi of France' discussed whether Adam was an hermaphrodite, and whether Aristophanes' myth in Plato's *Symposium* had been derived from Genesis.[55] In the garden, as another writer put it, man was 'then untouch'd with woman or her sinne'.[56] In an extended, and somewhat obscure metaphor, Richard Franck wrote that Adam 'steer'd both Sexes in one bottome' and that 'to Pilot the Helm of two distinct Vessels, and both at once in storm under Sail: Surpasses the skill and methods of Navigation'.[57] Despite such speculations, human sexuality was perhaps the one set-back consequent upon the Fall which few seventeenth-century writers showed any real interest in reversing. (Sir Thomas Browne was an exception, admitting in *Religio Medici*: 'I could be content that we might procreate like trees without conjunction, or that there were any way to perpetuate the world without this trivial and vulgar way of coition. It is the foolishest act a wise man commits in all his

---

[49] James Turner, *One Flesh: Paradisal Marriage and Sexual Relations in the Age of Milton* (Oxford: Clarendon, 1987), p. 54.

[50] See Pagel, *Paracelsus*, pp. 113–7, 215f.; Pierre Bayle, *Dictionnaire historique et critique*, s.v. 'Eve', note C; Fludd, *Tractatus theologico-philosophicus* (Oppenheim, 1617), pp. 85–97; F. M. van Helmont, *Quaedam Praemeditatae et Consideratae Cogitationes super Genesis* (Amsterdam, 1697), pp. 48–51.

[51] Boehme, *The Second Booke*, p. 219.   [52] Hill, *English Bible*, p. 239.

[53] Taylor, *Theosophick Philosophy*, p. 22.   [54] Pordage, *Mundorum*, p. 62.

[55] Havers (tr.), *General Collection of Discourses*, p. 578; Cf. Browne, *Religio Medici* I.21 (p. 24). Origen had also pondered the connexion between Genesis and the *Symposium*. *Contra Celsum* IV.39–40; *In Genesin*, I.15.   [56] Qu. in Prest, *Garden of Eden*, p. 82.   [57] Franck, *Philosophical Treatise*, p. 144.

life. . .' 'Spermiticall emission', he observed elsewhere, was 'an undeniable enemie unto longaeuity' and posed a serious threat to long life.
Browne lived to the age of seventy-seven.)[58]

The status of the marital relationship was thought by some to have
been altered in other ways. A minority of commentators believed that
prior to the Fall the relationship between Adam and Eve had been based
upon equality, reciprocity, mutual love and respect. The wording of
Eve's curse – 'your desire shall be for your husband, and he shall rule
over you' (Genesis 3.16) – implied that here was a new condition, one of
subordination, which had not obtained in the original bliss of paradise.
According to this reading, Eve was by nature Adam's equal, and her
subsequent subjection accidental. Even Augustine, whose reputation for
misogyny is not entirely misplaced, had argued on occasion that in
paradise all human persons were equal, and the only dominance to be
exercised there was that of man over beast.[59] In the seventeenth century,
Quaker Margaret Fell argued on the basis of the first chapter of Genesis
that God did not observe 'distinctions and differences as men do'. Daniel
Rodgers claimed that in the estate of marriage, 'couples should be
peers'.[60] This was by no means the standard position, however. The
more usual reading of the Fall narrative was that Eve was by nature
weaker than Adam, and on this account that she, and not Adam, had
been seduced by the Serpent.[61] This apparent higher degree of vulner-
ability to the wiles of Satan explains why women were vastly over-
represented in the ranks of witches in the sixteenth and seventeenth
centuries.[62] St Paul had reinforced this stance by commanding wives to
'be subject to your husbands' (Colossians 3.18; Ephesians 5.22). This
conception of the natural passivity of women also received support from
Aristotle who had stated bluntly that 'the female is as it were a deformed
male'. In Aquinas, the more standard biblical view and the Aristotelian
position were fused into a powerful synthesis which was rarely questioned. Thus the combined weight of scripture, Aristotle, and Aquinas,

---

[58] Browne, *Religio Medici* II.9 (p. 76); *Pseudodoxia Epidemica*, III. ix (I, 190).

[59] Augustine, *City of God*, XII. 22, 23, 28, XIV passsim. But cf. *De Genesi ad Litteram*, XII.16 (*PL* 34, 467),
in which Augustine suggests subordination before the Fall. Gregory the Great also put forward
the view that where there is no sin, all are equal. *Moralia in Job* XXI.15 (*PL* 76, 203); *De Regula
Pastorali* (*PL* 77, 34).   [60] Both qu. in Turner, *One Flesh*, p. 108.

[61] Thus Philo: 'But the Woman was more accustomed to be deceived than the man. For his
councils as well as his body are of a masculine sort, and competent to disentangle the notions of
seduction.' The natural weakness of woman was also the result of her having been formed out of
Adam: 'This was so ordained in the first place, that the woman might not be of equal dignity with
the man.' *Quaestiones in Genesin*, 1.27, 33 (pp. 796, 798).

[62] Thomas, *Religion and the Decline of Magic*, p. 520.

had long established the status of the woman as the man's natural inferior.[63] Alexander Ross expressed the standard seventeenth-century view when he wrote that even in the garden, wives would have been subject to husbands, on account of their inherent inferiority.[64] John Salkeld went further, opining that there would have been more men than women in paradise, since men are more perfect, and things in Eden would have tended to perfection. Thus even at their best, women had been inferior to men, though Salkeld hastens to add that the production of females does not always proceed from a 'defect of nature'.[65]

Adam, Eve, and their progeny were not the only ones to suffer as a result of that first transgression: the curse of the Fall was not discriminate in its effects. Animals, plants, even the earth itself, shared in the human punishment. A literal reading of the temptation of Eve, for example, presents us with a serpent which is 'subtle' and which is capable of speech. Some authorities believed that all animals, like the serpent, were capable of speech and reason.[66] With the Fall, animals lost the ability to speak, or possibly, as Philo conjectured, we lost the ability to understand them.[67] From the specific curse placed on the serpent – 'upon your belly you shall go, and the dust you shall eat' – it could be inferred that the serpent originally had stood vertically on its tail, that it had legs, or possibly even wings. Bede and other medieval thinkers had given the serpent the face of a virgin, an image reproduced in Michelangelo's depiction of the temptation in the Sistine Chapel.[68] Many seventeenth-century writers agreed upon the description given by William Nicholls, according to whom the serpent was 'that flying fiery sort, which are bred in *Arabia* and *Aegypt*, that are of a shining yellowish Colour, like that of Brass; which by the motion of their wings and the vibration of their Tails reverberating the Suns Beams, do afford a most glorious appearence'.[69]

---

[63] See discussion in Aquinas, *ST* 1a. 92 (XIII, 35–47); Aristotle: *Generation of Animals* 737a. Also see Jacques Lacqueur, *Making Sex: Body and Gender from the Greeks to Freud* (Harvard University Press, 1990) passim; Ian Maclean, *The Renaissance Notion of Woman* (Cambridge University Press, 1980), ch. 2; Turner, *One Flesh*, ch. 3.   [64] Ross, *An Exposition*, p. 26.

[65] Salkeld, *Treatise of Paradise*, p. 182. Salkeld thus allows sex in paradise.

[66] Josephus, *Antiquities*, i.i.4 (*Works*, p. 30.); Cf. Irenaeus, *Fragments*, xiv; Jean Le Clerc, *Twelve Dissertations*, pp. 142–5; Nicholls, *Conference with a Theist*, pp. 195f.

[67] Whiston, *Authentic Records*, pp. 908f.; Conyers Middleton, *An Encounter of the Bishop of London's Discourses . . . with a Farther Inquiry into the Mosaic Account of the Fall* (London, 1750) p. 176. Cf. Philo, *Quaestiones in Genesin*. 1.32.

[68] Henry Kelly, 'Metamorphoses of the Eden Serpent during the Middle Ages and Renaissance', *Viator* 2 (1971) 301–27.

[69] Nicholls, *Conference with a Theist*, p. 201. Similar descriptions are given by John Witty, *An Essay*, II, 115–18; Simon, *Commentary upon Genesis*, pp. 59–62, 72. For further discussions of the original nature of the serpent and the curse which befell it, see Joseph Mede, *Diatribe Discourses on Divers Texts of Scripture* (London, 1662), pp. 424–56; John Lightfoot, *A Few and New Observations upon the Book of Genesis* (London, 1642), p. 5; Hughes, *Analytical Exposition*, p. 37; Andrewes, Αποσπασματια Sacra,

In either event, Eve might easily have mistaken the serpent for an angel, a misfortune which, while not excusing her entirely, makes her succumbing to the blandishments of the creature more understandable. The fall of the animals is also an implication of that view which placed man at the centre of the creation. Timothy Willis thought that because 'Man in the Scripture is called *Omnis creatura*, euery creature', it was followed that when Adam fell, all the creatures of necessity fell with him.[70] The mutations caused in the creatures, as we have seen, were also regarded as a punishment for, and reminder of, the fallen state of the human race.

A minority held that following upon the Fall, fierce animals and hurtful plants made their first appearance. However, this flew in the face of the narrative of the days of creation, according to which God made no new creatures after the sixth day.[71] What could be allowed was that existing animals and plants underwent transformations for the worse.[72] George Walker wrote that 'All poison and unwholesome quality, taste and smell in herbes, plants, trees, and grasse, which hurt man or beast; came into the world by sin, and are bitter fruits of man's Fall and transgression.'[73] 'All the creatures', agreed Godfrey Goodman, 'forsaking their first and naturall vse, did serue for mans punishment, and rebelled against him.'[74] Du Bartas found poetic justice in these events: 'Rebellious *Adam* from his God revolting / Findes his yerst-subjects 'gainst himselfe insulting'. 'If he moves against God', agreed Andrewes, 'all move against him.' [75] Such a rebellion marked the end of natural

pp. 252, 674–8; John Richardson, *Choice Observations*, ch. 3; Pettus, *History of Adam and Eve*, pp. 132f. Browne, *Pseudodoxia Epidemica*, v.iv (I, 375f.); White, *A Commentary on Genesis* (London, 1656), Bk III, pp. 161f.; Salkeld, *Treatise of Paradise*, pp. 207–21; Ross, *An Exposition*, p. 59; Dunton, *The Athenian Oracle*, 3rd edn I, 36. [70] Willis, *The Search for Causes*, p. 43.

[71] Augustine at one time seemed to hold this view, but later changed his mind. *De Genesi contra Manichaeos* ch. 13; *De Genesi ad litteram*, ch. 8. Cf. Hakewill, *An Apologie* (3rd edn) p. 153.

[72] Patristic and Medieval sources to this effect include Augustine, *De Genesi contra Manichaeos*, 1.18; Bede, *Commentarii in Genesim*, 196C, 200A; Hugh of St Victor, *Adnotationes elucidatoriae in Pentateuchum*, 37D, Neckham, *De naturis rerum II*, 156, Abelard, *Hexaemeron*, 750D, Honorius Augustodunensis, *Hexaemeron*, 258D, Rupert of Deutz, *Commentarii in Genesim*, 231B, Vincent of Beauvais, *Speculum historiale* 1.29. [73] Walker, *History of the Creation*, p. 234.

[74] Goodman, *Fall of Man*, p. 280; Cf. Walker, *History of the Creation*, pp. 193, 229; Charron, *Of Wisdom*, p. 256; Taylor, *Theosophick Philosophy*, p. 28; Milton, *Paradise Lost*, x. 710–14; Mede, *Diatribe Discourses*, p. 445; Boehme, *The Second Book*, p. 216; Salkeld, *Treatise of Paradise*, pp. 123f.; Pordage, *Mundorum Explicatio*, p. 58. Patristic and Medieval sources for this view include Augustine, *City of God* XI.22, *De Genesi ad litteram* 3.16 (*CSEL* 28.3.2); Bruno of Segni, *Expositio* I (*PL* 164, 156A); Hildegard, *Scivias* I.ii.27; Augustine had claimed that history had repeated itself in his own times, observing that when rebellion broke out in Italy, domestic animals were loosed and turned into wild creatures. *City of God*, II.23.

[75] Du Bartas, *Divine Weeks and Works*, I.i.3, ll. 127f.; Andrewes, Αποσπασματια *Sacra*, p. 318. Also Willis, *The Search for Causes*, p. 42. Abelard remarked similarly that animals only became contemptuous of us, when we became contemptuous of God. *Expositio* I (*PL* 178, 766D–767A); Cf. Rupert of Deutz, *De sancta Trinitate* 1.182.

human domination of the world, and could as easily be regarded as the result of human misfortune. Edward Reynolds stated that 'Gods Image in Man, is by this Fall much weakened, as wee may observe by the Rebellion and Insurrection of the Creatures against him.'[76] 'Sin had so strangely disfigured and disguised him', concluded one author, 'that none of his Subjects could remember to know him, or think, or believe him to be their natural Prince.'[77]

The creatures rebelled not only against their erstwhile master. They also turned on each other. In paradise, Adam 'gave forth his edicts unto all the creatures his natural Subjects. The Golden Rule was kept amongst them, when every one did justice by kind'.[78] With their master's abdication, conflicts and strife arose amongst the creatures themselves, and for the first time, animals feasted on the flesh of their fellows. 'The Lyon did eat grasse before the fall', wrote Bishop Andrewes, for 'the ravening and preying of savage beasts came by Man's transgression.'[79] Many commentators held that carnivorous animals had originally been excluded from the garden, or that no animal had been by nature carnivorous.[80] Jacob Boehme actually believed that all antipathies, between various animals, plants, stones and even stars, could be traced back to the Fall. As a result of the Fall:

such untowardnesse is found to be in all Creatures, biting, tearing, worrying, and hurting one another, and such Enmity, strife, and hatred in all Creatures: and that every thing is so at odds with it selfe, as wee see it to be not onely in the Living Creatures, but also in the Starres, Elements, Earth, Stones, Metalls, in Wood, Leaves, and Grasse, there is a Poyson and Malignity in all things: and it is found that is must be so, or else there would be no like nor mobility. . .[81]

At special times during the course of human history God had seen fit to suspend these enmities, and restore for a time the peaceful relationships of Eden. The most spectacular of such occasions took place when all the animals, many of them patently ill-suited travelling companions, undertook their forced sojourn together with Noah aboard the ark.[82] There were other instances too: Elijah was fed by wild crows, Daniel survived the lions' den, Jonah was regurgitated intact by the whale, St Paul was

---

[76] Reynolds, *A Treatise of the Passions*, pp. 435f.   [77] Franck, *Philosophical Treatise*, p. 161.

[78] *Ibid.*, p. 161

[79] Andrewes, Αποσπασματια *Sacra*, p. 109. Cf. Du Bartas, *Divine Weeks and Works*, 1.i.3, ll. 48–103, Milton, *Paradise Lost*, x. 710–12; Boehme, *The Second Booke*, p. 216; Thomas Hodges, *The Creatures Goodness as they come out of God's Hands* (London, 1653), p. 30.

[80] Prest, *Garden of Eden*, pp. 24–6.

[81] Boehme, *The Second Book*, Preface. Cf. Franck, *Philosophical Treatise*, p. 159.

[82] Lightfoot, *Observations on Genesis*, p. 9

blessed with immunity to the poison of the viper. To these biblical witnesses could be added numerous reports from the period of the Christian persecutions which attested to 'the feare of the wilde Beasts towards many of the Martyrs'.[83] But for the most part, the moratorium on these natural enmities was postponed until the end of time when Isaiah's millennial vision would be fulfilled: 'The wolf will live with the lamb, the leopard will lie down with the goat, the calf and the lion and the yearling together; and a little child will lead them' (11.6).

The earth itself also suffered along with its inhabitants. 'Cursed is the ground because of you', the Lord tells Adam, 'thorns and thistles it shall bring forth to you' (Genesis 3.17f.). On account of this passage, Franck believed that 'In Edan's fair Fief, no brambles grew, nor was sterility known in her borders.' Now, however, the 'plastick power' of the earth was weakened, so that it could no longer bring forth perfect animals, but only insects and lesser creatures.[84] Such creatures as worms and flies, wrote Godfrey Goodman, are 'mixt imperfect creatures', a 'strange Sodomiticall brood' which were the 'fruits of corruption'.[85] Spontaneous generation from corrupted earth thus accounted for the existence of maggots, worms, annoying insects, and other imperfect creatures which God had not included in the first creation.[86] The weakening of the earth's fertility also meant that Adam and Eve were forced to grow their own food. In the state of innocence the earth had naturally produced sufficient for the dietary needs of our first parents.[87] Now, through 'the unhappy Lapse of our First Parents', they and their posterity 'were destin'd to . . . Laborious Tenure and Drudgery'.[88] Even seasonal change was thought to be a consequence of human sin. After the Fall, the seasons became 'very irregular and confused'.[89] As Shakespeare expresses it: 'Here feel we not the penalty of Adam, The seasons' difference'.[90]

[83] Reynolds, *Treatise of the Passions*, p. 437.
[84] Franck, *Philosophical Treatise*, p. 127; Robinson, *Anatomy of the Earth*, p. 4; Daneau, *Wonderfull Woorkmanship*, fol. 83v.   [85] Goodman, *Fall of Man*, pp. 17f.
[86] Hughes, *Analytical Exposition*, p. 9.; Goodman, *Fall of Man*, p. 19. Rupert of Deutz had suggested that new and monstrous creatures could be formed by unnatural unions (proscribed in Leviticus 19.19). Thus the viper courts the sea lamprey, luring her to the beach, and 'exciting her to conjugal intimacy'. The spawn of this illicit affair developed harmful attributes as a consequence of their aberrant origins. *De sancta Trinitate* 1.182.
[87] Cockburn, *An Enquiry*, p. 171; Ross, *An Exposition*, p. 72; Thomas Malvenda, *De Paradiso* (Rome, 1605), p. 202.
[88] Steven Switzer, *The Nobleman, Gentleman, and Gardener's Recreation* (London, 1715), p. 72.
[89] Thomas Sherlock, *The Use and Intent of Prophecy . . . in Six Discourses*, (London, 1725), p. 106; Pordage, *Mundorum Explicatio*, p. 58. But cf. Beaumont, *Considerations*, p. 87.
[90] *As You Like It*, II.i.5f.

THE DELUGE AND CONFUSION OF TONGUES

A second wave of transformations came upon the earth and its inhabitants with the Deluge. At this time, it was generally believed, the original garden of Eden was destroyed.[91] Indeed, the topological features of the earth's surface underwent monumental changes, as described in the theories of Burnet, Whiston, Woodward, and Robinson. There had been those of the ancients who thought that the earth might once have been smooth like an egg – an idea which found a degree of acceptance amongst the Fathers, medieval school-men, and even some of the moderns.[92] Poet Andrew Marvell described how 'the arched Earth does here / Rise in a perfect hemisphere!'[93] Thomas Burnet, as we have already noted, articulately defended the view that the earth's original form had been a perfect sphere.[94] Proponents of this view generally agreed that the Flood had disfigured the earth's once-perfect surface with mountains and valleys. 'Since the Flood', said Luther, 'mountains exist where fields and fruitful plains before flourished.'[95] Malebranche expressed the view that 'the visible world would be more perfect if the seas and lands made more regular figures'.[96] Some also maintained that the earth's geological stability was upset by the Flood, and that earthquakes and volcanoes made their first appearances after this event.[97] Still others, like the Abbé Pluche, believed that as a result of the Flood the earth's axis was tilted, leading to intemperate weather conditions, the succession of the seasons, and an abridgement of human life-span.[98]

---

[91] Joseph Hall, Contemplation III, *Works*, rev. edn, 12 vols., (London, 1837–9) I. 15; Hakewill, *An Apologie*, (3rd edn), p. 2; Ross, *An Exposition*, p. 42. The destruction of Eden as a consequence of the Flood was not universally accepted, for as we have seen some seventeenth-century writers attempted to locate the original site of paradise. See discussion in Salkeld, *Treatise of Paradise*, pp. 36–42.

[92] Burnet, *Sacred Theory*, I.v (p. 63); Ovid, *Metamorphoses*, I, XV; Marjorie Nicolson, *Mountain Gloom and Mountain Glory* (New York: Norton, 1963), pp. 78–80.

[93] Marvell, 'Upon Appleton House', stanza lcvi. Cf. Goodman, *Fall of Man*, p. 282; Louis Ginzberg, *The Legends of the Jews*, 7 vols., (Philadelphia: Jewish Publication Society of America, 1911–13) III, 31. This view was by no means universal, however. Raleigh had insisted that mountains and valleys had been from the beginning. *The Historie of the Worlde* (1614) I.iii.v. Both Du Bartas and Milton have mountains emerging at the time of the creation. *Divine Weeks and Works*, I.iii.23, 40 (I, 173); *Paradise Lost*, VII. 282–7. An alternative tradition suggested that the earth's surface became irregular at the time of the Fall. See Nicolson, *Mountain Gloom and Mountain Glory*, p. 82.

[94] Burnet, *Sacred Theory*, passim.

[95] Martin Luther, *Critical and Devotional Commentaries on Genesis* ed. J. M. Lenker, (Minneapolis, 1904) I, 164.   [96] Qu. in Passmore, *Man's Responsibility for Nature*, p. 37.

[97] Ray, *Wisdom of God*, p. 147.

[98] Pluche, *Spectacle*, III, 340. Cf. Genesis 8.22. Others, however, argued that the tilting of the earth on its axis was part of God's original design, see, e.g., More, *Antidote*, p. 41; Bentley, *Works*, III, 186f.

A number of theorists suggested that the Deluge had been brought about by a reversal of those ordering processes which had been at work in the original creation. The divine command which had separated the sea from dry land (Genesis 1.9) was held in abeyance, and the earth was again without form and void. Godfrey Goodman believed that at the time of the Flood 'the whole world did seeme to goe backward, and to returne to the first nothing'.[99] According to John Woodward, the Deluge effected the dissolution of all solids. John Hutchinson asserted that the Flood had the effect of 'reducing the Earth to its first State, and a Parallel Act to the first Foundation of it'.[100] Other changes wrought by the Deluge had direct effects on the fortunes of the human race, and indeed were linked by some to the deteriorating moral condition of humanity. Woodward believed that God had 'altered that Constitution of the Earth, by means of the Deluge . . . thereby adapting it more nearly to the present Exigencies of things, to the lapse'd and frail state of humane Nature'.[101] Fellow theorists Burnet and Whiston agreed that the incommodiousness of the earth which resulted from the Flood made it a more suitable habitation for fallen beings.[102] These changes that they referred to, of course, were for the worse. It was commonly believed that the Flood washed away the earth's rich topsoil. As a result of this erosion the post-diluvian earth was less fertile and proved unable to provide suitable vegetable aliment for food. For this reason, the human diet had to be supplemented with meat, and thus, only after the Flood did mankind receive divine dispensation to kill and eat animals (Genesis 9.3).[103] John Edwards believed that 'after that great Primitive Malediction' human bodies 'stood in need of some more than ordinary recruits, *viz.* the active and generous Spirits which are produced by feeding on Animals'.[104] Indeed, that the original human inhabitants of the earth

---

[99] Goodman, *The Fall of Man*, p. 281.

[100] Hutchinson, *Moses's Principia*, pt I, p. 47. Such views were not without their problems, however. As one of Woodward's critics pointed out, such an extreme catastrophe would have killed all the fishes, requiring Noah to have installed a fish-pond on the Ark. See Arbuthnot, *Woodward's Account of the Deluge*, pp. 12f.

[101] Woodward, *Essay*, pp. 61, 83, 90, 92. Cf, Derham, *Physico-Theology*, p. 83.

[102] Burnet, *Sacred Theory*, p. 126; Whiston, *New Theory*, pp. 168–74; 'Of the Mosaick History of the Creation', p. 91, *Ibid*. In the following century Thomas Sherlock, bishop of London, was to reject this idea entirely, suggesting that the 'the *old* Curse was fully executed and accomplished in the Flood.' Thus, there was a 'Restoration of the Earth after the Flood'. *Use and Intent of Prophecy*, pp. 101, 111.

[103] Goodman, *Fall of Man*, p. 281; Alexander Ross, *The Second Book of Questions and Answers upon Genesis* (London, 1622), pp. 56f.; Simon, *A Commentary*, p. 115; Burnet, *De Rerum Originibus*, p. 261, in *Doctrina Antiqua*; Thomas Robinson, *A Vindication*, p. 53, in *An Essay*; Luther, *Lectures on Genesis*, *Luther's Works* , II, 132.   [104] Edwards, *A Demonstration*, pt I, p. 185.

had been vegetarian was widely held. In man's original estate, wrote Pope, 'no murder cloth'd him, and no murder fed'.[105] Grotius thought that if men had eaten meat in the interval between Fall and Flood, it was because they were wicked, not because it was lawful.[106] Alexander Ross extended the prohibition even to the beasts themselves, so that up until their disembarkation, carnivorous animals also were restricted to a vegetarian regimen. Lions and other wild beasts had fed upon herbs, partly because in the Ark there would have been no meat to feed them. Meat-eating became necessary for both man and beast, because 'the temperature of the creature is not so sound now as it was before the flood'.[107]

The stature of living things also decreased at this time. The average height of human beings, according to William Whiston, had diminished over time. (The construction of such ancient monuments as Stonehenge seemed only credible on the assumption that our ancestors had been bigger and stronger. Philo had written that 'the first men received bodies of vast size reaching to a gigantic height', while Genesis 6.4 reports that 'there were giants in the land in those days'.[108]) Fossil evidence, too, suggested the existence of enormous creatures in the past – huge serpents and dragons – species which had since either become extinct, or whose dimensions had shrunk to more modest proportions.[109] In the wake of the Flood, the life-span of human beings also began to contract. It was apparently not uncommon for the first generations to live until well into their 900s. Adam had lived to the ripe age of 930, Seth to 912, and Methuselah, 969. Such longevity, it was generally held, was not owing to a shorter antediluvian year as some had suggested, but to a variety of environmental factors.[110] Adam's knowledge of physick and the virtues of herbs had been transmitted to the patriarchs, thus extending their life-expectancy. The fact that the Flood had diminished the fertility of the earth's soil, either by increasing its salinity or by eroding away the topsoil, also meant that the earth's vegetation had lost much of its power to sustain human life. Generally, then, it was thought natural

[105] Pope, *Essay on Man*, III, 154.
[106] Browne, *Pseudodoxia Epidemica*, III.xxv (I, 264); Grotius, *Annotata ad Vetus Testamentum*, Ad Genesin, 4.3, 9.3; Cf. Hughes, *Analytical Exposition*, p. 11; Pettus, *History of Adam and Eve*, p. 85; Walker, *History of the Creation*, p. 230. Patristic authorities include Tertullian, *De Ieuniis*, 4 (*PL* 2, 958f.); Jerome, *Adversus Jovinianum* i.18 (*PL* 23, 237). Also Luther, *Table Talk* 131 (p. 64). Hakewill thought this a vulgar error. *An Apologie*, (3rd edn), p. 2. Alexander Ross was equally sceptical about antediluvian vegetarianism. *The Second Book*, p. 37.   [107] Ross, *An Exposition*, p. 27.
[108] Philo, *Quaestiones in Genesin*, I. 32 (p. 797). The Hebrew term here is *nephilim*, understood in the seventeenth century to mean 'giant', but now more commonly translated 'fallen ones'.
[109] Whiston, *Authentic Records*, pp. 837, 930, 901, 924. Cf. Buffon, *Natural History*, II, 234.
[110] Pererius, *Commentariorvm in Genesin*, pp. 351–2; Hakewill, *An Apologie*, (3rd edn), pp. 42f.

that those who had lived closer to the birth of the world would have
been stronger, smarter, bigger, and longer-lived.[111]

The final great calamity to befall the human race was the confusion of
languages which took place on the plains of Shinar, site of the ill-fated
tower of Babel. This was Francis Bacon's 'second curse'.[112] Now the
linguistic link to the patriarchs was severed, and the wisdom of the first
ages lost forever. 'In the age after the flood', observed Bacon, 'the first
great judgement of God upon the ambition of man was the confusion of
tongues; whereby the open trade and intercourse of learning and knowledge was chiefly imbarred.'[113] For those who believed that the original
language had survived intact until Babel, this was perhaps the greatest
loss of all.[114] Thereafter, all languages were conventional, and their signs
merely arbitrary representations of the things they signified. No longer
could the nature of things be read from their names: the loss of the
language of Adam entailed the loss of the knowledge of Adam. The
peculiar advantages of natural language – in which words bear a real
rather than an arbitrary link to the things they signify – were now gone
forever.[115] After Babel, the human race was dispersed over the surface of
the earth, and civilisation had to begin all over again.

One of the more serious consequences of the confusion of languages,
in addition to the disappearance of the arts and sciences, was loss of the
original knowledge of Deity. Many seventeenth-century thinkers believed that Babel had spelt the end of a simple and unaffected mono-
theism. From this time on, different nations had professed belief in
different gods, on account of the various names for God which followed
the fall of language.[116] The religious accord which depended on com-

[111] Pluche, *Spectacle*, III, 340; Cockburn, *An Enquiry*, pp. 171–3; Goodman, *Fall of Man*, p. 281; Walsh, *The Antediluvian World*, pp. 31–52. Williams, *The Common Expositor*, pp. 146–7. It was also believed that the divine plan required the patriarchs to live longer: in order to populate the earth, to found the arts and sciences, and to preserve Adam's knowledge of the creation intact to the time of Moses. See e.g. Hakewill, *An Apologie*, (3rd edn), p. 42; Beaumont, *Considerations*, p. 95; Luther, *Table Talk* 160 (p. 73); Josephus, *Antiquities*, l.104–6 (*Works*, p. 34).
[112] Bacon, *Advancement of Learning*, II, XVI.4 (p. 132); John Wilkins, *Mercury, or, the Secret and Swift Messenger*, in *Mathematical and Philosophical Works*, 2 vols. (London, 1802), II, 53.
[113] Bacon, *Advancement of Learning*, I, VI.2 (p. 39).
[114] This was a contentious issue. Some thought that the original language was lost at the Fall; others thought it may even have survived Babel. See, e.g. Thomas Browne, *Of Languages* in *The Workes of Sir Thomas Browne*, 4 vols., (London: Faber and Faber, 1928–37) III, 70; Torneillus, *Annales sacri et profani* (Coloniae Agrippinae, 1622), p. 127; John Webb, *An Historical Essay, Endeavoring a Probability that the Language of the Empire of China is the Primitive Language* (London, 1669), pp. 16f.; Peter Heylin, *Cosmographie in Foure Bookes* (London, 1652), p. 18.
[115] Augustine, *On Christian Doctrine*, II.iv.5 (p. 36).
[116] John Seldon, *De dis syris syntagmata II*, (London, 1617), Prolegomena, pp. 52f.; John Hutchinson, *A New Account of the Confusion of Tongues*, in *An Abstract from the Works of John Hutchinson* (Edinburgh, 1753). Also see Harrison, *'Religion' and the Religions*, pp. 146–57.

mon articles of faith had thus disintegrated. Human conflicts in general, and the religious disputes rending Christendom in the seventeenth century in particular, were seen to result from confusions about the true meanings of words and concepts. Certainly, the recent controversies over the translation of scripture and the meanings of crucial passages bore out this contention. Moravian educationalist Johann Amos Comenius, for example, believed that religious differences were mostly about 'terms and meanings', 'not in fundamentals' but 'only in the manner of expressing them'. In his view, it was as a consequence of 'the multitude, the variety, and the confusion of languages', that the commonwealth of men had been 'torn to pieces'.[117]

REVERSING THE CURSE

For the seventeenth century, the Fall was neither an allegorical tale, nor a moral fable. It was an historical event which had taken place in, or around, 4004 BC.[118] Its consequences pertained not only to the spiritual condition and prospects of human beings in a future world, but also to the material conditions of the present world. While Christian religion had provided the means by which the spiritual losses of the Fall might be overcome, complete redemption involved an engagement with the material world which had also suffered along with its human inhabitants as a consequence of Fall and Flood. The physical losses which had attended the Fall were redressed in a number of ways. Attempts were made to 're-create' the earth by emulating God's creative activities; the knowledge and dominion once possessed by Adam were actively sought, as was the primitive language with its quasi-magical powers; the earth was brought under cultivation with a view to restoring it to its original fertility and usefulness. Collectively these activities were thought to be appropriate responses to the literal command given to Adam, and repeated to Noah, to replenish the earth, and have dominion over it.

Inasmuch as God's originally good creation had been unmade by Fall

---

[117] Comenius, *The Way of Light of Comenius*, tr. E. T. Campagnac, (London: Hodder and Stoughton, 1938), pp. 8, 198, 188.

[118] The chronological enterprises of the seventeenth century also bear witness to the newly emerged historicity of the events of sacred history. The best known chronology of this period is that of Archbishop James Ussher, *The Annals of the Old and New Testament* (London, 1658). Ussher pinpointed the moment of creation as 'the night preceding the twenty-third day of October, in the year of the Julian Caledar, 710 [i.e. 4004 BC] (p. 1). According to Ussher, Adam fell the very day he was created, which would have been 28 October. Ussher's dating of the creation attained an almost canonical status when it appeared in the margin of the Authorised Version at Genesis 1.1.

and Deluge, it was thought that the imitation of God's creative activities would go some way towards restoring the earth to its prelapsarian perfection. At the same time, fortuitously, through the imitation of God, the divine image within would be restored. The idea that mankind should imitate the activity of God, and restore the divine likeness motivated a range of pursuits from husbandry to alchemy. Edward Reynolds, observing that 'Mans Soul beareth an *Image* and dark resemblance' to the Deity, explained that 'in many . . . proceedings of Gods works there is some Analogie and Resemblance in the Works of Men'. Thus the works of man ought to be directed, in imitation of God, towards these three ends: 'either to the perfection of Men, such as are those, which informe the Understanding, and governe the life: or to his Conservation, as those directed to the furthering of his welfare and repairing, the decayes, or sheltering the weaknesses of Nature: or lastly to his Ornament, such as those Elegancies of Art, and Curiosities of Inventions'.[119] God's image could thus be restored in man through an emulation of divine activities, which included the repair of the decays of nature. Walter Blith, sometime Captain in Cromwell's army, argued that in cultivating the earth, men were following the example of the Deity. 'God', he wrote, 'was the Originall, and first Husbandman, the patern of all Husbandry, and first project of that great design, to bring that old Masse and Chaos of confusion unto so vast an Improvement, as all the world admires and subsists from.' According to Stephen Switzer, 'God almighty was not only the first Author and Founder, but also the Regulator and Planter of Gardens and Gardening.' Timothy Nourse believed that agriculture was 'the *Restauration of Nature*, which may be looked upon as a *New Creation* of things'. To imitate God in this respect would be to create a new world in the ruins of the old, for, as Blith would have it, 'the Improvement, or Advancement of the fruits and profits of the Earth by ingenuity, is little less than an addition of a new world'.[120]

---

[119] Reynolds, *Treatise of the Passions*, pp. 430f.

[120] Walter Blith, *The English Improver Improved or the Survey of Husbandry Surveyed*, (London, 1653), pp. 3, 4. Cf. Switzer, *Gardener's Recreation*, II, 2. Timothy Nourse, *Campania Fælix, or, a Discourse of the Benefits and Improvements of Husbandry* (London, 1700), p. 2. Cf. Flavell, *Husbandry Spiritualized: or The Heavenly use of Earthly Things* (London, 1669), pp. 2–11; Leonard Meager, *The Mystery of Husbandry* (London, 1697), pp. 1f. The idea of God as a husbandman can be traced to the Fathers. Hence Ambrose: 'The land was, therefore, unformed, since it was as yet unploughed by the industrious attentions of the farmer, for the cultivator had still to appear. It was unformed because it was devoid of growing plants. . . Correctly, then, was the land called unformed which was devoid of ornament and which did not present to view the linked rows of budding vine shoots. God wished to show us that the world itself would have no attraction unless a husbandman had improved it with varied culture.' *Hexameron*, I.viii.23 (pp. 30f.)

Poets thus described the Deity as the 'Gard'ner of the Universe', and the 'pre-eternal gardener'.[121] Christ, too, had links with the art of cultivation, for upon his first resurrection appearance Mary Magdalene had mistaken him for a gardener (John 20.15). Her mistake was incorporated into Christian iconography to such an extent that there are literally countless depictions of Christ as gardener. As Charlotte Otten reports: 'He appears on altars, ivory book covers, in Biblical illustrations; in choirs, stalls, windows; in sculpture, paintings, illuminations, engravings, woodcuts, metalcuts. Sometimes he wears a gardner's cap or cowl, frequently a halo. He is always equipped with a gardener's tool – hoe, spade, shovel, dibble – and sometimes he has a watering can.'[122] This identification was reinforced by the fact that Christ is represented in the Gospel of John as the 'Word' which had been the divine agent in creation (John 1.1–4, 14). Elaborating this theme, Gregory of Nyssa had described Christ as 'the true husbandman' who 'at the beginning in Paradise cultivated human nature, which the heavenly father planted'.[123] According to tradition, then, Father and Son had both been cultivators of the earth in some sense, and had thereby lent a sanctity to the activities of gardening and agriculture.

Alchemists similarly believed that in their activities they were following the same kind of procedure employed by God in the creation of the world.[124] In forming the world, the chief task of the creator had been the process of chemical separation, or of giving form to prime matter.[125] The business of transmutation proceeded along similar lines. Indeed, the physical and chemical reactions produced in the alembics of the alchemists were not only rehearsals of events in the creation, but they mirrored, in microcosm, transformations of the macrocosm. Allan Debus writes: 'The formation of the earth's crust could seemingly be duplicated in chemical flasks, mountain streams were explained in terms of earthly distillations, thunder and lightning were no less than the explosion of an aerial sulphur and nitre, duplicating gunpowder on a grand scale, and rains were due to macrocosmic circulations that imitated the heating of water in the alchemical pelican.'[126] In Thomas Vaughan's view, the goal of chemistry was the creation of useful sub-

---

[121] Samuel Gilbert, *The Florists Vade-Mecum* , 2nd edn, (London, 1693), p. 251.
[122] Charlotte Otten, *Environ'd with Eternity: God, Poems, and Plants in Sixteenth and Seventeenth Century England* (Lawrence: Coronado Press, 1985), p. 14.
[123] Gregory of Nyssa, *In Canticum canticorum* (*PG* 44, 1092D).
[124] Debus, *English Paracelsians*, pp. 24–6.
[125] See, e.g., Duchesne, *Chymicall and Hermeticall Physicke*, Epistle Dedicatory (by Thomas Tymme) and Sig. Hi.   [126] Debus, *English Paracelsians*, p. 29.

stances out of elemental chaos, and thus chemists were to a degree repeating the work of God in the creation.[127] Bacon's method too, on his own analysis, consisted in 'following therein . . . the example of the divine creation'.[128]

The idea of imitating the creative activities of the Deity struck many as rather too ambitious a project for a fallen creature. Seeking to be like God was, after all, the occasion of the original sin (Genesis 3. 5), and the pride of the alchemists was precisely the kind of hubris which had led to Babel. A more common reading of the practical implications of Adam's Fall was that human creatures should concern themselves with the less exacting goal of imitating the paradisal activities of Adam, or some of them, at any rate. 'All Bliss / Consists in this', wrote Traherne, 'To do as *Adam* did.'[129] But what was it that the first man had actually done? How had he occupied his time? Bacon thought that originally man had been placed in the garden to perform a kind of work, his primary activity being 'no other than work of contemplation'. He continues: 'Man's employment must of consequence have been matter of delight in the experiment, and not matter of labour from the use', for 'the first acts which man performed in Paradise consisted of the two summary parts of knowledge, the view of the creatures, and the imposition of names.'[130]

In the seventeenth century, 'the view of the creatures' – accumulation of knowledge of the natural world – was believed to serve two basic purposes: knowledge of God, and mastery of the world. On the first point it could be claimed that knowing the creatures was a means of coming to know the Creator. William Cowper had thought that in Eden, Adam's encyclopaedic knowledge of the creatures had been made possible by his knowledge of God:

Our father Adam was made Lord of the Creatures, and by the knowledge wherewith God endued him, he knew the Lord, and the Creature also. At one

---

[127] Thomas Vaughan, *Lumen de Lumine* qu. in J. B Leishmann, *The Metaphysical Poets* (New York: Russell and Russell, 1963), pp. 181f.

[128] *Novum Organum*, i.cxxi (p. 79). Bonaventure argued similarly that the means by which we come to a knowledge of the world bears a relation to the means by which it was first created. Knowledge comes in the form of six-fold illumination – the lights of scripture, sense perception, mechanical knowledge, rational philosophy, natural philosophy, moral philosophy: 'Wherefore, very fittingly may these six illuminations be compared to the six days of creation or illumination in which the world was made, the knowledge of Sacred Scriptures corresponding to the creation of the first day, that is, to the creation of light and so on one after the other in order. Moreover just as all these had their origin in the one light, so, too, are all these branches of knowledge ordained for the knowledge of Sacred Scripture . . .'*De Reductione artium ad theologiam*, 5, in *Philosophy in the Middle Ages*, eds. Arthur Hyman and James Walsh (Indianapolis: Hackett, 1974), p. 425.

[129] Thomas Traherne, 'The Apostacy', lines 37–9.

[130] Bacon, *The Advancement of Learning* i.vi.6 (p. 38).

Court, he imposed names to them all, according to their nature; the knowledge which he had of God, led him to the knowledge of the creature, and it was not by the creature, that he learned knowledge of the Creator.

In our present fallen condition, however, the order of knowledge is reversed: 'but now man is sent to the Schoole of the creature, and put backe, as we say, to his ABC, to learne the glory, goodnesse, and providence of the Creator, by looking to the creature'.[131] John Flavell put the matter more succinctly: 'man, who at first was led by the knowledge of God to knowledge of the Creature, must now by the Creatures learn to know God'.[132] Henry Reynolds relied upon the arcane idea of the chain of being to make the same point. The proper knowledge of nature would enable the diligent enquirer 'by linkes of that golden chaine of *Homer*, that reaches from the foote of *Iupiters* throne to the Earthe, more knowingly and consequently more humbly climb vp to him, who ought to bee indeed the only end and period of all our knowledge and vnderstanding'.[133] Investigation of the world became a theological activity. The physico-theological enterprises which we considered in the previous chapter were thus informed not only by the search for purposes of natural objects now bereft of symbolic meanings, but by the conviction that knowledge could bring about a reversal of the curse of ignorance, and the separation from God which resulted from it.

Knowledge of the creatures led to theological knowledge. But it served in addition to mitigate the consequences of the Fall and re-establish human dominion over nature. To use Flavell's words: 'By a skilful and industrious improvement of the creatures . . . we might have a fuller taste of heaven.'[134] Knowledge, in other words, gives rise to improvement of the human lot, reversing the process of deterioration set in train by the Fall, and transforming the earth into a paradisal anticipation of the life to come. According to John Pettus, 'we wilfully banish our selves out of the *Paradise* of Knowledge, either by not *seeing, trying, or inquiring* into the nature of our selves or other Creatures, or not freely *imparting* what we do know, or foolishly *condemning* or *censuring* the kind and laborious *impartments* of others'.[135] John Johnston insisted that the study of nature was not just a vain collation of knowledge, but rather a discipline which made possible manipulation of the world, and restored to the human race abilities lost through Adam's lapse:

[131] Cowper, *The Works of William Cowper* (London, 1629), p. 842.
[132] Flavell, *Husbandry Spiritualized*, Epistle Dedicatory, Sig A3r.
[133] Reynolds, *Mythomystes*, p. 71.
[134] Flavell, *Husbandry Spiritualized*, Epistle Dedicatory, Sig. A2v.
[135] Pettus, *History of Adam and Eve*, p. 61.

He is to me a true Son of Natural Philosophy who knows how to augment, and multiply the Winds, to produce new mettals, to make mineral Waters; Artificial, of Vitriol, Brimstone, Allum, &c. and to bring forth new plants and animals. He is a legitimate enquirer into Nature, who knows how to prolong life, keep back old age, change statures and complexions, reason the force of imagination upon any body, cure disease hitherto incurable, ease pains, and can hasten the times of maturity, clarification, putrefaction, concoction, and germination.[136]

Natural philosophy was thus a potential panacea for the ills which came after the Fall.

Members of the Royal Society expressed their aims in similar terms. Robert Hooke declared: 'And as at first, mankind fell by tasting of the forbidden Tree of Knowledge, so we, their Posterity, may be in part restor'd by the same way, not only by beholding and contemplating, but by tasting too those fruits of Natural Knowledge, that were never yet forbidden.'[137] It was the objective of the Society, according to its first historian Thomas Sprat, to enable mankind to re-establish 'Dominion over *Things*'.[138] Practice of the new philosophy was a re-establishment of the religion of Adam. The experimental philosopher, according to Sprat:

will be led to admire the wonderful contrivance of the *Creation*; and so to apply, and direct his praises aright: which no doubt, when they are offer'd up to *heven* [sic] from the mouth of one, who has well studied what he commends, will be more sutable [sic] to the *Divine Nature*, than the blind applauses of the ignorant. This was the first service, that *Adam* perform'd to his *Creator*, when he obey'd him in mustring, and naming, and looking into the *Nature* of all the *Creatures*. This had bin the only *religion*, if men had continued innocent in *Paradise*, and had not wanted a *redemption*.[139]

Adam's only religion had been the contemplation of the creatures. Those rites and doctrines which from the seventeenth century onwards were termed 'religion' had been necessitated by Adam's transgression. The new natural philosophy added a missing dimension to this religion: salvation prepares us for the next world, science makes amends for the damage we have wrought in this one. In an address to the Royal Society, Joseph Glanvill announced that the researches of that august body had led to 'the accelerating and *bettering* of *Fruits*, *emptying Mines*, *drayning Fens* and *Marshes*'. '*Lands*', he went on to say, 'may be *advanced* to scarce credible degrees of *improvement*, and innumerable other *advantages* may be obtained by an *industry* directed by *Philosophy* and *Mechanicks*.' The new

---

[136] Johnston, *Wonderful Things of Nature*, Sig. A3v.
[137] Hooke, *Micrographia*, Preface. On this general theme see Webster, *Great Instauration*, pp. 86, 100, and passim. [138] Sprat, *History of the Royal Society*, p. 62. [139] *Ibid.*, pp. 349f.

philosophy thus provided 'ways of *captivating Nature*, and making her *subserve* our *purposes* and *designments*' leading to the restoration of 'the *Empire* of *Man* over *Nature*'.[140] '*Experimental* and *Observational* knowledge', agreed Richard Neve, give man 'Power to Master Creatures'.[141]

Advances in knowledge did not merely help re-establish a lost dominion over nature. In addition, they provided ways in which recompense could be made for other losses suffered at the Fall. Adam, for example, had enjoyed the advantage of more acute organs of sensation. Robert Boyle believed that only in the millennium would the superior sensory faculties which Adam had once possessed be returned: 'it is likely that . . . all our faculties will, in the future blessed state, be enlarged and heightened; so will our knowledge also be'.[142] Until then, however, artificial aids – telescopes and microscopes – could augment the moderns' limited powers of observation. Adam had not needed a telescope, wrote Glanvill: 'The acuteness of his natural Opticles . . . shew'd him much of the Coelestial magnificence and . . . without Galilaeo's tube.'[143] By implication, seventeenth-century scientists, armed with the latest instruments for improving their meagre senses, could now enjoy the same heavenly prospects as Adam. Robert Hooke declared that through 'the addition of such artificial Instruments and methods, there may be, in some manner, a reparation made for the mischiefs, and imperfections mankind has drawn upon it self . . . The only way wich now remains for us to recover some degree of those former perfections, seems to be, by rectifying the operations of the Sense, the Memory, and Reason, since upon the evidence, the strength, the integrity, the right correspondence of all these . . . all our command over things is to be establisht.'[144] Hooke, along with many other Fellows of the Royal Society, thus believed that recent developments in mechanical philosophy along with the invention of various glasses and instruments could assist in overcoming the deformities which had blunted human enquiries since the Fall.

Adam's contemplation of the creatures was not the only feature of his prelapsarian existence which the seventeenth-century sought to emulate. Some went so far as to advocate the adoption of the dietary habits of Adam and Eve. Leaders of some of the radical groups which sprang up during the English revolution suggested that birds and beasts were our brothers, and ought not to be slaughtered for food. Familist Giles

[140] Glanvill, *Scepsis Scientifica*, Sigs b3v, b4r–v.
[141] T. Snow [i.e. Richard Neve], *Apopiroscipy*, (London, 1702), Prologemonon, Sig. b2v.
[142] Boyle, *The Christian Virtuoso*, *Works* vi, 789; cf. *Some Motives to the Love of God*, *Works* i, 283.
[143] Glanvill, *Vanity of Dogmatising*, p. 5.   [144] Hooke, *Micrographia*, Preface.

Randall, Ranter Giles Robins, and Roger Crab, the mad hatter of Chesham, all advocated the vegetarian regimen on these grounds.[145] The most notable vegetarian of the period, Thomas Tryon, explicitly linked the human propensity to violence with the practice of meat-eating which followed upon the Fall. Tryon conceded that 'the Lord did give the Nations liberty to kill and eat the Flesh of Inferior Creatures', but points out that 'this was not done until Mankind had departed out of his holy Law, and government of his divine Principle'.[146] Such views failed to attract much interest from the general populace, and the vegetarian cause was ill-served by the death from malnutrition of one of Crab's disciples, Captain Norwood. Even Tryon, himself a strict vegetarian, only recommended moderation in the consumption of meat to his readers. Meat-eating commentators pointed out that whatever situation had existed in Eden, Noah was later given explicit permission to eat the flesh of animals.[147] And in any case, vegetarianism was seen to conflict directly with the conviction that the whole sub-lunary world had been created for the use of the human race. Abbé Pluche thus scorned those who advocated abstinence from any food. Pythagoras and the Brachmins, he wrote, might well have shown 'Respect for the Blood of a Fly'. 'The Virtue of Man', he went on to say, 'does not consist in abstaining from every thing, notwithstanding his being sensible of his own Privileges; but in making use of every Thing with Moderation and Justice.'[148]

Some of the more radical groups went so far as to adopt Adam's original mode of dress, as the ancient Adamites had done.[149] In Bohemia a certain 'Picard' is reported to have attracted many followers all of whom discarded their customary attire to attend worship in places which they referred to as 'paradise'.[150] Ranters and Adamites, it was alleged, shed not only their clothes but their sexual inhibitions, claiming their behaviour to be sanctioned by the biblical injunction to 'be fruitful and multiply' and by St Paul's assurance that 'to the pure, all things are

---

[145] Thomas, *Man and the Natural World*, pp. 287–300; Christopher Hill, *Puritanism and Revolution*, (London: Secker and Warburg, 1958), ch. 11.

[146] Tryon, *The Good House-wife made a Doctor* (London, 1692), pp. 217f.; *Country-Mans Companion* (London, 1683), pp. 120f.

[147] Genesis 9.3; Willet, *Hexapla in Genesin* (Cambridge, 1605), p. 105. Benjamin Needler, *Expository Notes* (London, 1655), p. 16. [148] Pluche, *Spectacle*, v, 39, 42f.; iii, 320–2

[149] Andrewes, Ἀποσπασματια Sacra, p. 331. Cf. Epiphanius, *Adversus haereses* 52; Augustine, *De haeresibus*, 31.

[150] Richard Brathwait, *A Mustur Roll of the Evill Angels Embattled against S. Michael* (London, 1655), pp. 75–81.

pure' (Titus 1.15).[151] Anabaptists, against whom no accusation seems to have been withheld, were similarly charged. Quakers, too, went naked 'as a sign', courageously ignoring the fact that Eden had enjoyed a perpetual spring in a more temperate climate.[152]

The issue of the exercise of dominion of one man over another was also taken up by those wishing to recreate the original conditions of paradise. Genesis taught that in Eden human dominion was exercised only over the birds and beasts. As Milton put it: '. . . but Man over men / He made not Lord; such title to himself / Reserving, human left from human free'.[153] While it might be argued that human sin called for the institution of civil authorities, radical groups nonetheless pressed for that egalitarianism which they thought had reigned in Eden.[154] Gerrard Winstanley, leader of the Diggers, wrote in 1649 that when 'the great Creator Reason, made the Earth to be a Common Treasury, to preserve Beasts, Birds, Fishes and Man . . . not one word was spoken in the beginning That one branch of mankind should rule over another'.[155] John Heydon and François Poulain de la Barre also made pointed reference to the fact that 'the *Scripture* speaketh not a word o inequality'.[156] The subjugation of women to men was a related theme. As we have seen, the Quakers argued for equality in marriage on the basis of Adam and Eve's prelapsarian marital state. In a similar vein, Emilia

[151] R. Abbott, *The Young Mans Warning-piece* (London, 1657) Sig. a3r-4v; L. R., *The Ranters Ranting* (London, 1650); Thomas Hall, *Comarum ἀκοσμίαι. The Loathsomnesse of Long Hair . . . with an Appendix against Painting, Spots, Naked Breasts, etc.* (London, 1654) pp. 111–13; Hill, *World Turned Upside Down*, pp. 317f.; Turner, *One Flesh*, pp. 82–5.

[152] Calvin, *Treatises against the Anabaptists and against the Libertines*, tr. B. Farley (Eerdmans: Grand Rapids, 1982) pp. 263–5, 279–81. Williams, *The Common Expositor*, p. 219. The nakedness of the natives of America, well attested in the travel literature, could, by implication, sustain two interpretations. They were either innocent, or shameless. By and large, it was the latter interpretation which was adopted. See, e.g., Pererius, *Commentariorvm in Genesin*, pp. 236f.; Hill, *English Bible*, p. 244.

[153] Milton, *Paradise Lost*, XII. 69–71. Admittedly, divine talk of political hierarchies would seem a little premature in a garden which had only two human inhabitants. Those who opposed kingly rule, however, could adduce additional arguments from subsequent passages in Genesis. Nimrod, of the tainted line of Ham, was reputed to have been the first king, and a typical example of all that was wrong with monarchies (Genesis 10.8–11). Robert Filmer argued in his *Patriarcha* (1680) to the contrary, that Adam and the patriarchs enjoyed 'royal authority', 'lordship and dominion of life and death', and 'universal monarchy'. See discussion in Locke, *Two Treatises on Government*, in *Works*, 10th edn, 10 vols. (London, 1801), v, 215–20 and passim. Earlier writers had argued similarly that had there been children in paradise, there must also have been the exercise of parental authority, which was thus thought to provide the natural basis for political authority. See Salkeld, *Treatise of Paradise*, pp. 125–30; Ross, *An Exposition*, p. 25.

[154] See Williams, *The Common Expositor*, p. 220–4; Duncan, *Milton's Earthly Paradise*, pp. 165–75.

[155] Winstanley, *A Declaration to the Powers of England* (1649), *Works*, p. 251.

[156] Qu. in Turner, *One Flesh*, p. 108.

Lanier pleaded: 'Then let us have our Libertie again / And challendge to your selves no Sov'raigntie.'[157]

Despite the interest of various minority groups in egalitarianism, vegetarianism, and nudism, these things were not generally thought to encapsulate the essence of prelapsarian bliss. Thus whereas certain activities or relationships were conceded to have been appropriate in the perfection of paradise, they were not so regarded in the seventeenth century. In any case, there remained genuine uncertainty about the equality of the sexes in Eden; the eating of animal flesh had been explicitly permitted by God; and nakedness, while it might have well suited a tropically-situated paradise which had been exempted from seasonal extremities, seemed manifestly imprudent for those who had to endure harsh winters in the northern latitudes. On the other hand, there could be little doubt about the knowledge and dominion which Adam had once enjoyed, and these goals, for more optimistic seventeenth-century thinkers, seemed achievable. We have established that knowledge was thought crucial to dominion. Dominion itself was most often understood as the bringing about of physical transformations to the landscape of a fallen world.

REPLANTING THE GARDEN

While the image of Adam as a gentleman gardener was held up as the paradigm to be emulated, it was hard to forget that the legacy of the Fall was thorns and thistles, and an earth which required intensive labours to render it useful. It was one thing to the praise the charms of the pastoral life, but quite another to bring order to a barren and desolate wilderness, or an unkempt forest wasteland of trees, briars and brambles. Allied to the ideal of the contemplation of the creatures was the imperative to subdue the earth and to bring land under cultivation. This could be most easily achieved, it was thought, through the establishment of gardens. 'God *Almightie* first Planted a *Garden*', declared Francis Bacon, 'And indeed, it is the Purest of Humane pleasures.'[158]

If the gentle art of gardening were an undertaking appropriate for Adam in his innocence, it would scarcely need more to recommend it as a suitable past-time for his seventeenth-century descendants. Gardening

[157] Emilia Lanier, *The Poems of Shakespeares Dark Lady: Salve Deus Rex Judaeorum*, ed. A. L. Rowse (London: Cape, 1978), pp. 43, 102–5.
[158] Bacon, 'Of Gardens', *Essays*, ed. W. A. Wright (London: Macmillan, 1871) p. 186.

was lauded by its advocates as the 'oldest, happiest occupation', 'the best employment for the best of creatures', the 'ancientest of all trades', 'the first and best Vocation'.[159] Of all activities, thought Leonard Mascall, there is none 'that more doth refresh ye vital spirits of men, nor more engender admiration in the effects of nature . . . then is the skill of Planting and Grassying'.[160] 'When God almighty would have *Adam* to partake of a perfection of happinesses, even then when he stood innocent', wrote William Coles, 'he could find none greater under the sun, then to place him in a Garden.' [161] Tilling the earth, according to Richard Neve, was 'the most *Ancient*, most Noble, and most Useful of all the Practical *Sciences*'. Without it, on account of 'the unhappy *Fall* of our First *Parents*, and the *Curse* upon the Earth', no-one in town or country could live, other than as brutes.[162] An anonymous correspondent to *The Spectator* wrote that a garden is 'naturally apt to fill the Mind with Calmness and Tranquility, and to lay all its turbulent Passions at rest'; a garden 'gives us a great insight into the Contrivance and Wisdom of Providence, and suggests innumerable Subjects for Meditation'.[163] Stephen Switzer, whose enthusiasm for terraculture prompted him to advance the unlikely thesis that gardening was the central theme of Milton's 'Paradise Lost', described the garden as 'an Epitome of Paradise it self, where the Mind of Man is in its highest Raptures, and where the Souls of the Virtuous enjoy the utmost Pleasures they are susceptible of in this sublunary State'. Gardening was both a preparation for, and a foretaste of the joys of heaven.[164] Even Voltaire's world-weary Candide was eventually to seek peace in his garden. The serenity of the garden was frequently contrasted with the turmoil of the city. Abraham Cowley pointed out that 'God the first garden made, and the first city Cain', echoing William Cowper's observation that 'God made the country,

---

[159] Pareus, *In Genesin Mosis commentarius*, col. 344; A. Speed, *Adam out of Eden* (London, 1659), To the Reader; Conradus Heresbachius, *The Whole Art of Husbandry*, enlarged by Gervase Markham (London, 1631) p. 7. Moses Cooke, *The Manner of Raising, Ordering, and Improving Forrest-Trees* (London, 1676), p. 52. Cf. Abraham Cowley, 'Of Agriculture', in *Works*, ed. Richard Hurd, (London, 1809), III, 143–57; Samuel Hartlib, *The Reformed Husband-Man* (London, 1651), To the Reader; *Legacy of Husbandry*, p. 301.

[160] Leonard Mascall, *The Country-mans New Art of Planting and Grassing* (London, 1652), Epistle Dedicatory. Agriculture, wrote John Worlidge, 'quickened the Genius, recreated the spirits, and actuated the intellect.' *Systema agriculturae* (London, 1669), Preface.

[161] Coles, *Adam in Eden*, To the Reader.   [162] Neve, *Apopiroscipy*, ch. 2, p. 3.

[163] *The Spectator*, Saturday, 9 September 1712 (p. 683).

[164] Switzer, *Gardener's Recreation* (1715 edn), pp. iv, xvi, 39; *The Practical Fruit-Gardener*, 2nd edn (London, 1731), p. 3, qu. in Otten, *Environ'd with Eternity* p. 7. Also see C. A. Wimmer, *Geschichte der Gartentheorie* (Darmstadt: Wissenschaftliche Buchgesellschaft, 1989) pp. 154–65.

and man made the town'.[165] Many patriotic Englishmen regarded their homeland as uniquely placed to begin reinstating the conditions of paradise on earth. 'This very nation might be made the paradise of the World', exclaimed Walter Blith. English poets agreed that there was no better place to practise the art of gardening than in their own country. England was 'the garden of the world', 'this other Eden, demi-Paradise'; 'that renowned isle / Which all men Beauty's garden plot enstyle'.[166] For seventeenth-century muses it was a new Eden which was to appear in England's green and pleasant land.

Cultivated gardens were recreational in a more active sense than that with which we are familiar. The formal, enclosed garden could serve as systematic representation of those elements of nature which were presently scattered about in the ruins of a fallen world. The *Theatrum botanicum* (1640) of John Parkinson, who had served as apothecary to James I, was praised as 'a Botanicke Theatre' containing all the 'vegetables in the pride of beauty, ranged in their proper order', and constituting a 'compleat Paradise upon earth'.[167] Planned gardens brought together diverse species, and presented them systematically, as they might be presented in a botanical text. Such gardens thus represented not only an imposition of order, but were an expression of knowledge of plants and their uses. 'To make thee truly sensible of that happinesse which Mankind lost by the Fall of *Adam*', wrote Coles, 'is to render thee an exact *Botanick* . . . to reinstate thee in another *Eden*.'[168] These words were echoed by Coles' admirers:

> Court bounteous Nature, search into her deepest mysteries
> And seek that sovereign virtue that, in each Plant hidden lies.
> So may we the first Ages Innocence hope to revive,
> And long obscured Wisdom from her dark mists to receive.[169]

The seventeenth-century garden was both a living pharmacopoeia and 'a kind of surrogate Bible'.[170] The geometric formality of the seventeenth-century garden also bore witness to the god-like capacity of the gardener to bring order out of chaos – an order reproduced in George Herbert's 'Paradise':[171]

[165] Abraham Cowley, 'The Garden', v. William Cowper, 'The Task', *Works* (1836–7 edn.), I, 749.
[166] Blith, *The English Improver Improved*, sig. d3v, qu. in Webster, *Great Instauration*, pp. 482f. Andrew Marvell, Shakespeare, William Browne, all qu. in Hill, *English Bible*, p. 152.
[167] Parkinson, *Theatrum botanicum*, Opening Address, by John Speed.
[168] Coles, *Adam in Eden*, To the Reader.   [169] E. Philips, dedicatory poem in Coles, *Adam in Eden*.
[170] Prest, *Garden of Eden*, p. 23.
[171] On the introduction of geometric patterns into gardens see Thomas, *Man and the Natural World*, pp. 256f; Lovejoy, *Chain of Being*, pp. 15f.

> I blesse Thee, Lord, because I Grow
> Among Thy trees, which in a Row
> To Thee both fruit and order Ow

The Garden of Eden was similarly conceived of in these strict geometrical terms, as having 'clipt hedges, square parterres, strait walls, trees uniformly lopt, regular knots and carpets of flowers, groves nodding at groves, marble foundations, and water works'.[172] In Eden, wrote Joseph Beaumont, 'no crook-back'd Tree / Disgrac'd the place, no foolish scrambling Shrub, / No wilde and careless Bush, no clownish Stub'.[173] Thomas Browne believed that geometrical patterns were latent in living things, and that the planting of formal gardens was merely a reassertion of the natural state of affairs.[174] Neither is it a coincidence that the six most famous botanical gardens in Europe – Padua, Leyden, Montpellier, Oxford, Paris, and Uppsala – were established in the sixteenth and seventeenth centuries. As John Prest has ably demonstrated, 'contemporaries interpreted the foundation of these encyclopaedic Gardens in a context of the re-creation of the earthly Paradise, or Garden of Eden.'[175]

The garden derived much of its power as a symbol, or literal recreation, of paradise on account of the widespread belief that plants reproduced asexually. The garden was thus a place unsullied by sexual reproduction. It excluded not only animals, but indeed, all sexual beings.[176] Plants, it was imagined, were celibate creatures, undivided in their nature and not requiring a mate for completion.[177] Because the Garden of Eden had enjoyed perpetual spring, it also became incumbent upon the seventeenth-century gardener, through a judicious selection of plant varieties and by paying careful attention to planting times, to design a garden with evergreen plants and annuals which flowered in succession so that gardens were never wanting for foliage or flower. The importation of winter-flowering bulbs from Asia and the Americas played an important role in these attempts to emulate Eden.[178] The

---

[172] Passmore, *Man's Responsibility for Nature*, p. 36.
[173] Thomas, *Man and the Natural World*, p. 220.
[174] Browne, *The Garden of Cyrus*, p. 178, and passim.
[175] Prest, *Garden of Eden*. Also see Webster, *Great Instauration*, pp. 152, 163, 477–9; Michael Leslie and Timothy Raylor (eds.), *Culture and Cultivation in Early Modern England* (Leicester University Press, 1992). For the later influence of this idea, see Max Schultz, *Paradise Preserved: Recreations of Eden in Eighteenth and Nineteenth-Century England* (Cambridge University Press, 1985).
[176] Boehme, *The Second Booke*, p. 60; Malvenda, *De Paradiso*, p. 203.
[177] The single exception was the palm, known from the time of Theophrastus to reproduce sexually. The palm was for this reason considered a 'hieroglyphic of Nuptuals'. H. Hawkins, *Partheneia sacra* (Rouen, 1633), pp. 151–8; Prest, *Garden of Eden*, pp. 81f.
[178] Bacon, 'Of Gardens', *Essays*, p. 186; Prest, *Garden of Eden*, pp.

garden was also a place in which limited dominion could be exercised. 'In a garden', observed John Lawrence, 'a man is lord of all, the sole despotic governer of every living thing.'[179]

Gardens might have been symbols of Eden, small scale representations of how order might be restored to a disobedient nature. Literal compliance with the imperative to subdue the earth required something more, however. What gardens represented on a small symbolic scale, widespread agriculture and colonisation instantiated at a more grand and literal level.[180] Eden could not be truly restored until the whole earth could be brought under human dominion and made useful. God appointed Adam to subdue the earth, wrote John White in his commentary on Genesis, 'that is, by Culture and Husbandry, to Manure and make it fit to yield fruits and provision . . . which is done by Planting, Earing, Sowing, and other works of Husbandry'. 'God will have men do two things', agreed Lancelot Andrewes, 'the one to follow husbandry, the other to keep sheep and other cattell, for God's will is not that the earth shall be covered with nettles, like the slothful man's vineyard.'[181] In *The English Improver Improved* (1653), Walter Blith set out a plan for reclaiming land for cultivation, and proposed means for increasing the productivity or 'usefulness' of land already under cultivation. Adam had been set the task 'to till the Earth, and improve it', he wrote, urging his contemporaries to do likewise.[182] Sowing seed, planting trees, plowing, digging, dressing, these were, in the words of John Pettus, 'a replenishment of the first Creation'. Through these agricultural activities, man 'may be said to subdue the Earth, or conquer those extravagancies of nature'. Subduing the earth, agreed George Hughes, 'is by plowing, tilling, and making use of it'.[183]

Such activities, it is important to recognise, were not the encumbrance laid upon Adam as the result of his sin. Even in his original estate, Adam had been destined to be a worker. 'God made man', wrote Lancelot Andrewes, 'to labour, not to be idle, and therefore *Adam*, in the state of his innocencie, was put into the garden of Eden that he might dresse it and keep it.'[184] Work was one of the ends for which human beings had been

---

[179] John Lawrence, *The Gentleman's Recreation* (1716) qu. in Thomas, *Man and the Natural World*, p. 238.
[180] On the link between gardens and husbandry in seventeenth-century England, see John Hunt, 'Hortulan Affairs', in Greegrass et al. (eds.), *Samuel Hartlib*, pp. 321–42.
[181] White, *A Commentary*, bk I, pp. 113f. Andrewes, Ἀποσπασματια *Sacra*, p. 371.
[182] Blith, *The English Improver Improved* (London, 1653), p. 4.
[183] Pettus, *History of Adam and Eve*, p. 83; Hughes, *Analytical Exposition*, p. 11.
[184] Andrewes, Ἀποσπασματια *Sacra*, p. 104. Cf. Edwards, *Discourse concerning the Old and New Testaments*, III, 111f.; Geneva Bible (1607 edn), fol. IV, n. f. On the work-ethic in Eden, see Duncan, *Milton's Earthly Paradise*, p. 153.

created. According to Stephen Blake, 'all things are so ordained that [they] shall be no way usefull without knowledge and labour'. Indeed our ignorance of the nature of things makes us culpable in God's eyes: 'man should be accountable to God of what improvement he hath made of that measure of knowledge which was given him'.[185] Work, then, was not simply a means of sustaining life, a life directed towards some other, more spiritual, purpose: work was itself a divinely-ordained activity, and the ordinance which instituted it remained in essence unchanged by the Fall. This literal reading of Genesis 2.15 – 'The Lord God took the man and placed him in the Garden of Eden to till it and keep it' – meshed neatly with the Reformers' doctrine of the priesthood of all believers, according to which all human vocations were equally sacred. The most mundane occupations were thus imbued with a spiritual significance. Every calling was now considered a religious one. It has been plausibly argued, for this reason, that seventeenth-century sabbatarianism was less to do with resting on the sabbath than with working on the other six days.[186] The accumulation of capital surplus to immediate needs which resulted from this approach to labour was, as Weber famously pointed out, the key to understanding the emergence of capitalism in the early-modern world.[187]

If work had been intended as the original occupation of the human race, and if labour had been an end in itself, the Fall reinforced its necessity by providing additional motivations. For now the task was not merely one of maintaining the earth in its paradisal perfection, but of restoring it to its original condition, and of counteracting its new tendencies to corruption. 'It has therefore been the chief and laudible Understanding of the Wise and Virtuous in all Ages to endeavour a Reparation of that Loss', wrote Stephen Switzer of the curse which had been laid upon the earth through human transgressions, 'and so to manure, cultivate, dress and improve it.'[188] Husbandry, according to Timothy Nourse, restores ground suffering from 'the Original Curse of

---

[185] Stephen Blake, *The Compleat Gardeners Practice* (London, 1664), Epistle Dedicatory, (Sig. A3.r); Preface (Sig a.v).

[186] Christopher Hill, *Society and Puritanism in Pre-Revolutionary England* (London: Panther Books, 1964), pp. 141–211. Cf. Duffy, *Stripping of the Altars*, pp. 394f. The situation is well captured by Hill in the following exchange: 'Member of the Massachusetts General Court. – "You are not to do unnecessary work on the Sabbath". Indian Chiefs. – "That will be easy: we haven't much to do any day, and can well take our ease on the Sabbath."' (p. 141).

[187] Weber, *The Protestant Ethic and the Spirit of Capitalism* (1902); Carl Mitcham, 'The Religious and Political Origins of Modern Technology', in Paul Durbin and Friedrich Rapp (eds.) *Philosophy and Technology* (Dordrecht: Reidel, 1983), pp. 267–73.

[188] Switzer, *Gardener's Recreation*, p. 72.

Thorns and Bryers . . . to its Primitive Beauty in the State of Paradise'. Working the land was, he continued, recreation in two senses – because of 'the Refreshment it gives to the Mind', and on account of 'the *Restauration of Nature*, which may be looked upon as a *New Creation* of things'.[189] Refreshment of the mind was not the only boon to arise out of husbandry. Those who took seriously God's commands with respect to improving the earth would be materially rewarded for their pains. Our original dominion is in part renewed to us, said Edward Reynolds, on account of God's promise that '*The diligent hand maketh Rich*, and *hee that Ploweth his land, shall have plenty of Corne*.'[190] Dominion and economic incentive were thus not two distinct motivations, for it was natural that obedience to the Deity would be accompanied by earthly rewards.

Bringing land under cultivation was, in addition to reversing the curse which followed upon the Fall, a redress of the injury caused to the earth by the Flood. The Deluge, we recall, had increased the salinity of the soil, and had left mountains and marshes in its wake. Those who still subscribed to the ancient view of the perfection of the sphere regarded mountains as geological monstrosities, raised up in the wake of those cataclysms which had followed upon man's first disobedience.[191] John Wilkins wrote of those 'who thinke Mountaines to bee a deformity in the earth, as if they were either beate up by the flood, or else cast up like so many heaps of rubbish left at the creation'.[192] We do not have to search far to find representatives of this view. Andrew Marvell judged the surface of the present earth to be: 'But a rude heap together hurl'd / All negligently overthrown / Gulfes, Deserts, Precipices, Stone.' The gloomy Donne described mountains as 'warts and pockholes in the face / of th' earth'. 'The earth also is spotted', wrote William Cowper, 'like the face of a woman once beautiful, but now deformed with Leprosie.' Burnet, as we have seen, believed that 'the present Earth looks like a heap of Rubbish and Ruines'.[193] The Deluge had also left behind bogs and marshes which were equally incapable of sustaining agriculture. Ideally, swamps would be drained and mountains levelled. For want of

---

[189] Nourse, *Campania Fœlix*, p. 2.   [190] Reynolds, *Treatise of the Passions*, p. 437.
[191] Nicolson, *Maintain Gloom and Mountain Glory*, ch. III.
[192] Wilkins, *The Discovery of a World*, pp. 117f.
[193] Marvell, *Upon Appleton house*, stanza 96. Donne, 'The First Anniversary', lines 284–301. Cowper, *Works*, p. 114. This view, incidentally, was rejected by many of the physico-theologians. According to Ray, for example, mountains were 'most convenient for the entertainment of the various sorts of Animals' and for the 'putting forth of Plants'. Without mountains, moreover, there would be no rivers. Finally, 'Chains of Mountains are of great use for Boundaries and Limits to the Territories of Princes or Commonwealths, to secure them on those parts from sudden Incursions of Enemies.' *Miscellaneous Discourses*, p. 165.

the necessary technology, the latter seemed destined to await the end times, when, as Isaiah had prophesied, the earth would be returned to its original spherical perfection, 'every valley exulted, and every mountain and hill made low' (Isaiah 40.4). In the mean time, marshy ground could be reclaimed and placed under cultivation, and mountainous regions, too, where possible could be used for agriculture. Richard Burton wrote of his ideal estate: 'I will have no bogs, fens, marshes, vast woods, deserts, heaths . . . I will not have a barren acre in all my territories, not so much as the tops of the mountains: where nature fails, it shall be supplied by art.'[194]

In the seventeenth century, land not put to human use thus stood as a mute reminder that God's designs had yet to be fulfilled by a dilatory mankind. 'Those that have possessions in the earth', urged John White, 'must withall so manure and husband them that they may be useful and fruitfull.'[195] The spectacle of a wild and untamed nature filled the industrious husbandman with a deep repugnance. 'Wild and vacant lands' were representative of 'a deformed chaos', 'the very abstract of a degenerated nature'.[196] Such landscapes were a direct reflection of the degeneration of their inhabitants. If 'improving' the earth were a sign that God's purposes for the world were being fulfilled, and if material prosperity accrued to those who co-operated in the divine scheme of things, inhabited lands which showed little sign of cultivation and development were by implication occupied by those who seemed to be outside the divine plan. Failure to take part in the restoration of the natural world was attributed to various factors. An unhealthy papist preoccupation with the contemplative life, for example, would hinder the business of subduing the earth. George Walker referred to 'the beastly dotage of many Romish saints . . . who count it a high perfection to live in caves, and dennes, and cottages in the wilderness remote from all humane society'.[197] Men and women such as these would never subdue the earth. Papism combined with idleness was a particularly fatal combination, as the plight of the Irish seemingly bore witness. The inhabitants of Ireland were compared with the indolent natives of the

---

[194] Quoted in John Hale, *The Civilization of Europe in the Renaissance* (Sydney: Simon and Schuster, 1995), p. 511.   [195] White, *A Commentary*, p. 114.

[196] Thomas, *Man and the Natural World*, p. 255. In the eighteenth century, Buffon wrote that 'uncultivated Nature is hideous and languishing'. Without cultivation, 'the earth presents nothing but a disordered mass of grass herbage, and of trees loaded with parisitical plants. . . all the low grounds are occupied with putrid and stagnating waters, and miry lands, which are neither solid nor fluid, are impassible, and remain equally useless to the inhabitants of the earth'. *Natural History*, II, 252, III, 457, 455.   [197] Walker, *History of the Creation*, p. 195.

Americas – 'little better in their ways than the most remote Indians', according to Owen Roe O'Neill.[198] Ireland, like the New World, was a land of swamps and bogs, and this could but reflect ill on her impoverished inhabitants. 'A great part of *Ireland* lyes at present waste', observed Samuel Hartlib. There are 'Fens and waste grounds; besides Forests and Commons, which drained and improved might equalise in value some two or three counties in *England*.'[199] The remote Indians, to whom O'Neill compared the Irish, were, of course, the paradigm case of apathy and idleness, and were thus fully deserving of their savage and unfriendly surroundings. They were, moreover, a living example of the fate which might have befallen Europe had it not been for the religious industry of Christendom. 'Were it not for *Europes* agriculture, and industry', wrote Richard Franck, 'her florid Fields, and flourishing Pastures, would soon feel the fatal stroke of disorder; so become Forrests, and barren Desarts, fit only for bestial, and savage inhabitants.'[200] But America was not a wilderness beyond redemption, for with the settlement of diligent puritans it might now be transformed, in the words of Bostonian John Cotton, into 'a Paradise, as if this were the garden of Eden'.[201]

The activities of more 'advanced' human cultures were thus considered both a melioration of the effects of the curse, and a reward for industry. 'The Author of Mans Being and Faculties', declared John Ray, 'is well pleased with the Industry of Man in adorning the Earth with beautiful Cities and Castles, with pleasant Villages and Country Houses, with regular Gardens and Orchards and Plantations.' European civilisation thus played an important role in the fulfilment of the divine purposes, unlike the barbarous nations who had squandered their God-given resources:

[B]e it not preferred before a Barbarous and Inhospitable *Scythia*, without Houses, without Plantations, without Corn-fields or Vineyards, where the roving *Hords* of the savage and truculent Inhabitants, transfer themselves from place to place in Wagons, as they can find Pasture and Forage for their Cattle, and live upon Milk and Flesh roasted in the Sun at the Pomels of their Saddles; or a rude and unpolished *America*, peopled with slothful and naked *Indians*, instead of well-built Houses, living in pitiful Hutts and Cabans, made of Poles set endways . . .[202]

---

[198] Qu. in Hill, *English Bible*, p. 135.
[199] Hartlib, *Samuel Hartlib his Legacy of Husbandry*, 3rd edn (London, 1651), p. 291.
[200] Franck, *Philosophical Treatise*, p. 75.
[201] John Cotton, *A Brief Exposition . . . Upon the Whole Book of Canticles* (London, 1655) p. 164, qu. in Williams, *Wilderness and Paradise*, p. 100.   [202] Ray, *The Wisdom of God* pp. 117–18.

In Ray's assessment, these 'Indians' were no noble savages exemplifying the perfection of the human race in its original estate, but rather a race of rude beings, ignorant of divine purposes, and thus of their own place in the natural order.

The New World suffered not only on account of its indolent inhabitants. It also seemed patently unsuitable for large-scale cultivation, partly on account of its marshy terrain. This watery landscape was commonly regarded as a vestige of the Flood. Following the retreat of the floodwaters, it was thought that many regions of the earth had been left sodden and swampy. In civilised areas, human industry had already reclaimed lost ground, but in provinces recently inhabited or populated by those not motivated by the Protestant work-ethic, large bogs and marshes still rendered much land useless. 'And we may easily imagine', said Burnet, 'there were innumerable such Lakes, and Bogs . . . til the world begun to be pretty well stockt with people, and humane industry cleans'd and drain'd those unfruitful and uninhabitable places. And those countries that have been later cultivated, or by a lazier people, retain still, in proportion to their situation and soil, a greater number of them.'[203] The American continent, clearly, was inhabited by 'a lazier people'. Sentiments such as these were to form the basis of eighteenth-century discussions about the inferiority of all things American.[204]

The failure of aboriginal peoples to put their land to good use became one of the primary justifications for colonisation. The morality of establishing settlements in occupied lands was, according to George Walker, writing in 1641, a question 'much controverted among godly and learned divines'. The general issue was 'whether it bee lawfull, to send people, and to plant colonies in the vast countrie of the west-Indies, which are not replenished with men able to *subdue the Earth*, and to till it'. Walker clearly thought that such activities were justified, although he entertained certain reservations:

---

[203] Burnet, *Sacred Theory*, i.viii (pp. 86f.) Bacon attributed the soddenness of the American continent and the backwardness of its inhabitants to a second inundation, which came some thousands of years after the universal Deluge. *The Advancement of Learning and New Atlantis*, p. 277.

[204] Corneille de Pauw observed that the New World was 'covered with immense swamps, which render the air extremely unwholesome, and the soil productive of a prodigious number of poisonous vegetables'. This he attributed to the disposition of the native inhabitants. They were, he judged, 'utter strangers to industry', 'a race of men, of whom sluggishness was the chief characteristic', and whose nature approached the level of beasts. Corneille de Pauw, *Selections from Les Recherches Philosophiques sur les Americains*, tr. Mr Webb (Bath, 1789), pp. 1f. Also see Gerbi, *The Dispute of the New World*, pp. 1–79.

If wee bee Sons of *Adam*, the whole Earth is free for us, so long as it is not replenished with men and subdued. The ancient straggling inhabitants or any other, who have taken possession before, they have a right to so much as they are able to replenish and subdue, and bring under culture and tillage; and no other people have the right to *dispossesse* and expell them . . . except they have such *commission and warrant* as God gave to the Israelites to expell the *Canaanites* . . .'[205]

Walker did not believe that native peoples should be forcibly dispossessed of their lands in the manner of the Catholic Spaniards in South America. On the other hand, the condition cited by Walker – 'so much as they are able to replenish and subdue' – seemed to provide a possible sanction for colonisation. John Winthrop cited the authority of Genesis to support his view that the Indians who enclosed no land, had no settled habitations, 'nor any tame cattle to improve the land by', had 'no other but a natural right to these countries'. 'If we leave them sufficient for their own use', he concluded, 'we may lawfully take the rest.'[206] Richard Eburne argued in *A Plaine Path-way to Plantations* (1624) that the settlement of new-found lands, or the 'Doctrine of Plantations', as he called it, could be furnished with many proofs 'out of the Bible and Sacred Histories'. The chief warrant for colonisation 'was God's expresse commandment to *Adam, Genesis* 1.28. that hee should *fill the earth, and subdue it*'. By virtue of this charter, continued Eburne, 'hee and his haue euer since had the *Privilege* to spread themselves from place to place, and to *Hauve, hold, occupie, and enjoy* any Region or Countrey whatsoeuer.' The command was all the more compelling because it was repeated to Noah and his progeny: 'Replenish yee the earth, or fill it vp againe.'[207] Other passages of scripture also made mention of colonisation. The inhabitants of newly colonised lands would have taken little comfort from the words of Deuteronomy to which Walker alluded: 'When the Lord your God brings you into the land which you are entering to take possession of it, and clears away many nations before you . . . and you defeat them; then you must utterly destroy them; you shall make no covenant with them, and show no mercy to them' (7.1–2). Fortunately, this text rarely seems to have been used to justify the supplanting of a native people. The biblical warrant for colonisation was not so much the concept of a promised land for a chosen people, but rather the ethic of putting the natural world to use, and answering the ends which God had

---

[205] Walker, *History of the Creation*, pp. 222f. [206] Qu. in Hill, *English Bible*, p. 136.
[207] Richard Eburne, *A Plaine Path-way to Plantation* (London, 1624), sig,. B2v, pp. 16–18.

ordained for created things.[208] Such a justification might be turned
around, of course, and be used to highlight the wastage of lands at
home. In a book which set forth a number of schemes for more efficient
domestic production in England, Adolphus Speed declared that '*England*
affords Land enough for the Inhabitants, and if some men did but *indus-*
triously and *skillfully* improve it and manure it, we need not go to *Jamaica*
for new *plantations*.'[209] (One of Speed's projects for better utilising England's pastures involved a rabbit-breeding programme – a project
doomed to success if ever there was one.) But in the seventeenth and
eighteenth centuries it proved easier to establish colonies abroad than to
persuade land owners and the Crown to bring more land under the
plough.

Added impetus for the colonisation of apparently under-utilised land
came from developing theoretical conceptions of the relationship between land ownership and land use. During the English revolution
radical groups frequently drew attention to the fact that the landed
gentry left considerable tracts of land in their wild state. On Sunday, 1
April, 1649, in a mostly symbolic act of defiance, a group of poor
commoners gathered on St George's Hill, just outside London, and to
the consternation of local land owners, together began to dig the
earth.[210] The implication was clear: if the gentry were not to put their
land to use, it should be placed in the hands of the deserving, and in this
instance, the starving poor. Gerrard Winstanley, leader of the Diggers,
pointed out that one-third of the land of England was waste and barren,
drawing the obvious conclusion that such lands ought to be given to
those who could develop them.[211] The great Creator, said Winstanley,
'made the Earth to be a Common Treasury' and 'a Common Store-
house for all'.[212] These communist conceptions of land ownership were
also linked to the Old Testament notion of the Hebrew people as God's
tenants, and to that compassionate construct, the year of Jubilees

---

[208] It is perhaps worth alluding to an important difference between the exploratory and colonising
motives of those who settled, respectively, the north and south of the continent. The Spaniards
and Portugese, it might be said, set out from the old world in search of a terrestrial paradise, an
El Dorado. As mentioned in a previous chapter, Columbus actively sought the location of
paradise. To his royal patrons, he wrote: 'if I could pass the equinoctial line . . . I should find the
earthly paradise'; and of the continent of South America: 'there are great indications of this
being the terrestrial paradise'. The puritan settlers of the North, by way of contrast, saw their
mission not as the discovery of Eden, but as the transformation of a wilderness into a paradise.
On the ramifications of these contrasting approaches, see George Williams, *Wilderness and
Paradise*, pp. 100f.   [209] Speed, *Adam out of Eden*, To the Reader.
[210] Hill, *World Turned Upside Down*, p. 110, ch. 7 passim.   [211] Hill, *English Bible*, p. 133, cf. p. 166.
[212] Winstanley, *Declaration to all the Powers of England, Works*, pp. 251f.

(Leviticus 25.10–17). One did not have to subscribe to such collectivist notions of land ownership to recognise that commons could be put to better use. Samuel Hartlib observed that commons 'make poor by causing idleness', arguing that 'There are fewest poor, where there are fewest commons.'[213] Stephen Switzer repeated the principle, identifying Surrey as the county with most commons and most poor:

> ... the little cottages swarm with Children half naked, and, I had almost said, half starved too; but by the Help of a Wife's Spinning, added to that of a poor cow or two, and ten or twelve sheep, the Men live on entire idle Life, employing the whole day in smoking Tobacco, and perhaps the night in Thieving.[214]

Such images recall to mind the image of the lazy Irish and indolent Indians. Under-utilised land, wherever it was to be found, was a standing reproach to the idle poor, or indifferent rich.

More conservative readers of Genesis might concede to Winstanley that in Eden there had been no private ownership of land, without granting his conclusion that such a situation was now desirable. Bishop Lancelot Andrewes, one of the translators of the Authorised Version, had explained that 'The Earth was at first, as a dish of meat at a Table, where every man might bit where him pleased; but when one had cut forth his piece and laid it on his trencher, it became private.' The means by which land becomes private, Andrewes went on to say, is through the principle of *subjicite terram* – 'seising, keeping, and imploying of the Earth'. The principle was not applied domestically, but to unused land in the colonies: 'If we winne a Countrie, where no habitation hath been, or which hath not been habitable for [i.e. because of] wilde beasts, by chasing from thence the beasts, and by subduing that Countrie, it becometh our own by *subjicite terram.*'[215] A more formal account of the origin of property appeared in 1690. The ownership of land, wrote Locke in the second of his *Treatises of Government*, begins as a result of 'the taking any part of what is common, and removing it out of the state nature leaves it in'. Locke explained that 'as much land as a man tills, plants, improves, cultivates, and can use the product of, so much is his property', for inasmuch as 'God and his reason commanded him to subdue the earth, i.e. improve it for the benefit of life . . . he that in obedience to this command of God, subdued, tilled, and sowed any part of, thereby annexed to it something that was his property.' Improve-

---

[213] Hartlib, *Legacy of Husbandry*, pp. 42f.
[214] Switzer, *The Practical Husbandman or Planter*, 2 vols. (London, 1733), I, 4f.
[215] Andrewes, Αποσπασματια *Sacra*, p. 103.

ment by human labour thus became a criterion for ownership. Americans, Locke pointed out, 'are rich in land, and poor in all the comforts of life' because 'for want of improving it by labour, have not one hundredth part of the conveniencies we enjoy'.[216] These theoretical conceptions, ultimately based on literal readings of the phrase 'subdue the earth', thus played a central role in both efforts to develop and improve native land, and in the establishment of plantations abroad.

Finally, there were eschatological elements in the related visions of subduing the earth, and colonising it. 'Are not these the times of the Gospell prophesied', Ralph Austen wrote, 'when the *Wast and desolate places shall be inhabited.*'[217] The improvement of agriculture, said Blith, would constitute nothing less than 'an addition of a new world'.[218] Thomas Traherne agreed: 'The world had been a Wilderness overgrown with Thorns, and Wild Beasts, and Serpents: Which now by the Labor of many hands, is reduced to the Beauty and Order of *Eden.*'[219] And if new worlds at home were to come into being through the industry of husbandmen, the newly-discovered lands abroad, whose inhabitants seemed utter strangers to the art of agriculture, provided even greater scope for improvement. The preaching of the gospel to all the world – a condition to be satisfied before the millennium – was another motivation. Indeed, for Eburne, 'the principall end of Plantations, is, or should be, the enlargement of *Christ's Church* on earth'.[220] John White agreed that 'God especially directs this of creating Colonies unto the planting and propagating of Religion.'[221] This motive could be associated with millenarianism – for the Gospel had to be preached to the whole world before the end – or combined with the development ethic. Traherne, for example, thought that England, too, might have been a wilderness, 'a blind corner of brutish Americans' had it not been for the fact that the Gospel 'is owned and fully received'.[222] The effects of the Gospel thus pertained not only to the spiritual realm, but had brought about a transformation of the very landscape of Christian countries.

For the seventeenth century, the story of the Fall was literal and not allegorical. It was about the material world, not merely the spiritual. It contained an imperative, as well as an indicative. True, it portrayed the

[216] Locke, *Two Treatises, Works*, v, 354, 356, 362.
[217] Ralph Austen, *A Treatise of Fruit-Trees* (Oxford, 1653), Epistle Dedicatory.
[218] Blith, *The English Improver Improved*, p. 4.   [219] Thomas Traherne, *Christian Ethicks*, p. 103.
[220] Eburne, *Pathway to Plantation*, Sig. B2v.
[221] Qu. in Webster, *Great Instauration*, p. 45, cf. p. 223.   [222] Qu. in Hill, *English Bible*, p. 138.

past, but also held out a vision of the future, a future in which the human race could attain a perfect knowledge of nature, and with that, a mastery of the world. Having once been cast out of a divinely-created Eden, it was now time for mankind to make amends, and begin the reconstruction of a paradise made with human hands.

LEARNING THE LANGUAGE OF NATURE

The pursuit of scientific activities, it should be clear, was an integral part of the attempt to revisit Eden, for such endeavours resulted in the rediscovery of lost knowledge, which in turn, conferred dominion. For Adam himself, however, there had been no need for such labours, no need, as Robert South had put it, 'to exhaust his time and impair his health' in order to arrive at pitiful and controverted conclusions. In possession of the language of nature, Adam had known the secret essences of all things without recourse to study and experiment. In the sixteenth and seventeenth centuries, many of those who sought to regain control of nature, attempted also to rediscover the language of Adam, or some symbolic system which would fulfil the promise of such a language. The 'language of nature' was thus variously understood to be the language which Adam had originally spoken, a system of natural symbols which could be found on objects and which bespoke the essence of things which bore them, or a written language in which the characters bore a real, rather than an arbitrary relation to the things signified. But however this language was conceived, a common thread ran through discussions of its nature: the *lingua Adamica* was a potential tool by which the natural world could be known and subdued. Knowing, naming, and commanding were linked by a literal reading of Genesis 2.19, where it is recorded that after the creation of all the animals, God paraded them before Adam to be named. The particular denominations which Adam bestowed upon the animals were thought to have been part of a natural language in which words were not arbitrary tokens of the things they represented, but the expression of the true nature of things.[223] Luther had written of Adam's naming of the creatures that 'because of the excellence of his nature, he views all the animals and thus arrives at such a knowledge of their nature that he can give each one a suitable name that harmonizes with its nature'.[224] In the first half of the seventeenth

---

[223] Webster, *Academiarum Examen*, p. 30. Bacon, *Advancement of Learning*, 1.i.3 (p. 6). For dissenting views, see Mersenne, *Harmonie universelle* (Paris, 1636, 37) 1.47.65; Le Clerc, *Twelve Dissertations*, p. 188. Also see Bono, *Word of God*, ch. 8.   [224] Luther, *Luther's Works*, 1, 119–21.

century, this was still a common view. According to Robert Bostocke, Adam 'was endowed with a singuler knowledge, wisdom and light of nature, that assoone as he did behold any beast, he by & by did so exactly now all their natures, powers, properties and vertues, that he gaue them names, apt, meete, and agreeable to their natures'.[225] Our first father, said Reynolds, 'was able by Intuition of the Creatures to give unto them all Names, according to their severall Properties and Natures; and shew himselfe, as well a Philosopher, as a Lord'.[226]

This exegetical tradition conferred an almost magical status on the natural names of things. Those who aim at a universal knowledge of the creatures, wrote John Pettus, 'may by due inspection into them gain the whole Body of *Philosophy*; which doubtless were sooner obtained if we could be informed of the true *Primitive Names* of all Creatures'.[227] Francis Bamfield declared that 'several secrets in Nature' could be found in 'the Letter and Spirit of the Significancy of the Original Language'.[228] In his attack on the universities, John Webster opposed the traditional study of ancient texts 'the recovery and restauration of the Catholicke language in which lies hid all the rich treasury of natures admirable and excellent secrets'. To know the true name of an object, Webster believed, was to know its 'internal natures, vertues, effects, operations, and qualities'.[229] John Webb, who thought that Chinese characters might hold the secret of the original language, spoke of the 'GOLDEN-MINE of Learning, which from all ANTIQUITY hath lain concealed in the PRIMITIVE TONGUE'.[230] Knowledge of this language, furthermore, brought power. Luther had suggested that from Adam's ability to name the animals 'there also followed, of course, the rule over all the animals.' Adam's knowledge of names and natures thus enabled him 'to compel lions, bears, boars, tigers' with a single word.[231] Walker followed Luther in suggesting that it was because Adam knew the names of the animals, that he was able to

---

[225] Bostocke, *Auncient Phisicke*, Sig Fiiii.r – Gi.v; Lightfoot, *A Few and New Observations*, p. 4; Cf. Simon, *A Commentary*, p. 54.

[226] Reynolds, *Treatise of the Passions*, pp. 6, 438. These writers suggest that Adam's knowledge enabled him to give the creatures fit names. Some commentators stressed the converse: that from the names, would come knowledge. Thus, according to Donne, Adam 'was able to decipher the nature of every creature in the name thereof'. Sermon, CI, *Works*, ed. Henry Alford (London, 1839) 6 vols., IV, 340. Arnold Williams suggests that this latter emphasis was more common in the seventeenth century. *The Common Expositor*, p. 81.

[227] Pettus, *History of Adam and Eve*, p. 60.

[228] Francis Bamfield, *Miqra qadosh, The Holy Scripture* (London, 1684) Title page.

[229] Webster, *Academiarum Examen*, pp. 32, 30. Cf. Kircher, *Oedipus Aegyptiacus*, 3 vols. (Rome, 1653–4), II, 42–57; Walker, *History of the Creation*, pp. 192f.; Webb, *Historical Essay*, p. 147.

[230] Webb, *Historical Essay*, Epistle Dedicatory.   [231] Luther, *Luther's Works*, I, 119–21.

call them to him at will.[232] Francis Bacon agreed that 'the imposition of names' was one of the summary parts of knowledge, and that with such knowledge came dominion: 'whensoever he shall be able to call the creatures by their true names he shall again command them'.[233] Recovery of this original language, then, would enable not only a reversal of the losses incurred at Babel, but would also restore to the human race much that had been lost by the Fall.

The Renaissance doctrine of 'signatures' – that natural objects bore some sign indicating their use – was an early attempt to reconstruct the language of nature. The signatures of plants, explained Henry More, provide 'a certain Key to enter Man into the knowledge and use of the treasure of Nature'. More pointed out that 'several *Herbs* are marked with some *mark* or *sign* that intimates their virtue, what they are good for'. Signatures are thus 'like the *Inscriptions* upon Apothecaries Boxes, that the Master of the Shop sets on that the Apprentice may read them'.[234] One of the chief ways in which signs could indicate the use of the object which bore them was through their resemblance to some part of the body. In the words of John Edwards, one of the last exponents of the doctrine: 'the outward *Signature* or impression which is on some Plants, shews their inward Virtue; and . . . from the resemblance which they have to the parts of a Man's Body we may gather their secret power, and know to what particular part they are appropriated'.[235] The language of signatures also reinforced the notion that all the things of nature had been created for human use. Paracelsus wrote that 'It is not God's will that what he has created for our benefit, and the gifts he has given us should remain hidden.' Consequently, 'nothing is without external and visible signs which take the form of special marks, just as a man who has buried a treasure marks the spot so that he may find it again'. Matthew Barker reasoned in a similar fashion that 'when we observe in these fruits of the Earth such vertues and qualities that are both nourishing and *medicinal* to the Body of Man, and some of them have *signatures* and *Characters* upon them that declare their vertue, and

---

[232] Walker, *History of the Creation*, pp. 193, 229

[233] Bacon, *Advancement of Learning*, I.vi.6 (p. 38); Bacon, *Of the Interpretation of Nature*, 1, *Works*, III, 222.

[234] More, *Antidote*, p. 56. Cf. Dedicatory poem by Anthracium Botanophilum' in Coles, *Adam in Eden*:

> Kind Nature alwayes hath held forth her Book
> But few have thought it worth their pains to look
> Within those precious Leaves wherein each cure
> Is plainly legible in *Signature*.

[235] Edwards, *A Demonstration*, pt 1, p. 133.

what part of Mans Body they are useful to, it shewes they were created for the use of Man'.[236]

A favourite example was the walnut, which 'hath upon its Fruit the Signature of the Head and Brain'. Walnuts were thus prescribed for various ills of the head.[237] There were numerous other signature-bearing plants. Quincies, which are 'a downy and hairy fruit' were 'accounted good for the fetching again Hair that has fallen by the French Pox'. The Maiden-hair plant was also touted as a good hair restorer.[238] For the same affliction, William Coles suggested a 'Dedoction of the long Mosse that hangs upon Trees in a manner like hair'. Such a preparation was said to be 'very profitable to be used in the falling off of the hair, and this it doth by Signature'.[239] *Umbilicus veneris* and *Satyrions* were said to be 'powerful to provoke Lust' on account of their having 'evident resemblance of genital parts upon them'.[240] Della Porta informs us that the herb 'scorpius' resembles the tail of the scorpion and is good against the bite of the creature, and that 'the stone Ophites resembleth the species and spots of Serpents, and it cures their bitings'.[241] In like fashion, liverwort was said to be good for the liver; lungwort for the lungs, kidney beans for the kidneys.[242]

The rationale behind the efficacy of signatures was the ancient conception of the microcosm. Each aspect of the living environment was represented somewhere in the human body, and this correspondence accounted for the healing power of herbs. George Herbert wrote in the poem 'Man' that 'He is in little all the sphere; / Herbs gladly cure our flesh, because that they / Finde their acquaintance there.'[243] Nicholas Culpeper, author of one of the standard seventeenth-century herbals, agreed that the curative properties of herbs were related to the fact that the world was 'one united body, and man an epitome of it'. For Culpeper, however, the effectiveness of herbal cures was linked to the stars: 'he who would know the reason of the Herbs must look up as high

---

[236] Paracelsus, *Die 9 Bücher der Natura Rerum*, in *Sämliche Werke*, ed. Sudhoff, xi, 393. Barker, *Natural Theology*, p. 25. On paracelsian signatures as a language of nature, see Bono, *Word of God*, pp. 129–39.

[237] Edwards, *A Demonstration*, pt i, p. 134; Croll, *Of Signatures*, Preface; Coles, *Adam in Eden*, p. 3; Richard Saunders, *Saunders Physiognomie and Chiromancie, Metoposcopie*, 2nd edn (London, 1671), Preface.

[238] *Ibid.*, p. 56; Croll, *Of Signatures*, Coles, *Adam in Eden*, p. 3; Culpeper, *Complete Herbal*, pp. 156, 209.

[239] Coles, *Adam in Eden*, p. 31. [240] More, *Antidote*, pp. 56f.; Cf. Coles, *Adam in Eden*, p. 70.

[241] Della Porta, *Natural Magick*, p. 17. Cf. More, *Antidote*, p. 57.

[242] Croll, *Of Signatures*, Preface; Edwards, *A Demonstration*, pt i, p. 135; Culpeper, *Complete Herbal*, pp. 151, 154, 27; Paracelsus, *Werke* xiii, 376f. [243] George Herbert, 'Man', lines 23f.

as the stars, astrologically'.[244] Sympathies and antipathies thus extended out from this world into the celestial regions beyond. Oswald Croll, who devoted a complete work to the doctrine of signatures, linked a range of doctrines – the image of God in the creatures, hidden virtues and their manifest signs or signatures, astrological influence, analogy and sympathy, microcosm and macrocosm. These, together, pointed to 'the foot-steps of the invisible God in the Creatures, the Shadow and Image of the Creatour imprest in the Creatures, or that Internal force, and occult vertue of Operation, (which as Natures Gift is insited, and infused by the most high God, into the Plant or Animal, from the Signature and mutual Analogick Sympathy and harmonius concordance of Planets, with the Members of the Human Body)'. By virtue of these signatures of the Deity, 'All Herbs, Flowers, Trees, and other things which proceed out of the Earth, are Books, and Magick Signes.' [245]

Signatures, then, could reasonably be regarded as a language of nature, and were supposed by supporters of the doctrine to have been the means by which Adam had come into his knowledge. Boehmenist John Ellistone wrote that 'Nature hath given Marks and Notes to every thing, whereby it may be known; and this is *the language of Nature*.'[246] Boehme himself had written that Nature 'hath given Marks and Notes to every thing, whereby it may be known' and these marks are nothing less than '*the language of Nature*, which telleth for what every thing is good and profitable'.[247] Thomas Browne, despite reservations about signatures, still regarded them the most likely source of Adam's knowledge. 'The finger of God hath left an inscription upon all his works . . . that doth express their natures', he wrote . 'By these letters God calls the stars by their names, and by this alphabet Adam assigned to every creature a name peculiar to its nature.'[248] Webster agreed that Adam had once been able to read this language, 'wherein were hidden and involved . . . all the treasury of those *ideal*-signatures'. Adam had understood 'both their internal natures and external signatures'.[249] Webster thought that

---

[244] Culpeper, *Complete Herbal*, p. vi. Culpeper complains in this passage that fellow herbalists Gerrard and Parkinson were ignorant of the reasons for the efficacy of herbs, because they did not extend their investigations to the astrological basis of cures.

[245] Oswald Croll, *A Treatise of Oswaldus Crollius of Signatures* (London, 1669). Preface. Cf. Boehme, *Signatura Rerum*, p. 4; Barker, *Natural Theology*, p. 25; Saunders, *Physiognomie and Chiromancie*, Preface.

[246] Boehme, *Signatura Rerum*, Preface, Sig. A4r. Ellistone believed that this language could only be understood by the action of the Holy Spirit, for it was this spirit which had reversed the curse of Babel on the day of Pentecost, giving forth 'the true sence and meaning of all languages in one'.

[247] Boehme, *Signatura Rerum*, Sig A4r; Cf. p. 4; Boehme, *The Second Book*, Sigs. A3v–r.

[248] Browne, *Religio Medici*, ii.2 (p. 65).   [249] Webster, *Academiarum Examen*, pp. 26f., 29

we too might learn this language, and in some measure partake in the knowledge of Adam. As part-time poet Wharton put it: 'But that Vocal *Signatures* explain / The end of their *Production*, and *Restore* / To us, in part, what *Adam* knew before.'[250]

Despite, or perhaps because of, the strong support of the Paracelsians and Boehmenists, the doctrine of signatures was subjected to increasing criticism over the course of the seventeenth century.[251] Detractors pointed out that not all useful plants bore signatures, that poisonous plants exhibited what appeared to be signatures, and that the parts of plants which bore the supposed signatures varied widely. Henry More was unperturbed by such criticism, responding that 'the Theatre of the world is an exercise of Mans wit, not a laxy *Polyanthea* or book of Common-places'. To some degree, all things are obscure, explained More, in order 'that the sedulity of that divine Spark, the Soul of Man, may have matter of conquest and triumph, when he has done bravely by a superadvenient assistance of his God'.[252] Divine signatures give us ample hints, but for the rest we must conduct our own investigations. William Coles offered a similar defence. Signatures were 'the Books out of which the Ancients first learned the Vertues of Herbes; Nature or rather the God of nature, having stamped on divers of them legible Characters to discover their uses, though he hath left others also without any, that after he had showed them the way, they by their labour and industry, which renders every thing more acceptable, might find out the rest'.[253] Jacob Boehme attributed the apparently random nature of signatures to human failings. Our inability to decipher the language of nature was just another consequence of the Fall, one which could be overcome only through supernatural means: 'the Spirit doth open up unto him the *Signature*, then he understandeth'.[254]

Yet, even advocates of signatures were forced to concede that the doctrine led to many abuses and absurdities.[255] Sir Thomas Browne, although sympathetic, complained that many of the supposed resemblances proved on closer examination to be rather dubious. In many of the instances put forward by Croll and Della Porta, Browne argued that 'the semblance is but postulatory'.[256] Francis Bacon also distinguished 'the true signatures and marks set upon the works of creation' from

---

[250] Coles, *Adam in Eden*, dedicatory poem.
[251] Agnes Arbor, *Herbals, their Origin and Evolution, a Chapter in the History of Botany, 1470–1670* (Cambridge University Press, 1912), p. 208.   [252] More, *Antidote*, pp. 56f.
[253] Coles, *Adam in Eden*, To the reader.   [254] Boehme, *Signature Rerum*, p. 1.
[255] R. W. Crausius devoted a chapter of his work on signatures to what he considered abuses of the doctrine. *Dissertatio inauguralis medica de signaturis vegetabilium* (Jena, 1697). See Prest, *Garden of Eden*, p. 64.   [256] Browne, *Pseudodoxia Epidemica*, II.vi (I, 140).

'empty dogmas'.[257] The defence of More and Coles was in any case self-defeating. If, by human ingenuity, the uses of those plants which did not bear signatures could be determined, the practical applications of all plants could as easily be ascertained. More fatal for the doctrine than any of these factors, however, was the failure of the microcosmic principles on which it was based. In his attack on the doctrine of signatures Noah Biggs was to declare: 'I am assured by faith, that neither is *man* the Image of *nature*, nor *Nature* the image of *man*.'[258] With the demise of this reciprocal set of resemblances the doctrine of signatures simply slipped from sight. Like astrology, which according to Ann Geneva, was similarly positioned 'within the search for requisite linguistic norms of a natural philosophical language', it became extinct 'because it reflected a now extinct world of neo-Platonic interdependent harmonies'.[259]

Another suggestion involving physical, rather than spoken or written symbols, was the language of gesture.[260] John Webster suggested in a passing remark that the language of the 'deaf and dumb' might be an instance of a universal language.[261] In his *Chirologia* (1644), John Bulwer provided a systematic defence of the idea. Human gestures, he claimed, were 'naturall signes' which enjoyed many advantages over conventional speech. The motions of the hand, said Bulwer, 'proceed from the meere instinct of Nature, and all these motions and habits of the *Hand* are purely naturall, not positive; nor in their senses remote from the true nature of the things that are implyed'.[262] Bulwer pointed out that human gestures amounted to a natural language which had survived the confusion of Babel. They were traces of a paradisiacal past when man and beast comprehended each other's discourse. Such considerations were linked to Renaissance speculations about a general science of somatic signs, formalised in the disciplines of physiognomy and its related branches chiromancy, podomancy, metoscopy.[263] These pursuits dealt

---

[257] Bacon, *Novum Organum*, ii.23 (p. 31).

[258] Biggs, *Mataetechnia Medicinae Praxeos*, p. 33.

[259] Ann Geneva, *Astrology and the Seventeenth-Century Mind* (Manchester University Press, 1996), pp. 12f. On astrology as a language system, see pp. 263–85.

[260] For an illuminating discussion of natural or bodily languages, see Richard Kroll, *The Material World*, pp. 201–25.   [261] Webster, *Academiarum Examen*, p. 25.

[262] John Bulwer, *Chirologia: or the Naturall Langvage of the Hand* (London, 1644), pp. 2, 3.

[263] Physiognomy dealt with general bodily signs, chiromancy with signs on the hand, podomancy on the foot, metoscopy on the head. Some of the more influential works in the field were Michel Lescot, *Physionomie*, (Paris, 1540); Jean d'Indagine, *Chiromance* (Lyon, 1549); Barthélemy Coclès, *Physiognomonia* (Strasbourg, 1533); Giovambattista della Porta, *De humana physiognomia*, (Hanover, 1593); Robert Fludd, *Utriusque cosmi historia* (Oppenheim, 1619); Jerome Cardan, *Metoscopia* (Paris, 1658); Cureau de la Chambre's own *Discourse on the Principles of Chiromancy* (London, 1658); Charles Le Brun, *Conférence de M. Le Brun sur l'Expression Générale et Particulière* (1698).

with 'external or sensible signes' which were thought to make possible 'the knowledge of the inside by the outside'.[264] Physiognomy, Cureau de la Chambre explains in the first volume of *Les caractères des passions* (1658), concerns 'the exact knowledge deduced from physical effects'. These '*Effects*, or *Signs*, which are imprinted on the Body' are one of two kinds: 'one is *Natural*, which proceeds from the constitutions of the Body, and the Elementary Causes; the other, the *Astrological*, which proceeds from the Stars or Celestial Bodies'.[265] These bodily signs give a far more accurate indication of the disposition of the soul than any amount of verbiage. 'There cannot be an assured judgement made of the Soul's inclinations', insists Cureau, 'otherwise than by the proper and permanent Signs, and that these are commonly drawn from the Figure, the Air of the Countenance, the Motions, and the Fleshy parts of the Body'.[266] Animals, too, exhibited such signs, which could thus convey information about the interior motions of the soul of the beast. Wolfgang Franzius informs us that 'as horses shew their anger by hair, so do Lyons by their Tayls, which they strike against the ground when at any time that are angered; but when their passion is a little over, they strike their own backs with it'.[267] Such signs were believed by some to be nothing less than a complete language, and it was frequently alleged, in particular against the Cartesians, that the human inability to read these languages was a failing on our part rather than theirs. Once, we had enjoyed the ability to comprehend the languages of birds and beasts; now, as a result of the Fall, the events which took place at Babel, or simply on account of the artificial and affected structures of human languages, this ability had gone.[268]

Neither signatures nor bodily signs and gestures ultimately proved suitable to the framing, or rediscovery of a universal language. Spoken words and written symbols seemed more likely candidates, if for no other reason than that it had clearly been a common spoken tongue which had been confused at Babel. While signs and gestures might overcome some of the communication problems which had ensued after Babel, they were generally considered to be poor substitutes for a

---

[264] Havers, *Discourses of the Virtuosi*, pp. 139f. Boehme wrote that in the beasts, 'every thing as it is inwardly . . . so it is outwardly signed.' *Signatura Rerum*, p. 3, cf. p. 77.

[265] Marin Cureau de la Chambre, *Les caractères des passions*, I and II (Amsterdam, 1658); E. T., *The Art How to Know Men*, pp. 191f., 195, 204.

[266] la Chambre, *The Art How to Know Men*, pp. 191f., 195, 204.

[267] Franzius, *History of Brutes*, p. 52.

[268] Montaigne, *Essayes*, II, 159–61, 167, 181; Charron, *Of Wisdom*, p. 244. Cf. William Holder, *Elements of Speech* (London, 1669), pp. 5f.; Plutarch, *De sollertia animalium*, 973A; Porphyry, *De abstinentia* III.

common spoken or written system of communication. Some thought that a more promising prospect for a universal language lay in the hope that the tongue which Adam had originally spoken was still extant somewhere in the world, or had been preserved in written form either in ancient texts or in other monuments from the past. Thomas Browne sceptically recounted the common Renaissance view 'that children committed unto the school of Nature, without instruction, would naturally speak the primitive language of the world'. While the trial seems never to have been conducted, it was widely believed that this language would turn out to be Hebrew.[269] This accounts for the interest of the Cabbalists in the Hebrew language.[270] Herodotus had alluded to a similar scenario, but concluded that the children of nature would speak Phrygian.[271] Other contenders included Samarian (or Samaratan), Chaldean, and even such relatively modern languages as Low German.[272] What counted against these candidates, however, was the fact that their written form was alphabetical, and their words did not in any way resemble the things they referred to. However ancient they might have been they could not have been that language in which was encoded the true nature of things. As John Webb declared, 'In vain do we search for the PRIMITIVE Language to be remaining with those Nations whose Languages consist in Alphabets.'[273] And so the search for the primitive tongue gravitated towards the written forms of languages with real characters – Chinese and ancient Egyptian.

The 'real' nature of Chinese characters had originally been noted by Bacon. 'It is the use of China, and the kingdoms of the High Levant', he

---

[269] Browne, *Pseudodoxia Epidemica* v.xxiii; vi.i (i, 434f., 442). On the priority of Hebrew, see Gulielmus Postellus, *De originibus seu de Hebraicae linguae* (Parisiis, 1538), fols. Aiiir–Aivr; J. H. Heidegger, *De historia sacra patriarchum*, 2 vols. (Amstelodami, 1667–71), i, 462f.; Richard Simon, *A Critical History of the Old Testament* (London, 1682), i.xiv (pp. 97–101); John Selden, *De Synedriis . . . veterum Ebraeorum*, Prolegomenon, cap. iii; Thomas Brett, *A Chronological Essay on the Sacred History* (London, 1629), pp. 56–93; Simon Patrick, *A Commentary*, pp. 218f. Also see discussion in H. Pinard de la Boullaye, *L'Etude Compareé des Religions* (Paris: Gabriel Beauchesne, 1922) pp. 158–63.

[270] Cabbalists believed that the Hebrew words of scripture contained the knowledge of Adam encoded in some cryptic form. An interpreter in possession of the right key, could unlock the secrets of Adam's original knowledge. John Wilkins sceptically observed: 'And if you will believe the Jews, the holy spirit hath purposely involved in the words of scripture, every secret that belongs to any art or science, under such cabalisms as these. And if a man were but expert in unfolding of them, [sic] it were easy for him to get as much knowledge as Adam had in his innocency, or human nature is capable of.' *Mercury*, p. 41.　　[271] Herodotus, *Histories*, ii.4

[272] Nicholas Serarius, *Prolegomena biblicae* (Moguntiaci, 1612), pp. 7–16; Mathew Hale, *Primitive Origination*, p. 162; Johannes Becanus, *Origines Antwerpianiae* (Antverpiae, 1569), p. 534. Also see P. Cormelius, *Languages in Seventeenth- and Early Eighteenth-Century Imaginary Voyages* (Geneva, 1965), Ch. 1.　　[273] Webb, *Historical Essay*, p. 150.

observed, 'to write in characters real, which express neither letters nor words in gross.'[274] Thomas Browne pursued the matter further. In the brief essay 'Of Languages', he pointed out that because the confusion of languages only fell upon those who took part in the construction of the ill-fated tower, the primitive language might have been preserved in some remote corner of the globe. He then observed that the 'Chinoys, who live at the bounds of the earth' have a very ancient language by virtue of a 'common character', and that they could trace their written history back to 'Poncuus, who is conceived our Noah'.[275] However, Browne thought it more likely that Egyptian hieroglyphics were the written form of the ancient language, and pursued his enquiries into Chinese no further. The most outspoken apologist for the priority of the Chinese language in the seventeenth century was John Webb. In *An Historical Essay, Endeavoring a Probability that the Language of the Empire of China is the Primitive Language* (1669), Webb set out his reasoning. The language of our first parents, Webb believed, would have survived without alteration to the time of Babel. It followed that Noah 'carried the *Primitive Language* into the Ark with him'.[276] That the Ark had eventually settled somewhere in the East, had been proposed by Walter Raleigh, and confirmed by a number of seventeenth-century writers.[277] From this Webb concluded that Noah and his progeny had settled in China, and had established the original language there. Most important of all, however, the settlers of China had not taken part in the building project at Babel, and had thus not been subjected to the curse of confusion. On account of China's isolation and her early use of writing, the original language had been preserved virtually intact up until the present.[278]

Webb's thesis met with a luke-warm reception. Matthew Hale thought it 'a novel conceit'. Wilkins, despite an early enthusiasm for Chinese characters, claimed the Chinese language to be 'very imperfect' and thus unlikely to have been the language of Adam. The symbols were too equivocal, too difficult to draw, too numerous, and in the final analysis, not truly representative of the things they depicted.[279] Cave

---

[274] Bacon, *Advancement of Learning*, II.xvi.2 (p. 131).
[275] Thomas Browne, 'Of Languages, and Particularly of the Saxon Tongue', *Works*, ed. Geoffrey Keynes (London: Faber and Faber, 1928) III, 71. [276] Webb, *Historical Essay*, pp. 16f.
[277] Walter Raleigh, *The Historie of the World in Five Bookes*, (London, 1652), I.vii.10 (p. 96); Nathaniel Carpenter, *Geography Delineated Forth in Two Bookes*, 2nd edn (Oxford, 1635), p. 213; Heylyn, *Cosmographie*, p. 18; Patrick, *A Commentary*, pp. 145–7.
[278] Webb, *Historical Essay*, pp. 16f., 35–44, 143–5. Cf. Bacon, *New Atlantis*, p. 223.
[279] Wilkins, *Mercury*, pp. 106f., *Essay toward a Real Character*, (London, 1668), pp. 10, 451.

Beck, who like Wilkins was working on an artificial universal language of his own, also regarded Chinese characters as deficient in a number of respects.[280] Eventually Robert Hooke was commissioned by the Royal Society to investigate the Chinese language with a view to determining its antiquity, and the possibility that it was the language which Adam had spoken. Hooke decided that Chinese was probably the most ancient form of writing still in use, but concluded disappointingly that the present Chinese language had 'no Affinity at all with the Character, the true Primitive or First Language, or Pronunciation of it, having been lost'.[281] The characters of Chinese were, in any case, extremely difficult to master, and this had always stood against them. As William Wotton, author of *A Discourse concerning the Confusion of Languages at Babel*, sourly remarked, a language is anything but natural when 'eight or Ten of the best Years of a Man's life must be spent in learning to read'.[282] This was fair comment from Wotton who himself had been a precocious linguist, learning Latin and Greek from the age of four and Hebrew soon afterwards.[283]

Egyptian hieroglyphics were another favourite contender. The land of the Pharaohs was regarded by many as the cradle of civilisation – 'one of the most ancient schools of the world' as Bacon had put it – and her hieroglyphics were more obviously representative of natural objects than Chinese characters.[284] Athanasius Kircher thought that China had borrowed its language and form of writing from Egypt, making Egypt's hieroglyphics more ancient than China's.[285] Thomas Browne, as we have mentioned, also favoured ancient Egyptian over Chinese. However, these ancient symbols were deemed to suffer from the same defects as the Chinese, and the fact that they had successfully resisted all attempts at translation counted decisively against them.[286]

By the eighth decade of the seventeenth century, members of the Royal Society had all but abandoned the search for the primitive language. Not only did the practical difficulties seem insuperable, but the quest was also tainted with overtones of an undesirable mystical

---

[280] Cave Beck, *The Universal Character* (London, 1657) Preface; Hale, *Primitive Origination*, p. 163.
[281] Hooke, 'Some Observations, and Conjectures concerning Chinese Characters', *Philosophical Transactions of the Royal Society*, XVI (1696), 63–78. (65, 73).
[282] Wotton, *Reflections of Ancient and Modern Learning* (London, 1694), p. 154.
[283] Levine, *Dr. Woodward's Shield*, p. 19.
[284] Bacon, *Advancement of Learning*, I.vi.9 (p. 39); cf. II.xvi.2 (p. 131);
[285] Kircher, *Of the Various Voyages and Travels undertaken into China*, in Peter de Goyer and Jacob de Keyzer, *An Embassy from the east India Company of the United Provinces to the grand Tartar Cham Emperour of China* (London, 1669), pp. 75f. Cf. Kircher, *Oedipus Aegyptiacus*, pt II.
[286] See e.g. Beck, *Universal Character*, Preface.

cabbalism. Webster, for example, was accused by Ward and Wilkins, of 'canting Discourse about the language of nature', more appropriate to Boehme and 'the highly illuminated fraternity of the *Rosycrucians*'.[287] Despite such reservations, however, Ward and Wilkins, and indeed any number of fellows of the Royal Society, were enthusiastic about the prospects of inventing, as opposed to discovering, a universal language and a real character.[288] Between the years of 1653 and 1668 several schemes were proposed, both in England and abroad: Thomas Urquhart, *Logopandecteision, or An Introduction to the Universal Language* (1653), Cave Beck, *The Universal Character* (1657), George Dalgarno, *Ars Signorum* (1661), Athanasius Kircher, *Polygraphia nova et universalis ex combinatoria arte detecta* (1663), Gottfried Leibniz, *Dissertatio de arte combinatoria* (1666), and best known of all, John Wilkins, *Essay Towards a Real Character and a Philosophical Language* (1684).[289] The schemes were many and various. Beck used a dictionary in which terms were allocated a number. When the language was in use, the relevant numbers were preceded by letters which determined tense, gender, case, and number. 'Honour thy father and Mother', for example, would be rendered 'leb2314 p2477 and pf2477' – hardly the 'sweetest cadences' and 'Poetical figures' which Beck had promised.[290] Dalgarno had retained the use of words. In his system, the first verse of Genesis reads: 'Dan semu, Sava samesa Nam tun Nom.'[291] Wilkins' scheme relied upon symbols of his own devising, and the example he used was the Lord's Prayer.[292] But however the systems were conceived, their authors almost invariably announced that it was their design to ameliorate the consequences of the events which had long ago transpired on the plain of Shinar.

As early as 1646, Robert Boyle had written to Samuel Hartlib expressing an interest in the 'real character', and venturing the opinion that it would 'make amends to mankind for what their pride lost them at the tower of *Babel*'.[293] Cave Beck's supporters spoke of his achievements as a 'reprieve' from 'bable's curse', or as a second Pentecost.[294] A

[287] Ward, *Vindiciae academiarum*, p. 5. [288] *Ibid.*, pp. 20f.

[289] For a complete list see James Knowlson, *Universal Language Schemes in England and France: 1600–1800*, Appendix B, pp. 224–32. Also Clark Emery, 'John Wilkins' Universal Language', *Isis*, 38 (1947–8), 174–85; Theodore Singer, 'Hieroglyphs, Real Characters, and the Idea of a Natural Language in English Seventeenth-Century Thought', *JHI* 50 (1989) 49–70.

[290] In the lexicon 2477 is the number allocated to 'Father'; 'p' indicates substantive person male; 'pf' substantive person female. [291] Dalgarno, *Ars Signorum*, (London, 1661), p. 118

[292] Wilkins, *Real Character*, p. 395.

[293] Robert Boyle, Letter to Samuel Hartlib, March 19, 1646/7, *Works*, I, xxxvii.

[294] Beck, *Universal Character*, Preface and Dedicatory poems.

universal language would 'have repaired the ruines of *Babell*'. [295] Others spoke of the specific aspects of the curse which they believed would be overcome. It was certainly not insignificant that Beck, Wilkins, and Dalgarno had all used biblical texts to illustrate their systems. Wilkins thought that his universal language would 'contribute much to the clearing of some of our Modern differences in *Religion*, by unmasking many wild errors, that shelter themselves under the guise of affected phrases'. Beck believed that a universal language would help make the true religion universal once more, as it had been before Babel. The universal character would be 'a singular means of propagating all sorts of Learning and true Religion in the world'. [296] George Dalgarno similarly prescribed his language scheme for such activities as 'civilising barbarous Nations, Propagating the Gospel, and encreasing Traffique and Commerce'. [297]

The systems of Beck, Wilkins, and Dalgarno were thus ambitious, but in the final analysis, ambitious failures. Even so, the claims made on their behalf were far more modest than those which Webster and the Rosicrucians made for the language of Adam. These artificial constructs were to reverse the curse of Babel, but not necessarily that of the Fall. A universal language would facilitate universal communication, reduce ambiguities, promote understanding, liberate scholars from the linguistic errors to which they were particularly prone. But no-one thought any longer that such languages would somehow unlock the secrets of Adam's encyclopaedic knowledge. The best of the schemes offered a way of ordering and symbolising what human ingenuity had discovered, but they were unable to penetrate into the unknown. The organisation of Wilkins' *Real Character* offers of a glimpse of the future direction of such systems – taxonomy. [298]

The only real alternative to the rather unsatisfactory compromise which located the value of universal language schemes in their ability to classify natural objects, was to search for an alternative language of

---

[295] Webb, *Historical Essay*, pp. 24f. Beck, *Universal Character*, Preface.
[296] Wilkins, *Real Character*, Epistle Dedicatory; Beck, *Universal Character*, Preface. Bishop William Bedell cherished a similar hope. See Benjamin DeMott, 'Comenius and the Real Character in England', *PMLA* 70 (1955) 1068–81.
[297] Dalgarno, *Ars Signorum*, 'Letter of Recommendation', qu. in James Knowlson, *Universal Language Schemes in England and France 1600–1800* (University of Toronto Press, 1975), p.11.
[298] Mary Slaughter, *Universal Languages and Scientific Taxonomy in the Seventeenth Century* (Cambridge University Press, 1972); Vivian Salmon, *The Works of Francis Lodowick* (London: Longmans, 1972), pp. viif.

nature in the abstract formulae of mathematics.[299] The language of mathematics was not, it seemed, a constructed language, for mathematical relations seemed intrinsic in nature. And as James Knowlson has pointed out, it is surely no accident that many of those interested in the universal character – Ward, Wilkins, Wallis, Pell, Newton, Mersenne, Descartes, Peiresck, and Leibniz – were mathematicians.[300] When Boyle wrote to Hartlib in 1646/7 about the prospects of a real character, he clearly thought of a universal language as a kind of semantic equivalent of algebra: 'since our arithmetical Characters are understood by all Nations of *Europe* . . . I conceive no impossibility, that opposes the doing that in words, that we see already done in numbers'.[301] Robert Hooke expressed the similar hope that natural history be expressed, like analytical geometry, 'in a few letters or Characters'.[302] Galileo, of course, had already claimed that the language of nature was mathematics, and that only to mathematicians was given the privilege of a full understanding of the world.[303] Subsequently, Newton's *Philosophiae naturalis principia mathematica* (1686–7) was to provide the final, and most important, phase in the mathematisation of the physical universe. The nature of physical objects became insignificant in accounts of their behaviour. Order was to be imposed on the objects of nature, not through an understanding of their essential qualities, but through the discovery of the laws which they obeyed. These laws were external to their natures, and were demonstrably mathematical. Even the study of the *nature* of the forces which operated upon objects, a subject which Newton himself had not wholly abandoned, was eventually to be replaced by a new preoccupation with the *laws* of forces. The identification of mathematics as a language of nature was the final stage in the imposition of the new ordering principles to which physical objects were subject. It represents, on the one hand, the last stage in the evacuation of meaning from the natural world, and on the other the triumph of mathematical physics – the most conspicuous feature of the scientific achievement of the seventeenth century. If Galileo and Newton had been the prime movers in the discovery of the mathematical language of nature, the quest for that

---

[299] Foucault has made the interesting observation that knowledge in the early modern period is related to two kinds of ordering principles: 'When dealing with the ordering of simple natures, one has recourse to a *mathesis*, of which the universal method is algebra. When dealing with the ordering of complex natures . . . one has to constitute a *taxinomia*. . .' *Taxinomia* and *mathesis*, in other words, together constitute the ways in which classical knowledge is organised. *Order of Things*, p. 72.   [300] Knowlson, *Universal Language Schemes*, p. 23.

[301] Boyle, Letter to Hartlib, March 19, 1646/7, *Works*, I, xxxviii.

[302] Qu. in Markley, *Fallen Languages*, p. 67.   [303] *Discoveries and Opinions of Galileo*, pp. 237–8.

language was no better exemplified than in the biography of Leibniz, who shared with Newton the discovery of the differential calculus which was to prove to be one of the most powerful tools for the mathematisation of the natural world. In the words of Frances Yates:

Leibniz conducted his search, moving meditatively in the world of the past amongst the magic 'characters', the signs of the alchemists, the images of the astrologers, of Dee's monad formed of the characters of the seven planets, of the rumoured Adamic language, magically in contact with reality, of the Egyptian hieroglyphs in which truth was hidden. Out of all this he emerges, like his century emerging from the occultism of the Renaissance, finding the true *notae*, the characters nearest to reality in the symbols of mathematics.[304]

The seventeenth century quest for a language of nature, a real character, a universal language – signifies an awareness of the absence of ordering principles in nature. They are not merely attempts to revisit the encyclopaedic knowledge of an Adam, who through literal readings of Genesis had been reborn in the seventeenth-century imagination as polymath and scientist, but also to repair the gulf between words and things, a division which for the seventeenth century was the legacy of the Fall and Babel. Mathematics, it must be said, fulfilled only some of the functions of the ideal language. It did not penetrate to essences, it did not grasp natures, it did not provide meanings, it seemingly failed to grasp the full significance of living things. If Leibniz had satisfied himself that mathematics was the language of nature, Newton's own biography paints a different picture. Newton did not rest with his remarkable achievements in the field of mathematics, but devoted a substantial proportion of his considerable energies to alchemy and the study of scripture. It was his ambition to reunite the sciences of things and words, to unify science and biblical exegesis. This the greatest mind of the age failed to achieve.

At the very beginning of the medieval period, the book of nature was written in symbols which were laden with various meanings, but which were not related to each other in any systematic way. Nature was a vast lexicon in which objects were given meanings, but grammatical and syntactic linkages between the elements of the language were completely absent. By the end of the seventeenth century the wheel has come full circle. Natural objects have been stripped of their intrinsic meanings, and even their qualities and essences have gone. In the physics of Descartes and Newton, simple natural objects are denuded of all but

---

[304] *The Art of Memory*, p. 370.

basic quantitative properties. In this new language of nature, syntax has triumphed over semantics. Henceforth the science of nature will deal with the mathematical or classificatory rules which govern the relations between natural objects. The meaning of the things of nature will survive only in those vestigial, figurative expressions which are now the sole preserve of the poets. The two books, which were once of necessity read in unison and assigned meanings according to a single universal hermeneutics, now take separate paths. The seventeenth-century quest for natural language is the visible, historical consequence of the failure of this once powerful interpretive system. If my analysis has attributed to literalism the collapse of this system, for the seventeenth century thinkers whom we have considered it was instead symptomatic of the failure of all human systems of representation, a failure which with their renewed historical sense they attributed to the Fall and the confusion of tongues, and their pervasive and baleful influence.[305] As a result of these primordial events, it was believed, not only had their world been rendered mute, providing only minimal and indirect evidence of its divine author, but human discourses which sought to elucidate that world had been confounded and fragmented.

In his recent book on language and representation in the late seventeenth century, Robert Markley has argued that 'seventeenth-century religious and political controversies and the development of experimental science led to breakdowns of traditional systems of representation, specifically the Bible and the taxonomies of Aristotelian science.' He continues: 'this instant questioning of the semiotics of power also challenged the ecclesiastical and political authority of the Church and State, institutions which depended, in part, on their ability to monopolize and to disseminate their versions of an authoritative language'.[306] It is my contention that in the broader context of the changes which took place over the sixteenth and seventeenth centuries, the converse is true: that the development of experimental science was a response to the breakdown of traditional systems of representation, in particular as they were

---

[305] In an excellent book, *The Word of God and the Languages of Man*, which only came to my attention as I was completing final revisions for this chapter, James Bono has argued that Genesis accounts of the Fall and Babel became for the Renaissance and seventeenth century a 'master narrative' which informed the quest for a language of nature, eventually giving rise to scientific practices. (See esp. pp. 53–84.) The account he provides is more nuanced than the one I have given, and convincingly argues that different readings of Genesis promoted different scientific practices. Thus there were various interpretations of the Fall-Babel narrative, but on my account, all relied upon the historical or literal sense of text. The 'master narrative' became operative because it was at this time recognised to be a narrative, as opposed to an allegory or moral fable. [306] Markley, *Fallen Languages*, p. 25.

embodied in approaches to the biblical text. Faced with the anomic consequences of the failure of a longstanding hermeneutical framework, seventeenth-century thinkers viewed their situation in the light of the events of Eden and Babel, interpreting their only partially successful quest to discover a transparent language of nature in terms of the Babel event, and attempting to regain, at least in part, the kind of knowledge of nature enjoyed by the inhabitants of Eden. Both that predicament, and the categories used to characterise it, arose out of the new hermeneutical practices of the previous century.

Conclusion

I believe the intellectual life of the whole of western society is
increasingly being split into two polar groups. . . At one pole we
have the literary intellectuals . . . at the other scientists.

C.P. Snow, *The Two Cultures*.

In this book I have argued that the historical origins of two of the
hallmarks of modernity – the identification of the meaning of a text with
its author's intention, and the privileged status of scientific discourse –
were closely intertwined. The modern approach to texts, driven by the
agenda of the reformers and disseminated through Protestant religious
practices, created the conditions which made possible the emergence of
modern science. However much we might regret the passing of the old
certainties, one of the advantages of living in a post-modern world is that
it gives us a perspective from which to evaluate the previous age and
enables us to identify those features of modernity which up until its
apparent demise we had taken for granted. New approaches to texts
characteristic of the latter half of the twentieth century serve to remind
us of the historically-determined nature of all hermeneutical enterprises.
While the profusion of 'readings' characteristic of the post-modern age
might evoke a nostalgia for a time when all texts had a determinate
meaning, and there were clear criteria which enabled us to approach
that meaning, more importantly, they should also furnish us with
important insights into *pre*-modern readings of texts, and to the magnitude of the hermeneutical revolution which took place in the early-
modern period. Not only has post-modernism brought the identification
of meaning with authorial intention to an end: it also should make us
cognisant of the fact that this notion of meaning had a beginning. The
death of the author should remind us of the birth of the author, some
five hundred years ago. Whatever its merits, the modernist presumption
which equates meaning with authorial intention has, in my view, mas-
ked the true significance of those changes to methods of textual interpre-

tation which took place at the advent of the modern world, and which led in turn to new interpretations of the book of nature. Of course, at some level, we have always known that medieval exegetes relied upon an elaborate system of interpretation which seemed at best fanciful, and at worst, irrational, and in which author's intention or literal sense were but single elements amongst others. However, owing to the fact that the business of interpretation is currently restricted in its application to words, texts, and other human artifacts, and does not extend to things and physical systems, we have tended to overlook the ontological implications of the hermeneutics of the patristic period and the Middle Ages. Indeed, that there is now such a disparity between our approaches to words and things, that scientific and literary activities have become so alien to each other, that the 'two cultures' share increasingly less common ground, is owing largely to the break-down of that universal hermeneutics which, in pre-modern times, had informed the study of both the book of scripture and the book of nature. The transformations which brought on the birth of modernity moved western culture from the era of 'the two books' to that of 'the two cultures'.

Another reason that historians of early-modern science and religion have tended to overlook the impact of methods of biblical interpretation on the development of the sciences, I suspect, is to do with the contemporary association of biblical literalism with religious bigotry and hostility towards the sciences. Viewed from this perspective, a link between the emergence of biblical literalism and the development of modern science seems highly implausible. The real difficulty here is that the negative associations of biblical literalism are projected back into history, so that the differences between the Catholic Church and Galileo, to take a prominent example, are seen to amount to a difference between biblical literalists who had elevated the literal truth of the scriptures over the evidence of their own senses, and a scientist prepared to take a more liberal approach to the interpretation of scripture in order to accommodate his scientific convictions. In other words, the literal interpretation of the Bible is thought to have acted as an impediment to the advancement of the sciences. As I have argued, however, this seventeenth-century dispute was more to do with the rights of individuals to make their own determinations about how the books of nature and scripture were to be read. Galileo himself adopted a literal approach to scripture, albeit one which allowed for a certain amount of 'accommodation' on the part of the biblical authors. The mistaken premise of this version of history is the assumption that to read the Bible literally is to consider the Bible to be literally true. On the contrary, the triumph of the literal approach to scripture opened up for the first time in the history of biblical interpretation the real possibility that parts of the Bible could be false. In order to see the force of this, we need only consider the conditions which led to the implementation of allegorical readings of scripture in the first place. Origen attempted to put in place a system which virtually guaranteed the truth of every word of scripture. Medieval exegetes, too, saw as their task that of reconciling biblical texts with each other and with known truths. Resort to allegory and tropology made this possible. It is not surprising that with the dismantling of the *quadriga*, the text of scripture was for the first time exposed to the assaults of history and science. While the Protestants' insistence that passages of scripture be given a determinate meaning proceeded from the purest of religious motives, they were inadvertently setting in train a process which would ultimately result in the undermining of that biblical authority which they so adamantly promoted.

The thesis I have outlined also, I trust, adds a missing dimension to standard accounts of the rise of modern science. Some of the more typical transitions assumed to have taken place in the early modern period are those in which, for example, Ptolemaic astronomy gave way to Copernican astronomy, or Aristotelian dynamics capitulated to Newtonian dynamics. This familiar picture makes sense of changes in beliefs about the world – people once thought that the sun revolved around the earth but now believe the reverse – but at the same time disguises the different roles which such beliefs might play, and crucially, whether both might be said to form part of a scientific discourse. We must therefore ask whether both beliefs occupy comparable, but interchangeable, positions within a particular thought structure, or whether instead they are indicative of fundamentally distinct ways of viewing the world. Belief that the earth lay immobile at the centre of the cosmos was not, in the sixteenth century, merely a matter of giving assent to a geocentric theory of the solar system. It was linked to a set of commitments of metaphysical, moral, religious, and anthropological import, not least of which was to do with the dignity of human beings and their place in the cosmos. The 'Copernican revolution', on this account, was not a matter of one paradigm displacing another. The success of the heliocentric view was made possible not by the failure of the alternative scientific hypothesis, but by the disintegration of that set of non-scientific commitments in which the geocentric cosmos had played a particular part. The same point can be made in another way. It is a commonplace that during the Middle Ages science was a handmaiden to theology. The full implication of this, however, is that inasmuch as science was subservient to theology, it was not science at all. My concern has been to show that what we might regard as medieval science, and natural history in particular, assisted in the elucidation of the meanings of sacred scripture – the central theological task of the Middle Ages – and thus is better classified not as a science but as one aspect of biblical hermeneutics. The contentions of John Ray about what constitutes proper natural history, spelt out in the introduction, also support this conclusion. According to Ray, the problem with previous natural histories was not so much their content, as the framework of the human sciences in which that content appeared, and the role it played within that framework. For the historian to strip away morals, emblems, fables, hieroglyphics, things pertaining to divinity, and identify some residue as medieval natural science, is to fail to discern the hidden integrating structures of medieval knowledge, and to trivialise at the same time the revolutionary nature of the contributions of figures such as Ray. The revolution which gave rise to a proper natural history was not the result of new facts or observations, nor of the discarding of irrelevant and extraneous material, but of a change to the mental field in which generally accepted facts were located.

We might turn again, at this point, to the further question of why science arose in the West, and why in the seventeenth century. This is a big question, but not on those grounds an inadmissible one. A complete answer, of course, would require a consideration of other contenders such as Islamic and Chinese cultures, something which others have attempted, but which is beyond the scope of the present work. However, the themes discussed in the present book provide at least some provisional answers. The Christian doctrine of creation assumes an intelligible world, created to be understood by its human inhabitants, and to serve their needs. Throughout the patristic and medieval periods, the book of God's works was interpreted, like scripture, and served both spiritual and physical needs. A change took place in the sixteenth century which challenged the assumption that the purpose of the material world lay in its referential or symbolic functions. Henceforth the quest for the divinely-instituted purpose of nature is diverted solely into the search for its practical utilities. The literal approach to texts precipitated this change of attitude towards the world, while the literal content of key passages of the Bible further motivated natural philosophers in their quest to master nature. In particular, narratives

relating to dominion over the earth were now read as literal imperatives, attempts were made to restore the original paradise once enjoyed
by Adam, and the lost language of nature was actively sought. The
negative consequences of these latter developments have been drawn
to our attention by Lynn White Jr. It should be apparent, in view of the
preceding chapter, that I cannot concur with the judgement of Jeremy
Cohen, who concludes on the basis of an exhaustive study of the
reception of the Genesis text, that 'the ecologically oriented thesis of
Lynn White and others can now be laid to rest'. Cohen is correct to
point out that passages of scripture referring to domination of the earth
were rarely, if ever, used by pre-modern Jews and Christians 'as a
license for the selfish exploitation of the environment'.[1] Cohen's study,
however, concludes precisely at that point in Western history when the
imperatives in Genesis were read in a new light, and were used to
sanction the human control of nature. What remains to be contested,
however, is whether, on balance, more harm than good resulted from
these new interpretations. Aspects of the Christian tradition contributed to the development of modern science; inevitably they led also to
the exploitation of nature. It is not clear that the former could have
occurred without the latter, for science is motivated by the same instrumental view of the world which led to environmental degradation.

It might be perceived to be a weakness of the thesis of this book that
we still encounter in the seventeenth century significant survivals of the
old symbolic world order, supposedly overturned in the hermeneutical
revolution of the previous century. These are not restricted to margins
of intellectual life, moreover, but are manifest even in figures supposedly
representative of the new, non-emblematic world view. Traces of the
old mentality are evident in the last great resurgence of Neoplatonism in
the middle decades of the seventeenth century, in the survival of astrology, in the vogue for the philosophy of Boehme and Paracelsus. It is
apparent, too, in seventeenth-century lives: in Thomas Browne's commitment to 'the philosophy of Hermes' and the view 'that this visible
world is but a picture of the invisible', in Kenelm Digby's experiments
with resurrection, in Robert Fludd's fascination with cabbala, in the
attempts of Henry More and Joseph Glanvill to prove empirically the
existence of witches and spirits, in Robert Boyle's insistence that 'the
great volume of nature is full of real hieroglyphicks, where . . . things
stand for words, and their qualities for letters', and in Newton's private

---

[1] Cohen, *'Be Fertile and Increase'*, pp. 5, 309.

obsessions with alchemy and biblical prophecies.[2] These instances, I would suggest, are indicative of an unconscious reluctance to admit the failure of the old world picture, combined with deep misgivings about the partial and fragmentary sciences which were proposed in its place. Faith in the language of mathematics, confidence in the possibilities of the human intellect, the growing assurance of the superiority of the new knowledge over that of the ancients, these things were accompanied by an acute sense of loss and a yearning for the certainties provided by the old world, now evacuated of meaning. This accounts for what is in many ways is the most remarkable feature of seventeenth-century science – the unwillingness of its practitioners to abandon those things which, in their eyes, had given a deeper significance to the natural world. Theirs were not the activities and beliefs of men marching towards a brave new world of empirical science without a backward glance, but rather of individuals with an inchoate awareness of the full implications of their new readings of the world, and of the relative impoverishment of a view of nature in which legitimate knowledge was reduced to mathematical relations and systems of classification. To the optimism generated by the remarkable achievements of the seventeenth century we must juxtapose the 'dread' experienced by Pascal as he contemplated the eternal silence of the new cosmos. The affirmation of the new science was tentative, rather than triumphalist, tinged always with a consciousness of the contingency of the human condition, and a growing awareness of the arbitrary nature of all structures of meaning in a post-Babel world. Cast over the millennial hope of the new Eden was the ever-present shadow of the Fall.

This ambivalence towards the mechanical world, though muted, remains with us. Throughout the seventeenth century, vestiges of the old world view remained in the common conviction that evidence of God's designs could be found in living creatures, and the less common assertion that nature could still teach us moral lessons. But these convictions suffered further setbacks in the eighteenth and nineteenth centuries. In the second half of the eighteenth century, David Hume put forward a persuasive case for the distinction between values and facts, insisting that we cannot derive the former from the latter. The notion that nature retained something of its moral authority was put to rest, though perhaps not finally, by Hume's recognition that factual claims about states of affairs cannot provide us with the basis for making moral

---

[2] Browne, *Religio Medici*, 1.12 (p. 13); Boyle, *Some Considerations, Works* II, 29.

judgements. Hume added insult to injury by dealing a telling blow to the argument from design: not only is nature a moral vacuum, but no theological conclusions of any consequence may be drawn from its features. To these philosophical claims, Darwin was to add scientific substance one hundred years later. The wonderful mechanisms of living creatures do not bear testimony to a divine designer, but rather embody the end-results of millions of years of fortuitous accidents. The Darwinian theory of natural selection spelt the end of the physico-theological impulse which had driven the natural science of the seventeenth century. The quest for benevolent adaptations in the natural world was now almost totally subsumed by already-existing utilitarian considerations. Still, the misgivings of the seventeenth century about the adequacy of scientific discourse to provide a satisfactory account of the natural world have resurfaced in our own era. There are those who wish to assert that the natural world has some intrinsic value, independent of theological considerations. Such assertions, and the arguments presented in their support, have generally not proven persuasive, although they bear witness to the human propensity to seek value and meaning in the physical world which we inhabit. Revivals, or perhaps, survivals of astrology, numerology, various aspects of physiognomy, the Gaia hypothesis (reminiscent of the idea of the world-soul), and other 'new age' tendencies also signify a desire to be reconnected with the natural world. Even sober scientific practitioners themselves have spoken of evidence of design, not in biological structures, but in the laws and constants of the physical universe. If in our own era, for the most part still thoroughly imbued with a belief in the supremacy of scientific accounts of reality, we encounter such sentiments, we should not be surprised that those who stood at the threshold of the modernity took the occasional backward glance.

In proposing a link between the interpretation of the Bible and the study of nature I hope to have made some contribution to that body of literature devoted to the more general question of the historical relations between science and religion. In concluding, it is worth reflecting briefly on that general theme. While it is commonly acknowledged that modern science had its origins in the seventeenth century, it is less frequently appreciated that modern religion, too, emerged at this time. Of course, the practices and beliefs said to constitute various religions had existed for some time. During the early modern period, however, the term 'religion' took on a new meaning – that with which we are most familiar – and came to denote something like 'subscribing to a particular set of beliefs'. Protestant religion in particular emphasised the importance of the acquisition of knowledge, for redemption was to be attained through the instrument of 'saving knowledge'.[3] The mainspring of religion thus ceased to be the performance of ritual acts presided over by an ecclesiastical hierarchy – baptism, confirmation, penance, the mass. Instead, religion came to be identified with systems of belief. Various 'religions' were thus distinguished by the beliefs of their adherents. The seventeenth century, it might be said, witnessed a dramatic reversal. 'Science', prior to this, had largely been a matter of subscribing to particular doctrines; Christian religion, on the other hand, had been to do with the performance of certain activities. Now science has become primarily an activity, while religion is a matter of subscribing to unchanging dogmas. In a sense, then, the performative aspects of medieval, other-worldly, Catholic religion were transformed by Protestants into this-worldly scientific activities. The investigation of the material world became a priority which displaced medieval rituals concerned with a spiritualised and sacramental cosmos. Moreover, the secularisation of the scientific impulse which is increasingly evident from the beginning of the eighteenth century deprived Protestant religion (and arguably Catholicism, too) of its active component, leaving it with only a body of doctrines with which to concern itself. The collapse of the complex system of similitudes which had characterised pre-modern knowledge also brought a new shape to the Western quest for redemption. No longer was salvation considered to be a process in which the divine image in mankind was restored. Instead, the impulse to restore the divine likeness within was redirected outwards into the natural world, and scientific activity became an increasingly material means of obtaining secular salvation.

[3] See, e.g. Smith, *The Meaning and End of Religion*, pp. 48–50, and passim; Harrison, '*Religion' and the Religions*, pp. 19–28.

References

PRIMARY SOURCES

Classical and Patristic sources in the collections *ANF, CCSL, CSEL, FC, LCL, NPNF* I, *PG,* and *PL,* have not been listed separately.

Abbot, George, *An Exposition on the Prophet Ionah,* (London, 1600).
Abbott, R., *The Young Mans Warning-piece* (London, 1657).
Agrippa von Nettesheim, Henricus Cornelius, *Opera Omnia,* 2 vols. (Hildesheim: G. Olms, 1975).
    Three Books of Occult Philosophy (London, 1651).
Albertus Magnus (Albert the Great), *Man and the Beasts: De Animalibus (Books 22–26),* tr. James Scanlan (Binghamton, Medieval and Renaissance Texts and Studies, 47, 1987).
    Opera Omnia, 38 vols., ed. Augustus Borgnet (Paris, 1890–99).
    The Book of Minerals, tr. Dorothy Wyckoff, (Oxford: Clarendon, 1967).
    The Book of Secrets , ed. M. Best and F. Brightman, (Oxford: Clarendon,1973).
Aldrovandi, Ulisse, *De quadrupedibus solidipedibus* 6 (Francofurti, 1623).
Andrewes, Lancelot, Αποσπασματια *Sacra* (London, 1657).
Anonymous, *Philiatros, or, The Copy of an Epistle . . . to a Young Student of Physicke* (London, 1615).
    Seder Olam (London, 1694).
    Two Remarkable Paradoxes (London, 1681).
Apsley, Allen, *Order and Disorder: or The World Made and Undone* (London, 1679).
Aquinas, St Thomas, *Commentary on Aristotle's Physics,* tr. R. Blackwell et al. (London: Routledge and Kegan Paul, 1963).
    Sancti Thomas Aquinatis in Aristotelis Librum de Anima Commentarium, ed. M. Pirotta (Turin, 1925).
    Summa theologiae , Blackfriars edn. 60 vols., ed. Thomas Gilby (London: Eyre & Spottiswoode, 1964–76).
Arbuthnot, John, *An Examination of Dr Woodward's Account of the Deluge* (London, 1697).
Athanasius, *Contra gentes and De incarnatione,* tr. R.W. Thomson (Oxford University Press, 1971).
Augustine, *Against the Academics,* tr. J. O'Meara (Westminster: Newman Press, 1950).

The City of God, tr. Marcus Dodds (New York: Random House, 1950).

Confessions, tr. Henry Chadwick (Oxford University Press, 1991).

On Christian Doctrine, tr. D. Robertson (Indianapolis: Bobbs-Merrill, 1958).

On Free Will, in *Augustine: Earlier Writings*, tr. John Burleigh (London: SCM, 1953).

Opera Omnia, 11 vols. (Parisiis: Gaume Fratres, 1836–9).

Austen, Ralph, *A Treatise of Frvit-Trees, together with The Spiritual vse of an Orchard* (Oxford, 1653).

Ayloffe, William, *The Government of the Passions, according to the Rules of Reason and Religion* (London, 1700).

Bacon, Francis, *The Advancement of Learning and New Atlantis*, ed. Arthur Johnston (Oxford: Clarendon, 1974).

Essays, ed. W.A. Wright (London: Macmillan, 1871).

Novum Organum, in *The English Philosophers from Bacon to Mill*, ed. E. A. Burtt (New York: Random House, 1967).

The Works of Francis Bacon, 14 vols., ed. James Spedding, Robert Ellis, Douglas Heath (London: Longman and Co., 1860).

Bacon, William, *A Key to Helmont* (London, 1682).

Bamfield, Francis, *Miqra qadosh, The Holy Scripture* (London, 1684).

Barker, Matthew, *Natural Theology, or, The Knowledge of God, from the Works of Creation* (London, 1674).

Barrough, Philip, *The Method of Physick* (London, 1652).

Barrow, Isaac, *The Theological Works of Isaac Barrow*, 9 vols., ed. Alexander Napier (Cambridge University Press, 1839).

Bartholomew Anglicus, *Batman vppon Bartholome, his Booke, De Proprietatibus Rerum* (London, 1582).

Baxter, Richard, *A Christian Directory*, 2nd edn (London, 1678).

The Judgement of Non-conformists, of the Interest of Reason in Matters of Religion (London, 1676).

Bayle, Pierre, *Dictionnaire historique et critique*, 4 vols. (Rotterdam, 1697).

Beaumont, John, *Considerations on a book entituled The Theory of the Earth* (London, 1693).

Becanus, Johannes, *Origines Antwerpianiae* (Antverpiae, 1569).

Beck, Cave, *The Universal Character* (London, 1657).

Bedford, Arthur, *The Scripture Chronology deomnstrated by Astronomical Calculations* (London, 1730).

ben Israel, Manasseh, *The Hope of Israel* (London, 1651).

Bentley, Richard, *The Works of Richard Bentley DD*, 3 vols., (London: Macpherson, 1838).

Bergerac, Cyrano de, *Cyrano de Bergerac's Voyages to the Moon and The Sun*, tr. John Aldington (London: Folio Society, 1991).

Bernard, Richard, *The Faithfoll Shepheard* (London, 1607).

The Bible: translated according to the Ebrew and Greeke (London, 1607). (The 'Geneva Bible', 1st edn, Geneva, 1560).

Biggs, Noah, *Mataetechnia Medicinae Praxeos. The Vanity of the Craft of Physick* (London, 1651).

Blake, Stephen, *The Compleat Gardeners Practice* (London, 1664).

Blith, Walter, *The English Improver Improved or the Survey of Husbandry Surveyed* (London, 1653).

Blount, Charles, *Miscellaneous Works* (London, 1695).

Blount, Sir Thomas Pope, *A Natural History* (London, 1693).

Bock, Hieronymous, *Hieronymi Tragi, De stirpium, maxime earum quae in Germania nostra* (Argentorati, 1552).

Boehme, Jacob, *Mysterium Magnum, or An Exposition of the First Book of Moses called Genesis* (London, 1654).

Signatura Rerum: or the Signature of all Things (London, 1651).

The Second Booke: concerning The Three Principles of The Divine Essence (London, 1648).

Bonaventure, *Opera Omnia*, 15 vols. (Parisiis: A.C. Pelier, 1864–71).

Bonnet, Charles, *The Contemplation of Nature*, 2 vols. (London: T. Longman, T. Becket, and P.A. de Hondt, 1766).

Oeuvres d'histoire naturelle et de philosophie, 18 tom. (Neuchatel, 1779–83).

The Book of Beasts, tr. T.H. White (London: Jonathan Cape, 1954).

Borel, Pierre, *A New Treatise Proving a Multiplicity of Worlds* (London, 1658).

Bostocke, Robert, *The Difference between the auncient Phisicke . . . and the Latter Phisicke* (London, 1585).

Boyle, Robert, *Some Physico-Theological Considerations about the Possibility of the Resurrection* (London, 1675).

The Works, 6 vols., ed. Thomas Birch (Hildesheim: Georg Olms, 1966). Reprint of 1772 London edn.

A Disquisition about the Final Causes of Natural Things (London, 1688).

Bradley, Richard, *A General Treatise of Husbandry and Gardening*, 2 vols. (London, 1726).

Bradshaw, William, *English Puritanisme* (London, 1605).

Brathwait, Richard, *A Mustur Roll of the Evill Angels Embattled against S. Michael* (London, 1655).

Brett, Thomas, *A Chronological Essay on the Sacred History* (London, 1629).

Browne, Sir Thomas, *Pseudodoxia Epidemica*, ed. Robin Robbins, 2 vols. (Oxford: Clarendon, 1981).

Religio Medici, Hydriotaphia, and *The Garden of Cyrus*, ed. Robin Robbins (Oxford: Clarendon, 1982).

The Workes of Sir Thomas Browne, 4 vols., (London: Faber and Faber, 1928–37).

Buffon, Louis, *Natural History, General and Particular*, tr. William Smellie, 20 vols., (London 1812–).

Bulwer, John, *Chirologia: or the Naturall Langvage of the Hand* (London, 1644).

Bunyan, John, *A Book for Boys and Girls* (London, 1686).

Pilgrim's Progress (London, 1678).

Burnet, Thomas, *Archaeologiae philosophicae* (London, 1692).

Doctrina Antiqua de Rerum Originibus, tr. Mead and Foxton (London, 1736). ET of *Archaeologiae philosophicae*.

A Review of the Theory of the Earth and of its Proofs, especially in Reference to Scripture (London, 1690).

The Sacred Theory of the Earth (London: Centaur Press, 1965), reprint of the 1690/1 edn.

Burton, Robert, *The Anatomy of Melancholy*, 8th edn (London, 1676).

Butler, Joseph, *The Analogy of Religion to the Constitution and Course of Nature* (London: Religious Tract Society, n.d.).

Calvin, John, *Commentary on the First Book of Moses called Genesis*, tr. J. King, (Grand Rapids: Baker, 1984).

Institutes of the Christian Religion, tr. Henry Beveridge, 2 vols., (London: Clarke, 1953).

Treatises against the Anabaptists and against the Libertines, tr. B. Farley (Grand Rapids Eerdmans: Grand Rapids, 1982).

Cardan, Jerome, *Metoscopia* (Paris, 1658).

Carpenter, Nathaniel, *Geography Delineated Forth in Two Bookes*, 2nd edn (Oxford, 1635).

Carver, Marmaduke, *A Discourse of the Terrestrial Paradise* (London, 1666).

Chambers, E., *Cyclopedia*, 2 vols. (London, 1728).

Charleton, Walter, *Natural History of Nutrition, Life, and Voluntary Motion* (London, 1659).

Physiologia Epicuro-Gassendo-Charltoniana (London, 1654).

Charron, Pierre, *Of Wisdom* (London, 1697).

Cheyne, George, *Philosophical Principles of Religion: Natural and Revealed*, 2nd edn. (London, 1714).

Cicero, *On the Nature of the Gods*, tr. H.C.P. McGregor (Ringwood: Penguin, 1972).

Clarke, Samuel, *A Mirour or Looking Glass*, 4th edn (London, 1671).

Clarke, Samuel, *The Works of Samuel Clarke, DD*, 4 vols. (London, 1738).

Cockburn, Patrick, *An Enquiry into the Truth and Certainty of the Mosaic Deluge* (London, 1750).

Coclès, Barthélemy, *A Brief and Most Pleasant Epitomye of the Whole Art of Physiognomie* (London, 1556).

Physiognomonia (Strasbourg, 1533).

Coles, William, *Adam in Eden: or, Natures Paradise* (London, 1657).

Collyer, David, *The Sacred Interpreter* (London, 1732).

Comenius, Johann Amos, *The Way of Light of Comenius*, tr. E.T. Campagnac (London: Hodder and Stoughton, 1938).

Conway, Anne, *Conway Letters*, ed. M.H. Nicolson (Yale University Press, 1930).

The Principles of the Most Ancient and Modern Philosophy (London, 1692).

Cooke, Moses, *The Manner of Raising, Ordering, and Improving Forrest-Trees* (London, 1676).

Coverdale, Miles, *Remains of Miles Coverdale*, ed. George Pearson (Cambridge University Press, 1846).

Cowley, Abraham, *The Works in Prose and Verse*, 3 vols., ed. Richard Hurd (London: Pr. for John Sharpe, 1809).

Cowper, William, *Works*, 15 vols., ed. Robert Southey (London: Baldwin, 1836–7).

The Works of William Cowper (London, 1629).

Crashawe, William, *Falisificationvm Romanarvm / Romish Forgeries and Falsifications* (London, 1606).

Crausius, Rudolphus W., *Dissertatio inauguralis medica de signaturis vegetabilium* (Jena, 1697).

Croll, Oswald, *De signatums* (1609), E.T., *A Treatise of Oswaldus Crollius of Signatures of Internal Things; or A True and Lively Anatomy of the Greater and Lesser World* (London, 1669).

Cudworth, Ralph, *True Intellectual System of the Universe*, ed. John Harrison, 3 vols. (London: Thomas Tegg, 1845).

Culpeper, Nicholas, *Complete Herbal and English Physician Enlarged* (Ware: Wordsworth, 1995).

Culpeper, Thomas, *Morall Discourses and Essayes* (London, 1655).

Culverwel, Nathaniel, *An Elegant and Learned Discourse of the Light of Nature* (London, 1652).

Cureau de la Chambre, Marin, *Discourse on the Principles of Chiromancy* (London, 1658).
  Les caractères des passions, I and II (Amsterdam, 1658); E.T., *The Art How to Know Men* (London, 1665).

Dalgarno, George, *Ars Signorum, vulgo character universalis et lingue philosophica* (Londini, 1661).

Daneau, Lambert, *The Wonderfvll Woorkmanship of the World* (London, 1578).

Dean, Richard, *An Essay on the Future Life of Brutes, Introduced with Observations upon Evil, its Nature, and Origin*, 2 vols. (Manchester, 1767).

Della Porta, Giovambattista, *De humana physiognomia* (Hanover, 1593).
  Natural Magick (London, 1658).

Denzinger, Henrici (ed.), *Enchiridion symbolorum*, 37th edn (Friburgi Brisgoviae: Herder, 1991).

De Pauw, Corneille, *Selections from Les Recherches Philosophiques sur les Americains*, tr. Mr Webb (Bath, 1789).

Derham, William, *Astro-Theology: or a Demonstration of the Being and Attributes of God from a Survey of the Heavens* (London, 1715).
  Physico-Theology (London, 1713).

Descartes, René, *Philosophical Letters*, tr. and ed. A. Kenny (Oxford: Clarendon, 1970).
  The Philosophical Writings of Descartes, 3 vols., tr. J. Cottingham, R. Stoothoff, and Douglas Murdoch (Cambridge University Press, 1984–).
  Principles of Philosophy, tr. V. Miller and R. Miller (Dordrecht: D. Reidel, 1983).

D'Espagnet, Jean, *Enchyridion physicae restitutae; or, The Summary of Physics Recovered* (London, 1651).

Dickerman, S.O., *De argumentis quibusdam e structura hominis et animalium petitis* (Halle, 1909).

Diderot, Dennis, *Philosophical Thoughts*, in *Diderot's Early Philosophical Works*, ed. and tr. Margaret Jourdain (Chicago: Open Court, 1916).

Digby, Kenelm, *A Discourse Concerning the Vegetation of Plants* (London, 1661).

D'Indagine, Jean, *Chiromance* (Lyon, 1549).

Diodati, John, *Pious and Learned Annotations upon the Holy Bible*, 2nd edn (London, 1648).

Donne, John, *Complete English Poems*, ed. C.A. Patrides (London: Dent, 1994).

Essayes in Divinity, ed. Evelyn Simpson (Oxford: Clarendon, 1952).

The Sermons of John Donne, ed. G. Potter and E. Simpson, 10 vols. (University of California Press, 1953–62).

The Works of John Donne: with a memoir of his life, ed. Henry Alford (London, 1839).

Dove, John, *Confutation of Atheism* (London, 1605).

Drelincourt, Charles, *A Collection of Texts of Scripture . . . Against the Principal Popish Errors* (London, 1686).

Dryden, John, *Dryden's Poems*, ed. Bonamy Dobrée (London: Dent, 1964).

Du Bartas, William, *The Divine Weeks and Works of Guillaume de Saluste Sieur du Bartas*, 2 vols., tr. Joshua Sylvester, ed. Susan Snyder (Oxford Clarendon, 1979).

Du Moulin, Pierre, *The Elements of Logick* (Oxford, 1647).

Duchesne, Joseph, *The Practise of Chymicall, and Hermeticall Physicke*, tr. Thomas-Tymme (London, 1605).

Dunton, John (ed.), *The Athenian Oracle*, 3rd edn. (London, 1728).

The Young Student's Library containing Extracts of the Most Valuable Books printed in England (London, 1692).

Durham, James, *Clavis Cantici: or, an Exposition of the Song of Solomon* (Edinburgh, 1662).

Eburne, Richard, *A Plaine Path-way to Plantation* (London, 1624).

Edwards, John, *Brief Remarks upon Mr. Whiston's New Theory of the Earth* (London, 1697).

A Demonstration of the Existence and Providence of God, From the Contemplation of the Visible Structure of the Greater and the Lesser World (London, 1696).

A Discourse concerning the Authority, Stile, and Perfection of the Books of the Old and New Testament, 2 vols. (London, 1694).

Erasmus of Rotterdam, *Enchiridion militis christiani* (London, 1533).

Escalante, Ferdinande de, *Clypevs concionatorvm versi dei* (Hispali, 1611).

Ferguson, James, *An Idea of the Material Universe, Deduced from a Survey of the Solar System* (London, 1754).

Ficino, Marcilio, *Opera*, 2 vols. (Basileae, 1576).

Filmer, Robert, *Patriarcha, or the Natural Power of Kings* (London, 1680).

Flavell, John, *Husbandry Spiritualized: or The Heavenly use of Earthly Things* (London, 1669).

Fludd, Robert, *Mosaicall Philosophy Grounded upon the Essential Truth or Eternal Sapience* (London, 1659).

Robert Fludd: Essential Readings, ed. R. Huffman (London: Harper Collins, 1992).

Utriusque cosmi historia, 2 vols. (Oppenheim, 1619).

Tractatus theologo-philosophicus (Oppenheim, 1617).

Fontenelle, Bernard, *Conversations on the Plurality of Worlds* (Dublin, 1687).

Fowler, Edward, *The Principles and Practices of Certain Moderate Divines of the Church of England* (London, 1670).

Foxe, John, *The Actes and Monumentes of John Foxe*, ed. G. Townsend and S. Cattley (London, 1837–41).

Franck, R., *A Philosophical Treatise of the Original and Production of Things* (London, 1687).

Franck, Sebastian, *The Forbidden Fruit* (London?, 1640).

Franzius, Wolfgang, *A History of Brutes; or, a Description of Living Creatures*, tr. N.W. (London, 1670).

Fuchs, Leonard, *De historia stirpium commentarii insignes* (Basilae, 1542).

Fulke, William, *The Text of the New Testament. With a Confutation of the Rhemists' Translation* (London, 1617).

Gale, Theophilus, *The Court of the Gentiles*, 4 vols. (Oxford, 1669–77).

Galileo Galilei, *Discoveries and Opinions of Galileo*, tr. Stillman Drake (New York: Anchor, 1957).

Gee, Elizabeth, and Kratzmann, Gregory (eds.), *The Dialoges of Creatures Moralysed* (Leiden: Brill, 1988).

Gesner, Konrad, *Catalogus plantarum Latine, Graece, Germanice, et Gallice* (Tiguri, 1542).

Historiae animalium, 5 vols. (Tiguri, 1551–87).

Gilbert, Samuel, *The Florists Vade-Mecum*, 2nd edn (London, 1693).

Gilbert, William, *On the Loadstone and Magnetic Bodies and on the Great Magnet of the Earth*, tr. P. Fleury Mottelay (Chicago: Encyclopaedia Britannica, 1952).

Glanvill, Joseph, *Essays on Several Important Subjects in Philosophy and Religion* (London, 1676).

Lux Orientalis, in *Two Choice and Vseful Treatises* (London, 1682).

Scepsis Scientifica (London, 1665). Includes the 2nd edn of *The Vanity of Dogmatising*.

Goodman, Godfrey, *The Creatvres Praysing God* (London, 1622).

The Fall of Man (London, 1616).

Grosseteste, Robert, *Hexameron*, ed. Richard C. Dales and Servus Gieben (London: British Academy, 1982).

Grotius, Hugo, *Annotata ad Vetus Testamentum*, 3 vols. (Paris, 1644).

Hakewill, George, *An Apologie*, 3rd edn (Oxford, 1635).

Hakluyt, Richard, *The Principal Navigations, Voyages, and Discoveries of the English Nation* (London, 1589).

Hale, Matthew, *The Primitive Origination of Mankind Considered and Examined According to the Light of Nature* (London, 1677).

Hall, John, *An Humble Motion to the Parliament of England concerning the Advancement of Learning and the Reformation of the Universities* (London, 1649).

Hall, Joseph, *The Invisible World, Discovered to Spirituall Eyes* (London, 1659).

Works, rev. edn, 12 vols. (London: Pr. 1837–9).

Hall, Thomas, *Comarum ἀκοσμίαι. The Loathsomnesse of Long Hair . . . with an Appendix against Painting, Spots, Naked Breasts, etc.* (London, 1654).

Vindiciae Literarum. The Schools Guarded (London, 1654).

Hammond, Henry, *A Paraphrase and Annotations upon all the Books of the New Testament*, 4 vols. (London, 1653).

A Paraphrase and Annotations upon the Books of the Psalms, 2 vols. (London, 1659).

Hare, H., *The Situation of Paradise Found Out* (London, 1683).

Harris, John, *Remarks on Some Late Papers Relating to the Universal Deluge* (London, 1697).

Hartlib, Samuel, *Samuel Hartlib his Legacy of Husbandry*, 3rd edn (London, 1651).

The Reformed Husband-Man (London, 1651).

Harvey, William, *An Anatomical Disquisition on the Motion of the Heart and Blood in Animals*, (Chicago: Encyclopaedia Brittanica, 1951).

Anatomical Exercises on the Generation of Animals, tr. Robert Willis (Chicago: Encyclopaedia Brittanica, 1951).

The Circulation of the Blood and Other Writings, tr. K. Franklin (London: Dent, 1963).

A Second Disquisition to John Riolan (Chicago: Encyclopaedia Brittanica, 1951).

Havers, G. (tr.), *A General Collection of Discourses of the Virtuosi of France* (London, 1664).

Hawkins, H., *Partheneia sacra* (Rouen, 1633).

Hearne, Thomas, *Ductor Historicus* (London, 1698).

Heidegger, J.H., *De historia sacra patriarchum*, 2 vols. (Amstelodami, 1667–71).

Herbert of Cherbury, Edward, First Lord, *A Dialogue between a Tutor and his Pupil* (London, 1768).

Herbert, George, *The Works of George Herbert*, ed. Tim Cook (Ware: Wordsworth Poetry Library, 1994).

Heresbachius, Conradus, *The Whole Art of Husbandry*, enlarged by Gervase Markham (London, 1631).

Hermanus, Phillipus, *An Excellent Treatise teaching howe to cure the French Pockes*, tr. John Hester (London, 1590).

Hermes Trismegistus, *Die Kyraniden*, ed. Dimitris Kaimakis, Beitrage der Klassischen Philologie, Heft 76 (Meisenheim am Glan: A Hain, 1976).

Hermetica, ed. B.P. Copenhaver (Cambridge University Press, 1992).

Hester, John, *The Pearle of Practise* (London, 1594).

Heylyn, Peter, *Cosmographie in Foure Bookes* (London, 1652).

Mikrokosmos. A Little Description of the Great World (Oxford, 1629).

Heywood, Thomas, *The Hierarchie of the Blessed Angels* (London, 1635).

Hobbes, Thomas, *Leviathan*, ed. Michael Oakeshott (New York: Collier, 1962).

Works, ed. William Molesworth (Aalen: Scientia, 1962).

Hodges, Thomas, *The Creatures Goodness, as they came out of God's Hands* (London, 1653).

Holder, William, *Elements of Speech* (London, 1669).

Hooke, Robert, *Micrographia: or Some Physiological Descriptions of Minute Bodies made by Magnifying Glasses* (London, 1665).

'Some Observations, and Conjectures concerning Chinese Characters', *Philosophical Transactions of the Royal Society*, xvi (1696), 63–78.

Hopkinson, John, *Synopsis paradisi* (Rotterdam, 1693).

Howard, Edward, *Remarks on the New Philosophy of Descartes* (London, 1700).

Hugh of St Victor, *On the Sacraments of the Christian Faith*, tr. Roy Deferrari (Cambridge, Mass.: Mediaeval Academy of America, 1951).

The Didascalicon of Hugh of St Victor, tr. and intr. Jerome Taylor (New York: Columbia University Press, 1961).

Hughes, George, *An Analytical Exposition of the first Book of Moses* (London, 1672).

Hutchinson, John, *An Abstract from the Works of John Hutchinson* (Edinburgh, 1753).

A New Account of the Confusion of Tongues, in *An Abstract from the Works of John Hutchinson* (Edinburgh, 1753).

Moses's Principia (London, 1724–7).

Isidore of Seville, *Etymologiae* (Strasbourg, 1470).

Isidore of Seville: The Medical Writings., ed. and tr. William Sharpe (Philadelphia: American Philosophical Society, 1964).

James, Thomas, *A Manuduction, or Introduction unto Divinitie* (London, 1625).

A Treatise of the Corruption of Scripture, Councels, and Fathers, by the Prelates, Pastors, and Pillars of the Church of Rome (London, 1611).

Jenkin, Robert, *Reasonableness and Certainty of the Christian Religion*, 2nd edn (London, 1700).

Johnson, Samuel, *Lives of the English Poets*, 2 vols. (London: Dent, 1950).

Johnston, John, *An History of the Wonderful Things of Nature* (London, 1657).

A Description of the Nature of Four-Footed Beasts (Amsterdam, 1678).

Josephus, Flavius, *The Works of Josephus*, tr. William Whiston (Peabody: Hendrickson, 1993).

Josselyn, John, *New-Englands Rarities Discover'd . . . together with The Physical and Chyrurgical Remedies* (London, 1672).

Keach, Benjamin, *Troposchåemalogia: Tropes and Figures* (London, 1692).

Keill, John, *An Examination of Dr Burnet's Theory of the Earth* (Oxford, 1698).

An Examination of the Reflections on The Theory of the Earth together with A Defence of the Remarks on Mr Whiston's New Theory (Oxford, 1699).

Kepler, Johannes, Introduction to *Astronomia nova*, in *The Great Ideas Today 1983* (Chicago: Encyclopaedia Britannica, 1983), pp. 309–23.

Epitome of Copernican Astronomy, tr. Glenn Wallis, (Chicago: Encyclopaedia Britannica, 1952).

Gesammelte Werke, 20 vols. (Munich: C.H. Beck, 1937–45).

King, William, *De origine mali* (London, 1702); E.T. *An Essay on the Origin of Evil*, (London, 1731).

Kirby, William, *On the Power, Wisdom and Goodness of God as manifested in the Creation of Animals*, 2 vols. (London: Pickering, 1835).

Kircher, Athanasius, *Arca Noë in tres libros digesta* (Amstelodami, 1675).

Athanasii Kircheri Fuldensis Buchonii e Societate Iesu, Magnes seu de arte magnetica opus tripartitum (Rome, 1641).

Of the Various Voyages and Travels undertaken into China, in Peter de Goyer and Jacob de Keyzer, *An Embassy from the east India Company of the United Provinces to the grand Tartar Cham Emperour of China* (London, 1669).

Oedipus Aegyptiacus, 3 tom. (Rome, 1653–4).

La Mothe le Vayer, François de, *Politique du Prince, Petits traites ou lettres*, Lettre LIV, *Opuscule ou Petit Traite sceptique sur sette commmune facon de parler, N'avoir pasle sens commun*, in *Oeuvres*, 2 vols. (Paris, 1654).

Lanier, Emilia, *The Poems of Shakespeares Dark Lady: Salve Deus Rex Judaeorum*, ed. A. L. Rowse (London: Cape, 1978).

La vie parfaite: Points de vue sur l'essence de la vie religieuse (Paris: Turnhout, 1948).

Lawrence, John, *The Gentleman's Recreation* (London, 1716).

Le Brun, Charles, *Conférence de M. Le Brun sur l'Expression Générale et Particulière* (Amsterdam and Paris, 1698).

Le Clerc, Jean, *Five Letters concerning the Inspiration of the Holy Scriptures* (London, 1690).

　　Twelve Dissertations out of Monsieur Le Clerc's Genesis, tr. Mr Brown (London, 1696).

le Fabure, Nicasius , *A Compleat Body of Chemistry* (London, 1664).

Leibniz, Gottfried W., *Discourse on Metaphysics, Correspondence with Arnauld, and Monadology*, tr. George Montgomery (Chicago: Open Court, 1902).

　　Essais de Théodicée , 2 vols. (Amsterdam, 1734).

Leibniz, Gottfried W., and Clark, Samuel, *The Leibniz Correspondence*, ed. H.G. Alexander (Manchester University Press, 1976).

Lemnius, Levinus, *An Herbal for the Bible*, tr. Thomas Newton (London, 1587).

Lescot, Michel, *Physionomie* (Paris, 1540).

Lesser, Friedrich C., *Théologie des Insectes, ou Demonstration des Perfections de Dieu dans tout ce qui concerne les Insectes*, tr. P. Lyonnet, 2 vols. (La Haye, 1742).

Lightfoot, John, *A Few and New Observations vpon the Book of Genesis*, (London, 1642).

Locke, John, *Works*, 10th edn, 10 vols. (London, 1801).

Luther, Martin, *Critical and Devotional Commentaries on Genesis* ed. J.M. Lenker, (Minneapolis, 1904).

　　Luther's Works, 55 vols., ed. Jaroslav Pelikan and Helmut Lehman (St Louis:Concordia, 1955–75).

　　Table Talk, tr. William Hazlitt (London: Harper Collins, 1995).

　　Three Treatises (Philadelphia: Fortress Press, 1970).

Mackaile, Matthew, *Terra Prodromus Theoricus* (Aberdeen, 1691).

Macrobius, *Commentary on the Dream of Scipio*, tr. William Stahl (Columbia University Press, 1952).

Malebranche, Nicolas, *Oeuvres complètes*, ed. G. Rodis-Lewis (Paris: J. Vrin, 1958–70).

　　Father Malebranche his Treatise Concerning the Search After Truth, 2nd edn, tr. T. Taylor (London, 1700).

Malvenda, Thomas, *De Paradiso* (Rome, 1605).

Marten, Anthony, *The Common places of . . . Peter Martyr* (London, 1583).

Marvell, Andrew, *The Complete English Poems*, ed. Elizabeth Donno (London: Allen Lane, 1974).

Mascall, Leonard, *The Country-mans New Art of Planting and Grassing* (London, 1652).

Mather, Samuel, *The Figures and Types of the Old Testament* (Dublin, 1683).

Meager, Leonard, *The Mystery of Husbandry* (London, 1697).

Mede, Joseph, *Diatribe Discourses on Divers Texts of Scripture* (London, 1662).

Mersenne, Marin, *Harmonie universelle*, 2 vols. (Paris, 1636, 37).

· Middleton, Conyers, *An Encounter of the Bishop of London's Discourses . . . with a Farther Inquiry into the Mosaic Account of the Fall* (London, 1750).

Migne, Jacques-Paul (ed.), *Patrologiae cursus completus*, Series Graeca, 162 vols. (Paris, 1857–1912).

(ed.) *Patrologiae cursus completus*, Series Latina, 217 vols. (Paris, 1844–1905).

Milton, John, *Complete Prose Works of John Milton*, 7 vols. (Yale University Press, 1953–74).

The Poetical Works of John Milton, ed. T.H. Buckley (London: Routledge, 1893).

Moffett, Thomas, *Insectorum sive minimorum animalium theatrum* (London, 1634).

Theatrum Chemicum (Argenterati, 1613).

Monardes, Nicholas, *Joyfull Nevves out of the Newe Founde Worlde*, tr. John Frampton (London, 1577).

Montaigne, Michel Eyquem de, *The Essayes of Michael Lord of Montaigne*, tr. John Florio, 3 vols. (Oxford University Press, 1951).

More, Henry, *Annotations upon the Two Foregoing Treatises, Lux Orientalis . . . and The Discourse of Truth* (London, 1682).

Antidote against Atheism 2nd edn (London, 1662).

A Collection of Several Philosophical Writings of D. Henry More, 2nd edn. (London, 1662).

Democritus Platonissans; or, An Essay upon the Infinity of Worlds out of Platonic Principles (Cambridge, 1646).

Divine Dialogues, 2 vols. (London, 1668).

An Explanation of the Grand Mystery of Godliness (London, 1660)

Observations upon Anthroposophia Themagica and Anima Magica Abscondita (London, 1650).

Theological Works (London, 1708).

More, Thomas, *A Dyaloge of Syr Thomas More . . . wherein be treated dyuers matters* (London, 1529).

Morgan, Thomas, *The Moral Philosopher*, 2nd edn. 3 vols. (London, 1738–40).

Needler, Benjamin, *Expository Notes* (London, 1655).

Neville, Francis De, *The Christian and Catholike Veritie* (London, 1642).

Newton, Isaac, *The Correspondence of Isaac Newton*, 7 vols., ed. H.W. Turnbull et al. (Cambridge University Press, 1959–77).

Sir Isaac Newton's Theological Manuscripts, ed. Herbert McLachlan, (Liverpool University Press, 1950).

Optics, 4th edn (New York: Dover, 1952).

Nicholls, William, *A Conference with a Theist* (London, 1696).

Nicolaus of Cusa, *De Ludo Globi* (Paris, 1514).

Niewentydt, Bernard, *The Religious Philosopher*, 3 vols. (London, 1718).

Nourse, Timothy, *A Discourse of Natural and Reveal'd Religion* (London, 1691).

Campania Fœlix, or, a Discourse of the Benefits and Improvements of Husbandry

(London, 1700).

Origen, *On First Principles*, tr. G.W. Butterworth (Gloucester, Mass.: Peter Smith, 1973).

 The Song of Songs, Commentary and Homilies, tr. R.P. Lawson, (London: Longmans, Green and Co., 1957). *Ancient Christian Writers* XXVI.

Paley, William, *Natural Theology* (Edinburgh: Oliver and Boyd, 1817).

Paracelsus, *A Hundred and Foureteene Experiments and Cures . . . collected by John Hester* (London, 1596).

 Four Treatises of Theophrastus von Hohenheim called Paracelsus, tr. C. Lilian Temkin et al. (Johns Hopkins University Press, 1941).

 Of the Supreme Mysteries of Nature (London, 1655).

 Sämliche Werke, ed. Karl Sudhoff and Wilhelm Matthiessen, 15 vols. (Munich: R. Oldenburg, 1922–33).

 Selected Writings, ed. Jolande Jacobi (New York: Pantheon, 1951).

Pare, Ambroise, *On Monsters and Marvels*, tr. Janis Pallister (University of Chicago Press, 1982).

Pareus, David, *In Genesin Mosis commentarius* (Francofurti, 1609).

Parkinson, John, *Theatrum Botanicum: The Theatre of Plantes* (London, 1640).

Pascal, Blaise, *Pensées*, tr. A. J. Krailsheimer (Ringwood: Penguin, 1976).

Pasquier, Etienne, *Les Lettres d'Etienne Pasquier* (Paris, 1586).

Patrick, Simon, *A Commentary upon the First Book of Moses, Called Genesis* (London, 1695).

Peacock, W. (ed.), *English Prose*, 5 vols. (Oxford University Press, 1949).

Pererius, Benedictus, *Commentariorum in Genesin*, 4 vols. (Coloniae Agrippinae, 1601).

Perkins, W., *Works* (Cambridge, 1603).

Pettus, John, *Volatiles from the History of Adam and Eve* (London, 1674).

Philo of Alexandria, *The Works of Philo*, tr. C.D. Younge (Peabody: Hendrickson, 1993).

Physiologus, tr. Michael J. Curley (Austin: University of Texas Press, 1979).

Pinnell, Henry, *Philosophy Reformed and Improved in Four Profound Tractates* (London, 1657).

Plato, *The Collected Dialogues*, ed. Edith Hamilton and Huntington Cairns (Princeton University Press, 1982).

Plotinus, *Enneads*, tr. Stephen Mackenna and B.S. Page (Chicago: Encyclopaedia Britannica, 1952).

Pluche, Noël Antoine, *Spectacle de la Nature: or Nature Display'd*, 5th edn revised and corrected, 7 vols. (London, 1770).

Pope, Alexander, *Poems*, Twickenham edn, ed. John Butt, 11 vols. (Yale University Press, 1950–69).

Pordage, S., *Mundorum Explicatio* (London, 1661).

Porphyry, *On Abstinence from Animal Food*, tr. Thomas Taylor, ed. Esme Wynne-Tyson (London: Centaur, 1965).

Postellus, Gulielmus, *De originibus seu de Hebraicae linguae* (Parisiis, 1538).

Power, Henry, *Experimental Philosophy* (London, 1664).

R., L., *The Ranters Ranting* (London, 1650).

Raleigh, Walter, *The Historie of the World in Five Bookes* (London, 1652).
The Historie of the Worlde in Five Bookes (London, 1614).

Ray, John, and Willughby, Francis, *The Ornithology of Francis Willughby* (London, 1678).

Ray, John, *Miscellaneous Discourses Concerning the Dissoution and Changes of the World* (London, 1692).
Three Physico-Theological Discourses, 2nd edn. (London, 1693).
The Wisdom of God Manifested in the Works of Creation (London, 1691).

Réaumur, René Antoine Ferchault de, *Memoirs pour servir à l'histoire des Insectes*, 6 vols. (Paris, 1734–42).
The Natural History of Bees (London, 1744).
The Natural History of Ants, tr. W.M. Wheeer (London, Knapp, 1926).

Reynolds, Edward, *A Treatise of the Passions of the Soul of Man* (London, 1647).

Reynolds, Henry, *Mythomystes: Wherein a Short Survey is taken of the Nature and Valve of Trve Poesy* (London, 1632).

Richardson, John, *Choice Observations and Explanations upon the Old Testament* (London, 1655).

Robbins, F., *The Hexaemeral Literature* (University of Chicago Press, 1912).

Roberts, Francis, *Clavis Bibliorum. The Key of the Bible* (Edinburgh, 1649).

Robinson, Thomas, *The Anatomy of the Earth* (London, 1694).
An Essay towards a Natural History of Westmoreland and Cumberland . . . to which is annexed A Vindication of the Philosophical and Theological Paraphrase of the Mosaic History of the Creation (London, 1709).
New Observations of the Natural History of this World of Matter, and of this World of Life (London, 1696).

Rondelet, Guillaume, *Gulielmi Rondeletii doctoris medicinae in schola Monspeliensiprofessoris regii libri de piscibus marinus* (Lyon, 1554).

Ross, Alexander, *An Exposition on the Fourteene first Chapters of Genesis* (London, 1626).
The Second Book of Questions and Answers upon Genesis (London, 1622).

Rust, George, *A Letter of Resolution concerning Origen and the Chief of his Opinions* (London, 1661).

Salkeld, John, *A Treatise of Paradise* (London, 1617).

Salmon, William, *Clavis Alchymiae* (London, 1691).

Sanderson, Robert, *Thirty-Six Sermons* (London, 1689).

Saunders, Richard, *Saunders Physiognomie and Chiromancie, Metoposcopie*, 2nd edn (London, 1671).

Schaff, Philip, (ed.), *The Creeds of Christendom*, 4th edn, 3 vols. (New York: Harper, 1919).

Selden, John, *De synedriis et praefectiuris juridicis veterum Ebraeorum*, (Amsterdam, 1679).
Joannis Seldeni I.C. de dis syris syntagmata II, (London, 1617).

Senault, Jean François, *De L'Usage des Passions* (1641), E.T. *The Use of the Passions*, tr. Henry, Earl of Monmouth (London, 1671).

Man Becom Guilty, Or, the Corruption of Nature by Sinne, according to St Augustin's Sense (London, 1650).

Natural History of the Passions (London, 1674).

Serarius, Nicholas, *Prolegomena biblicae* (Moguntiaci, 1612).

Shakespeare, William, *The Complete Works*, ed. Stanley Wells and Gary Taylor (Oxford: Clarendon, 1986).

Sherlock, Thomas, *The Use and Intent of Prophecy . . . in Six Discourses* (London, 1725).

Sidney, Philip, *An Apology for Poetry* (1595), in *English Critical Essays*, ed. E. Jones (Oxford University Press, 1963).

Simon, Patrick, *A Commentary upon the First Book of Moses, called Genesis* (London, 1698).

Simon, Richard, *A Critical History of the Old Testament* (London, 1682).

Smith, Henry, *God's Arrow against Atheists* (London, 1656).

Smith, John, *Select Discourses* (London, 1660).

Snow, T., (pseud. for Richard Nerve), *Apopiroscipy* (London, 1702).

South, Robert, *Twelve Sermons preached upon Several Occasions*, (London, 1692).

Sermons Preached on Several Occasions, 7 vols. (Oxford: Clarendon, 1823).

The Spectator 1711–14, ed. Joseph Addison and Richard Steele et al. (London: Hamilton, 1808).

Speed, A., *Adam out of Eden* (London, 1659).

Spenser, Edmund, *The Faerie Queen*, ed. A.C. Hamilton (London: Longmans, 1977).

Sprat, Thomas, *History of the Royal Society of London* (London, 1667).

Steno, Nicolaus, *The Prodromus to a Dissertation concerning Solids Naturally contained with Solids* (London, 1671).

Stephens, P., and Brown, W., *Catalogus Horti Botanici Oxoniensis* (Oxonii, 1658).

Sterry, Peter, *The Appearance of God to Man in the Gospel* (London, 1710).

Discourse of the Freedom of the Will (London, 1675).

The Rise, Race and Royalty of the Kingdom of God in the Soul of Man (London, 1683).

Stillingfleet, Edward, *Origines Sacrae* (London, 1662).

Origines Sacrae (London, 1664).

Origines Sacrae, 7th edn (Cambridge, 1702).

Swammerdam, Jan, *Ephemera vita or the Natural History and Anatomy of the Ephemeron* (London, 1681).

Historia insectorum generalis (Utrecht, 1669).

The Letters of Jan Swammerdam to Melchisidec Thévenot, tr. G.A. Lindeboom (Amsterdam: Smuts and Zeitlinger, 1975).

Swan, John, *Speculum mundi. or, a Glasse Representing the Face of the World* (London, 1665).

Swift, Jonathan, *Gullivers Travels* (Ringwood: Penguin, 1991).

Swinden, Tobias, *An Enquiry into the Nature and Place of Hell*, 2nd edn (London, 1727).

Switzer, Stephen, *The Nobleman, Gentleman, and Gardener's Recreation* (London, 1715).

The Practical Fruit-Gardener, 2nd edn (London, 1731).

The Practical Husbandman or Planter, 2 vols. (London, 1733).

Symmons, Edward, *Scripture Vindicated* (Oxford, 1644).

Taylor, Edward, *Jacob Behmen's Theosophick Philosophy Unfolded* (London, 1692).

Thomas Aquinas, St., see Aquinas, St Thomas.

Thomas à Kempis, *The Imitation of Christ* , tr. Leo Sherley-Price (Harmondsworth: Penguin, 1952).

Thomas of Cantimpré, *De natura rerum*, Br. Mus. MS Egerton, 1984.

Thorowgood, Thomas, *Jews in America: or probabilities that the Americans are of that race* (London, 1650).

Toland, John, *Letters to Serena* (London, 1704).

Topsell, Edward, *The Historie of Foure-Footed Beasts* (London, 1607).

The History of Four-Footed Beasts and Serpents (London, 1653).

Torneillus, Augustinus, *Annales sacri et profani* (Coloniae Agrippinae, 1622).

Tournefort, Joseph Pitton de, *Elémens de botanique, ou Méthode pour connaître les plantes* (Paris, 1694).

Traherne, Thomas, *Centuries, Poems, and Thanksgivings*, ed. H.M. Margoliouth, 2 vols. (Oxford: Clarendon, 1958).

Christian Ethicks: or Divine Morality (London, 1675).

Tryon, Thomas, *Country-Mans Companion* (London, 1683).

The Good House-wife made a Doctor (London, 1692).

Turner, Richard, *A View of the Heavens*, 2nd edn (London, 1783).

Turner, William, *A New Herbal, wherein are conteyned the names of Herbes* (London, 1568).

Tyconius, *The Book of Rules of Tyconius*, ed. F.C. Burkitt (Cambridge University Press, 1894).

Tymme, Thomas, *A Dialogue Philosophicall* (London, 1612).

Tyson, Edward, *Philological Essay Concerning the Pygmies*, appended to *Orang-Outang, sive Homo Sylvestris, or the Anatomy of a Pygmie* (London, 1699).

Ussher, Archbishop James, *The Annals of the Old and New Testament* (London, 1658).

Van Helmont, F.M., *A Cabbalistic Dialogue* (London, 1682).

Quaedam Praemeditatae et Consideratae Cogitationes super Genesis (Amsterdam, 1697).

Van Helmont, Jean Baptist, *Oriatrike or, Physick Refined*, tr. John Chandler (London, 1662).

Vaughan, Henry, *The Complete Poetry of Henry Vaughan*, ed. French Fogie (Garden City: Anchor Books, 1964).

Vaughan, Thomas, *The Works of Thomas Vaughan*, ed. Alan Rudrum (Oxford: Clarendon, 1984).

Vincent of Beauvais, *Speculum naturale*, in *Speculum Quadruplex*, 4 vols. (Graz: Akademische Druck-u Verlagsanstalt, 1964–5). Repr. of Douai edn, 1624.

Vossius, Gerhardus J., *Vossius de vera etat mundi*, 2nd edn, printed with *De Septuaginta interpretibus* (The Hague, 1661).

Walker, George, *The History of the Creation* (London, 1641).

Walsh, Francis, *The Antediluvian World; or, A New Theory of the Earth* (Dublin, 1743).

Ward, Seth, *Vindiciae Academiarum* (Oxford, 1654).

Warren, Erasmus, *Geologia: Or, A Discourse concerning the Earth before the Deluge* (London, 1690).

Webb, John, *An Historical Essay, Endeavoring a Probability that the Language of the Empire of China is the Primitive Language* (London, 1669).

Webster, John, *Academarium Examen* (London, 1654).

Westmacott, William, *Historia vegetabilium sacra* (London, 1695).

Whichcote, Benjamin, *Moral and Religious Aphorisms* (London, 1930).

The Works of the Learned Benjamin Whichcote, DD, 4 vols. (Aberdeen, 1751).

Whiston, William, *A Collection of Authentic Records belonging to the Old and New Testaments* (London, 1727).

The Eternity of Hell Torments Considered (London, 1740).

A New Theory of the Earth (London, 1696).

A Vindication of the New Theory of the Earth (London, 1698).

The Accomplishment of Scripture Prophecies, 2nd edn (Cambridge, 1708).

Astronomical Principles of Religion, Natural and Reveal'd (London, 1717).

Whitaker, William, *Disputatio de sacra Scriptura* (Cantabrigiae, 1588).

White, John, *A Commentary upon the First Three Chapters of the First Book of Moses called Genesis* (London, 1656).

Whitelock, Bulstrode , *An Essay in Defence of Pythagoras* (London, 1692).

Wilkins, John, *The Discovery of a New World in the Moone* (London, 1638).

The Discovery of the New World, or, a Discourse Tending to Prove that there may be another Habitable World in the Moon, 5th edn (London, 1684).

An Essay toward a Real Character and a Philosophical Language, (London, 1668).

Mercury, or, the Secret and Swift Messenger, in *Mathematical and Philosophical Works*, 2 vols. (London: Pr. by C. Wittingham, 1802).

Ecclesiastes, or, A Discourse concerning the Gift of Preaching (London, 1647).

Willet, Andrew, *Hexapla in Genesin* (Cambridge, 1605).

Synopsis Papismi, that is, A General View of Papistry (London, 1592).

William of Auvergne, *Opera Omnia*, 2 vols. (Parisiis: Apud Andraeam Pralard, 1674).

William of Normandy, *The Bestiary of Guillaume Le Clerc*, George Druce (Ashford: Headley Brochers, 1936).

Willis, Timothy, *The Search for Causes Containing A Theosophicall Investigation of the Possibilitie of Transmutatorie Alchemie* (London, 1616).

Winstanley, Gerrard, *The Mysterie of God, Concerning the Whole Creation* (London, 1648).

The Works of Gerrard Winstanley, ed. George Sabine (Cornell University Press, 1941).

Wither, George, *Choice Emblems, Divine and Moral* (London, 1681).

Witty, John, *An Essay towards a Vindiction of the Vulgar Exposition of the History of the World*, 2 vols. (London, 1705).

Woodward, John, *An Essay toward a Natural History of the Earth* (London, 1695).

Worlidge, John, *Systema agriculturae* (London, 1669).

Wotton, Edward, *Edoardi Wottoni Oxoniensis de differentiis animalium libri decem* (Paris, 1552).
Wotton, William, *Reflections of Ancient and Modern Learning* (London, 1694).
Wright, Thomas, *The Passions of the Minde* (London, 1601).
Zanchius, Hieronymous, *De operibus Dei intro spacium sex dierum creatis* (1591), in *Perum Theologicorum* (Geneva, 1613).

SECONDARY SOURCES

Abraham, G.A., 'Misunderstanding the Merton Thesis: a Boundary Dispute between History and Sociology', *Isis* 74 (1983) 368–87.
Aiken, Pauline, 'The Animal History of Albertus Magnus and Thomas of Cantimpré', *Speculum* 22 (1947) 205–25.
Allen, Don Cameron, *The Legend of Noah: Renaissance Rationalism in Art, Science, and Letters* (Urbana: University of Illinois Press, 1949).
Allen, Phyllis, 'Medical Education in 17th-Century England', *Journal of the History of Medicine*, 1 (1946), 115–43.
  'Scientific Studies in the English Universities in the Seventeenth Century', *JHI* 10 (1949) 238.
Allers, R., 'Microcosmos from Anaximandros to Paracelsus', *Traditio* 2 (1944) 318–407.
Almond, Philip C., 'The Contours of Hell in English Thought, 1660–1750', *Religion* 22 (1992) 297–311.
  Heaven and Hell in Enlightenment England (Cambridge University Press, 1995).
  'Henry More and the Apocalypse', *JHI* 54 (1993) 189–200.
Althaus, Paul, *The Theology of Martin Luther* (Philadelphia: Fortress Press, 1966).
Anderson, Lorin, *Charles Bonnet and the Order of the Known* (Dordrecht: D. Reidel, 1982).
Arbor, Agnes, *Herbals, their Origin and Evolution, a Chapter in the History of Botany, 1470–1670* (Cambridge University Press, 1912).
Ashworth, William, 'Natural History and the Emblematic World View', in David Lindberg and Robert Westman (eds.), *Reappraisals of the Scientific Revolution* (Cambridge University Press, 1990).
Aston, Margaret, *England's Iconoclasts*, vol. 1 (Oxford: Clarendon, 1988).
Attfield, Robin, *The Ethics of Environmental Concern* (Oxford: Blackwell, 1983).
Auerbach, Eric, *Mimesis*, (Princeton University Press, 1968).
Bailey, M.L., *Milton and Jacob Boehme* (New York: Oxford University Press, 1914).
Barbour, Ian (ed.), *Western Man and Environmental Ethics: Attitudes towards Nature and Technology* (Reading, Mass.: Addison-Wesley, 1973).
Barr, James, 'The Ecological Controversy and the Old Testament', *Bulletin of the John Rylands Library* 55 (1972) 9–32.
Bath, M., 'Recent Developments in Emblem Studies', *Bulletin of the Society of Renaissance Studies*, 6 (1988), 15–20.

Bauer, Karl, *Die Wittenberger Universitätstheologie und die Anfänge der Deutschen Reformation* (Tübingen, 1928).

Bauer, Walter, *A Greek-English Lexicon of the New Testament and Other Early Christian Literature*, 2nd edn (University of Chicago Press, 1979).

Baur, L., 'Die Philosophie des Robert Grosseteste', *Beiträge zur Geschichte der Philosophie des Mittelalters* 9 (1912) 59.

Baylor, *Action and Person: Conscience in Scholasticism and the Young Luther* (Leiden: Brill, 1977).

Beckwith, Sarah, *Christ's Body: Identity, culture and society in late medieval writings* (London: Routledge, 1993).

Beierwaltes, Werner, 'Negati Affirmatio, Or the World as Metaphor', *Dionysius* 1 (1977) 127–59.

Benin, Stephen, *The Footprints of God: Divine Accommodation in Jewish and Christian Thought* (Albany: SUNY Press, 1993).

Bennett, H.S., *English Books and Readers, 1603–1640* (Cambridge University Press, 1970).

Blackwell, R., *Galileo, Bellarmine, and the Bible* (University of Notre Dame Press, 1991).

Boas, George, *The Happy Beast in the French Thought of the Seventeenth Century* (New York: Octagon, 1966).

Boehmer, Heinrich, *Luthers erste Vorlesung* (Leipzig, 1924).

Bono, James, *The Word of God and the Languages of Man: Interpreting Nature in Early Modern Science and Medicine*, vol. 1 (Madison: University of Wisconsin Press, 1995).

Born, L.K., 'Ovid and Allegory', *Speculum* 9 (1934) 362–79.

Bossy, John, *Christianity in the West, 1400–1700* (Oxford University Press, 1985).

Boüard, Michel de, "Encylopédies médiévales. Sur la 'connaissance de la nature et dumonde' au moyen âge", *Revue des questions historiques*, series 3, 16 (1930) 258–304.

Bowler, Peter, 'Preformation and Pre-existence in the Seventeenth Century', *JHB* 4 (1971) 221–44.

Bray, Gerald (ed.), *Documents of the English Reformation* (Cambridge: James Clarke, 1994).

Brigden, Susan, *London and the Reformation* (Oxford: Clarendon, 1989).

Brooke, John Hedley, *Science and Religion: Some Historical Perspectives* (Cambridge University Press, 1991).

Brown, Peter, *The Body and Society: Men, Women and Sexual Renunciation in Early Christianity* (London: Faber and Faber, 1990).

Brown, Stuart, 'Leibniz and More's Cabbalistic Circle', in Sarah Hutton (ed.), *Henry More (1614–1678) Tercentenary Studies* (Dordrecht: Kluwer, 1990) pp. 77–95.

Bruns, Gerald L., *Hermeneutics Ancient and Modern* (Yale University Press, 1992).

Buckley, Michael, *At the Origins of Modern Atheism* (Yale Univeristy Press, 1987).

Bynam, Caroline Walker, *Holy Feast and Holy Fast* (University of California Press, 1988).

Byrne, Peter, *Natural Religion and the Nature of Religion* (London: Routledge, 1989).

Camelot, P-Th., "'Sacramentum'. Notes de théologie sacrementaire augustinienne", *Revue thomiste* 57 (1957) 429–49.

Cassirer, Ernst, *The Platonic Renaissance in England*, tr. James Pettigrove (London: Nelson, 1953).

Charbonneau-Lassay, Louis, *The Bestiary of Christ* (New York: Arkana, 1972).

Chenu, Marie-Dominique, 'Cur homo? Le sous-sol d'une controverse au xiie siècle', *Mélanges de science religieuse*, 10 (1953) 197–204.

Nature, Man and Society in the Twelfth Century (University of Chicago Press, 1968).

Cizewski, Wanda, 'Reading the World as Scripture: Hugh of St Victor's *De tribus diebus*', *Florilegium* 9 (1987) 65–88.

'Beauty and The Beasts: Allegorical Zoology in Twelfth-Century Hexaemeral Literature', in H.J. Westra (ed.), *From Athens to Chartres: Neoplatonism and Medieval Thought* (Leiden: Brill, 1992) 289–300.

Clark, Anne, *Beasts and Bawdy* (London: Dent, 1975).

Clark, W.B., and McMunn, M.T. (eds.), *Beasts and Birds of the Middle Ages: The Bestiary and its Legacy* (University of Pennsylvania Press, 1989).

Clark, Willene, *The Medieval Book of Birds: Hugh of Fouilloy's Aviarum* (Birmingham, N.Y.: Medieval and Renaissance Texts and Studies, 1992).

Clarke, Kenneth, *Animals and Men* (London: Thames and Hudson, 1977).

Cohen, Jeremy, *"Be Fertile and Increase, Fill the Earth and Master It": The Ancient and Medieval Career of a Biblical Text* (Cornell University Press, 1989).

Conger, G.P., *Theories of Macrocosmos and Microcosmos in the History of Philosophy* (New York: Columbia University Press, 1922).

Copenhaver, Brian, 'A Tale of Two Fishes: Magical Objects in Natural History from Antiquity through the Scientific Revolution', *JHI* 52 (1991) 373–98.

Cornelius, P., *Languages in Seventeenth- and Early Eighteenth-Century Imaginary Voyages* (Geneva: Librairie Droz, 1965).

Courcelle, Pierre, 'Tradition Néo-Platonicienne et Traditions Chrétiennes de la "Region de Dissemblance"', *Archives d'Histoire Doctrinale et Littéraire du Moyen Age* (1957) 5–33.

Cox, Patricia, 'The *Physiologus*: A *Poiesis* of Nature', *Church History* 52 (1983) 433–43.

Cressy, David, *Literacy and the Social Order* (Cambridge University Press, 1980).

Crombie, A.C., *From Augustine to Galileo* (London: Heinemann, 1957).

Science, Optics and Music in Medieval and Early Modern Thought (London: Hambledon Press, 1990).

Crouse, R.D., 'Honorius Augustodunensis: The Arts as *Via ad Patriam*', in *Arts Libéraux et Philosophie au Moyen Age* (Paris: Vrin, 1969).

'*Intentio Moysi*: Bede, Augustine, Eriugena and Plato in the *Hexaemeron* of Honorius Augustodunensis', *Dionysius* 2 (1978) 137–57.

Curry, Patrick, *Prophecy and Power: Astrology in Early Modern England* (Princeton Unversity Press, 1989).

Curtius, E. R., *European Literature and the Latin Middle Ages* (London: Routledge and Kegan Paul, 1953).

Dales, Richard, 'A Twelfth-Century Concept of the Natural Order', *Viator* 9 (1978) 179–92.

Daly, Peter, and Callahan, Virginia (eds.), *Andreas Alciatus: The Latin Emblems and Emblems in Translation*, 2 vols. (University of Toronto Press, 1985).

Daniélou, Jean, *Origène*, (Paris: La Table Ronde, 1948).

Philon d'Alexandrie (Paris, 1958).

Davies, Godfrey, 'Arminian versus Puritan in England *c.* 1620–1650', *Huntington Library Bulletin* 5 (1934), 157–79.

Davies, Gordon, *The Earth in Decay: A History of British Geomorphology 1578–1878* (London: Oldsbourne, 1969).

Debus, Allen, *The English Paracelsians* (London: Osbourne, 1965).

Man and Nature in the Renaissance (Cambridge University Press, 1978).

De Lubac, Henri, *Exégèse Médiéval: Les Quatres sens de l'écriture*, 2 vols. (Paris Auber, 1959–64).

De Mott, Benjamin, 'Comenius and the Real Character in England', *PMLA* 70 (1955) 1068–81.

Diehl, H. 'Graven Images: Protestant Emblem Books in England', *Renaissance Quarterly*, 39 (1986), 49–66.

Dithmar, Reinhard (ed.), *Martin Luther's Fabeln and Sprichworter* (Darmstadt: Wissenschaftliche Buchgesellschaft, 1995).

Drake, Stillman, *Galileo at Work: His Scientific Biography* (University of Chicago Press, 1978).

Dronke, Peter, 'Platonic-Christian Allegories in the Homilies of Hildegard of Bingen', *From Athens to Chartres: Neoplatonism in Medieval Thought*, ed. H. J. Westra (Leiden: Brill, 1992).

Duffy, Eamon, *The Stripping of the Altars: Traditional Religion in England, c.1400 – c.1580* (Yale University Press, 1992).

Dunbar, H. Flanders, *Symbolism in Medieval Thought and its Consummation in the Divine Comedy* (New York: Russell and Russell, 1961).

Duncan, Joseph E., 'Paradise as the Whole Earth', *JHI* 30 (1969) 171–86.

Milton's Earthy Paradise: A Historical Study of Eden (Minneapolis: University of Minnesota Press, 1972).

Durbin, Paul, and Rapp, Friedrich (eds.) *Philosophy and Technology* (Dordrecht: Reidel, 1983).

Ebeling, G., 'Die Anfänge von Luthers Hermeneutik', *Zeitschrift für Theologie und Kirche*, 48 (1951) 162–230.

Luther: An Introduction to his Thought (London: Collins, 1970).

Ehrman, Bart, *The Orthodox Corruption of Scripture* (Oxford University Press, 1992).

Eisenstadt, S.N. (ed.), *The Protestant Ethic and Modernization* (New York, 1968).

Eisenstein, Elizabeth, *The Printing Press as an Agent of Change*, 2 vols. (Cambridge University Press, 1979).

The Printing Revolution in Early Modern Europe (Cambridge University Press, 1983).

294 *References*

Emery, Clarke, 'John Wilkins' Universal Language', *Isis* 38 (1947–8), 174–85.

Evans, E.P., *Animal Symbolism in Ecclesiastical Architecture* (New York: Henry Holt, 1896).

Evans, G.R., *The Language and Logic of the Bible: The Road to Reformation* (Cambridge University Press, 1985).

Philosophy and Theology in the Middle Ages (London: Routledge, 1993).

Fahlbusch, Erwin et al. (eds.), *Evangelisches Kirchenlexicon*, 3rd edn, 4 vols. (Göttingen: Vandenhoeck & Ruprecht, 1986–96).

Farington, B., *The Philosophy of Francis Bacon*, (Liverpool, 1964).

Findlen, Paula, *Possessing Nature: Museums, Collecting, and Scientific Culture in Early Modern Italy*, (Berkeley: University of California Press, 1995).

Fisch, H., 'The Scientist as Priest: A Note on Robert Boyle's Natural Theology', *Isis* 44 (1953) 252–65.

Fletcher, Angus, *Allegory: The Theory of a Symbolic Mode* (Cornell University Press, 1964).

Foa, Anna, 'The New and the Old: The Spread of Syphilis (1495–1530)' in *Sex and Gender in Historical Perspective*, ed. Edward Muir and Guido Ruggiero (Johns Hopkins University Press, 1990).

Fontaine, Jacques, 'Isidore de Séville et l'astrologie', *Revue des études Latines* 31 (1953) 283–5.

'Isidore de Séville et la Mutation de l'Encyclopédisme Antique', *Cahiers D'Histoire Mondiale* 9 (1966) 519–38.

Force, James, *William Whiston: Honest Newtonian* (Cambridge University Press, 1985).

Foucault, Michel, *The Order of Things* (London: Tavistock, 1987).

Fraenkel, Peter, *Testimonia Patrum: The Function of the Patristic Argument in the Theology of Philip Melanchthon* (Geneva: Droz, 1961).

Freeman, Rosemary, *English Emblem Books* (London: Chatto and Windus, 1967).

Frei, Hans, *The Eclipse of Biblical Narrative*, (Yale University Press, 1974).

Funkenstein, Amos, *Theology and the Scientific Imagination* (Princeton University Press, 1986).

Garin, Eugenio, 'Alcune Osservazione Sul Libro Come Simbolo', in *Umanesimo e Simbolismo*, Archivio de Filosophia (Padua, 1958), pp. 93–102.

Gascoigne, John, *Cambridge in the Age of Enlightenment: Science, Religion and Politics from the Restoration to the French Revolution* (Cambridge University Press, 1989).

Gaukroger, Stephen (ed.), *The Uses of Antiquity* (Dordrecht: Kluwer, 1991).

Gaukroger, Stephen, and Schuster, John (eds.), *Descartes' Natural Philosophy*, vol. 1 (Oxford University Press, forthcoming).

Geneva, Ann, *Astrology and the Seventeenth-Century Mind* (Manchester University Press, 1996).

Gerbi, Antonello, *The Dispute of the New World: The History of a Polemic, 1750–1900*, tr. Jeremy Moyle (University of Pittsburgh Press, 1973).

Giard, Luce, 'Remapping Knowledge, Reshaping Institutions', in Pumfrey et al. (eds.), *Science, Culture, and Popular Belief*, pp. 28–32.

Gieben, S., 'Traces of God in nature according to Robert Grosseteste, with the text of the *Dictum, Omnis creatura speculum est'*, *Franciscan Studies* 24 (1964) 144–58.

Gillespie, Neal, 'Natural History, Natural Theology, and Social Order: John Ray and the "Newtonian Ideology"', *JHB* 20 (1987) 1–49.

Gilson, Ettiene, *The Christian Philosophy of Saint Augustine* (London: Victor Gollancz, 1961).

History of Christian Philosophy in the Middle Ages (London: Sheed and Ward, 1972).

Ginzberg, Louis, *The Legends of the Jews*, 7 vols. (Philadelphia: Jewish Publication Society of America, 1911–13).

Glass, Bentley, 'Heredity and Variation in the Eighteenth Century Concept of the Species', in *Forerunners of Darwin 1745–1859*, ed. B. Glass, Owsei Temkin, and L. Strauss Jr. (Johns Hopkins University Press, 1968).

Gohau, *A History of Geology*, tr. A. and M. Carozzi (New Brunswick: Rutgers University Press, 1991).

Gowan, Donald and Shumaker, Millard, *Subduing the Earth: An Exchange of Views* (Kingston, Ont.: The United Church of Canada, 1980).

Grafton, Anthony, *New Worlds, Ancient Texts*, (Cambridge, Mass.: Harvard University Press, 1992)

Graham, Victor, 'The Pelican as Image and Symbol', *Revue de la littérature comparée* 36 (1962) 235–43.

Grant, Edward, *Planets, Stars, and Orbs: The Medieval Cosmos, 1200–1687* (CambridgeUniversity Press, 1995).

Greaves, Richard, *The Puritan Revolution and Educational Thought* (New Brunswick: Rutgers University Press, 1969).

'Puritanism and Science: The Anatomy of a Controversy', *JHI* 30 (1969) 345–68.

Green, Ian, *The Christian's ABC: Catechisms and Catechising in England, c. 1530–1748* (Oxford: Clarendon, 1996).

Greenblatt, Stephen, *Marvellous Possessions: The Wonder of the New World* (University of Chicago Press, 1991).

Greengrass, Martin, Leslie, Michael and Raylor, Timothy (eds.) *Samuel Hartlib and Universal Reformation* (Cambridge University Press, 1994).

Greetham, D.C., 'Bartholomaeus Anglicus on Nature', *JHI* 41 (1980), 663–78.

Gregory, Tullio, *Anima mundi: la filosophia di Guglielmo di Conches e la scuola di Chartres* (Florence, 1955).

Guerlac, H., and Jacob, M., 'Bentley, Newton, and Providence', *JHI* 30 (1969), 307–18.

Hale, John, *The Civilization of Europe in the Renaissance* (Sydney: Simon and Schuster, 1995).

Hall, A. Rupert, *The Revolution in Science* (London: Longman, 1983).

Häring, Nikolaus, 'Commentary and Hermeneutics', in Robert Benson and Giles Constable (eds.) *Renaissance and Renewal in the Twelfth Century* (Cambridge, Mass.: Harvard University Press, 1982).

'The Creation and Creator of the World According to Thierry of Chartres and Clarenbaldus of Arras', *Archives d'Histoire Doctrinale et Littéraire du Moyen Age* 22 (1955) 184–200.

Harms, W., 'On Natural History and Emblematics in the Sixteenth Century', Allan Ellenius (ed.), *The Natural Sciences and the Arts* (Uppsala: Almqvist and Wiksell, 1985), pp. 67–83;

Harrison, Peter, 'Animal Souls, Metempsychosis and Theodicy in Seventeenth-Century English Thought', *JHP* 31 (1993) 519–44.

'Newtonian Science, Miracles, and the Laws of Nature', *JHI* 56 (1995) 531–53.

'Religion' and the Religions in the English Enlightenment (Cambridge University Press, 1990).

Haskins, C.H., *Studies in the History of Medieval Science* (New York: Ungar, 1960).

Hastings, Hester, *Man and Beast in French Thought of the Eighteenth Century* (Johns Hopkins University Press, 1936).

Hendricks, Donald, 'Profitless Printing: Publication of the Polyglots', *The Journal of Library History* 2 (1967) 98–115.

Henry, J., 'Atomism and Eschatology: Catholicism and Natural Philosophy in the Interregnum', *BJHS*, 15 (1982), 211–46.

Hick, John, *Evil and the God of Love* (London: Macmillan, 1968).

Hicks, Carola, *Animals in Early Medieval Art* (Edinburgh: University of Edinburgh Press, 1993).

Hill, Christopher, *Collected Essays of Christopher Hill*, 3 vols. (Amherst: University of Massachusetts Press, 1986).

The English Bible and the Seventeenth-Century Revolution (Ringwood: Penguin, 1994).

Puritanism and Revolution (London: Secker and Warburg, 1958).

Society and Puritanism in Pre-Revolutionary England (London: Panther Books, 1964).

The World Turned Upside Down (Ringwood: Penguin, 1975).

Hoeniger, F.D. and J.F.M., *The Development of Natural History in Tudor England* (Charlottesville: University Press of Virginia, 1969).

Hoopes, Robert, *Right Reason in the English Renaissance* (Cambridge, Mass: Harvard University Press, 1962).

Hooykaas, R., *Religion and the Rise of Modern Science* (Grand Rapids, Eerdmans, 1972).

'Science and the Reformation', in *The Protestant Ethic and Modernization*, ed. S.N. Eisenstadt (New York, 1968) pp. 211–39.

Huff, Toby, *The Rise of Early Modern Science: Islam, China, and the West*, (Cambridge University Press, 1993).

Hunter, Michael, (ed.), *Robert Boyle Reconsidered* (Cambridge University Press, 1994).

Science and Society in Restoration England (Cambridge University Press, 1981).

Hunter, Michael, and Schaffer, Simon (eds.), *Robert Hooke: New Studies* (Woodbridge: Boydell, 1989).

Hutchison, Keith, 'Dormative Virtues, Scholastic Qualities, and the New Philosophies', *History of Science* 29 (1991) 245–78.

'What Happened to Occult Qualities in the Scientific Revolution?', *Isis* 73 (1982) 233–53.

Hutin, S. *Les disciples anglais de Jacob Boehme au XVII et XVIII siècles* (Paris: Denoël, 1960).

Hutton, Sarah (ed.), *Henry More (1614–1687): Tercentenary Studies* (Dordrecht: Kluwer, 1990).

Huysmans, Joris Karl, *La Cathédrale* (Paris: Plon, 1968).

Hyman, Arthur, and Walsh, James, (eds.) *Philosophy in the Middle Ages* (Indianapolis: Hackett, 1974).

Ives, Samuel, and Lehman-Haupt, Helmut, *An English 13th Century Bestiary: A New Discovery in the Technique of Medieval Illustration* (New York: Kraus, 1942).

Jackson, Darrell, 'The Theory of Signs in Augustine's *De Doctrina Christiana*', in *Augustine: A Collection of Critical Essays*, ed. Markus, pp. 92–147.

Jacob, James R, 'Boyle's Circle in the Protectorate: Revelation, Politics and the Millennium', *JHI* 38 (1977), 131–40.

Jacob, James R. and Margaret C., 'The Anglican Origins of Modern Science: the Metaphysical Foundations of Whig Constitution', *Isis* 71 (1980) 251–67.

Jacob, Margaret C., *The Newtonians and the English Revolution* (Hassocks: Harvester Press, 1976).

'Millennarianism and Science in the late Seventeenth Century', *JHI* 37 (1976) 335–41.

James, M.R., *The Bestiary*, (Oxford: Roxburghe Club, 1928).

Jeauneau, E. (ed.), *Jean Scot: Homélie sur le prologue de Jean* (Paris, 1969).

Jones, R.F., *Ancients and Moderns: A Study in the Scientific Movement in Seventeenth-Century England* (St Louis, 1936).

Kearney, Hugh, 'Puritanism and Science: Problems of Definition', in Webster (ed.), *Intellectual Revolution*, pp. 254–61.

Scholars and Gentlemen: Universities and Society in pre-Industrial Britain, 1500–1700 (London: Faber and Faber, 1970).

Kelly, Henry, 'Metamorphoses of the Eden Serpent during the Middle Ages and Renaissance', *Viator* 2 (1971) 301–27.

Kelmsley, Douglas, 'Religious Influences in the Rise of Modern Science', *Annals of Science* 24 (1968) 199–226.

Kenny, Anthony, *Aquinas on Mind* (London: Routledge, 1993).

Klaaren, Eugene, *Religious Origins of Modern Science* (Grand Rapids: Eerdmans, 1977).

Knowlson, James, *Universal Language Schemes in England and France 1600–1800* (Toronto: University of Toronto Press, 1975).

Korshin, Paul, *Typologies in England, 1650–1820* (Princeton University Press, 1982).

Kroll, Richard, *The Material World: Literate Culture in the Restoration and Early Eighteenth Century* (Johns Hopkins University Press, 1991).

Kroll, Richard, Ashcroft, Richard, and Zagorin, Perez (eds.), *Philosophy, Science, and Religion in England 1640–1700* (Cambridge University Press, 1992).

Kubrin, David, 'Newton and the Cyclical Cosmos', *JHI* 28 (1967) 325–46.

Kuhn, Albert, 'Glory or Gravity: Hutchinson vs. Newton', *JHI* 22 (1961) 303–22.

Kuhn, Thomas, *The Structure of Scientific Revolutions*, 2nd edn (University of Chicago Press, 1970).

Kusukawa, Sachiko, *The Transformation of Natural Philosophy: The Case of Philip Melanchthon* (Cambridge University Press, 1995).

la Boullaye, H. Pinard de, *L'Etude Comparée des Religions* (Paris: Gabriel Beauchesne, 1922).

Lacqueur, Jacques, *Making Sex: Body and Gender from the Greeks to Freud* (Cambridge, Mass.: Harvard University Press, 1990).

Ladner, Gerhard, 'Medieval and Modern Understanding of Symbolism: A Comparison', *Speculum* 54 (1979) 223–56.

Lamont, William, *Godly Rule, Politics and Religion 1603–60* (London: Macmillan, 1969).

Lauchert, F., *Geschichte des Physiologus* (Strassburg: Karl Trübner Verlag, 1889).

La vie parfaite: Points de vue sur l'essence de la vie religieuse (Partis-Turnhout, 1948)

Leclercq, Jean, *The Love of Learning and the Desire for God* (New York: Fordham University Press, 1974).

Leff, G., *Paris and Oxford Universities in the Thirteenth and Fourteenth Centuries* (New York: 1968).

Le Goff, Jacques, *Medieval Civilization*, tr. Julia Barrow (Oxford: Blackwell, 1988).

The Medieval Imagination, tr. A. Goldhammer (University of Chicago Press, 1988).

Leishmann, J.B., *The Metaphysical Poets* (New York: Russell and Russell, 1963).

Lemoine, Michel, 'L'oeuvre encyclopédique de Vincent de Beauvais', *Cahiers D'Histoire Mondiale* 9 (1966) 571–9.

Lennon, T., Nicholas, J., and Davis, J. (eds.), *Problems of Cartesianism* (Kingston and Montreal: McGill-Queens University Press, 1982).

Leslie, Michael, and Raylor, Timothy (eds.), *Culture and Cultivation in Early Modern England* (Leicester University Press, 1992).

Levi, Anthony, *French Moralists* (Oxford: Clarendon, 1964).

Levine, Joseph M., *Dr Woodward's Shield: History, Science, and Satire in Augustan England* (Cornell University Press, 1991).

Lewis, Jack P., *A Study of the Interpretation of Noah and the Flood in Jewish and Christian Literature* (Leiden: Brill, 1978).

Lindberg, David, and Numbers, Ronald (eds.), *God and Nature: Historical Essays on the Encounter between Christianity and Science* (University of California Press, 1986).

Lindberg, David and Westman, Robert (eds.), *Reappraisals of the Scientific Revolution* (Cambridge University Press, 1990).

Linden, S., 'Alchemy and Eschatology in Seventeenth Century Poetry', *Ambix* 31 (1984), 102–24.

Lockridge, Kenneth, *Literacy in Colonial New England* (New York, 1974).

Lovejoy, A.O., *The Great Chain of Being* (New York: Harper, 1960).

Maclean, Ian, *The Renaissance Notion of Woman* (Cambridge University Press, 1980).

Madsen, William G., *From Shadowy Types to Truth: Studies in Milton's Symbolism* (New Haven: Yale University Press, 1968).

Mâle, Emile, *Religious Art in France: The Twelfth Century*, tr. Marthiel Mathews, (Princeton University Press, 1978).

Mandelbrote, Scott, '"A Duty of the Greatest Moment': Isaac Newton and the writing of biblical criticism", *BJHS* 26 (1993) 281–302.

Manuel, Frank, *The Religion of Isaac Newton* (Oxford: Clarendon, 1974).

Markley, Robert, *Fallen Languages: Crises of Representation in Newtonian England, 1660–1740* (Cornell University Press, 1993).

Markus, R.A. (ed.), *Augustine: A Collection of Critical Essays*, (New York: Doubleday, 1972).

Marrone, Steven P., *William of Auvergne and Robert Grosseteste* (Princeton University Press, 1983).

Martz, Louis, *The Paradise Within: Studies in Vaughan, Traherne, and Milton* (New Haven: Yale University Press, 1964).

Matthias, Peter (ed.), *Science and Society 1600–1900* (Cambridge University Press, 1972).

McColley, Diane, *A Gust for Paradise: Milton's Eden and the Visual Arts* (Urbana: University of Illinois Press, 1993).

McCulloch, Florence, *Medieval Latin and French Bestiaries* (Chapel Hill: University of North Carolina Press, 1962).

McEvoy, J., 'Microcosm and Macrocosm in the Writings of St. Bonaventure', *Commissio Internationalis Bonaventurianae S. Bonaventura. Volumen Commemorativum . . . Cura et Studio Commissionis Internationalis Bonventurianae* (Roma: Padre di Editori di Quaracchi, 1972–4).

The Philosophy of Robert Grosseteste (Oxford: Clarendon, 1982).

McGrath, Alister, *The Intellectual Origins of the European Reformation* (Blackwell: Oxford, 1987).

McGuire, J.E., and Rattansi, P.M., 'Newton and the Pipes of Pan', *Notes and Records of the Royal Society of London*, 21 (1966) .

McKough, Michael, *The Meaning of the Rationes Seminales in St Augustine* (Washington: Catholic University of America, 1926).

Meinhold, Peter, *Luthers Sprachphilosophie* (Berlin: Lutherisches Verlagshaus, 1959).

Merchant, Caroline, *The Death of Nature* (San Francisco: Harper and Row, 1980).

Merton, Robert K., 'Puritanism, Pietism, and Science', *The Sociological Review* 28 (1936) 1–30.

Science, Technology and Society in Seventeenth-Century England (New York: Harper, 1970).

Milton, Anthony, *Catholic and Reformed: The Roman and Protestant Churches in English Protestant Thought 1600–1640* (Cambridge University Press, 1995).

Mitcham, Carl and Grote, Jim (eds.), *Theology and Technology: Essays in Christian Analysis and Exegesis* (New York: University Press of America, 1984).

Moeller, Bernt, 'Scripture, Tradition, and Sacrament in the Middle Ages and in Luther', in *Holy Book and Holy Tradition*, ed. F.F. Bruce and E.G. Rupp (Manchester: Manchester University Press, 1968), pp. 113–35.

Muckle, J.T., 'The *Hexameron* of Robert Grosseteste. The First Twelve Chapters of Part Seven', *Medieval Studies* 6 (1944) 151–74.

Mulligan, Lotte, 'Anglicanism, Latitudinarianism, and Science in Seventeenth-Century England', *Annals of Science* 30 (1973) 213–19.

'Puritanism and English Science: A Critique of Webster', *Isis* 71 (1980) 456–69.

'Robert Boyle, "Right Reason", and the Meaning of Metaphor', *JHI* 55 (1994) 235–57.

Musurillo, Herbert, 'The Problem of Ascetical Fasting in the Greek Patristic Writers', *Traditio* 12 (1956) 16–28.

Needham, Joseph, *Science and Civilisation in China*, 7 vols. (Cambridge University Press, 1954–84).

Nellas, Panayiotis, *Deification in Christ: Orthodox Perspectives on the Nature of the Human Person* (Crestwood, NY: Vladimir's Seminary Press, 1987).

Nelson, Benjamin, *On the Roads to Modernity: Conscience, Science and Civilizations*, ed. Toby Huff (Totowa, N.J.: Rowan and Littlefield, 1981).

Nicolson, Marjorie Hope, *Mountain Gloom and Mountain Glory* (New York: Norton, 1963).

Noble, Paul, 'The *Sensus Literalis*', *Journal of Theological Studies*, (NS) 44 (1993), 1–23.

Norton, David, *The History of the Bible as Literature*, 2 vols. (Cambridge University Press, 1993).

Ong, W.J., *Ramus: Method and the Decay of Dialogue* (Cambridge, Mass: Harvard University Press, 1958).

Osler, Margaret J., 'From Immanent Natures to Nature as Artifice: The Reinterpretation of Final Causes in Seventeenth-Century Natural Philosophy', *The Monist* 79 (1996), 388–407.

Ott, L., 'Die platonische Weltseele in der Frühscholastik', in *Parousia: Studien zur Philosophie Platons und zur Problemgeschichte des Platonismus* (Frankfurt, 1965), 307–31.

Otten, Charlotte, *Environ'd with Eternity: God, Poems, and Plants in Sixteenth and Seventeenth Century England* (Lawrence: Coronado Press, 1985).

Pagel, Walter, *Paracelsus: An Introduction to Philosophical Medicine in the Era of the Renaissance* (Basel: Karger, 1958).

'Religious Motives in the Medical Biology of the XVIIth Century', *Bulletin of the Institute of the History of Medicine* 3 (1935) 97–128, 213–31, 265–312.

Pagel, Walter, and Rattansi, P., 'Vesalius and Paracelsus', *Medical History* 8 (1964) 309–34.

Pagels, Elaine, *Adam, Eve, and the Serpent* (New York: Vintage, 1989).

Panaccio, Claude, 'From Mental Word to Mental Language', *Philosophical Topics* 20 (1992) 125–43.

Panofsky, E., *The Life and Art of Albrecht Dürer*, 4th edn (Princeton University Press, 1955).

Passmore, John, *Man's Responsibility for Nature* (London: Duckworth, 1974).

Patrides, C.A., 'The Upright Form of Man', *Premises and Motifs in Renaissance Thought and Literature* (Princeton University Press, 1982).

Pelikan, Jaraslov, *The Reformation of the Bible, the Bible of the Reformation* (New Haven: Yale University Press, 1996).

Peter, Walter, *The Renaissance* (London: Macmillan, 1910).

Peuckert, W.E., *Paracelsus, Die Geheimnisse. Ein Lesebuch aus seinen Schriften* (Stuttgart, 1941).

Piltz, Anders, *The World of Medieval Learning*, tr. David Johnes (Oxford: Blackwell, 1981).

Popkin, Richard, and Force, James, (eds.), *The Books of Nature and Scripture: Recent Essays in Natural Philosophy, Theology, and Biblical Criticism in the Netherlands of Spinoza's Time and the British Isles of Newton's Time* (Dordrecht: Kluwer, 1994).

Porter, Roy, *The Making of Geology: Earth Science in Britain 1660–1815* (Cambridge University Press, 1977).

Post, G. (ed.), *Studies in Medieval Legal Thought* (Princeton University Press, 1964).

Prest, John, *The Garden of Eden: The Botanic Garden and the Re-Creation of Paradise* (New Haven: Yale University Press, 1981).

Pumfrey, Stephen, Rossi, Paolo, and Slawinski, Maurice (eds.), *Science, Culture and Popular Belief in Renaissance Europe* (Manchester University Press, 1991).

Rabb, T.K., 'Puritanism and the Rise of Experimental Science in England', *Cahiers d'Histoire Mondiale* 7 (1962).

Rashdall, Hastings, *The Universities of Europe in the Middle Ages*, 2nd edn, 3 vols. (Oxford: Clarendon, 1936).

Raven, C.E., *Natural Religion and Christian Theology* (Cambridge University Press, 1953).

Reallexicon für Antike und Christentum, ed. Ernst Dassmann (Stuttgart: Anton Hiersemann, 1950–).

Redondi, Pietro, *Galileo: Heretic*, tr. Raymond Rosenthal (London: Penguin, 1987).

Reeds, Karen, 'Renaissance Humanism and Botany', *Annals of Science* 33 (1976) 519–43.

Reedy, Gerard, *The Bible and Reason: Anglicans and Scripture in Late Seventeenth-Century England* (Philadelphia: University of Pennsylvania Press, 1985).

Reeves, Eileen, 'Augustine and Galileo on Reading the Heavens', *JHI* 52 (1991) 563–79.

Reventlow, Henning Graf von, *The Authority of the Bible and the Rise of the Modern World* (Philadelphia: Fortress Press, 1985).

References

Ritter, J., (ed.), *Historisches Wörtebuch der Philosophie* (Basel: Schwabe, 1971–).

Robbins, F., *The Hexaemeral Literature* (University of Chicago Press, 1912).

Roberts, L. (ed.), *Approaches to Nature in the Middle Ages* (New York: Medieval and Renaissance Texts and Studies, 16, 1982).

Roger, Jacques, *Les Sciences de la Vie dans la Pensée Française du XVIIIᵉ Siècle*, 2nd edn (Paris: Armand Colin, 1971).

Rosenfield, Leonora, *From Beast-Machine to Man-Machine* (New York: Octagon, 1968).

Rossi, Paolo, *The Dark Abyss of Time: The History of the Earth and the History of Nations from Hooke to Vico* (University of Chicago Press, 1984).

Rubin, Miri, *Corpus Christi: The Eucharist in Late Medieval Culture* (Cambridge University Press, 1991).

Ruestow, Edward, 'Piety and the defence of natural order: Swammerdam on generation', in Margaret Osler and Paul Farber (eds.) *Religion, Science, and Worldview* (Cambridge University Press, 1985).

Runia, David, *Philo in Early Christian Literature* (Minneapolis: Fortress Press, 1993).

Rupp, Gordon, *The Righteousness of God: Luther Studies* (London: Hodder and Stoughton, 1953).

Russell, D., 'Alciati's emblems in Renaissance Europe', *Renaissance Quarterly* 34 (1981) 534–54.

Salmon, Vivian, *The Works of Francis Lodowick* (London: Longmans, 1972).

Salt, Leo, 'Puritanism, Capitalism, Democracy, and the New Science, *American Historical Review* 73 (1967) 18–29.

Schaffer, Simon, 'Newton's Comets and the Transformation of Astrology', in Patrick Curry (ed.) *Astrology, Science and Society: Historical Essays* (Woodbridge: Boydell Press, 1987), 219–43.

Schaper, J., 'The Unicorn in the Messianic Imagery of the Old Testament', *Journal of Theological Studies*, NS, 45 (1994) 117–36.

Schmidt, Charles, 'Perennial Philosophy: from Agnostino to Leibniz', *JHI* 27 (1966) 505–32.

Schultz, Max, *Paradise Preserved: Recreations of Eden in Eighteenth- and Nineteenth-Century England* (Cambridge University Press, 1985).

Sells, A.L., *Animal Poetry in French and English Literature and the Greek Tradition* (London: Thames and Hudson, 1957).

Shapin, Steven, *A Social History of Truth: Civility and Science in Seventeenth-Century England* (University of Chicago Press, 1994).

'Robert Boyle and Mathematics: Reality, Representation, and Experimental Practice', *Science in Context* 2 (1988) 23–58.

Shapin, Steven, and Schaffer, Simon, *Leviathan and the Air-Pump: Hobbes, Boyle, and the Experimental Life* (Princeton University Press, 1985).

Shapiro, Barbara, 'Latitudinarianism and Science in Seventeenth-Century England', in Webster (ed.), *Intellectual Revolution*, 286–316.

Probability and Certainty in Seventeenth-Century England (Princeton University Press, 1983).

Shumaker, Wayne, *The Occult Sciences in the Renaissance* (Berkeley: University of California Press, 1972).

Singer, Theodore, 'Hieroglyphs, Real Characters, and the Idea of a Natural Language in English Seventeenth-Century Thought', *JHI* 50 (1989) 49–70.

Slaughter, Mary, *Universal Languages and Scientific Taxonomy in the Seventeenth Century* (Cambridge University Press, 1972).

Smalley, Beryl, *Studies in Medieval Thought and Learning* (London: Hambledon Press, 1981).

The Study of the Bible in the Middle Ages, (Oxford: Blackwell, 1952).

Smith, Wilfred Cantwell, *The Meaning and End of Religion* (London: SPCK, 1978).

Snow, C.P., *The Two Cultures and the Scientific Revolution* (Cambridge University Press, 1959).

Southern, R.W., *Robert Grosseteste: the Growth of an English Mind in Medieval Europe* (Oxford: Clarendon, 1986).

Spring, David and Eileen (eds.), *Ecology and Religion in History* (New York: Harper and Row, 1974).

Spurr, John, 'Rational Religion in Restoration England', *JHI* 50 (1989) 563–85.

Stannard, Jerry, 'The Herbal as a Medical Document', *Bulletin of the History of Medicine* 43 (1969) 212–20.

'Medieval Herbals and their Development', *Clio Medica* (1974) 23–33.

Steffen, Lloyd H., 'In Defence of Dominion', *Environmental Ethics* 14 (1992) 63–80.

Stimson, Dorothy, 'Puritanism and the New Philosophy in 17th century England', *Bulletin of the Institute of the History of Medicine* 3 (1935) 321–4.

Stock, Brian, *The Implications of Literacy* (Princeton University Press, 1983).

Myth and Science in the Twelfth Century (Princeton University Press, 1972).

Stone, Lawrence, 'Literacy and Education in England, 1640–1900', *Past and Present* 42 (1969) 67–139.

Tawney, R.H., *Religion and the Rise of Capitalism* (New York: Harcourt, Brace, and Co., 1926).

Taylor, G.C., 'Shakespeare's Use of the Idea of the Beast in Man', *Studies in Philology*, 62 (1945) 531–2.

Thibodeau, Timothy, '*Enigmata Figurarum*: Biblical Exegesis and Liturgical Exposition in Durand's *Rationale*', *Harvard Theological Review* 86 (1993) 65–79.

Thomas, Keith, *Man and the Natural World* (Ringwood: Penguin, 1983).

Religion and the Decline of Magic (New York: Charles Scribner's Sons, 1971).

Turner, James, *One Flesh: Paradisal Marriage and Sexual Relations in the Age of Milton* (Oxford: Clarendon, 1987).

Tuveson, Ernest, 'Swift and the World Makers', *JHI* 11 (1950) 54–74.

Tyacke, Nicholas, 'Puritanism, Arminianism, and Counter-Revolution', in *Origins of the English Civil War*, ed. Conrad Russell (London: Macmillan, 1973).

Van den Abeele, Baudouin, 'L'*exemplum* et le monde animal: Le cas des oiseaux chez Nicole Bozon', *Le Moyen Age* 94 (1988) 51–72.

Van Engen, John, *Rupert of Deutz* (University of California Press, 1983).

Vartanian, Aram, 'Trembley's Polyp, La Mettrie, and Eighteenth-Century French Materialism', *JHI* 11 (1950) 259–86.

Vickers, Brian (ed.) *Occult and Scientific Mentalities in the Renaissance*, (Cambridge University Press, 1984).

Walker, D.P., *The Ancient Theology*, (Cornell University Press, 1972).

  'Orpheus the Theologian and Renaissance Platonists', *Journal of the Warburg and Courtauld Institutes*, 16 (1953) 100–20.

Weber, Max, *The Protestant Ethic and the Spirit of Capitalism*, tr. T. Parsons (New York: Charles Scribner's Sons, 1930).

Webster, Charles, *From Paracelsus to Newton* (Cambridge University Press, 1982).

  The Great Instauration: Science, Medicine, and Reform, 1626–1660 (London: Duckworth, 1975).

  (ed.), *The Intellectual Revolution of the Seventeenth Century* (London: Routledge and Kegan Paul, 1974).

  'Puritanism, Separatism, and Science', in Lindberg and Numbers (eds.), *God and Nature*, pp. 192–217.

Wellmann, Max, 'Der *Physiologus*, Eine Religions geschichtlich-Naturwissenschaftliche Untersuchung', *Philologus*, Supplementband 22, Heft 1 (1930), 1–116.

Westfall, Richard, *The Life of Isaac Newton* (Cambridge University Press, 1994).

  Science and Religion in Seventeenth-Century England (New Haven: Yale University Press, 1958).

Westmen, Robert, 'Nature, Art, and Psyche', in Vickers (ed.), *Occult and Scientific Mentalities*, 177–229.

White, Lynn, 'The Historical Roots of our Ecological Crisis', *Science*, 155/3767, March 1967, 1203–7.

Whitney, Elspeth, 'Lynn White, Ecotheology, and History', *Environmental Ethics* 15 (1993) 151–69.

Wilkinson, L.P., *Ovid Recalled* (Cambridge University Press, 1955).

Williams, Arnold, *The Common Expositor: An Account of the Commentaries on Genesis, 1527–1633* (Chapel Hill: University of North Carolina Press, 1948).

Williams, George H., *Wilderness and Paradise in Christian Thought* (New York: Harper, 1962).

Wimmer, C.A., *Geschichte der Gartentheorie* (Darmstadt: Wissenschaftliche Buchgesellschaft, 1989).

Wind, Edgar, 'The Revival of Origen', in *Studies in Art and Literature for Belle da Costa Greene*, ed. Dorothy Miner (Princeton University Press, 1954), 412–24.

Wolfson, H.A., *The Philosophy of the Church Fathers*, 2 vols., 2nd edn (Harvard University Press, 1964).

Wright, J.K., *The Geographical Lore of the Time of the Crusades* (New York, 1965).

Yates, Frances A., *The Art of Memory* (London: Pimlico, 1992).

  Giordano Bruno and the Hermetic Tradition (University of Chicago Press, 1964).

Yoder, A., *Animal Analogy in Shakespeare's Character Portrayal* (New York, 1947).

Zambon, Francesco, '*Figura bestialis*. Les fondements théoretiques du bestaire médiéval', in *Epopeé animale, fable, fabliau*, ed. G. Bianciotto and M. Salvat (Paris: Publications de l'Université de Rouen, 1984).

Index

Abelard, Peter, 68, 110n
accommodation, 133–8, 160, 267
Adam, 61, 206, 207, 208, 209, 226, 232, 233,
  234, 235, 236, 239, 270; an androgyne,
  215–16; encyclopaedic knowledge of, 61,
  62, 137, 211–13, 229, 253, 265; fall of,
  212–21, 229, 230, 237; language of, 225,
  226, 249, 250, 253, 258, 261, 263; mastery
  of nature, 209, 219, 229, 250-1; naming
  of the creatures; 61, 211, 231, 249, 250-1,
  253
Adamites, 233
Adelard of Bath, 63, 68
Aelian, 24, 86, 188, 190, 191
aetiologia, 27
agriculture, 207, 239, 248; *see also* husbandry
Alanus de Insulis, 34
Albert the Great, *see* Albertus Magnus
Albertus Magnus, 38, 64–6, 68, 71, 72, 73, 88
alchemy, 106, 227, 228–9, 263, 271
Aldrovandi, Ulisse, 73, 77, 88
Alexandrian theology, 12, 15
Allan of Lille, 35, 44
allegoria, *see* allegorical interpretation
allegorical interpretation, 9, 18–19, 45, 48, 57,
  123, 268; applied to things, 3–4, 28–9;
  criticism of, 108–11, 126, 197; decline of,
  4, 29, 91, 113, 129, 268
allegory, 3–4, 18, 108, 109, 114, 122, 268; as
  literary form, 91, 192–3
Ambrose of Milan, 12–13, 17, 21, 22, 23, 25, 29,
  48–9, 128, 209
America, *see* New World
Anabaptists, 234
anagogia, 26, 27, 28, 114, 122
anatomy, 79, 80, 83, 86, 102
Andrewes, Lancelot, 210, 219, 220, 239, 247
anima mundi, *see* world soul
animals, fabulous or mythical, 65–6, 71, 74, 76,
  77, 86, 88–9; harmful or venomous, 20-1,
  84, 162–6, 175; as moral exemplars, 22–3,

43, 91, 186–93; as natural signs, 21, 25–6,
  31, 80, 91–2, 162, 230; wild, 32, 49, 164,
  209, 219–21
Anselm of Canterbury, 36–7, 38n
anthropocentrism, 177, 182
antipathy, 58n, 89, 253
Antipodes, 82, 112–13
Aquinas, St Thomas, 34, 36, 44, 70, 172–3,
  177–8, 217–8; theory of interpretation, 28,
  110; theory of knowledge, 38, 52–3
Arbuthnot, John, 125
Aristotelian science, 24, 25, 102–7, 138–9, 154,
  167, 169, 194, 268
Aristotle, 7, 15, 66, 67, 71, 73, 83, 97, 119, 139,
  161, 172–3, 177, 217–18; criticism of, 82,
  102, 104, 105, 106, 107; medieval influence
  of, 65, 66, 69, 70, 101, 102
Ark, Noah's, 128, 258
Arnobius of Sicca, 20
asceticism, 36
Asclepius, 40, 56
Aston, Margaret, 115
astrology, 52, 53, 54, 106, 144, 179, 253, 255, 256,
  263, 270, 272
Auerbach, Eric, 30-1
Augsburg Confession, 117, 124
Augustine of Hippo, 11, 20, 21, 31–3, 34, 38,
  39, 54, 58, 62, 82, 92, 116, 128, 162–3,
  177, 179; on Genesis, 46, 123, 207, 208–9,
  217; on knowledge of nature, 13, 25–6,
  32, 62; theory of interpretation, 25–6,
  28–30, 110, 132, 133; theory of signs, 28,
  29, 30
Austen, Ralph, 195, 196, 248
authorial intention, 113, 120, 123, 125, 129,
  168–9, 266, 267

Babel, *see* confusion of tongues
Bacon, Francis, 64, 90, 136, 137, 140, 167, 203,
  225, 229, 235; on dominion over nature,
  61, 205, 251; on final causes, 182, 183, 184;

306